Japanese Historians and the National Myths, 1600-1945

Japanese Historians and the National Myths, 1600-1945

Note on Usage

All Japanese names are given in Japanese word order. That is, surnames precede personal names, the opposite of Western practice: for example, the name of Hayashi Razan, the first to appear in the book. Hayashi was his family name and Razan his personal name. The only exceptions are references to works in English by writers with Japanese names. No notice is taken of pen names.

In the romanization of Japanese, macrons over vowels are used to indicate the long vowels ō and ū. The short vowels are just o and u. The distinction is critical for meaning in Japanese. This convention is observed except for a few words that are well known in English, such as Tokyo, Kyoto, Osaka, Shinto, Shogun. They ought to be Tōkyō, Kyōto, Ōsaka, Shintō, and Shōgun, but English convention allows the elimination of the macrons.

The only abbreviation used in this work is TZKS, which stands for Tsuji Zennosuke Kankei Shiryō [Historical Materials Related to Professor Tsuji Zennosuke], in the Historiographical Institute, Tokyo University. These references indicate file and document numbers. For example, the first reference, TZKS 114-11, means Tsuji Zennosuke Shiryō, file number 114, document number 11. Once inside the document, the references are easy to find.

Translations and glosses in square brackets are mine, not those of the original authors.

Elsewhere, I thank the following for reading the manuscript or portions of it:

David Abosch, professor, State University of New York at Buffalo
Fumiko Ikawa-Smith, professor, McGill University
James McMullen, professor, Oxford University
Yasko Nishimura, research associate, Institute for the History of Science and
   Technology, University of Toronto.

Others whom I thank for supporting the project are:

Harold Bolitho, professor, Harvard University
Robert Borgen, professor, University of California at Davis
Neil McMullin, associate professor, University of Toronto
Klaus Pringsheim, president, Canada-Japan Trade Society, Ottawa
Karl Steenstrup, professor, München University.

Acknowledgments

I express my gratitude to Professor Kanai Madoka, Professor Emeritus, Historiographical Institute, Tokyo University, for encouragement and great practical assistance. Without him, this book would not have been possible. Professor Miyachi Masato, Historiographical Institute, Tokyo University, guided me to many valuable materials. Professor Gonoi Takashi of the Overseas Materials Section, Historiographical Institute, Tokyo University, was a genial and patient host of the foreign scholars. Professor David Barrett of McMaster University closely edited the manuscript, for no reward.

Others in Japan whom I thank are:

Hayashiya Tatsusaburō, professor emeritus, Kyoto University
Hiraizumi Wataru, former member of the House of Representatives for Fukui
  Prefecture
Ienaga Saburō, professor emeritus, former Tokyo Educational University
Imai Osamu, lecturer, Waseda University
Inoue Kiyoshi, professor emeritus, Kyoto University
Kano Masanao, professor, Waseda University
Kuroita Nobuo, and his wife Nagai Michiko, novelist, of Tokyo
Ishida Ichirō, professor emeritus, Tōhoku University
Miyazaki Michio, former professor, Kokugakuin University
Naramoto Tatsuya, professor emeritus, Ritsumeikan University
Takasaki Jikidō, board chairman, Tōhō Gakkai
Tanaka Takashi, former president and professor emeritus, Ise Kōgakkan
  University
Tokoro Isao, professor, Kyoto Industrial University
Tsuji Tatsuya, professor emeritus, Yokohama City University
Yamamoto Takeo, professor emeritus, Historiographical Institute, Tokyo
  University.

Illustrations

Contents

Published in Japan by University of Tokyo Press

Printed in Canada on acid-free paper ∞

ISBN 0-7748-0644-3 (UBC Press)
ISBN 4-13-027031-1 (University of Tokyo Press)

Canadian Cataloguing in Publication Data

Brownlee, John S.
Japanese historians and the national myths, 1600-1945

   Includes bibliographical references and index.
   ISBN 0-7748-0644-3

   1. Japan – History – To 645 – Historiography. 2. Japan – Historiography. I. Title.

DS834.7.B76 1998   952'.01'072   C97-911036-X

This book has been published with the help of a grant from the Humanities and Social Sciences Federation of Canada, using funds provided by the Social Sciences and Humanities Research Council of Canada.

UBC Press gratefully acknowledges the ongoing support to its publishing program from the Canada Council for the Arts, the British Columbia Arts Council, and the Department of Canadian Heritage of the Government of Canada.

UBC Press
University of British Columbia
6344 Memorial Road
Vancouver, BC V6T 1Z2
(604) 822-5959
Fax: 1-800-668-0821
E-mail: orders@ubcpress.ubc.ca
http://www.ubcpress.ubc.ca

University of Tokyo Press
7-3-1- Hongo, Bunkyo-ku
Tokyo 113, Japan

John S. Brownlee

Japanese Historians and the National Myths, 1600-1945: The Age of the Gods and Emperor Jinmu

UBCPress / Vancouver

UNIVERSITY OF TOKYO PRESS

Introduction

In this book, I examine how Japanese historians between 1600 and 1945 dealt with the ancient myths of their origins as a people and of the imperial house. The subject has not been studied hitherto by Western scholars and not in a comprehensive way by Japanese scholars. The discussion ends in 1945 because of the defeat of Japan and the end of the imperial state, in which the sovereignty of the emperor of Japan was based on the myths.

The myths arose in primitive times and were recorded in Japan's first histories, *Kojiki* [Record of Ancient Matters, 712] and *Nihon Shoki* [also known as *Nihongi*; Chronicles of Japan, 720]. They tell of the creation of Japan by deities, the activities of the deities during the Age of the Gods, the founding of the imperial line by the Sun Goddess, and the reign of the first emperor, Jinmu, a direct descendant of the Sun Goddess, beginning in 660 BC according to *Nihon Shoki*.

Both *Kojiki* and *Nihon Shoki* start with spurious tales of the creation of the world that were adopted from Chinese books, and they do not reflect Japanese ideas of creation. *Nihon Shoki* begins:

> Of old, Heaven and Earth were not yet separated, and the In and Yō [Chinese: Yin and Yang] not yet divided. They formed a chaotic mass like an egg which was of obscurely defined limits and contained germs.
>
> The purer and clearer part was thinly drawn out, and formed Heaven, while the heavier and grosser element settled down and became Earth.
>
> The finer element easily became a united body, but the consolidation of the heavy and gross element was accomplished with difficulty.
>
> Heaven was therefore formed, and Earth was established subsequently.
>
> Thereafter Divine Beings were produced between them.[1]

We will encounter some of these terms again in discussing the Japanese scholars of the seventeenth century, who took up the formal study of Confucianism. They attempted to integrate the Chinese concepts with traditional Japanese Shinto ideas.

In the eighth century, however, such abstract discussion was of interest only to elite scholars. *Kojiki* and *Nihon Shoki* swiftly abandon the Chinese story of the origins of Heaven and Earth. They offer an account of creation that was accepted by Japanese society of the early eighth century and that satisfied most Japanese minds until 1945 and many minds to the present. The two books really start with the divine beings that *Nihon Shoki* says were produced by Heaven and Earth.

Japanese deities, variously and exuberantly named, created the Japanese islands and somewhat obscurely created the people who live on them. Creation processes were various and mostly improbable. The most comprehensible process was sexual intercourse between deities, but the offspring were not uniform – they ranged from Japanese islands to heavenly bodies such as the sun and the moon and natural elements such as fire. Other creation processes defy comprehension. For example, the deity Izanagi lost his wife when she gave birth to fire; angered, he killed the fire-child. But when he washed the sword of death, new deities sprang to life from each part of the sword – the hilt, the guard, the blade. No Western theologian has cared to deal with that event, while Japanese theologians were interested only in its genealogical importance. They needed to know the precise order in which the deities appeared.

It is pointless to ask standard theological questions about the Japanese gods – questions about omnipotence, omniscience, benevolence, the necessity of their existence – because no Japanese ever asked those questions, and hence there are no answers. The world in which the creating deities lived was taken for granted, and Japanese theologians did not attempt to determine first causes. Instead, traditional scholars paid attention to the genealogies of the creating gods, their ancestors, and their offspring. These were studied in great detail, because in ancient times Japanese families competing for place and profit claimed as their ancestors the deities of the Age of the Gods. In the eighth century, the government of Japan explicitly acknowledged the importance of these genealogies, and a government department carefully examined submissions from ambitious families claiming such descent. Who begat whom in the Age of the Gods had to be thrashed out in the Department of Civil Affairs in order to determine precedence.[2] While those matters of place and profit were settled in their time, the subsequent thirteen centuries of study of these subjects have produced little clarification of the genealogies of the gods, and we shall not be concerned with them.

According to *Kojiki* and *Nihon Shoki,* the Age of the Gods led directly to the age of humans. The Sun Goddess sent her Heavenly Grandchild down from the Plain of High Heaven to the Central Land of Reed Plains, which is Japan. The place of the descent of the Heavenly Grandchild of the Sun

Goddess was identified as Takachiho. It is a high mountain in southern Kyushu, towering over its neighbouring peaks and therefore an obvious site for the heavenly descent, being the easiest to get to from the Plain of High Heaven. Today it is still recognized as such by the local inhabitants, and it is furnished with a major shrine, Kirishima Jinja, to venerate the heavenly descent. Materials explaining the descent of the Heavenly Grandchild are available at the shrine. When the Sun Goddess dispatched her Heavenly Grandchild to Japan, she declared,

> This Reed-plain-1500-autumns-fair-rice-ear Land is the region which my descendants shall be lords of. Do thou, my August Grandchild, proceed thither and govern it. Go! and may prosperity attend thy dynasty, and may it, like Heaven and Earth, endure for ever.[3]

Up to 1945, every Japanese school child was obliged to memorize this oath in archaic Japanese. It was considered the foundation of Japan's unique national essence [*kokutai*], centred upon the eternal line of emperors, whose everlasting prosperity was vouchsafed by the oath.

Some generations after the descent of the Heavenly Grandchild, the first human emperor, Jinmu, subdued all resistance to the heavenly founded imperial line and unified the Japanese nation. The martial nature of this first emperor, whose name means 'divine warrior,' was not lost upon the Japanese nation up to 1945. Although nothing in *Kojiki* and *Nihon Shoki* marked the passage from gods to humans, all scholars before 1945 saw the transition occurring with the reign of Emperor Jinmu. According to *Nihon Shoki*, Emperor Jinmu declared his ascension to the imperial throne at Kashihara, near Nara, in 660 BC. At present, Kashihara Shrine both worships Emperor Jinmu and celebrates his founding of the Japanese empire; 1995 was the 2,655th anniversary of the founding. In prewar Japan, all students memorized the list of emperors starting from Jinmu: Jinmu, Suizei, Annei, Itoku, Kōshō, and on to the reigning Shōwa emperor, 124th in the line by official count.

These foundation myths were accepted universally as historical truths and were repeated as such by all historians up to the Tokugawa period. Before this period, there was no reason for anyone to challenge them. Buddhism entered the country in the sixth century, but it was a comprehensive and tolerant religion, so Japanese did not have to renounce Shinto in order to take up Buddhism. Confucianism also came, but it was an ethical system and only partly a religion. For Japanese up to 1600, Confucianism was a set of social and moral principles put forth by a revered founder, Confucius, and not a system of metaphysics. Confucianism was forever vague about the existence of deities, so it offered no challenge to the Japanese founding myths. Christianity was brought to Japan in 1549 by St. Francis Xavier and survived for a century. But it was extirpated by the Tokugawa government before it could offer a serious challenge to established belief.

In any case, belief in the Age of the Gods was socially reinforced by the existence of Shinto shrines everywhere, ranging from the great shrines of Ise and Izumo, which worship the Sun Goddess and the Master of the Land (Ōkuninushi) respectively, to thousands of lesser shrines, many of which worship deities from the Age of the Gods. Kyoto in particular is full of shrines worshipping these deities, which remain part of the living religion of Japan.

In many ways, Japan entered a new era in 1600, when my study begins. The endless medieval wars were settled by a final battle at Sekigahara in 1600, and the Tokugawa victors went on to establish a firm peace under their tyrannical government. Buddhism died an intellectual death as the result of defeat of its militant sects in late-sixteenth-century battles. A revived secular Chinese Confucianism was deliberately imported and supported by the Tokugawa regime as an ideological support, and this proved to be the most fruitful opening in Japanese intellectual history.

This book takes up historical thought in the new Tokugawa era, dealing first with the development of rationalism in Confucian historical writing. I discuss the main scholars who took up the question of Japan's origins and the beginning of the imperial house: Hayashi Razan (1583-1657), the Mito scholars who wrote *Dai Nihon Shi* [Great History of Japan], Arai Hakuseki (1657-1725), Yamagata Bantō (1748-1821), and Date Chihiro (1802-77). These scholars by no means exhaust the list of those who were concerned with ancient history, but they fairly represent major trends. Through sheer rationalism, in an isolated society, they divested themselves, collectively and incrementally, of an ancient mythical understanding of Japan's origins.

In the Tokugawa period, this was mainly a negative operation that cast doubt on the origins of Japan and its imperial house. The only positive suggestion, hotly disputed, was that a Chinese ruler named Wu Taibo, and not Emperor Jinmu, had come to Japan to start the imperial line. The scholars involved in the dispute were well aware of the significance of grounding the imperial house in a line of humans and not descended from the Japanese gods. Even so, this dispute about whether the founder of the imperial house was an improbably descended Emperor Jinmu or an improbably derived Wu Taibo would not occur in modern society. It was not until the late nineteenth century, when Japan opened up to the world, that scholars were able to give more convincing positive explanations of the origins of Japanese society and institutions by turning to the social sciences of the West.

In the Tokugawa period, the Confucian scholars were resisted by scholars of National Studies, who reaffirmed the literal truth of the ancient myths; here I mainly discuss Motoori Norinaga (1730-1801). The battle was then carried on in the early Meiji period (1868-1912) between the new scientific historians of Tokyo Imperial University and latter-day National Scholars and political Shintoists, whose beliefs had not changed.

In outward form only, this struggle between ideologies resembled that between science and the Bible in the West. In Europe and North America, great intellectual battles raged in the eighteenth and nineteenth centuries over the evolution of species and the dating of societies by geology, geography, and archeology. The struggle was fierce and fought on many fronts, with many unexpected results, as scholars took wrong turns, went into blind alleys, and yet made great triumphs. In Europe and America, the Bible lost its authority as the result of intellectual exchange, and Adam and Eve in the Garden of Eden gradually receded from the beliefs of scholars and intellectuals. Apart from a few exceptions such as the 1925 Scopes trial in Tennessee, USA, modern states did not try to defend religious belief and establish the Bible as the sole authority on ancient history.

In Tennessee a law was passed on 21 March 1925 to prohibit the teaching of evolution in state-funded schools: 'Be it enacted – that it shall be unlawful for any teacher in any of the universities, normals, and all other public schools which are supported in whole or in part by the public school funds of the state, to teach any theory that denies the story of the Divine Creation of man as taught in the Bible, and to teach instead that man has descended from a lower order of animals.'[4] John T. Scopes, a young biology teacher, agreed to be a defendant in order to test the law. The resulting trial attracted wide attention, with reporters from all over the United States pouring into Dayton, Tennessee. Many of them heaped ridicule upon the law and upon the society and government of Tennessee. Scopes was found guilty, but on appeal the verdict was reversed on a technicality. There were no further prosecutions, though the antievolution law was not repealed until 1967. In 1968 an antievolution law in Arkansas was found unconstitutional by the United States Supreme Court, bringing the matter to an end.[5]

In Japan modern scientific history was adopted from the West around 1890 to reinforce the doubts of Confucian scholarship, generating fierce attacks on traditional beliefs. This happened at precisely the same time as the Meiji Constitution of 1889 defined the modern Japanese state.

The Constitution placed sovereignty in the emperor. This power was based squarely on the ancient myths about the origins of Japan and the unbroken line of emperors, which had been reaffirmed by the National Scholars in the Tokugawa period. Nothing besides these myths was available in Japanese political theory for the purpose. Moreover, on the basis of these myths, the emperor was described in the Constitution as 'sacred and inviolable.' Thus, the state necessarily became a supporter of the ancient myths; unlike in the West, the debate over their validity could not be confined to scholars.

The critical study of *Kojiki* and *Nihon Shoki* was not prohibited, and no list of censored topics was issued. However, the government of Japan tried on occasion to limit discussion. In 1892 it responded to public protest and fired Professor Kume Kunitake (1839-1931) from Tokyo Imperial University for unacceptably sceptical writing on Shinto, which was closely associated with the imperial house. At the time, Kume received no support from his colleagues at Tokyo Imperial University. However, most postwar Japanese scholars have condemned the action of the government and have seen in the Kume incident the origins of a taboo on discussion of the Age of the Gods and the early emperors.

The government was also sensitive about the history of the emperors in historical times; thus, in 1911 the interpretation of an imperial schism in the fourteenth century also became a matter for government intervention into university affairs. This cowed the scholars even further. To some extent, academic development between 1890 and 1945 is the story of conflict and accommodation between government and scholars. The tendency of scholars was toward accommodation to government restrictions.

However, government oppression is not the whole story. It is not true that the prewar government continuously oppressed scholars of history and forced them to conform to official truths. Compared to the harsh treatment handed out to communists and Marxists, who went to jail merely for possession of proscribed works after 1925, the professional historians were only lightly touched. Most modern Japanese historians, including the fired Kume Kunitake, thought that they had achieved freedom of scholarship undreamed of in the Tokugawa period. With this understanding, they proceeded to develop the historical profession, which they considered a science, in a thoroughly modern way. If professors did not proceed to a root-and-branch attack on the official truths, it was partly because they were nationalists and voluntarily accepted limits on thought and research that seemed compatible with their civic duty as Japanese and as civil servants [*kōmuin*]. Mikami Sanji (1865-1939) of Tokyo Imperial University is the prime example of a scholar who believed that professional historians must freely pursue their research. But he thought that scholars had no business teaching pure scholarly truth to the nation when the government deemed that it required invigorating myths. Pure scholarly truth must be confined among scholars. Mikami's position was obviously filled with difficulties, but he never acknowledged them.

Scholars in the twentieth century were divided on interpretation of the Age of the Gods. Two main positions developed. The first was represented by Hoshino Hisashi (1839-1917) of Tokyo Imperial University, who held that the founding myths were historically true. By the time of his death in 1917, there were few in the academic world who agreed with him. The second was represented by Kume Kunitake, who remained active after his dismissal from Tokyo Imperial University and who held that the myths were allegorical. This position was developed further by Mikami Sanji and Kuroita Katsumi (1874-1946) of Tokyo Imperial University, the most influential scholars of their generation. They held that the myths must be studied by the whole arsenal of twentieth-century methods, including linguistics, anthropology, folklore studies, and so on. However, Mikami and Kuroita believed that there was some historical reality at the bottom of the myths, which it was their job to uncover. Their position was the most common among academic historians.

As for Emperor Jinmu, scholars refrained from destroying him because they all thought that he had actually existed. However, even the most conservative prewar historians disagreed with the state on the date of Emperor Jinmu's ascension, which the government celebrated as 660 BC. By the 1930s, half a century of cumulative research had convinced the historians that the proper date was 40 BC. But in 1940, they surrendered their autonomy and participated in the extensive national ceremonies and projects celebrating the 2,600th anniversary of Emperor Jinmu. Those who had reservations did not express them.

In the 1930s and 1940s, some young scholars, such as Inoue Kiyoshi (b. 1913) and Ienaga Saburō (b. 1913), were outraged by the attitudes of the mainstream historians toward the Age of the Gods and Emperor Jinmu, thinking that they amounted to the propagation of lies. These young scholars had little influence.

Some on the other side, latter-day National Scholars, thought that the professional historians did not go far enough in affirming the myths as historical truth and supporting the great enterprises of the imperial state. This group, led by the militarist and imperialist Professor Hiraizumi Kiyoshi (1895-1984) of Tokyo Imperial University, became dominant in the 1930s. They pushed the historical profession toward formal affirmation of the historicity of the founding myths, which most of its members privately disbelieved as a result of cumulative modern scholarship.

Some historians went beyond affirmation to hearty participation. The most prominent were Professors Mikami Sanji and Kuroita Katsumi of Tokyo Imperial University, members of the committee that wrote *Kokutai no Hongi* [Cardinal Principles of the National Entity of Japan] in 1937. This was a hodgepodge of myths, legends, and specious reasoning to support the authoritarian imperial state and bore little resemblance to the scholarly views that they held during long and distinguished professional careers. Tsuji Zennosuke (1877-1955) of Tokyo Imperial University, the third outstanding scholar of his generation, took a longer route toward affirmation of the founding myths but arrived there in 1940. In that year, Tsuji published an article on the significance of the 2,600th anniversary in which he affirmed the historical truth of the founding myths and their significance for Japan's war against China.

In summary, the mainstream scholars were all nationalists. The modernization of Japan since the Meiji period had been carried out to save Japan; the adoption of Western methods was intended to preserve Japanese national independence and identity. All Japanese were encouraged to share in the great national project, and the few dissidents were handled by the state. Thus, Japanese historians developed the historical profession as a science, but by the 1930s they had come to understand it as a science in the service of the Japanese nation. When confronted by ultranationalism that insisted on the literal truth of the founding myths, they could see no alternative but to betray that science and to agree.

This theme of conflict and accommodation between scholars on one side and government and society on the other is followed through a series of incidents that highlight the problems: the Kume Kunitake affair in 1890-2; the Southern and Northern Courts controversy of 1911; the celebration in 1940 of the '2,600th anniversary' of the founding of the empire by Emperor Jinmu in 660 BC; the legal prosecution of the dissenting historian Tsuda Sōkichi in 1941. The work focuses on the historians and how they reacted to pressures and trends. I did not intend to write a general study of historiography, but it was necessary to introduce some of the developments of historiography in order to show where the historians stood. In particular, it was necessary to explain the development of Japanese historical writing in relation to that of the West in order to evaluate the degree of the fall from scientific history to nationalistic history. Similarly the general development of 'fascist' government and nationalist ideology is briefly discussed to make clear the political situation in which the historians found themselves.

Fortunately the historians wrote clearly, and we are spared some of the problems of interpreting the thought of literary writers and philosophers. For example, the Kyoto school of philosophy, led by Nishida Kitarō (1870-1945), Nishitani Keiji (1900-90), and Tanabe Hajime (1885-1962), fully supported Japan's militarism and imperialism. Yet these philosophers expressed themselves in profundities so obscure that some later interpreters think that they can detect covert opposition to militarism and imperialism.

The story of the historians has a happy ending. With the fall of the empire in 1945 and the promulgation of the democratic Constitution of Japan in 1947, the greatest barrier to the modernization of historical thought was removed: the imperial government. In the postwar era, academic historians carried to its conclusion the work of reassessing the ancient history of Japan. Not only have the scholars divested themselves of ancient mythical understanding of origins; their ideas have also been accepted throughout modern society. School textbooks now begin with geography, geology, and archeology, not with the Sun Goddess. They culminate in uninteresting propositions about an ancient society that are indistinguishable from those about ancient societies everywhere. Students may be bored by the unheroic materials, but they may be learning the truth. In light of Japan's modern history under the old myths, any boredom must be accounted a good thing. Lingering resistance to contemporary historical interpretation is noted, but it is no more important in Japan than creationism in North American science.

Under the democratic state, historical scholarship proceeded without hindrance to complete the rationalization and secularization of the origins of Japan and its emperors that were begun in the Tokugawa period. The single, irrefutable myth of origins, justifying political institutions and requiring obedience, supported by government authority and social belief, no longer stands. Its displacement has been part of the development of Japan into a modern liberal society. This does not fully explain why Japanese society is liberal, but it is an important constituent, hitherto not examined by Western scholars. Japanese people no longer think that they are the descendants of gods or that their emperor is divine. Their government must proceed under constitutional law that provides for democracy. These aspects are related to each other.

The rationalization and secularization of Japanese thought are also important for other people. Modern Japanese nationalism based on the myths was not benign. It led to imperialism and militarism, with wars against China in 1937 and then against the United States, the British Empire, France, the Netherlands, and the territorial possessions of all of them, affecting the people of many nations. Again, the force of the Japanese myth does not constitute a full explanation of this imperialism and militarism, but it was an important constituent. The incompleteness of the endeavour to rationalize and secularize Japanese thought before 1945 was costly to many other people. Its completion since 1945 is one of many factors making Japan the least aggressive of the powerful nations.

I wish to make two points about terms and methods. First, the term 'scientific history' appears frequently in my discussion of the historical method of Japanese scholars during the last century. The term was universally used by professional Japanese historians to characterize the methods in use between 1890 and 1945, and it still finds wider acceptance in Japan today than elsewhere. In Europe and North America, the term is obsolete at best or derided at worst. Almost every Western historian thinks that historical method is organized and systematic, and proceeds under the rigorous scrutiny of members of the historical profession, but that it does not amount to science. Since 1960, most Western historians have acknowledged subjectivity and no longer aspire to objectivity; they are happy to write from an acknowledged position, sometimes to urge a social purpose. My use of the term reflects that of Japanese historians and not my belief that their methods were scientific. It would be tiresome to express reservations by repeated qualifications (placing the term in quotation marks, naming it so-called or purportedly scientific history, and so forth), so I have just called it scientific history.

Second, the historians under study in this book raised numerous theories about the origin of the Japanese people and the beginning of the state. Kume Kunitake, Naka Michiyo, Mikami Sanji, Kuroita Katsumi, Tsuji Zennosuke, Tsuda Sōkichi, and many others tried obsessively to pin down the precise origins of Japan. They used a wide range of materials and methods, including anthropology, archeology, linguistics, myth studies, and racial theory to produce ever more complex and sophisticated explanations. Most of those explanations are now dead and buried. To deal with the thought of these historians, I have not found it necessary to exhume and evaluate all their theories about the origins of Japan. To do so would distract attention from the main thesis of this book. My purpose is to explain not the origins of Japan but the thought of the historians who dealt with those origins.

Part 1
The Tokugawa Period

1
Hayashi Razan (1583-1657) and Hayashi Gahō (1618-80): Founders of Modern Historical Scholarship

The World of Neo-Confucianism

A new era began in Japan in 1600. In that year, a final victory in battle was achieved by an eastern alliance of warlords, led by Tokugawa Ieyasu (1542-1616), over a western alliance, and peace came upon the land for the first time since 1333. Tokugawa Ieyasu went on to found a new and powerful government, the Tokugawa Bakufu [Military Government], which survived under Ieyasu's descendants and kept the peace until 1868. The government was new, but its form was old, for the first bakufu had been established in 1192. The legitimacy of the Tokugawa Bakufu also rested on ancient foundations. Its head, the shogun, was officially appointed by the emperor of Japan, who retained sovereignty over the nation.

Although Japan's governing institutions were ancient, a new intellectual era was born with the establishment of the Tokugawa Bakufu. Japan was a populous country, estimated at twelve to eighteen million, and its people were well versed in both practical skills and high arts. Its old traditions and ways of thinking had proved inadequate, yielding centuries of civil war, and the people were ready for new ideas. The old ways of thinking had little to offer. Medieval Shinto had worked its way into the repetition of esoteric mysteries and had nothing to contribute to the need to reorganize. Buddhism had become identified with militant sects that had been defeated in military battle, and the defeat weighed heavily on the Buddhists, deadening their intellects. But at hand lay Neo-Confucianism, imported from China, a fully developed, systematic, rational philosophy that explained and justified all things. Neo-Confucianism affected every aspect of Japanese thought in the Tokugawa period, including the study of history, and brought new life to that subject.

Modern historical writing in Japan began with Hayashi Razan. He is described as 'the founder of modern historical scholarship. With Razan, historical scholarship emerged from the middle ages and changed into one

Hayashi Razan (1583-1657), Confucian scholar,
offered a rational alternative to the divine
ancestry of Emperor Jinmu. (From Hori Isao,
Hayashi Razan [Tokyo: Yoshikawa Kōbunkan
1964], courtesy of the publisher)

that was permeated by positivism, rationalism, and a critical spirit.'[1] This
view is representative of modern Japanese historians.

Razan began his career at the age of thirteen in 1595, like many young
Japanese men, by entering a Zen Buddhist monastery, the Kenninji in Kyoto.
In 1597 he left the monastery for secular life, citing his filial duty toward
his mother, and in later writings he criticized Buddhism for disrupting the
social order with demands such as the renunciation of filial piety.[2] In 1604,
at the age of twenty-two, he enlisted as a student under Fujiwara Seika (1561-
1619), then Japan's leading Confucian scholar. Hayashi Razan proved to be
a brilliant student, eventually succeeding Fujiwara Seika as the preeminent
Confucian of his time. He became a scholarly administrator at the Tokugawa
Bakufu and a teacher at the highest level; at the end of his career, he instructed the Shogun Ietsuna. In 1630 he received a grant of land from the

bakufu and established an academy that claimed to be the official bakufu school.[3] The Hayashi academy, known as Sage's Hall, did become the official bakufu school in 1789, when the bakufu disciplined it for allowing heterodox doctrines to creep in. It was then renamed The Academy at Shōhei Slope [Shōheizaka Gakumonjo] and slightly outlasted the Tokugawa Bakufu, surviving until 1871. Under the hereditary guidance of Razan's descendants, the academy played a major role in the formation of Japanese Confucian thought and produced a history of the bakufu, *Tokugawa Jikki* [Veritable Records of the Tokugawa], completed in 1849.

Razan's primary interest as a Confucianist was not in writing history but in establishing and propagating the teachings of Chinese Confucianism of the Zhu Xi school, generally known as Neo-Confucianism.[4] The orthodox Japanese version of Neo-Confucianism contained little that was original; nor did its teachers aspire to originality. As put by Inoue Tetsujirō (1855-1944), a famous scholar of philosophy at Tokyo Imperial University, 'Anyone wishing to belong to the Chu Hsi [Zhu Xi] school had to stick faithfully to Chu Hsi's theories. In other words, he had to be Chu Hsi's spiritual slave. As a result we can read volumes of the Chu Hsi's scholars' works and find that they all say the same thing.'[5] Of Hayashi Razan, Inoue wrote, 'Razan's theories about the Supreme Ultimate, Yin and Yang, the Mandate of Heaven, and the mind were all derived from Zhu Xi ... There is nothing of Razan's own devising. With respect to philosophy and ethics, he does nothing more than describe or enlarge upon the ideas of Zhu Xi.'[6]

Neo-Confucianism became the dominant philosophy of the Tokugawa period. Three principles had a direct bearing on the writing of history. First, the universe was held to be systematically and rationally ordered. Its fundamental principles could be grasped by thought and its detailed workings understood by correctly placing its constituents into relational order. That it was correctly understood could be confirmed by the investigation of things. There was nothing ultimately mysterious about the universe, nothing that might cause human intelligence to doubt its capacities. Hence, the great philosophers, such as Zhu Xi, could write with unchallenged confidence. The constituents of the universe – the Supreme Ultimate (太極), Yin and Yang (陰陽), Principle (理), and Ether (気 , also translated as material force) – were all givens in the philosophy, and the task of thinkers was to refine knowledge of their relationships with each other. This task gave rise to endless speculation since the world contains myriad things, and there was no end to philosophical writing. However, Hayashi Razan and most Japanese Confucians agreed that such refinement of knowledge had already been attained by the principal philosophers of China, and their duty was to transmit it to Japan.

Second, the philosophy of Neo-Confucianism was complete. Its unifying principles extended uniformly from metaphysics, through the physical order, through the social order, and into the personal realm. This was particularly advantageous for philosophers, since the essential principles, once grasped, explained everything. The link between the metaphysical realm and the social order was especially attractive in the Tokugawa period. It meant that the Japanese social and political order, of recent devising, was as necessary and inevitable as the metaphysical and physical realms, which were eternal. The Tokugawa Bakufu leaders were not explicit, but their unwavering support of the Neo-Confucian philosophy indicates that they understood its utility for a regime established by conquest and seeking legitimation. Neo-Confucianism proved that the universe wanted the Tokugawa leaders to govern in the way that they did. This helps to explain why they were so concerned about the correct understanding of Neo-Confucianism that they banned unorthodox teachings from the Hayashi academy in 1790.

These systematic and comprehensive aspects of Neo-Confucianism appealed to Hayashi Razan, who had left the Zen monastery because of dissatisfaction with its teachings. In Neo-Confucianism the Supreme Ultimate creates Heaven and humans from the outside, but it simultaneously governs them from within. There was no need for religious withdrawal from society to control desires and no need for religious rites to affect matters.[7]

Third, one of the forms of investigation that demonstrated the correctness of Neo-Confucianism was historical study. In China there was a long tradition of historical writing that had already influenced Japan in ancient times, in the production of the Six National Histories between 720 and 901.[8] After 901, Japan developed independent genres of historical writing, deviating from the Chinese models. First came Historical Tales of the Heian period: *Eiga Monogatari* [A Tale of Flowering Fortunes], *Ōkagami* [The Great Mirror], and *Imakagami* [Mirror of the Present Day]. With the transition to military society in the twelfth century came War Tales of the medieval period (dozens of major and minor works). Then the political problems of the relations between the imperial government and the bakufu produced works of Historical Argument: *Gukanshō* [Miscellany of an Ignorant Fool, 1219] and *Jinnō Shōtōki* [Record of the Legitimate Descent of the Divine Sovereigns, 1339].

In the meantime, Chinese historical writing also moved ahead in different ways. The forms of historical writing and the modes of explanation became firmly categorized, and methods of research were improved. These became subsumed under the general philosophy of Neo-Confucianism, as was every branch of knowledge, and historians understood that their conclusions supported the general principles of the philosophy. Most obviously Heaven rewarded good rulers and punished bad ones; the historical signs of both types of rulers were agreed upon. To demonstrate these truths, historians in the Song dynasties (960-1279) developed methods of research based on documents. They rejected some received interpretations and dismissed the irrational, the fabulous, and even the uncertain or improbable in the knowledge that historical truth would only confirm the accepted philosophy and never undermine it. Their confidence was never shaken by untoward examples, such as the unhindered prosperity of unqualified or even wicked men, or the failure of excellent men, which could always be disposed of by special explanations.[9]

This method of historical research (考証学 Chinese *kaozhengxue*, Japanese *kōshōgaku*) is translated as 'evidential research' in Chinese Studies and as 'positivistic research' in Japanese Studies. *Kaozhengxue* was practised by a Qing dynasty school of textual scholarship founded by Huang Zongyi (1610-95) and Gu Yanwu (1613-82). It included textual analysis to determine early and late texts and forgeries; the use of mathematics, astronomy, and even archeology to confirm textual information; and epigraphy.[10] Having digressed into their own forms of historical writing after the Heian period, the Japanese caught up with this positivistic research in the Tokugawa period, primarily through the works of Hayashi Razan and the Mito scholars.

The influence of Chinese historical writing on Japan in the Tokugawa period was based on the acceptance of Neo-Confucian philosophy by Japanese scholars, who were convinced of its truth. Hayashi Razan, having accepted it, was greatly impressed by an early example of Chinese historical writing, the *Chunqiu* [Spring and Autumn Annals], which in his day was still ascribed to Confucius and described events in the period 722-481 BC. It was probably the attribution to Confucius that most impressed him; as noted below in the discussion of Emperor Jinmu, he took the standards of Confucius as his model. Later works that especially impressed him were *Tangjian* [Mirror of the Tang Dynasty] and Zhu Xi's *Zizhi tongjian gangmu* [Summary of the Comprehensive Mirror for the Aid of Government].[11] The original *Zizhi tongjian* [General Mirror for the Aid of Government] by Sima Guang in 1084 covered the history of China from the fifth century BC to the tenth century AD, and it is universally acknowledged as a great product of Chinese scholarship.[12] Zhu Xi's summary of the work, *Zizhi tongjian gangmu*, was considered a tour de force.[13]

Honchō Tsugan [General Mirror of Japan]

Hayashi Razan's most important historical work was *Honchō Tsugan* [General Mirror of Japan]. It was written in Classical Chinese, and Razan and his successors went to the trouble of rendering into Classical Chinese passages that had originally been written in Japanese. The title also reflects the influence of Chinese historical writing, taking the term 'general mirror' from Sima Guang's *Zizhi tongjian*. In fact this title was given to the work by Razan's third son, Hayashi Gahō (also known as Shunsai, 1618-80).

Razan began the work in 1644 at the request of the Shogun Iemitsu and called it *Honchō Hennen Roku* [Annalistic Record of Japan], and, using the methods of positivistic research, he carried the record through the reign of Emperor Uda (r. 887-97). That is, he got one reign further than the last of the Six National Histories, *Nihon Sandai Jitsuroku* [Veritable Records of Three Reigns of Japan, 901]. The Shogun Iemitsu died in 1651, and Razan died in 1657; moreover, his manuscript was burned in the same year in the great fire of Meireki. However, the new Shogun Ietsuna asked Gahō to continue the work from another manuscript, and he completed it in 1670. Gahō is generally regarded as the intellectual heir of his father, and the finished work faithfully reflects the ideas and methods of Razan.[14]

Honchō Tsugan consists of a main narrative, written by Razan, reaching from the first emperor, Jinmu (r. 660-585 BC), through the fifty-ninth emperor, Uda (r. 887-97).[15] Hayashi Gahō contributed all the rest. He organized the work, did some of the writing himself, and parcelled out portions to his two sons and two disciples, Hitomi Tomomoto and Sakai Hakugen. They also had the help of eight clerks.[16] They wrote the preliminary narrative covering the Age of the Gods; the continued narrative from the sixtieth emperor, Daigo (r. 897-930), to the 107th emperor, Go Yōzei (r. 1586-1611); and a summary of the main narrative and the continued narrative, after the model of Zhu Xi's *Summary of the General Mirror for the Aid of Government*. Also included are appendices on the gods of Heaven and Earth and on civil and military offices and their incumbents.[17] All in all, it is a thorough history of Japan despite this cumbersome structure dictated by the Chinese models. Devoted attention is required to read it.

Except for one reign, all the history that Razan dealt with was contained in the Six National Histories. Apparently Razan accepted the standard narrative of those works as adequately conforming to the requirements of Confucian history, and he added little. As noted, the Six National Histories had been written under the influence of the first wave of Chinese thought in ancient times, and in Razan's view they had mostly gotten it right the first time. As in *Nihon Shoki*, Emperor Nintoku (r. 313-99) continues in *Honchō Tsugan* as the model ruler, giving tax remission to the people. In the same way, Emperor Buretsu (r. 498-506) carries on as the perfectly evil ruler, still pulling out men's fingernails and then making them dig up yams, along with committing other abominations. Positivistic research was not applied to these cases, which had no basis in historical fact, because Chinese historiography recognized the existence of both good and evil rulers. It seemed perfectly natural to the Japanese scholars that such rulers should also exist in Japan.

The assassination of Emperor Sushun (r. 587-92), which might be expected to elicit discussion, passed without comment. Razan wrote only that 'They assassinated the emperor in the bed chamber; the ministers were greatly astonished.'[18] The assassination was first recorded in *Nihon Shoki*, which simply noted the event as an incident of clan politics, with no remarks on its morality or political significance. In all the succeeding centuries of historical writing, not a single work took umbrage over the assassination, and apparently Hayashi Razan simply followed in this tradition. However, other Confucians in the Tokugawa period treated the matter more critically. Razan's Confucian contemporary, Kumazawa Banzan (1619-91), forcefully criticized Prince Shōtoku, a saintly ruler traditionally beyond criticism, for his role in the affair.[19]

Hayashi Gahō similarly skipped over contentious matters with little comment. Gahō handled the fourteenth-century division in the imperial house into Southern and Northern Courts almost impartially. He gave the history of the Southern Court in the continued narrative, but he listed chapters under both the Southern and Northern emperors in the summary. In his own work *Nihon Ōdai Ichiran* [Survey of the Sovereigns of Japan], he recognized the Northern Court after the reign of Go Daigo, mainly because it occupied Kyoto and exercised some power. As we shall see, these matters of the two courts became extremely contentious in the twentieth century.

Thus, it cannot be said that the Hayashi, father and son, went out of their way to make fresh moral points about history; rather, they seemed to accept those that were already established. Despite being bakufu scholars, they seemed simply to accept the coexistence of the imperial house and the bakufu as historical reality and were not over-anxious to promote the supremacy, or even the legitimacy, of the bakufu. However, such acceptance of historical coexistence was itself a kind of legitimation.

Razan made great strides in positivistic research in some areas. Comparing the accounts in the Six National Histories and *Kojiki* with Chinese sources on the same period, he discovered major anachronisms. For example, the *History of the Later Han* gave an account of the disordered land of Wa, taken since ancient times to be Japan, and a Queen Himiko, but in Razan's calculation the time corresponded to the reign of Emperor Seimu (r. 131-90), when Japan was at peace. Razan suggested that the authors of the *History of the Later Han* had misplaced the events of the reign of Empress Regent Jingū (r. 201-69), taking her as Queen Himiko. He also wrestled with the inconsistencies in *Nihon Shoki*, in matters of birth dates and ages of emperors.[20]

A Failure of Positivistic Research: The Account of the Jōkyū War of 1221

Honchō Tsugan contains three major examples of the failure of positivistic research, two of which have already been raised. First, convincing Confucian paradigms of explanation rendered the Hayashi scholars unaware of the problems surrounding the good Emperor Nintoku and the evil Emperor

Buretsu. They failed to notice that the accounts of these emperors were taken straight from Chinese books. Second, Japanese traditions of historical writing seem to have made them uninquisitive about the assassination of Emperor Sushun. The original account in *Nihon Shoki* gave it little space. Third, loyalty to the emperor prevented positivistic research in another remarkable case, where it might have been employed to good effect. This was the Jōkyū War of 1221, in which Retired Emperor Go Toba (r. 1183-98; retired 1198-1221) declared Hōjō Yoshitoki (1163-1224) a traitor and an enemy of the imperial government and called for his destruction.

Oddly the question of loyalty to an emperor attracted more attention than the assassination of an emperor. In fact *Nihon Shoki* passed over the assassination of not one but two emperors with little comment. While murder excited little discussion, Japanese have taken most seriously the matter of political and personal obedience. It is no accident that Japanese, who borrowed Confucianism from China in ancient times and revived it in the Tokugawa period as a universal ideology, paid no attention to Mencius, one of the major figures in the development of Chinese Confucianism. Mencius is well known for a doctrine of justifiable revolution. According to his teaching, the only remedy for irremediably bad governance, whose signs were well known in Chinese thought, was revolution. Japanese revulsion for revolution was no doubt the reason that the Jōkyū War of 1221, containing the potential for revolution, excited discussion, while the assassination of emperors did not.

Hōjō Yoshitoki was no ordinary traitor, for he headed the Kamakura Bakufu founded by Minamoto Yoritomo (1147-99), and Yoshitoki's destruction would have entailed that of the warrior government. But Yoshitoki and the other Kamakura leaders resisted, led forces against Kyoto, and easily defeated the imperial army. Kamakura then deposed the child Emperor Chūkyō (r. 1221); sent into exile retired Emperor Go Toba and two of his sons, who were also retired emperors; punished with death and banishment a number of Go Toba's aristocratic advisers; confiscated some property for redistribution to its own vassals; and set up a Kamakura government office in Kyoto. Nothing of this scale had ever happened in Japan.

The most shocking measures were those taken against the imperial family, because it was universally believed to be divinely founded and divinely protected. The events of 1221 called forth some rare political tracts discussing the propriety of the Kamakura actions: a passage in *Myōe Shōnin Denki* [Biography of Saint Myōe, thirteenth century] and echoing passages in *Masukagami* [The Clear Mirror, ca. 1370] and *Baishōron* [Argument of the Plums and Pines, ca. 1349]. These tracts depicted as historical fact an imaginary conversation between Hōjō Yoshitoki and his son Yasutoki (1183-1242), in which Yasutoki professed unwillingness to proceed against the emperor. Yoshitoki persuaded him to go to the fight, claiming that the doctrine of good government, which he said the Hōjō practised, was superior to the doctrine of imperial sovereignty. He did not refer to any authorities for this assertion. Moreover, Yoshitoki claimed that he had no intention of interfering with the imperial succession, and therefore he held that his actions were not without precedent in Japanese history.[21]

Left unresolved was the theory of the imperial state and the question of whether or how it could accommodate the bakufu. It is not clear why anonymous medieval writers constructed this imaginary dialogue between Yoshitoki and Yasutoki. It appears that they were in a muddle about political and constitutional theory and meant to have it two ways. On the one hand, according to Yoshitoki, the emperor was an absolute sovereign and must be obeyed if it was obvious that his command was his personal wish and if he personally led his forces into battle. There would be no alternative to humble surrender. On the other hand, barring this singular and unexpected case of the former emperor of Japan leading his forces into battle, resistance to the retired emperor was justified because the cause of the bakufu was righteous.

Honchō Tsugan did not seize the opportunity to clarify the situation through research; presumably Hayashi Gahō was responsible for the writing in this section. Instead of critically evaluating the sources, which would probably have led to dismissal of these passages in *Myōe Shōnin Denki*, *Masukagami*, and *Baishōron*, he merely wove them together into a narrative. The passage in *Honchō Tsugan* on the Jōkyū War used as basic sources *Azuma Kagami* [Mirror of the East, latter thirteenth century] and *Jōkyūki* [Record of the Jōkyū War, thirteenth century], which are considered more or less trustworthy, but also *Myōe Shōnin Denki* and *Masukagami*. Furthermore, positivistic research did not extend to the identification of sources; later Confucian scholars, notably the Mito scholars and Arai Hakuseki, did name their sources.

The *Honchō Tsugan* account first follows *Azuma Kagami* and *Jōkyūki*. When hostilities began, councils were held in Kamakura; at these councils, doubts were expressed about resisting the emperor, but they were dispelled, and armies were sent forth. Hōjō Yasutoki set off after a touching farewell from his father, but then he returned to Kamakura and presented a startling case. It was taken from *Masukagami* and converted from Classical Japanese into Classical Chinese:

> Yasutoki said, 'Supposing we encounter the imperial army, with the emperor's carriage going in front, flying the imperial banner: What should we do, advance or retreat?
>
> Yoshitoki reflected, and then said, 'An excellent question! If the emperor himself is leading an offensive against the Kanto, then you cannot attack. You must remove your helmet, cut your bowstring, and kneel at

the roadside, respectfully confessing your crime to the emperor. You must then accept his decree. But if he has remained in the capital, protected by his forces, then you must fight heedless of death.'

Yasutoki listened submissively, and then departed.[22]

The narrative then resumes without any comment or analysis, and the episode leaves unresolved the issues that it raises.

In its uncritical acceptance of the medieval sources and its impotency to clarify a solution, this passage fails as both positivistic research and political philosophy. Thus, this first modern history of Japan had shortcomings. I opened with a statement that Hayashi Razan's scholarship was 'permeated by positivism, rationalism, and a critical spirit.' Significantly these qualities were enfeebled in passages related to the imperial house. In the case of the Jōkyū War of 1221, Hayashi Gahō may have been unaware of the force of belief in the imperial house, causing his betrayal of positivism, rationalism, and the critical spirit. But as we shall see, there is evidence that Hayashi Razan deliberately restrained his rationalism when dealing with the founding myths.

The Age of the Gods and Emperor Jinmu
We need to examine yet the rationalism of Hayashi Razan and its implications for the staple beliefs about ancient history, the existence of the Age of the Gods, and the divine founding of the imperial line. Razan had doubts about the Age of the Gods because of the sheer irrationality of the stories. In this he was not alone: others who had doubts included the Mito scholars Asaka Tanpaku (1656-1737) and Fujita Yūkoku (1774-1826), Yamaga Sokō (1622-85), Kumazawa Banzan, and Arai Hakuseki – Confucians all.[23]

Razan was lightly sceptical of the gods in general. For example, he dismissed the idea that Sugawara Michizane (845-903), believed to have died in anger and dismay because of undeserved political disgrace, became a god of lightning and struck down his enemy Fujiwara Kiyoyuki and others. Razan applied to this the rationalism of the Confucian universe, stating that the idea of a lightning god is 'a vulgar idea, and not worthy of acceptance. Lightning occurs when Yin and Yang clash; thunder occurs when Yin and Yang attack each other.'[24]

He was also dubious about the Age of the Gods, because Neo-Confucianism made no mention of the creator gods of Japanese tradition in its explanation of the forces that created the world. Thus, he held that humans were generated by the Ether of Heaven and Earth, and he proposed a view of early society that is not wholly objectionable to modern people: 'In ancient times when Heaven and Earth opened up, humans were generated. They killed birds and beasts, ate their flesh, drank their blood, used their fur as clothing, and wore their skins. There were not yet rituals involving clothing and food.'[25] This view of early human society was based not on anything resembling anthropological research but on ancient Chinese and Japanese texts. They contained abundant materials on society before the civilizing work of the sages and emperors and on barbarian societies. Most important, this view left no room in historical narrative for the gods of Japan, and accordingly Razan began his history with the first human emperor, Jinmu.

Razan's views on Emperor Jinmu are most important. In an essay entitled 'Jinmu Tennō Ron' [Essay on Emperor Jinmu], Razan presented sympathetically a well-known story that the founder of the Japanese imperial line was actually a Chinese named Wu Taibo.[26] Most significant for our purposes is that Razan rejected the Age of the Gods, and the direct succession of the first Japanese emperor from the gods, in favour of the founding of the imperial line by humans. That they came from China, home of the respected philosophers of a great civilization, probably elevated the importance of the story for Hayashi Razan. Bitō Masahide says that Razan was placing Japanese history onto a universal basis, instead of the narrow and singular basis claimed for it by *Kojiki* and *Nihon Shoki* and emphasized in the middle ages by *Jinnō Shōtōki* [Record of the Legitimate Descent of the Divine Sovereigns, 1339].[27]

The original story of Wu Taibo (Japanese: Go Taihaku) was told by the Chinese historian Sima Qian in the *Shiji* [Records of the Historian, ca. 100 BC]. Wu Taibo was an uncle of the founder of the Zhou dynasty, one of the states of the Spring and Autumn era (722-481 BC). Wu Taibo left his own country, renouncing his succession to the throne in favour of his more capable younger brother, an act that was much lauded by Confucians. He went somewhere else – vaguely south – where he lived among barbarians, who made him their king. There were many points of resemblance between these barbarian people and the ancient Japanese as described by Chinese historians, and there were some points of congruence with the Japanese records of Emperor Jinmu. It was not difficult for Japanese historians to suggest that Wu Taibo and Emperor Jinmu were related.

The story of Wu Taibo was not included in *Kojiki* or *Nihon Shoki*, but it was known in the middle ages. In *Jinnō Shōtōki*, Kitabatake Chikafusa (1293-1354) raised the theory in order to deny it.[28] In 1341 a Zen monk, Chūgan Engetsu (1300-75) is said to have produced an edition of *Nihon Shoki*, or a history of Japan, that was ordered burned by the imperial court for mentioning the theory. The theory was again rejected as distorted by Ichijō Kanera (1402-81) in his *Nihon Shoki Sanso* [Interpretations of *Nihon Shoki*].[29] It emerged again in the Tokugawa period, with Hayashi Razan the first to take it up in detail.

It is clear that Razan did not believe in the Age of the Gods and the divine antecedents of Emperor Jinmu, and it would have made considerable difference to subsequent Japanese thought if he, the leading scholar of his day, had said so. He did not. In his 'Essay on Emperor Jinmu,' he noted that Confucius himself favoured an unorthodox view of the origins of the Xia dynasty (1989-1523 BC?) and discussed it with his disciples. But when he wrote the *Spring and Autumn Annals*, he used the official source. Thus, said Razan, Confucius distinguished between public and private matters – and so did Razan. He declined publicly to refute the established historical orthodoxy, and the story of Wu Taibo is raised in *Honchō Tsugan* only to be scotched.[30] 'Essay on Emperor Jinmu' was known by other scholars of the time, but it was a personal essay and did not have the stature of *Honchō Tsugan*, the great authoritative history based on the Chinese models.

Hayashi Razan did not give any reasons for preserving a distinction between public and private matters. Neither did Confucius, but the example of Confucius was enough to persuade Razan. He was so committed to the public interest that he wrote the exact opposite of his belief in the human and Chinese origin of the imperial house. Around 1648 he wrote *Shintō Denjū* [Instructions on Shinto] and sent it to Sakai Tadakatsu (1587-1662), an elder of the bakufu; in its surviving form, it is known as *Shintō Denjū Shō* [Selections from Instructions on Shinto]. It is a short, comprehensive, and clearly written work in which Hayashi Razan interpreted Shinto in terms of Confucian metaphysics.

For example, creation occurred when Ether divided to become Yang and Yin, which he then identified as the creator gods of Shinto, Izanagi, and Izanami. They gave birth to all things, which are classified as either Yang – heaven, sun, fire, day – or Yin – earth, moon, water, night. The five elements served for further classification, given by a table.[31] The Plain of High Heaven, where the gods dwelt in the Age of the Gods, is extravagantly described by three of the most important elements in Confucian thought, Heaven, Principle, and Supreme Ultimate: 'In the ritual prayers it is recited that the gods dwell in the Plain of High Heaven. The Plain of High Heaven is Heaven (*Ten*). It is Principle. It is the Supreme Ultimate. It is a place without form where the gods by nature dwell.'[32] No one had ever described the Plain of High Heaven in that way.

In dealing with Shinto, Razan was obliged to take up history as well as metaphysics and to discuss the Age of the Gods and the origins of the imperial house. He did so in a completely orthodox way, citing the record first given in *Kojiki* and *Nihon Shoki* of the seven generations of heavenly gods and the five generations of earthly gods, leading to the Heavenly Grandchild of the Sun Goddess, who descended from the Plain of High Heaven. 'The successive generations of emperors to the present are his descendants. The accession ceremony for the emperor celebrates this descent of the Heavenly Grandchild from Heaven.'[33] A Confucian emphasis is given to the imperial regalia of mirror, jewel, and sword, but their historical provenance and significance are affirmed: 'They are the treasures received from the Sun Goddess and held by the successive generations of emperors.' They represent wisdom, compassion, and courage, and 'With the three regalia the kingly way is carried out. The principle of the kingly way and Shinto is the same.'[34] In this work, there is no trace of doubt about the truth of these things. Thus, Razan accepted the fundamental historical account of the origins of Japan and the imperial house, while converting it into the Confucian terms acceptable in his day.

In this way, Hayashi Razan presented two versions of the creation of the world and the origins of the imperial house and suppressed the version that seemed more congenial to his Confucian rationalist thinking. Why? Although the positions stated above are nonsensical, no one thinks that he was merely confused.

Before proceeding to an answer, we must take note of three cautions. First, Herman Ooms has claimed in an influential work that Hayashi Razan was searching in a complicated fashion for an affirmative philosophy for Japan's new political and social order. Thus, his purpose in taking up the Wu Taibo theory was not intended as a denial of Emperor Jinmu's descent from the Sun Goddess. 'Razan's theory of the Chinese ancestry of the imperial house, for instance, was not intended to desacralize a myth but to link Japan genealogically (physically) with the Way,' which was Chinese in origin.[35] Second, David A. Dilworth has pointed out that Hayashi Razan was far from alone in mingling Confucianism with Shinto: 'this mythological, or religious element is a common thread running through such diverse figures as Razan, [Nakae] Tōju, [Yamazaki] Ansai, and [Kumazawa] Banzan in the seventeenth century, and even Ogyū Sorai and Kokugaku in the eighteenth century.'[36] Third, there was an ancient intellectual tradition of mingling Buddhism with Shinto, to the satisfaction of both Buddhists and Shintoists; now it was time to mingle Confucianism with Shinto.

Yet Hayashi Razan was conscious of his suppression of the theory of Wu Taibo. In order to justify his position, he put forward the model of Confucius, who subscribed to the accepted theory of the origins of Xia despite doubts.

The explanation is provided by Ishida Ichirō, who says in his commentary on *Shintō Denjū Shō* that the Tokugawa Bakufu in its early stage possessed little of the theory of autonomous power that developed in its latter stages, thanks to the efforts of scholars such as Arai Hakuseki. In its early stage, the bakufu was still using borrowed legitimacy from the imperial house. The imperial house originated from the Sun Goddess and was the legitimate sovereign of Japan, but it had delegated its power to the Kamakura, Muromachi, and Tokugawa Bakufu in succession. Thus, the Tokugawa Bakufu in Hayashi Razan's time had little choice but to emphasize the sacred descent of the emperors, who in turn authorized the bakufu to govern.[37] But

Razan was a Confucian, so all this had to be expressed in the Confucian terms of the new Tokugawa era. Hence, the Plain of High Heaven, which had never been problematic in Japanese thought, became Heaven (*Ten*), Principle, and the Supreme Ultimate, according to Razan.

It was in this sense that he understood perfectly the distinction between private and public, suppressing his private view of the human and Chinese origins of the imperial house in favour of the public view of its founding by the gods of Japan.[38] Hayashi Razan is widely regarded as the first modern historian of Japan, but he would not be the last to censor his private rational beliefs for the public interest.

2
Dai Nihon Shi
[History of Great Japan]

The Imperial Loyalism of Tokugawa Mitsukuni

It is strange that one of the most powerful statements of imperial loyalism came from a branch family of the Tokugawa, which was the hereditary ruling family of the bakufu. It took the form of a history, *Dai Nihon Shi*, begun by Tokugawa Mitsukuni (1628-1700), *daimyo* of Mito domain. Although not completed until 1906, its main features and political position were well known early in the eighteenth century, as the bulk of the work, consisting of the basic annals and the biographies, was presented to the bakufu in 1720.

Dai Nihon Shi was unmatched in the time taken to complete it, but this was an era when men spent many years on beloved scholarly projects, sometimes extending over generations. Motoori Norinaga (1730-1801) spent thirty years writing *Kojiki Den* [Commentary on *Kojiki*], and the work was carried on after his death to its completion in 1832. Kawamura Hidene (1723-92) spent his life writing commentaries on the Six National Histories, which were carried on by his sons Shigene and Masune. There were others. *Dai Nihon Shi* was not unusual in this respect.

The imperial loyalism inherent in the project was significant because of the latent antagonism between the imperial house and the bakufu. This antagonism was structural: the establishment of the bakufu in the thirteenth century had necessarily diminished imperial sovereignty, and the imperial house never forgot it. In medieval times, the imperial house had twice tried to destroy the bakufu and reassert complete sovereignty, in the Jōkyū War of 1221 and in the Kenmu Restoration of the 1330s. Both times it had failed, yet the problem persisted because none of the successive bakufu (Kamakura, Muromachi, Tokugawa) developed a theory of sovereignty that was independent of the imperial house. The political theories of Neo-Confucianism that flourished in the Tokugawa period helped out the bakufu somewhat, with Arai Hakuseki contributing the most to an independent theory of bakufu sovereignty.[1] Yet such theories were feeble compared to those available to governments in China and the West, which granted full and righteous dominion to a government that had displaced a predecessor. The weakness in Japanese theory stemmed mainly from the Kamakura Bakufu's decision not to terminate the imperial line after the bakufu's military victory in 1221. This removed any need for the bakufu to consider justification of revolution. Instead, the Kamakura, Muromachi, and Tokugawa Bakufu all had to continue seeking self-legitimation while at the same time subscribing to imperial sovereignty. In the end, they convinced no one. In 1868 the bakufu fell to imperial loyalist forces asserting that 700 years had produced no justification for it.

Given this persistence of imperial sentiment, one might expect the Tokugawa Bakufu to be sensitive to expressions of pure imperial loyalism and unlikely to tolerate them in its midst. It was indeed sensitive, as shown by two incidents in the mid-eighteenth century. It punished courtiers at the imperial court who apparently hoped to disestablish the usurping bakufu. In the Hōreki Incident (1758-9), Takenouchi Shikibu (1712-67) was punished by exile, and in the Meiwa Incident (1766), Yamagata Daini (1725-67) was executed and about thirty others were punished. But the Tokugawa took no measures to clear out imperial loyalism from within their own ranks.

Indeed, the opposite was true: the bakufu, which derived its legitimacy from the emperor, had no alternative but to proclaim its sincere imperial loyalism. Thus, it is possible that the bakufu decided to let *Dai Nihon Shi* stand as its own statement of imperial loyalism when it accepted the annals and biographies of the project presented by the Mito domain in 1720. Moreover, it must have seemed safe to do so, for *Dai Nihon Shi* was produced by a family related to the Tokugawa rulers. It could not possibly be linked to intended military action against the bakufu. However, we cannot go beyond speculation on this point, because we lack evidence about the ideas of the bakufu officials who accepted *Dai Nihon Shi*.

It is even more strange that this statement of imperial loyalism came in the complex form of a major work of historical writing begun in 1657 and not completed for 250 years. But history was at the heart of imperial sovereignty, and no theory of government ever took its place. The imperial house claimed that it was a fact of history that the Sun Goddess had launched the imperial line and had promised to protect it forever. Hence, historical writing was the best expression of imperial loyalism.

Dai Nihon Shi was the inspiration of Tokugawa Mitsukuni. His first idea was to write history; loyalist history developed later. The preface to *Dai Nihon Shi*, by Tokugawa Tsunaeda, Mitsukuni's adopted son, says,

> At the age of eighteen, my father read the biography of Po I. He rose to his feet with the admiration he felt at Po I's high devotion to duty. Fondling the book, he said with a sigh, 'If this book did not exist, one could not find

out about the history of early China. If one had no histories to rely on, one could not cause future ages to know what should be emulated.' Hereupon, he sighed and conceived the determination to compile a history.[2]

The book was *Shiji* by Sima Qian. As explained by Herschel Webb,

Po I and his brother Shu Ch'i were princes of a certain Chinese state enfeoffed under the Yin dynasty. They were praised as models of fraternal deference for having yielded the throne to each other upon their father's death. In the end neither became ruler, and both went to seek refuge with the prince of the Chou state. When the latter overthrew the Yin dynasty, Po I and Shu Ch'i refused to aid him or accept his rule, preferring death by starvation on a certain 'western mountain' to service under a usurper.[3]

The story was inspiring to Tokugawa Confucians, and it may have been relevant to Mitsukuni's personal situation. Mitsukuni inherited the Mito domain despite being the third son of his father, but he then passed on the succession, not to his son but to his elder brother's line.

So lasting was the impression of the Chinese example that, when the mature Mitsukuni organized his history project, he set it up on the model of *Shiji*. It was written in Chinese and followed the same format of basic annals of the emperors, biographies, tables, and essays. This was known as the annals-biographies form [*kidentai*] of historical writing; *Dai Nihon Shi* was the first Japanese work to use it. The Six National Histories of ancient times and *Honchō Tsugan*, also written in Chinese, had used the annals for-mat [*hennentai*]. As discussed below, it was partly through adroit use of the annals-biographies format that the authors of *Dai Nihon Shi* were able to display their imperial loyalism.

Imperial loyalist history emerged next in Mitsukuni's mind, and there is no good explanation for this. Nothing in his family background, regional history, political situation, or personal circumstances caused him to become more of an imperial loyalist than anyone else. On the other hand, there was no reason why he, or any other educated Japanese of the seventeenth cen-tury, should not be. His loyalism was pure and apparently adopted out of belief in its truth and importance, in the same way that men might sub-scribe to the ideals of the way of the warrior or to a religion. In fact, since the bakufu governed Japan and took care of all the difficult details of real life, the distant and secretive court of the emperors might have seemed all the more pure.

Pure imperial loyalism of the type displayed by Mitsukuni is generally found among those who supported, as Mitsukuni did, the Southern Court in the Southern-Northern Courts schism of the fourteenth century. In 1333 Emperor Go Daigo overthrew the tottering Kamakura Bakufu by force and proclaimed an imperial restoration. However, Ashikaga Takauji (1305-58) withdrew his support and set up a new bakufu, known as the Ashikaga Bakufu after its founder, or the Muromachi Bakufu after its location in Kyoto. Ashikaga Takauji proceeded to install a rival line of the imperial house as emperor in Kyoto (the Northern Court), and war ensued against Go Daigo's line in Yoshino (the Southern Court). It lasted from 1333 to 1392, through five emperors of the Northern Court and four emperors of the Southern Court, and was finally settled through a compromise.

Loyal and selfless supporters of the Southern Court, or at least men portrayed as such, sprang into action from the beginning of the war: such were the warrior Kusunoki Masashige (1294-1336), who died by suicide in a hopeless battle, and Kitabatake Chikafusa, author of the powerful and idealistic *Jinnō Shōtōki* (1339). There are about fifteen Shinto shrines in Japan, dating from the Meiji period, devoted to the worship of men who contributed notably to the cause of the Southern Court. There appear to be none honouring those who supported the Northern Court. In addition, there is a major government-supported shrine, Yoshino Shrine, to worship Emperor Go Daigo, who started the schism; there is no such shrine for any emperor of the Northern Court. It is not clear why the Southern Court gathered such a mantle of legitimacy and such capacity for inspiration. Nor is it clear which came first in Mitsukuni's case: imperial loyalism, or overwhelming preference for the Southern Court. The tradition of selfless devotion to the Southern Court was fully established by Mitsukuni's time, and it may well have attracted him, an idealistic youth.

In addition to organizing a loyalist history, Mitsukuni manifested his imperial loyalism, for example, in his New Year's observances. Each year he put on his court dress and worshipped in the direction of the emperor in Kyoto, saying, 'My lord (*shukun*) is the emperor. The present shogun is the head of my family (*soshitsu*). One must take care not to misunderstand the situation.'[4] He was also active in the preservation of loyalist historical sites. In 1692 he sent a retainer, Sasa Jitsuchika, to repair the grave of the celebrated Kusunoki Masashige.[5] In 1694 he sent a petition to the bakufu asking for repairs to the tomb of Emperor Jinmu, but apparently nothing came of it.[6]

Probably imperial loyalism was linked with nationalism. Mitsukuni, like other scholars, became acutely aware of the historical differences between China and Japan and found that they were best illustrated by the history of Japan's singular imperial house. Like the National Scholar Motoori Norinaga, Mitsukuni argued that Japanese should stop referring to China as the Middle Kingdom: 'It is appropriate for the people of China to call their country the Middle Kingdom. But Japanese should not call it that. The capital of Japan should be referred to as the Middle Kingdom. Why should Japanese call a foreign country the Middle Kingdom? There is no justification for it.'[7]

What is striking about Mitsukuni's loyalism is its pure, abstract, disinterested quality. It must have been apparent to everyone that his loyalism had no connection with any political interests or plans. Hence, the bakufu, formally committed to the same ideology, could not disapprove, since Mitsukuni could present a threat only through the intensity, and not the nature, of his belief.[8]

Structure and Organization of *Dai Nihon Shi*

The ideology of imperial loyalism governed the structure and organization of *Dai Nihon Shi*. Basic annals covered the reigns of the emperors, and they came first. The only difficulty arose when it came to criticizing the emperors. Chinese precedent included the writing of assessments [*ronsan*] of the emperors, and the Japanese scholars originally set out to prepare assessments. Bitō Masahide notes that early Mito thought was deeply Confucian and disposed scrupulously to follow the Chinese models of historical writing, and hence the scholars were prepared to write the assessments. But Mito thought was later influenced by the Japanese Confucian school of Ogyū Sorai and by the National Studies school, both of which recommended deviation from the Chinese models.[9] Thus, the assessments were first included and then deleted. After formal deletion from the official version, they still had an effect, as they were seen by later historians, including Arai Hakuseki and Rai Sanyō (1780-1832).[10]

Assessments were written by one of the prominent early Mito scholars, Asaka Tanpaku (1656-1737), a skilled historian and a systematic rationalist. However, in 1803 they were ordered deleted by the Mito lord Harutoshi, on the ground that almost all the Mito scholars agreed upon: assessments were inappropriate for the history of Japan. They had originated in the historical practice of China, where dynasties rose and fell by the decree of Heaven, and it was plain for Chinese historians to see that those who rose had been virtuous and those who fell had not been. But this did not apply to Japan, where there had only been one dynasty, and where there would never be another dynasty. Any other outcome was unthinkable. As put earlier by Miyake Kanran (1674-1718) in his *Ronsan Bakugo* [Refutation of Assessments], 'In the history of our country all the rulers have been from a single family. Thus, the content of our histories differs from that of China, in which the new dynasty evaluates the preceding one.'[11]

A more extreme view was expressed by Takahashi Tanshitsu (1771-1823), one of the prime movers to delete the assessments: 'Assessments are fine, but sometimes there are parts that have too much plain speaking about the emperor. However much one tries to write assessments in accordance with the principles of *taigi meibun* [supreme duty of righteousness and correspondence of name and status], it will not do for a subject to do too much plain speaking. Therefore, it is proper that they were deleted from *Dai Nihon Shi*.'[12]

Another factor causing deletion was that, over the years, the historians had turned their attention to three significant interpretive questions, known as the three special features of *Dai Nihon Shi*. They made the assessments less valuable for clarifying these points. The three special features are always raised when *Dai Nihon Shi* is discussed. The Mito historians set themselves to resolve unsettled points about legitimate sovereigns, and their conclusions are always regarded as important. Yet there is almost no sign that previous historians had been worried about these points or even interested in them, and one must conclude that it was the Mito historians themselves who assigned great importance to these issues and their resolution of them.

The person most concerned about these three interpretations was Tokugawa Mitsukuni himself. The first involved Empress Regent Jingū (r. 209-69), on whose status *Nihon Shoki* was unclear. In *Dai Nihon Shi,* Jingū was made into a regent and taken out of the list of emperors, from which she has remained excluded. The determining influence was probably not the Chinese bias against female rulers but the wish to tidy up the historical record.

Second was the case of Emperor Kōbun (r. 671-2). His status was also unclear in *Nihon Shoki*, which does not say whether or not there was an accession ceremony. *Nihon Shoki* was presented to the throne by Prince Toneri (676-735), a son of Emperor Tenmu, who displaced Kōbun. Prince Toneri may have feared showing his father as a rebel against a legitimate emperor, Kōbun, so *Nihon Shoki* left open the question of his legitimacy. Mitsukuni explicitly held that Prince Toneri had concealed the truth, and he proceeded to restore Kōbun to the list of legitimate emperors,[13] where he has remained. This judgment cannot be considered unreasonable, but based on a careful investigation of the evidence available.

The third of Mitsukuni's decisions was to declare the Southern Court the legitimate line in the Southern-Northern Courts schism of the fourteenth century. The various theories are too detailed for review here, but we may render our judgment that Mitsukuni's view was no more or less worthy of acceptance than any other. For example, Asaka Tanpaku held, with equal cogency, that the five emperors of the Northern Court should be included in *Dai Nihon Shi* since they were the ancestors of the reigning emperor and thus gave legitimacy to Tokugawa Ieyasu.[14] Mitsukuni's singular devotion to the throne, which was especially pronounced among supporters of the Southern Court, dictated his conclusion. The issue of legitimacy could not be left unresolved because of loyalist political belief that there could have been a single day in history when the country was without a legitimate sovereign.

With all problems of the emperors solved, the rest of history fell into place. The shoguns, unique to Japanese history, were allotted a separate category of biographies and were treated even-handedly. This even extended to including Ashikaga Takauji and his son Yoshiaki (1329-67) in the list of shoguns, despite their appointment as shogun by the Northern Court, which was not recognized as legitimate by the Mito school. Thus, the Mito scholars in no way considered that shoguns might be disloyal. Hence, I suggested that the bakufu had no difficulty in accepting the work in 1720. The category of rebels [*hanshin*] included more than a dozen men, none of them shoguns, and only three were included in the category of traitors [*gyakushin*]: Soga Umako (?-626), who had assassinated Emperor Sushun in 587, and his son Emishi (?-645) and his grandson Iruka (?-645), who together had supposedly tried to usurp imperial powers in the seventh century and had been overthrown in the Taika Reform of 645.

The compilers even resisted the temptation to place among rebels the villainous men who had led forces against the imperial house in the Jōkyū War of 1221, defeating it and sending emperors into exile. Thus, Hōjō Yoshitoki and his son Yasutoki were included in biographies of retainers of the shogun. In the assessment of Yoshitoki, the compilers pointedly explained why he was placed in this category and not among rebellious subjects. When the line of Minamoto shoguns ended in 1219, Yoshitoki chose an imperial prince to be shogun. 'Thus, while inwardly filled with wickedness and tampering with authority, outwardly he displayed honour to the emperor.'[15] They went on to praise Yoshitoki for rightly resisting Emperor Go Toba, whose government was not virtuous, and for helping the suffering people of Japan; however, he was condemned for his interference with the imperial succession after the Jōkyū War. Here the compilers made clear that benevolent public administration was required but was insufficient without a correct attitude toward the imperial succession. Thus, they combined the political philosophies of Chinese Confucianism and Japanese imperial loyalism.

Hōjō Yasutoki's government was regarded as exceedingly virtuous. His assessment noted that, when he led forces against Go Toba, it was due to the prompting of his father, so Yasutoki was absolved from blame. In conclusion, the assessment endorsed the judgment of *Jinnō Shōtōki*: '"His argument at the time of the Jōkyū War was superior. Yasutoki carried on the achievements of Yoshitoki, encouraged the spirit of peace and order, and took nothing for himself." This is the accepted view.'[16]

Treatises and tables were written long after the basic annals and biographies and are generally not given due credit for their accuracy and usefulness. Modern scholars concentrate instead on the more interesting political questions about the imperial house that are raised in the basic annals and biographies. As Nakamura Kōya noted, the basic annals and biographies are inseparable, providing complementary sources for historical understanding. However, the treatises could be extracted from *Dai Nihon Shi* to form a distinct work of cultural history. Tables similarly could constitute a separate reference work.[17]

Evaluation of Mito Scholarship

The positivistic research conducted by the Mito scholars was unprecedented in Japan and unrivalled until the establishment of the Historical Bureau of the early Meiji government. They did everything about texts that could be done: collecting copies of old works such as *Kojiki* and *Nihon Shoki,* studying variants, comparing characters and styles, determining authenticity, and so on. Beyond that, they were the first Japanese scholars to conduct historical research in the modern style, making field trips to find documents and then applying the methods of positivistic research to these materials.

Travel for research was especially intensive between 1676 and 1693, when thirteen teams were sent out, equipped with letters of introduction from Tokugawa Mitsukuni. They were especially interested in temple documents related to the history of the Southern Court, but they also scoured the country for all manner of sources for the biographies, calling on scholars, visiting shrines and battle sites, and so on. All of Japan was covered, and one research team headed by Sasa Jitsuchika in 1685 visited forty-five provinces.[18]

The results were brought back to the *Dai Nihon Shi* compilation office, called the Shōkōkan, which first opened in 1657. The name was taken from a phrase in the preface to the ancient Chinese history *Zuo Zhuan,* 'Shōō kōrai – Elucidate the past and consider the future.' Thirty to forty people were normally employed there, reaching fifty at one point in the Genroku era (1688-1704). The high expense, consuming one-third of the Mito domain budget, provoked criticism.[19] The project not only employed people from Mito but also attracted scholars from elsewhere in Japan. The energy and efficiency of the project are plain to see in the basic annals and biographies.

However, despite their thorough checking of sources, the Mito scholars were sometimes unable to detect obvious historical fabrications that lay before their eyes. Most notable are the accounts of Emperor Nintoku, considered virtuous ever since *Kojiki* and *Nihon Shoki* were written, and Emperor Buretsu, the perfect model of the wicked emperor according to *Nihon Shoki.* These were the same emperors whose authenticity went unchallenged in *Honchō Tsugan.* The accounts in *Kojiki* and *Nihon Shoki* are full of Chinese rhetoric, detailing good and bad acts by rulers, and modern Japanese scholars have identified the sources in Chinese works. The stereotyped figures of the good first ruler who won the mandate of Heaven and founded the dynasty, and the bad last ruler who lost the mandate and caused its ruin and downfall, were common in Chinese histories. In Japan there was no change of dynasty, but Nintoku marked the beginning of a lineage within the imperial house, and Buretsu marked its end. Hence, in ancient times the historians applied the stereotypes and borrowed materials from Chinese works to create a narrative of the actions of these emperors.

It appears that in reality the historians in ancient times knew almost nothing about Nintoku and Buretsu. It is surprising that the Mito historians, who were very familiar with Chinese history and literature, did not detect these borrowings. The only explanation is that they, as devout Confucians, were convinced by these tales about sublime virtue in a good ruler and utter wickedness in a bad one. The existence of such rulers fit into the paradigm of Confucian historical explanation, and so the Mito scholars thought that the tales were historically true.[20]

Another major failure of positivistic research has already been noted in discussing Hayashi Razan – namely the events of the Jōkyū War in which Hōjō Yoshitoki and Hōjō Yasutoki are shown in a quandary about the emperor. Unlike *Honchō Tsugan*, *Dai Nihon Shi* names its sources, giving *Myōe Shōnin Denki*, *Azuma Kagami*, *Jōkyūki*, and *Masukagami* as references for different parts of the story. Nevertheless, *Dai Nihon Shi* tells the same old story. Once more Yasutoki suggests the absolute sovereignty of the emperor and holds out surrender and seeking a pardon as their only option. Yoshitoki replies that the bakufu is more virtuous than the emperor and that he does not intend to change the imperial line. Yasutoki goes away satisfied but returns alone to ask what to do in case the emperor himself leads his forces into battle. Yoshitoki agrees for the last time in these histories that there is no alternative in such circumstances but to surrender to the emperor. If, however, the emperor does not appear but sends forces to represent him, they must all fight those forces to the death.[21] As in *Honchō Tsugan*, all this is rendered from the original Classical Japanese into Classical Chinese, which carried more authority for Confucians.

The intentions of the authors of the original texts in the thirteenth and fourteenth centuries were difficult to interpret.[22] In *Dai Nihon Shi* as well, we cannot be certain of the intentions of the compilers. Which is the most important: Yasutoki's idea of the absolute sovereignty of the emperor, requiring surrender? Yoshitoki's contention that the government of the bakufu was more virtuous, justifying resistance? Yoshitoki's claim that they were not really doing anything unprecedented since they were not changing the imperial line? Or the final agreement of the two to the unlikely idea that they must surrender if the emperor himself leads his forces? *Dai Nihon Shi* gives a factual narration but provides no answers. It seems that the overwhelming importance of events touching the emperor caused them to forsake their critical faculties. As in *Honchō Tsugan*, this is a failure of both positivistic research and political philosophy.

The Age of the Gods and Emperor Jinmu

In light of the dedication of the Mito scholars to positivistic research, which was inherently rational, one might expect a critical attitude toward the Age of the Gods and the origins of the imperial line. In fact Tokugawa Mitsukuni himself expressed difficulties with the Age of the Gods, saying, 'The matters of the Age of the Gods are all strange and hard to include in the chronicle of Emperor Jinmu.' Asaka Tanpaku was more emphatic, saying, 'The matters of the Age of the Gods are far-fetched and insignificant and should be disregarded.'[23]

Were rationalist principles of historical research and interpretation applied to the Age of the Gods and Emperor Jinmu? Only in part, because of the imperial loyalism that inspired the entire project in Tokugawa Mitsukuni's time and to which the Mito scholars were committed after his death. Political belief, and not historical method, determined their attitude. The existence of Emperor Jinmu, the originator of the imperial line, was necessary to the belief in the imperial house. No one in Japan, not even the leaders of the three successive bakufu, had ever devised another political framework than the succession of emperors. While some, such as Hayashi Razan, were prepared to reconsider some details about the imperial ancestors, most people were not, apparently believing that to question details would bring the entire framework into question.

This holistic attitude was held by Tokugawa Mitsukuni, who was said – without much evidence – to have been outraged by Hayashi's views on Emperor Jinmu and sought to have *Honchō Tsugan* suppressed by the bakufu. Notwithstanding his enthusiasm for things Chinese, he was a Japanese nationalist and detested the theory of Wu Taibo. It is reported that he urged the bakufu that 'The Hayashi family should be ordered immediately to retract this evil theory and revise the work according to the standard histories.'[24] The story is difficult to assess since *Honchō Tsugan* does not relate as history the story of Wu Taibo. However, this is probably not because Mitsukuni succeeded in having it deleted but because Hayashi Razan never intended to include it.

Thus, Mitsukuni was committed to starting his history of the imperial line with Emperor Jinmu, but this landed him in difficulties with the Age of the Gods. In *Kojiki* and *Nihon Shoki*, the reign of Emperor Jinmu follows directly after the Age of the Gods, with nothing to mark the boundary between the time of gods and the time of humans. According to those chronicles, therefore, Emperor Jinmu's ancestors were divinities. This not only offended the rationalism of the Mito scholars but also made for exceptional difficulties in determining Jinmu's lineage, because the genealogies of the Age of the Gods were so disordered.

A good summary of these problems was given in 1842 by a later Mito scholar, Fujita Tōko (1806-55), in *Kōdōkan Jutsugi* [The Rationale of the Kōdōkan]. The Kōdōkan was a domain school set up by the Mito daimyo

Tokugawa Nariaki (1800-60) and was devoted to imperial loyalism and resistance to foreign intrusion. Fujita gave a commentary on one phrase in Tokugawa Nariaki's writing, *Kōdōkan Ki* [Record of the Kōdōkan], which went, 'For what purpose is the Kōdōkan established? It is to study how, in most ancient times, the gods established the highest standards and transmitted them to their descendants.'[25] This, said Fujita, was not as easy as it sounded because of confusion in the original texts, compounded by centuries of tendentious scholarship.

First, said Fujita, the numbers of the gods in the ancient texts, and discussed in works such as *Engi Shiki* [Procedures of the Engi Era, 901-23], are beyond counting. Second, *Nihon Shoki* and *Kojiki* differ in their accounts of the gods. *Nihon Shoki* proposes Kunitokotachi no Mikoto as the first deity to come into existence, while *Kojiki* gives Ame no Minaka Nushi no Mikoto. Third, and particularly troublesome, was that

> some of the later interpreters of antiquity followed *Nihon Shoki*, and some followed *Kojiki*, while others blended the two, claiming that Ame no Minaka Nushi and Kunitokotachi were the same deity, but under different names. The same kind of arguments were applied to the differences in the sequences of the deities. With respect to the deeds and the virtues of the gods, the various theories were confused, with distortion of facts and twisted meanings, leading nowhere.

This confusion, says Fujita, existed even when *Nihon Shoki* was written. Prince Toneri, the main compiler, could not sort it out and so wrote down variant versions to indicate the discrepancies in the accounts. But the matter was important because it was necessary to make clear the origins of the imperial house.

> It is usual to measure the past by the present, exaggerating what is only dimly and poorly known, with the terrible consequence of passing on absurdities. Therefore, our lord Tokugawa Mitsukuni compiled the history, starting with the reign of Emperor Jinmu, and at the head of this chapter he placed the essentials of the Age of the Gods, thereby making clear the origins of the imperial house. In doing so, he intended to straighten out these absurdities.[26]

Fujita makes clear the necessity of clarifying the deities in order to explain the origins of the imperial house. Because of the difficulties in doing so, *Dai Nihon Shi* limits itself, as he notes, to 'the essentials.' This was as far as the Mito scholars could bring themselves. Driven into this corner, they included the Age of the Gods only as a collapsed genealogy at the head of the chapter on Emperor Jinmu and then left it alone. The following citation is long, but of the 3,399 pages in the printed edition of *Dai Nihon Shi*, this is all that they could devote to the Age of the Gods:

> Emperor Jinmu's personal name was Hikohohodemi, and his childhood name was Sanu.
>
> The Heavenly Ancestor ruled the Plain of High Heaven; this is Amaterasu Ōmikami, the Sun Goddess. Her son Masaka Akatsu Kachihayabi Ama no Oshi Omimi no Mikoto married Takuhata Chichi Hime, the daughter of Takami Musubi no Mikoto, and they gave birth to Amatsu Hikohikoho no Ninigi no Mikoto.
>
> The Heavenly Ancestor commanded the assembled deities to pacify the land below, and thereupon she sent down her heavenly grandchild to dwell as ruler in the Central Land of Reed Plains. She gave to him the three sacred regalia of eight-sided jewel, eight-hand mirror, and grass-cutting sword, saying,
>
>> This Reed-plain-1500-autumns-fair-rice-ear Land is the region which my descendants shall be lords of. Do thou, my August Grandchild, proceed thither and govern it. Go! and may prosperity attend thy dynasty, and may it, like Heaven and Earth, endure for ever and ever.
>
> Thereupon the Heavenly Grandchild left his Heavenly Rock Seat and descended to the Peak of Takachiho in Hyuga and went to Ata, where he married Konohana no Sakuya Hime, the daughter of O-yama Tsumi; and they gave birth to Hiko Hoho Demi no Mikoto. Hiko Hoho Demi no Mikoto married Toyotama Hime, the daughter of the Sea God, and they gave birth to Hiko Nagisa Take Ukaya Fukiaezu no Mikoto ... Emperor Jinmu was the fourth son of Fukiaezu no Mikoto.[27]

I have called this a collapsed genealogy, devised to solve problems faced by the Mito historians. However, what remained in *Dai Nihon Shi* for readers was not an impression of the difficulties faced by the Mito scholars in trying to reconcile their rationalism with their loyalist political beliefs. Only insiders could know that story. Instead, *Dai Nihon Shi* starts on the first page with the gods. It stands as an affirmation of the imperial house, based on its origins in the Age of the Gods and its unbroken succession from Emperor Jinmu. This was standard belief among educated and uneducated alike. The intellectual struggles among the Mito scholars had yielded nothing in the final text.

The Mito scholars were superb historians, unsurpassed until the late nineteenth century. But there were at least three points on which their rationalism and positivism failed, for different reasons.

First, we have seen that they could not overcome their Confucian training and beliefs in order to examine more thoroughly the fraudulent histories of Emperor Nintoku and Emperor Buretsu in the fourth and fifth centuries. Although capable of such examination, they perpetuated fabricated history because they accepted the Confucian paradigms of the first good emperor and the last evil emperor. Emperor Nintoku was the first good emperor of the lineage, and Emperor Buretsu was the last bad emperor of the lineage. According to their Confucian thinking, the throne necessarily shifted to another lineage because of the moral failure of Emperor Buretsu. This made sense to them. Hence, they accepted, without investigation, the stories of the benevolent Emperor Nintoku, and the stories of the evil Emperor Buretsu, which were taken from Chinese sources.

Second, their support for the imperial house in the Jōkyū War of 1221 muddled their thinking about the Hōjō, who defeated and punished the imperial house. The point of their account of the war was confused.

Third, in the text of *Dai Nihon Shi*, they affirmed the Age of the Gods despite widespread disbelief among the Mito scholars. Tokugawa Mitsukuni's hostility to the theory of Wu Taibo had closed off the only other explanation of the origins of the imperial house – that it was started by a human from China. There was no other recourse than a collapsed genealogy of the Age of the Gods. They had to do it in order to explain the origins of the revered first emperor, in whose existence they believed without question.

Rationalism in Mito historical writing had not overcome the powerful demands of Confucianism and imperial ideology. Yet the inherent rationalism of their great Confucian historical project was influential. Positivistic research was firmly established in Japan by this huge work, raising the standards of scholarship far beyond those of the Japanese middle ages and even beyond the Hayashi scholars. Standards could not be further elevated until the advent of Western scientific method in the late nineteenth century. Then it would be possible to question more thoroughly the Age of the Gods, though surprisingly not the existence of Emperor Jinmu.

3
Arai Hakuseki (1657-1725) and Yamagata Bantō (1748-1821): Pure Rationalism

Lives

The lives of Arai Hakuseki and Yamagata Bantō were quite disparate since they came respectively from the highest and lowest classes of the Tokugawa social order, the samurai and the merchants. Both overcame adversity to become successful.

Arai Hakuseki was a *rōnin*, or masterless samurai, because his father had fallen into disgrace, but he rose in stature because of his great intelligence and hard work. Hakuseki was a child prodigy, of a type common in China and Japan, who could read the Chinese classics at a young age and remember them all.[1] This scholarly excellence was the source of his continued advancement as a scholar and teacher at several domains until he was employed by the bakufu in 1694, instructing the future Shogun Ienobu (r. 1709-12) until Ienobu's death in 1712. According to Hakuseki's own records, he was an indefatigable lecturer on Chinese and Japanese history, spending 1,299 sessions with Ienobu over a period of nineteen years.[2] The endurance of both teacher and pupil is remarkable.

Hakuseki was a Confucian by training and conviction, being a disciple of a much renowned scholar, Kinoshita Jun'an (1621-98). Kinoshita's scholarly descent was from Matsunaga Sekigo (1592-1657), who was in turn a disciple of the celebrated Fujiwara Seika (1561-1619). But while Hakuseki knew all the Chinese classics, he had no interest in abstract philosophy and never troubled himself much about the constituents and processes of the Confucian universe. He simply accepted tradition; for example, while believing that Heaven [*Ten*] grants or withdraws its mandate to rulers on the basis of their virtue or lack of it, he never explained what Heaven is. It was not necessary, because by his time Confucian scholars of China and Japan thought that they had reached a clear, common understanding of such things. Hakuseki simply accepted that understanding. Instead of philosophy, he devoted his energy primarily to his bureaucratic career and secondarily to the study of the history of Japan and China. Viewing history through

Arai Hakuseki (1657-1725), Confucian scholar, gave a euhemerist interpretation of the Age of the Gods. (From Miyazaki Michio, ed., *Arai Hakuseki no Gendaiteki Kōsatsu* [Modern Interpretations of Arai Hakuseki] [Tokyo: Yoshikawa Kōbunkan 1985], courtesy of the publisher)

the eyes of an orthodox Confucian, he was therefore concerned with matters of state and morality. He believed without doubt that ethics are the motive power of history, since Heaven invariably rewarded the good and punished the bad. More important for our discussion, he was a rationalist in the Confucian tradition and impatient with superstition and error. Thus, he set out to correct many errors about the ancient history of Japan.

If Arai Hakuseki was impatient with superstition and error, Yamagata Bantō was angered by them and set out to destroy them viciously and absolutely. As a youth, he studied at the Kaitokudō [Hall of Virtuous Cultivation] in Osaka, the most prominent of schools founded by members of the merchant class, and went on to study Dutch Learning. Yamagata was the first Japanese scholar to study history from the point of view of both Confucianism and Western scientific learning, and this helps to account for the relentless nature of his attacks on what he saw as the absurd beliefs of Japan and China.

As Albert Craig observed, 'Bantō's life as an Osaka merchant is a Horatio Alger-like story of initial adversity overcome by frugality and hard work, and of subsequent success and honor.'[3] As an adviser to the Sendai feudal domain, he placed its finances on a sound footing and gained much for his own family, dying a wealthy man. But he also went blind over the last twenty years of his life. During that period, he composed *Yume no Shiro* [Instead of Dreaming], dictating it to his son and others. Completed in 1820, it contained his views on a wide range of subjects, including astronomy, geography, political philosophy, religion, and history.

Arai Hakuseki's Historical Studies
Hakuseki proved himself as a working historian with *Hankanpu* [Chronology of the Domains, 1701], a record of the major daimyo houses between 1600 and 1680. Scholars are generally not interested in the work for its method, regarding it as a straightforward, competent compilation of existing records. Three works of Hakuseki have drawn scholarly interest, for both their substance and their method: *Tokushi Yoron* [A Reading of History, 1712], *Koshitsū* [The Essence of Ancient History, 1716], and its companion work *Koshitsū Wakumon* [Questions and Answers on the Essence of Ancient History].

Not many criticisms are made of his exercise in positivistic research. His histories did not take up the gods and the more dubious emperors to whom deeds were attributed by the authors of *Kojiki* and *Nihon Shoki*. Hakuseki also regarded *Kujiki* [Chronicles of Ancient Matters] as an authentic source for ancient history, but in the eighteenth century that work was discredited by scholars. Dealing with figures whose historical reality is not doubted, he confined himself to documents and narratives from mainly reliable histories and stayed away from such implausible subjects as the discussions held by the Kamakura leaders on the eve of the Jōkyū War. At most he is faulted for failing to cite his sources; for example, he borrowed extensively from Hayashi Gahō's *Nihon Ōdai Ichiran* and did not always acknowledge it.[4] More generally his view of history is criticized by moderns for its acceptance of the causative and ordering role of Heaven, which unquestionably influenced his decisions about the selection and omission of materials, as it did all Confucianists of Japan and China.

The Age of the Gods and Emperor Jinmu in Arai Hakuseki's Works
The salient point about the Age of the Gods and Emperor Jinmu in *Tokushi Yoron* is that they are not discussed at all. Arai Hakuseki was the first historian to break free from the framework for discussion that was established in ancient times with the writing of *Kojiki* and *Nihon Shoki*. Both those books began with the Age of the Gods, passed on to Emperor Jinmu as the first human emperor, and proceeded chronologically through all the emperors to date. Every historian thereafter took for granted the historical truth of this record and found it necessary to recapitulate it in some form, no matter what his own interest. Hayashi Razan started at Emperor Jinmu and struggled privately with doubts about Wu Taibo as his ancestor, but Razan's son

Gahō backed up and included the Age of the Gods in an appendix. As we have seen, the Mito historians were the first for whom acceptance was difficult. They accepted Jinmu as the first emperor, but they wrestled mightily with the Age of the Gods and ended up by reducing it to a genealogy of Emperor Jinmu. Arai Hakuseki was the first to pass over these matters, though he was well acquainted with their content and meaning.

As I have argued elsewhere, this was because Hakuseki focused on the location of political power, and not its derivation, as the important point about history.[5] Taking it for granted that power in the imperial state originally lay with the emperors, he did not chronicle them but started his history in the reign of the fifty-sixth emperor, Seiwa (r. 858-76), with the first shift of political power, namely to the Fujiwara family in 858. He then followed power through its historical location in the courts of the retired emperors, and then in the several forms of government of the military clans, culminating in the Tokugawa Bakufu. He did not seem to think that power would ever shift again, away from the Tokugawa Bakufu. In all these shifts, he detected the Confucian will of Heaven, causing power to move away from the morally deficient to the morally superior. He concluded that there had been nine periods of imperial history and five periods of warrior history leading up to his own time. Except for his ideas about causation by the will of Heaven, this periodization on the basis of political power has a pleasing modernity to it.

Hakuseki was not especially concerned about the derivation of Emperor Jinmu. He knew all the details of the theory of Wu Taibo but saw no reason to take them seriously. This was partly because of the instinctive nationalism shared by many Japanese Confucianists, who felt uncomfortable about applying Chinese theories to the history of Japan.[6] More important, Hakuseki did not need the theory of Wu Taibo in order to rationalize the origins of the imperial house. A proper interpretation of the Japanese records sufficed.

A correct approach to the Japanese records meant viewing the Age of the Gods as a record of the actions of humans. The method, called euhemerism, is well known but no longer popular in the West; it was first practised in ancient times by a Greek writer named Euhemerus (third century BC). Euhemerus claimed to have discovered, on a remote island, physical evidence that Zeus was a human being. It is not clear why Hakuseki should have been the first to develop the method in Japan, but it was an extension of a more general preoccupation among Confucian scholars with the reality or otherwise of gods and spirits of the dead.

Because of its fundamental rationalism, Confucianism often contained doubts about gods and spirits. Zhu Xi himself was not clear, saying, 'Where ghosts and spirits are concerned, even the Sages found it hard to explain the principles [governing them]. One should not say there is not really something; yet one should not say there is really something.'[7] For beating around the bush, that statement is hard to top. Japanese Confucian scholars eager to rationalize gods and spirits, and impatient with the vapid theories of medieval Shintoists, tended to see them as manifestations of the universal forces of nature identified in standard Neo-Confucianism. Thus, scholars such as Hayashi Razan, Yamaga Sokō, and Yamazaki Ansai spoke of gods and spirits as forms of Principle, Ether, Yin and Yang, and the Five Elements.[8]

In *Kishinron* [Essay on Ghosts and Spirits], Hakuseki also adopted such approaches. The traditional Shinto gods of Japan were known as the gods of Heaven and the gods of Earth, and to complete the discussion Hakuseki dealt with *tama,* spirits, which generally indicated the spirits of the dead. Citing Chinese books, he argued that the traditional gods of Heaven, whatever that meant in ancient Shinto, were associated with the Heaven of Confucianism; the gods of Earth in traditional Shinto were associated with the Earth of Confucianism; and tama were associated with humans. However, he then proceeded to complicate the issue by invoking Yin and Yang, associating tama with Yin and the gods of Heaven with Yang. Next, tama were associated with 'returning': one type of tama returns to Heaven after death, and another to Earth.[9] The argument thereafter becomes ever more complex.

For the modern reader, this clarifies nothing, since no terms were defined and the meaning of association was not discussed, although books and scholarly theories were cited. However, according to Miyazaki Michio, Hakuseki's discussion was orthodox Confucianism, drawing its central point from the Book of Rites, its reasoning from Zhu Xi's *Essay on Ghosts and Spirits,* and its major premise from the words of Confucius in the *Analects.*[10]

Hakuseki's euhemerism was reserved only for the gods mentioned in the chapters on the Age of the Gods in *Kojiki* and *Nihon Shoki* and not for the thousands of gods worshipped locally throughout the shrines of Japan. As a Confucian official, he appreciated the importance of rites in government and society. As a scholar, he saw that Shinto contained elements of the Confucian way of the ruler, that Confucian virtues could be discovered in the Age of the Gods, and that some universal aspects of Shinto were demonstrable by comparison with China. Thus, the practice of Shinto was quite tolerable.[11] Unlike that of Euhemerus, his method was not based on alleged discovery of physical evidence of the humanity of the gods but on linguistic analysis of the records of the Age of the Gods, which were well known to all scholars. His fundamental dictum in *Koshitsū* was 'What are called the gods were human beings' [*Kami to wa hito nari*], and he offered linguistic explanations of how the records of humans in ancient times had come to be misunderstood as the records of deities: 'In the common usage of Japan, respected persons are called *kami* 化美 [the characters have no meaning]. The word is the same in ancient and modern language and means "superior." But when modern orthography is used, there is a distinction between *kami* 神 [meaning deity or divine] and *kami* 上 [meaning superior].'[12]

Hakuseki claimed that confusion in orthography since ancient times had led to the belief that divinities rather than human beings were referred to at the beginning of history. In another work, *Tōga* [The Japanese *Erya*, a medieval Chinese dictionary, covering from the Chou to the Han dynasties], he amplified the point: 'In antiquity there were people called *kami* 神 [divinities]. In *Nihongi* the characters for "spirit sage" 神聖 and "godly person" 神人 were pronounced *kami*. Now in general Japanese usage, *kami* signifies reverence. Thus, rulers, palace heads, and so forth are called *kami*. Hence, it was an appropriate term for godly persons; they were called *kami* to indicate reverence.'[13] The main point was that the godly persons of ancient times were persons, no matter what peculiarities of orthography and pronunciation prevailed. On this basis, Hakuseki proceeded in considerable detail to a euhemerist interpretation of ancient history.

In *Koshitsū* Hakuseki presented twenty-five points of reinterpretation of the Age of the Gods. They are based on a reasonable and thoughtful analysis of linguistic history according to *Kojiki* and *Nihon Shoki* and on the nature of language in general. However, they are also often speculative, occasionally forced, and frequently unconvincing even when they are difficult to challenge. Whether or not he was correct in detail is moot and need not concern us. Let us take one example.

The Plain of High Heaven

Generally Hakuseki's reinterpretations are based on place names or words describing the qualities of the characters mentioned. Typical is his discussion of the main location of the Age of the Gods, called the Plain of High Heaven [Takamagahara], which he identified as an actual place in Hitachi Province.

> We see that 'according to the theory of the teacher in *Nihongi Shiki* [Private Commentary on *Nihongi*], Takamagahara 高天原 means "Heaven," but it is more likely that it refers to the sky.'[14] Later scholars are in agreement with this interpretation. However, they all attempt to explain its meaning on the basis of the Chinese characters that are currently used.
>
> In general, when reading the books of ancient Japan, understanding should be based on the meaning of the ancient words, and not on the Chinese characters that are used.
>
> The character for High 高 was read as 'Taka,' and the pronunciation is found in the name of the ancient province of Taka 高 in *Sendai Kuji Hongi* [Basic Annals of Events of Former Ages] and of Taka 多珂 in *Hitachi no Kuni Fudoki* [Geographical Record of Hitachi Province],[15] and this latter usage is found in present-day Taka District in Hitachi Province.

The character for Heaven 天 in *Kojiki* is glossed as 'Ama' 珂麻. When the ancients said 'Ama,' they meant the ocean. 'Ame' 阿海 meant Heaven; but through phonetic change, this character came to be pronounced 'Ama' 珂麻 [hence, 'Ama' refers to the ocean].

The character for Plain 原 was read as 'Hara' 播羅. What the ancients meant by 'Hara' was 'on top of, above.'

Putting it all together, the ancient word Taka-Ama-no-Hara meant a maritime location called Taka.

> Note: I have said that the ancient word 'Hara' meant 'on top of, above.' This is found, for example, in *Nihon Shoki*, where the word for 'upstream' 川上 is read as 'Kahara' 箇播羅.[16]
>
> At the present day, there are places in Kaijō District 海上 in Hitachi Province with names such as Takamaura 高天浦 and Takamagahara 高天原.[17]

Thus, Hakuseki concluded that the term 'Plain of High Heaven' in the Age of the Gods referred to a place name in Hitachi Province. By such means, he grounded the gods in actual places in ancient Japan and proceeded in similar ways to rationalize their activities as those of humans.

Hakuseki retained his respect for these actors in ancient times because of their great work of founding state and society. He found no difficulty in retaining respect for the Shinto shrines that recognize them as deities, especially the shrines of Ise, which worship the Sun Goddess; Izumo, which worships Ōkuninushi [The Master of the Land]; and Atsuta, which worships several of the founding deities.[18]

In his euhemerism, Hakuseki edged toward the position that the myths of the Age of the Gods had been concocted in order to support the legitimacy of the imperial house. There is no such suggestion in his historical works, but a hint can be found in a 1721 letter to Sakuma Dōgan (1652-1736). He says that the Japanese imperial house dated from the end of the Chou dynasty in China (third century BC) but that there was physical evidence that humans, and not gods, existed in Japan before that: bells had been excavated. In order to support the imperial house, said Hakuseki, the Age of the Gods was invented to confuse the issue.[19] He did not pursue the point and may have made it inadvertently. To contend that the Age of the Gods was concocted to support the imperial house was quite different from arguing that it had come to be misunderstood through linguistic confusion.

What shall we make of it? In the Tokugawa period, it made little difference to the prevailing scholarship, and certainly none at all to the Japanese populace at large, that one scholar had rationalized the gods into humans. In modern Western societies, the general reinterpetation of the beginning of things took place over centuries of effort by thousands of scholars, with many wrong beginnings and blind alleys, amateur mistakes, disputes and refutations, dire predictions of social disaster, and consequences both intended and unintended. In Japan Hakuseki was alone in his own time. Hardly anyone knew how to respond to him, except those such as Motoori Norinaga – who issued learned and detailed affirmations of the truth of the Age of the Gods. However, when seen in the context of an ongoing development from Hayashi Razan's doubts about Emperor Jinmu, and the vexations about origins that afflicted the Mito scholars, Hakuseki's work forms part of a scholarly trend toward rationalizing and secularizing the origins of Japanese society.

The Militant Rationalism of Yamagata Bantō

In the preface to *Yume no Shiro*, Yamagata said that he realized that he was passing his life pointlessly by resting whenever he felt like it, so he disciplined himself to write instead of just drifting off every day. Hence the title of his book: Instead of Dreaming. This much he owed, he thought, to his teachers at the Kaitokudō, Nakai Chikuzan (1730-1804) and his younger brother Nakai Riken (1732-1817), to whom he attributed all his good ideas. But he absolved them from any blame for the fact that his writing touched on sensitive, even dangerous, topics:

> The sections on astronomy and geography were written initially with respect for the ancient laws, but in the end it was necessary to explain the rotation of the earth on its axis, which is prohibited. I also ended up freely proposing hypotheses, but if readers are confused, it is all my fault for simply following where my thoughts led me. There ought not to be any doubts. In the section on the Age of the Gods, I have destroyed the ancient theories that were handed down to the present day. I cannot escape from the charge that I have argued against the foundations of the august imperial house. In the section on the historical succession of emperors, I have criticized the national histories, including the theory of the divine ancestors; for this I repeatedly apologize. For this reason, the book should not be widely circulated.[20]

The two dangerous topics, astronomy and geography, and the Age of the Gods, were connected. It was partly his knowledge of Western science and geography that led Yamagata into extensive criticism of Japanese religion and history.

Like most Tokugawa scholars, Yamagata was thoroughly trained in Confucianism. At the beginning of *Yume no Shiro*, he thoughtfully listed the books from which he had quoted; they consisted of about 370 titles, ranging over the major and minor works of China and Japan in philosophy and history. He cited the exact words of the works that he attacked, and it must be said that he knew his enemies. But the list also contained works of science.

If Confucianism contributed to his rationalism, as it did to that of other scholars, Western science gave him factual knowledge that was lethal to many established beliefs. Hayashi Razan dismissed strikes of lightning as having nothing to do with a lightning god. So did Yamagata; but while Hayashi Razan went on to explain lightning as a product of Yin and Yang, Yamagata scoffed at such ideas, because he knew the scientific facts. Beyond that, the rationalism and the method of inquiry in science led him to question basic Confucian concepts. Whereas Confucianists accepted Heaven, Principle, Ether, Yin and Yang, and the Five Elements as basic elements and forces of the universe, and applied rationalism within that framework, science asked whether their reality could be demonstrated by experimental method. A clash between Confucianism and science, inevitable at some point in Japanese intellectual history, occurred in the thought of Yamagata Bantō.

Mainly because of his scientific knowledge, Yamagata was an atheist. He lived in the midst of what he considered profound and universal ignorance and superstition. Perhaps it was necessary, at that stage of the intellectual history of Japan, for someone to go out of his way to attack ideas of gods, ghosts, and spirits: Chapters 10 and 11 of *Yume no Shiro* are called 'Mukiron' [Atheism]. Minamoto Ryōen's general observation applies to these chapters: 'What distinguished his thought was not so much its depth or elaborateness as the scathing nature of his criticisms, and his clarity.'[21] Chapter 10 bases most of the discussion on Chinese works, while Chapter 11 takes up the major shrines of Japan, as well as goblins and ogres.

Yamagata's interest was in exposing falsehood and superstition and in establishing truth; he had no objection to the social purposes of Confucianism. Thus, he attacked the concept of life after death because it could not be demonstrated scientifically or even rationally, but he thought that parents should be remembered and honoured. This had no connection in his mind with ghosts and spirits.

Despite his rejection of Confucian metaphysics and popular belief in gods, Yamagata was explicit on the point that the Confucian social order was excellent. *Yume no Shiro* concludes, 'As I see it, there are various teachings, but nothing as good as Confucianism. Let the ruler be the ruler, and the subject the subject; let the father be the father, and the son the son. What more could one seek?'[22]

Chapter 3 of *Yume no Shiro* is an extended discussion of the Age of the Gods in which Yamagata demolishes it from the point of view, first, of general rationalism, in which the deities and their acts were inherently improbable; second, of major errors, inconsistencies, and anachronisms in the

standard accounts of the Age of the Gods; and third, of unacceptable interpretations by Japanese scholars through the ages up to his own time. However, these three aspects are not separated in his text. 'No matter what the
subject,' wrote Yamagata, 'we must doubt what is doubtful, and refute what
must be refuted.'[23]

The first, the inherent improbability of the deities and their acts, was
perhaps the easiest critique to make, and it can be applied to most traditional religions. For a person learned in geography, the stories of the creation of Japan in *Kojiki* and *Nihon Shoki* were ridiculous, consisting, for example, of sexual intercourse by deities to produce islands. Other acts of
creation were equally risible, such as Izanagi's cleansing himself of pollu-
tion and thereby producing more deities by acts such as washing his eyes
and nose. Yamagata was not interested in euhemerism or any other kind of
interpretation of these stories: they were presented as truth, and he thought
that they should be dispensed with.

The second concern, errors and anachronisms in the ancient texts, involved a more scholarly approach. It was apparent that Yamagata had studied *Kojiki* and *Nihon Shoki* as deeply as anyone and would not be caught
with inconsistencies of his own or in the failure to consider some of the
evidence. One obvious target was chronology, which contained internal
contradictions and on which the ancient sources did not agree; nor did
they square at all with Chinese sources, which were generally considered
reliable. Merely to point out the problems in chronology was sufficient to
expose their absurdity. For example, Yamagata noted that medieval books
based on *Kojiki* and *Nihon Shoki* stated that the deity Fukiaezu died at the
age of 836,042. Not only that, since the year that he died was the forty-fifth
year of the reign of his fourth son, Emperor Jinmu, it also meant that he
had produced a child at the age of 835,998.[24] And in *Nihon Shoki* itself,
Emperor Jinmu noted in 667 BC, 'From the date when our Heavenly ancestor descended until now it is over 1,792,470 years.'[25] Such matters were
studied by scholars in the Meiji period who worked out a more acceptable
chronology, if not for the Age of the Gods, then at least for the established
list of emperors, culminating in the work of Naka Michiyo (1852-1908) in
1897.

Refutation of scholarly views, Yamagata's third point, concerned the reliability of historical evidence. The Age of the Gods and the history of the
early emperors were based on oral records of an illiterate society, and
Yamagata held that they were not reliable; indeed, they were entirely dis-
missible. According to *Nihon Shoki*, the Chinese writing system was adopted
in Japan during the reign of Emperor Ōjin (r. 270-310), providing a written
record for history after that time. Interestingly historians continue to accept the reign of Emperor Ōjin as a reasonable date for the beginning of
Chinese writing in Japan. 'The theory is,' wrote Yamagata, 'that the legends

were transmitted from ancient times, but since, according to Emperor Jinmu, 1,700,000 years had elapsed since the beginning, no credence should be given to that. Since writing did not exist from Emperor Jinmu until Empress Regent Jingū (r. 201-269), those events cannot be known.'[26] Anthropological knowledge hardly existed in his time, but Yamagata was able to say with confidence that 'Even at the present day there are countries without writing systems. In such countries, events of two or three reigns previous are transmitted orally, but before that they cannot be known.'[27] He did not say which countries he had in mind.

These views about historical documents brought him into direct conflict with the views of the major National Scholar, Motoori Norinaga, by then deceased. Norinaga's massive study *Kojiki Den* [Commentary on *Kojiki*, 1798] affirmed the literal truth of the Age of the Gods and held that the record in *Kojiki* was based on perfect oral tradition, transmitted without alteration from the Age of the Gods. Yamagata attacked Norinaga on many points involving this acceptance of oral tradition. Furthermore, he went on to ridicule Norinaga's other beliefs – for example, that the sun is a deity and had been born in Japan, which gave a special distinction to the Japanese nation. For a man like Yamagata, persuaded of heliocentricity, such an idea was preposterous beyond imagination. Of Norinaga's belief that the sun was a female deity, he wrote, 'Why, oh why, should a man with such wide learning in the study of Shinto go to such an extreme of stupidity?'[28] Norinaga also accepted the truth of tales such as the descent of the deity Hiko Hoho Demi to the bottom of the sea, where the Sea God lived in his castle and where he met a maiden who drew water from a well with a jewelled vessel. Did Norinaga really think, asked Yamagata, that there is a castle at the bottom of the sea? That there is a well at the bottom of the ocean?[29] And so on.

Since writing was unknown in ancient Japan, but was indeed known in China, Yamagata rejected the theory of Wu Taibo as the originator of the Japanese imperial house:

Writing was known in China in the time of Wu Taibo. If he came to Japan and established the country, why did he not propagate writing? After all, it is by means of writing that the state comes into being. After writing has become known, it is not possible to conceal its existence. [Therefore, it is evident that Wu Taibo never came to Japan.] The family history of the Wu is perfectly clear in *Shiji*, which says, 'Taibo died without heirs. He was succeeded by his younger brother Yuzhong.'[30]

Having destroyed the theory of the origins of the Japanese state in the Age of the Gods, and the theory of Wu Taibo set forth to rationalize such myths, Yamagata felt no need to offer an alternative. With destruction, his work was done.

Because of his lack of interest in saying how the Japanese state had actually developed in history, Yamagata Bantō has been disregarded by most modern scholars and is largely a forgotten figure. However, it is often noted that he was an intellectual predecessor of Tsuda Sōkichi (1873-1961), who covered much of the same ground and on whose research much of the history of ancient Japan has been based in the postwar period. Tsuda was tried and convicted in 1942 for insulting the imperial dignity by casting doubt on the existence of the Age of the Gods and the early emperors. In his written defence at the trial, Tsuda noted his scholarly predecessors, and Yamagata Bantō was prominent among them.[31]

4
Date Chihiro (1802-77):
Three Stages in the History of Japan

Hayashi Razan's turning away from Buddhism to Confucianism is said to symbolize the transition to modern scholarship.[1] But as we have seen, Hayashi Razan drew back from making public his doubts about Emperor Jinmu, so much remained to be done in order to rationalize Japanese history and place it on a universal basis.

The Mito historians carried out the best study based on positivistic research that developed within Confucianism, but they trembled at facing up to their doubts about the Age of the Gods. So far as any reader could tell, they affirmed the Age of the Gods on the first page of the first volume by giving the genealogy of Emperor Jinmu.

Arai Hakuseki turned the gods of ancient Japan into human beings, and doing so permitted him to dismiss them as a special factor in history that enfranchised forever the imperial house. This freed him to try to legitimate the Tokugawa Bakufu in fresh ways. More important for our purposes, he was able to think creatively about the history of humans in Japan and to arrive at a new periodization based on the location of political power. This was the greatest step in traditional Japan toward the development of social science.

Yamagata Bantō completed the secularization of Japanese history with his denial that gods and spirits exist. Euhemerism, the process of converting incredible and garbled tales of deities into acceptable stories about humans, was unnecessary because the stories about the Age of the Gods simply contained no truth. However, Yamagata Bantō stopped with the destruction of the ancient myths and did not provide an alternative explanation.

It remained for Date Chihiro to produce the first constructive account of Japanese history based on the rationalism that had developed to such a striking degree in Tokugawa Japan. Date's *Taisei Santenkō* [literally Thoughts on Three Turning Points in the Times, rendered here as Three Stages in the History of Japan] was the first Japanese work to consider the underlying social and economic conditions of life as the basis for periodization of history.

Date was a financial official in Kishū han, governed by the Tokugawa, and he wrote *Taisei Santenkō* in 1848, by lamplight at night, in the intervals of a busy official life. The work is significant as the culmination of rationalist and secular trends in the Tokugawa period. However, it was not published until 1873, so its influence on modern historiography was minor.

After 1848 Date Chihiro suffered setbacks as he supported a losing side in han politics and spent the years from 1852 to 1861 under house arrest.[2] After his release, he went to Kyoto to become involved in Restoration politics, not to much effect, and was forced to resume incarceration in his han, to be released after the Meiji Restoration. His biographer has little to say about his involvement in Restoration politics. Politics was not actually his passion; he was a literary gentleman, deeply read in the Japanese classics, who wrote poems, essays, miscellanies, and travel books. He was a disciple of the National Scholar Motoori Ōhira (1756-1833), the adopted son of Motoori Norinaga. Yet while Date appreciated the literary insights of the National Scholars, he did not share their dogmatic views of history, and he may best be seen as an independent rationalist. In 1870, at the age of sixty-nine, he wrote:

> In all things, one should not stick to a single view. Each country has something in which it excels. It is by observing and listening widely that the way of civilization opens up ... In the past, Confucianism and Buddhism were supreme in our country. But now the way of the West is opening up, bringing success and abundance. By holding only to Confucianism, or by putting on nothing but Buddhism, or by firmly clinging to National Studies, nothing great will be accomplished.[3]

Taisei Santenkō does not even mention the Age of the Gods, thereby revealing its modern viewpoint. It starts, like *Tokushi Yoron*, with a simple statement about the periodization of Japanese history: in Japan there have been three periods of history, named according to their dominant social and political characteristics. They are the age of *kabane*, or Clans; the age of *tsukasa*, or Offices in the Imperial Government; and the age of *na*, or names indicating Status in Feudal Society.

Thus, Date proposed a new periodization of history based on social and political materials other than the records of the imperial house used by traditional historiography or the narrative of political power as outlined by Arai Hakuseki. The three periods, says Date, correspond to upper, middle, and lower divisions of history. Ishige Tadashi has pointed out that at least eight other Tokugawa scholars used similar terms of upper, middle, and lower to periodize history, including both Confucian scholars such as Yamaga

Sokō and Arai Hakuseki and National Scholars such as Kamo Mabuchi.[4] However, none used them in Date Chihiro's sense of periods based on social and political data.

The time spans for each period are close to those used by modern historians, with the upper age of Clans extending from Emperor Jinmu to the late seventh century, the middle age of Offices in the Imperial Government going from the establishment of the *ritsuryō* state around 700 to the establishment of the Kamakura Bakufu in 1185, and the lower age of Status in Feudal Society covering from 1185 to 1848. Such periodization seems simple and obvious to modern readers, yet it was by no means so in 1848.

Date considered the first era, the age of Clans, to have originated spontaneously in Japan. It had none of the features of the two later eras. At the time, there was no writing in use to describe it.[5] However, Date trusted the account given in *Nihon Shoki* and cited it extensively to illustrate the nature of social organization and the sources of authority in the most ancient period. Using passages from the successive reigns of emperors, Date covered all the institutions of ancient times, showing clearly that clans were hereditary, regional, and specialized and did not draw their authority from appointment by the emperor. The emperor regulated the clans by confirming leaders, but this differed from imperial appointments in the age of Offices in the Imperial Government. Under the latter system, appointments were given to individuals for civil and military purposes, within the capital and without, and these offices were not transmitted to the descendants of the holders. In the Clan system, clans retained authority in their regions and kept the positions hereditarily. Their land was their own and not granted by the court.[6]

The first part of Date's work thus consists mainly of the citation of passages from *Nihon Shoki*. This makes for exceedingly dry reading, and for this reason it is unlikely that *Taisei Santenkō* will ever be translated. Yet Date was the first historian to notice that the narrative in *Nihon Shoki* illuminated the social and political basis of ancient society, and his citations were aptly made to this end. He was especially at pains to cite materials illustrating the autonomy of the clans, even when they were described in *Nihon Shoki* in the context of imperial action. He showed how they differed from apparently similar materials describing imperial action, such as appointments to office, in the next age of Offices in the Imperial Government.

The Clan system was broken up by the emperors, starting with the establishment of court ranks in the reign of Empress Suiko (r. 592-628) and the Seventeen-Article Constitution of Prince Shōtoku in 604. Date emphasized Article 12, which announced imperial sovereignty: 'Let not the provincial authorities or the Kuni no Miyakko levy exactions on the people. In a country there are not two lords; the people have not two masters. The sovereign is the master of the people of the whole country. The officials to whom he gives charge are all his vassals. How can they, as well as the Government, presume to levy taxes on the people?'[7] The system of Offices in the Imperial Government began in 645 with the first imperial appointments to offices in the central government; these offices were accompanied by land grants. Thus, governance of land was regulated for the first time by the imperial court and not by the authority of its holders.[8] The process was completed by Emperor Tenmu in 684 with his reordering of the Clan system into eight grades of family ranks, determined and awarded by the court.[9]

Most important is Date's assessment of the underlying causes of this change: 'In most ancient times, the people were simple and affairs were not major. But the country gradually extended in size, the population increased, and matters became more complex, inevitably making government difficult without a strict system.'[10] This statement is now unexceptional, but Date was the first person in Japan to make it. He made a similar rational point about the fabled expeditions of Empress Regent Jingū (regent 201-69) to conquer Korea, observing that among the causes was a need to obtain gold and silver.[11] But Date was not equipped by the Japanese tradition of historiography to develop his rational insight any further; that remained for future generations of social scientists. Having stated his view of essential causation, he pressed on with his narrative of the development of the age of Offices in the Imperial Government.

However, Date went on to compromise his explanation for modern readers. He was ambivalent about the role of the gods in history and was not sure whether to yield to them ultimate causative power.

> The imperial decrees broke up the old system, a drastic measure by the emperors. Since the Clan system was devised by the ancients, and the system of Offices in the Imperial Government represented a shift to Chinese ways, it might seem regrettable that the ancient system of imperial Japan was destroyed. Yet whether the phenomenon of change in the times is an autonomous principle of Heaven and Earth, or whether it is in accordance with the plans of the gods, cannot be fathomed by ordinary minds. In the end, human intellect and strength do not extend that far.[12]

All Japanese commentators have fastened on this passage, and Ozawa Ei'ichi is representative in arguing that Date was not free from medieval ideas and the influence of Tokugawa-period National Studies, both of which affirmed historical causation by the gods of Japan.[13] Arakawa Kusuo, a latter-day National Scholar, claims Date outright for that school, though he notes where Date differed from the master, Motoori Norinaga.[14]

If Date shared belief in the will of the gods with the National Scholars, he differed in his positive assessment of the departure from the ancient system to the Chinese-influenced imperial system. He maintained that, in addition to population increase and accompanying material problems, there was a need for governing techniques, and so Buddhism and Confucianism necessarily came to Japan. It was as natural, said Date, as the succession of the seasons.[15]

Thus, he disagreed profoundly with the National Scholars, for whom it was an article of faith that the shift in ancient times to the foreign, Chinese system was entirely regrettable. They held that it had resulted from some fundamental error in history in which the pure and beautiful Japanese of ancient times had been somehow deceived or misled. Moreover, Date turned against the National Scholars their belief that everything that happened in history was the result of the plans of the gods, thus exposing the fundamental weakness of their position: if everything was willed by the gods, how can anything be criticized? However things have gone, did not the gods will it? The shift from the Clan system to the Chinese-style system of Offices in the Imperial Government must have been ordained by the gods. Their works are unfathomable by human intellect and beyond criticism by it. Clearly the gods had meant the ancient Japanese to turn to the Chinese system, because that is what happened.

However, Date did not define the respective spheres of competence of gods and humans, the reasons why the gods might intervene, the duration of their activity, or any other aspect of their work. In this he was not alone: no National Scholar ever produced a systematic theology that clarified these points. Motoori Norinaga made the most organized efforts in this direction, but he was unable to maintain his distinction between the sacred sphere and the secular sphere.[16] Date did not even attempt a distinction; he simply had a belief in the gods that he could not avoid mentioning. Late in life, he reiterated this belief in ultimate causation, saying, 'After all, the changes in the world are mysterious, and human intellect does not extend that far,' and 'The natural changes in the times are mysterious and outside of ordinary human discourse.'[17]

However, if we weigh these statements against the structure and narrative of *Taisei Santenkō*, written more than twenty years earlier, it is clear that secular causation is primary in that work. In addition, the discussion of the ages of Offices in the Imperial Government and Status in Feudal Society is devoid of the kind of generalization about causation given above for the age of Clans and relies instead on cumulative historical description. Apparently it was only the most ancient history of Japan that was likely to tempt authors into speculation about the will of the gods. Otherwise, Ishige Tadashi sums up Date's method with an awkward but correct term, *genjitsu-teki ōhen shugi*, 'realistic expediency.'[18]

The second age, Offices in the Imperial Government, is given in some detail, proceeding through all its major institutions of ranks and offices, the addition of extra-legal institutions such as the Kurōdo-dokoro [Emperor's

Private Office] and Kebiishi [Capital Police], the Fujiwara Regency, and the government of the retired emperors. The main reason that Date gives for the downfall of the system of Offices in the Imperial Government is the separation of military offices from the civil government, which was subsequently overwhelmed by the military. He makes no reference to the gods.

Next Date discusses the age of Status in Feudal Society, which began in 1185 when Minamoto Yoritomo (1147-99) received permission from the court to establish stewards in the manors of the country and constables in the provinces. Yoritomo's power was based on the feudal families that had developed in the late period of Offices in the Imperial State, when the imperial court appointed regional families to conduct its northern wars. Date praises Minamoto Yoritomo for his wisdom in separating his power base from Kyoto, not taking imperial office like his failed predecessor Taira Kiyomori (1118-1181). Yoritomo concentrated instead on the governance of the military families, under the title of shogun. But Date's coverage of the transition from the age of Offices in the Imperial State to that of Status in Feudal Society does not contain any sudden insight, as does his discussion of the transition from Clans to Offices in the Imperial State. His most illuminating observation is that, whereas the change from Clans to Offices in the Imperial State was initiated from above by the emperors, the change to Status in Feudal Society came from below by the warrior families.[19]

Otherwise, his discussion of the age of Status in Feudal Society is disappointing for its brevity and complete lack of analysis of the Tokugawa system. He gives a quick survey of the deeds of Oda Nobunaga and Toyotomi Hideyoshi in the sixteenth century, the advent of the Tokugawa, and then a sudden conclusion: 'History has come to the present peaceful regime, with the system of Status in Feudal Society flourishing greatly.'[20] It is not clear why Date could not deal at all with the Tokugawa period; few scholars have dealt with the question.[21]

Despite this unsatisfying finish, Date's work remains as a great accomplishment of the development of rational, secular historical writing in Japan. It followed *Tokushi Yoron* in not dealing with the Age of the Gods, but it advanced beyond that work in not discussing the relations between the imperial court and the bakufu as the most important thing in history. *Taisei Santenkō* is the first work to deal with the history of the social and political organization of the Japanese nation, thus providing a new perspective on ancient problems. It is not, of course, a social history of the Japanese people, since it is about elites and how they were organized. But it did foreshadow some of the concerns of Meiji authors such as Fukuzawa Yukichi (1834-1901) and Taguchi Ukichi (1855-1905), who insisted that the history of 'civilization,' and not the deeds of emperors and generals, was the proper concern of historians.

The periodization of *Taisei Santenkō* was the culmination of the trends toward secularism and rationalization in Tokugawa thought. Yet it is apparent that, although impressive in retrospect, *Taisei Santenkō* did not have much significance in the development of modern Japanese historical thought. Published in 1873, it came out just at the wrong time.

In the period of Civilization and Enlightenment of early Meiji (the 1870s), those who sought rationalist foundations for modern Japan turned to the thought of the modern West. They regarded all the rationalist works of the Tokugawa period that we have surveyed as of a piece with the fusty, narrow, crabbed Confucian intellectualism that sought to uphold the institutions of a backward era. Fukuzawa Yukichi, the father of Civilization and Enlightenment, had scathing words for one of the greatest rationalist works, *Tokushi Yoron* by Arai Hakuseki. The nine stages of imperial history and the five stages of military history, said Fukuzawa, were only demarcations in elite politics and told nothing about the history of the Japanese nation. 'Throughout the whole twenty-five centuries or so of Japanese history, the government has been continually doing the same thing; it is like reading the same book over and over again, or presenting the same play time after time. Thus, when Arai Hakuseki talks about "nine stages" and "five stages" in the general spirit of the country, he is just presenting the same play fourteen times over.'[22] In place of this self-interested and irrelevant learning, Fukuzawa and the other scholars of the Enlightenment proposed an exciting view of Japan in world history, locating its position on the edge of great advances in civilization.

Yet the Confucian rationalism of the Tokugawa period, scorned in the 1870s and early 1880s, would make its return in scholarly historical thought in the 1890s, in alliance with Western historical method. The combination of Confucian rational method and Western scientific method laid the basis for modern historical thought and method to the present day.

5
The Resistance of the National Scholars

Motoori Norinaga

Before discussing the fate of rationalist scholarship in the Meiji period, I must pause to note the strength of National Learning [*kokugaku*], whose proponents were well aware of the trends outlined above and vehemently opposed them. National Learning became ever stronger and more articulate in the late eighteenth and nineteenth centuries, while in comparison the thread of rationalist scholarship appeared weak and tenuous.

National Learning began with a natural and somewhat inarticulate notion that the Confucian scholarship that overwhelmed intellectual society in the early Tokugawa period was inappropriate to Japan, whose political and social traditions were vastly different from those of China. I have already noted this in Tokugawa Mitsukuni and other Mito scholars, themselves Confucian, who felt uncomfortable with the application of Chinese historical theory to the Japanese emperors. Outside the entire field of Confucian studies, there gradually emerged a school of National Learning, which developed by the nineteenth century into a learning equally as scholarly and sophisticated as Confucianism. However, it took as its starting point the literal truth of the ancient Japanese myths rather than the universal principles of the Neo-Confucian synthesis.

The lineage of National Scholars is well known. The first prominent name is the monk Keichū (1640-1701), who worked quietly in Kyoto on ancient poetry and began studies in Japanese philology. He was followed by Kada Azumamaro (1669-1736), whose championship of Japanese studies against Chinese studies appears to have been expressed publicly. He is said to have petitioned the bakufu to support a school of Japanese studies, in the same way as it supported orthodox Neo-Confucianism in the Hayashi school. Nothing came of it.[1] Next came Kamo Mabuchi (1697-1769), who concentrated on ancient poetry and professed to find in the ancient words a Japanese Way; that is, a way of life that arose spontaneously in ancient Japan, was more natural than any Chinese Way, and superior. Mabuchi studied the ancient poetry collection *Man'yōshū* [Collection of Ten Thousand Leaves, 759] as the source of this way. He met his disciple, Motoori Norinaga (1730-1801), on only one occasion, in 1763, a night of unparalleled intellectual excitement.

Motoori Norinaga lived in Matsuzaka, near the great shrine of Ise, which worships the Sun Goddess; living there probably influenced his beliefs. He had no interest in continuing the family's commercial business and trained instead as a doctor. Doctors had the status of samurai and the privilege of wearing swords, but he had no inclination toward the martial way and even criticized the samurai ideology. Visiting Kyoto he was attracted by the literary scholarship of that ancient seat of learning, but – in his thirties – he had not yet found his calling in life. When he met Mabuchi in Matsuzaka, they discussed the ancient literature and the ancient Way of Japan. Mabuchi said that he had intended to extend his studies to *Kojiki* but that not enough time remained in his life. Therefore, he urged Norinaga to take up the task. This famous 'Meeting in Matsuzaka,' his only encounter with the master, marked the turning point in Norinaga's life, and he was inspired to spend the rest of his own life studying *Kojiki*. He finally completed his *Kojiki Den* [Commentary on *Kojiki*] in 1798. Thus, with Norinaga the National Scholars finally came to the point of addressing the fundamental historical myths of Japan found in *Kojiki*.

Kojiki Den follows the text of *Kojiki* from the beginning to the end. Norinaga reconstructed the script that had been invented for *Kojiki* and subsequently abandoned. By doing so, he showed modern readers how it should be read aloud. He then proceeded to deep philological studies of the passages and the individual words, clarifying their meanings in ancient times. This philology was based on extensive knowledge of ancient Japanese and Chinese works, and in case after case he showed how understanding had been distorted by misreadings accumulated over the centuries. Where appropriate he proceeded to disquisitions on the institutions and beliefs of ancient society. The work was a tour de force, and current scholars of *Kojiki* cannot neglect it.

Norinaga's research methods were remarkably close to those of the Confucians. Yet he consistently and forcefully opposed Chinese learning in general, saying that it consisted of a vain and unwarranted exercise of human intellect on matters that could not possibly be known. The human mind, he argued with considerable logic, is small and weak and cannot extend to an understanding of the principles of the universe. In an age that lacked science, his contention carried great force. Norinaga claimed that Confucian scholars who discussed the Supreme Ultimate, Principle, Ether, Yin and Yang, the Trigrams, and so on were dealing with nothing but their own intellectual inventions; these things had no existence in reality. Worse, they were not even aware of their errors and their pretensions. Japanese scholars, he said, should be aware of this Chinese spirit and protect themselves against it by adopting the Japanese spirit. This involved admitting the weakness of intellect and a humble recognition that the truth of things had already been known in Japan in the Age of the Gods. But here he departed from logical discussion and entered his own world of belief. The tales of the Age of the Gods, he held, were literal truth; they had been handed down without error or alteration by oral transmission and had fortunately been copied into writing in 712 in *Kojiki*. Since that time, they had been neglected and forgotten because of the unfortunate influence of Chinese culture on Japan, but with dedicated scholarly study in the Japanese spirit, they would yield the essentials of the Japanese Way, which was pure, clear, natural, without contradictions, and superior to the Chinese Way. Norinaga undertook such scholarly study and presented his conclusions not only in *Kojiki Den* but also in numerous other studies and tracts.[2]

Norinaga was a brilliant, systematic, and thorough scholar whose work had the effect of elevating the study of *Kojiki* to the same level as the study of the Chinese classics. *Kojiki* had always been accepted as an authoritative work on the Age of the Gods with respect to genealogy, and we have seen how the devoted labours of scholars over the centuries had led to the proliferation of theories that baffled the Mito scholars. With the work of Norinaga, *Kojiki* also became a source of religious, ethical, social, and political values unique to Japan. Norinaga showed how it could be interpreted to make the underlying principles of the Age of the Gods relevant to contemporary life.

With twentieth-century hindsight, we can see clearly that National Learning was based on a historical fallacy. National Scholars believed that Japanese civilization had originated independently and had not been influenced by Chinese civilization until the reign of Emperor Ōjin (r. 270-310). Then *Nihon Shoki* records the entry of the written Chinese language into Japan and thereafter many particulars of the advent of high classical civilization. Only through this fallacy could National Learning's insistence on the singular importance of the Age of the Gods make sense. A quite different picture is displayed by scholarship in post-World War II Japan, in which Japanese civilization is seen as developing progressively under the continuous influence of Chinese civilization, often transmitted through Korea, during all of the prehistoric periods of Japan (Jōmon, Yayoi, Kofun). In the modern picture, it is difficult to isolate the origins of characteristics considered specific to Japanese society.

Motoori Norinaga was well aware of the efforts of Confucian scholars to rationalize the Age of the Gods and of the euhemerist interpretations of Arai Hakuseki. However, while Norinaga repeatedly castigated Confucian scholars in general for their misguided intellectualism, he did not attack the views of the major scholars in detail. The following, criticizing both Confucian scholars and the Shintoist scholars who were influenced by them, is typical of his general broadside attack:

> People of later times who have interpreted these sacred works (*Kojiki* and *Nihon Shoki*) have fabricated divine mysteries transmitted by oral teachings; they have taught empty falsehoods and have adhered to theories from foreign countries. Incapable of believing in the profound truths of the Age of the Gods, they cannot even understand that the principles of the world are all to be found in the events of the Age of the Gods. They try to judge these principles on the basis of theories from foreign lands. As a result, where the materials are not in accord with the precepts of the foreign theory, such people present, unwarranted, twisted interpretations of their own liking that are based on their own ideas. They theorize that the Plain of High Heaven was merely the capital city, and was not in the heavens. They even declare that the Sun Goddess was not the sun but just the distant founder of the court, a divine-like person who lived on this earth. All these people extravagantly praise empty foreign theories, and egotistically try to make them fit; they regard the ancient legends as limited and trivial. And so the importance of these ancient legends is not widely disseminated, their essential meaning is lost, and the purpose of the sacred texts is grossly violated.[3]

For the most part, instead of refuting the Confucian scholars in detail, Norinaga presented his own interpretations in *Kojiki Den* and let them stand on the foundation of his own superior scholarship.

But there were some things that he could not let go. Norinaga was well acquainted with the theory of Wu Taibo as the founder of the Japanese dynastic line, but he did not attack its main proponent, Hayashi Razan. Instead, his fiercest barbs were directed at one of the weaker arguments for the theory, *Shōkōhatsu* [Contrary Views, 1781) by Tō Teikan (1732-97). Tō's career was similar to that of Hayashi Razan, as he left a Buddhist monastery in his youth to take up a life of Confucian scholarship. He was more eclectic than Razan, having taken an interest in National Learning, but he was best known for his positivistic research. In *Shōkōhatsu*, Tō made his contribution to the rationalizing of *Nihon Shoki* by dealing with its chronology, suggesting an adjustment of 600 years to make it square with Chinese and Korean sources. He also appeared to favour the theory of Wu Taibo and thus attracted the wrath of Norinaga. Tō laid out the descent of Emperor Jinmu from Wu Taibo on the basis of 'a certain record,' which he did not name, but variant versions of *Nihon Shoki* were often identified in this way. The record that he cited even had worm holes in it, obliterating some characters and making its interpretation difficult except in the hands of experts such as Tō. Norinaga attacked the 'certain record' as fraudulent because it was inconsistent with the way in which genealogies were given in ancient texts. Norinaga knew all the ancient texts, and irregularities could not slip past his notice. He also thought that the alleged worm holes were nothing but a clever trick. Norinaga went on to a thorough destruction of Tō's argument.[4]

Such attacks were necessary to establish the academic credentials of National Learning. However, the positive emphasis of the National Scholars on the ancient political institutions and cultural values of Japan was more important than their criticisms of Confucian critical scholarship. None of Norinaga's successors was as talented as he, but the school had tapped into a deep source of Japanese nationalism, bringing forth fundamental ancient values at a time when the security and sovereignty of the nation were felt to be threatened. In the 1790s, Japan's policy of isolation began to break down as British and Russian ships arrived in Japanese waters; and as the nineteenth century proceeded, it became apparent that Japan could not defend itself against the superior navies from the industrialized West. The value of the ancient tradition, and the need for a strong military to defend that tradition, came to be seen as inseparable. In 1825 Aizawa Seishisai's *Shinron* [New Theses] proposed improved defence for Japan and spoke to Japan's national values. Aizawa expounded at length on the special virtues of the Sun Goddess and the superior qualities that she imparted to the Japanese nation, without any indication that Confucian scholarship in the Tokugawa period had rendered these ideas problematic.[5] By 1850 everyone involved in political discussion knew how to invoke the national essence [*kokutai*] of the imperial nation [*kōkoku*] and to back it up with references to the divine founding in the Age of the Gods. Each tried to outdo the rest in patriotic expression, and all else but nationalist sentiment was swept from the field. National Learning cannot be held responsible for this development, but it did bring forward what were believed to be native Japanese values, founding them in a document, *Kojiki*, newly regarded as scripturelike, and expounding at length on their significance. The result was to give sophisticated credibility to the ancient myths and thus to make it plausible for modern people to conceive of a new and strengthened nation based upon them.

The Fate of Confucianism and National Studies

For most of the nineteenth century in Japan, as in European and North American debates over evolution and the Garden of Eden, there was no arbiter between the contending versions of national origins held by the Confucians and the National Scholars. After the Constitution of 1889, the imperial state necessarily became a supporter of the national founding myths as the basis for imperial sovereignty, but until then the contenders were on their own. The victor would be determined by the trend of the times and the vigour of the opponents, not by the exercise of authority. If it were a race, then the National Scholars seemed far ahead in 1868, for their version was favoured when the bakufu was destroyed and the emperor was restored to full sovereignty in the Meiji Restoration. No other basis for this sovereignty was claimed than the uninterrupted descent of the emperors from Emperor Jinmu, under the protection of the Sun Goddess as recorded in *Kojiki* and *Nihon Shoki*. This the National Scholars had affirmed.

Yet in the 1870s, Japan began the search abroad for knowledge to strengthen the foundations of imperial rule, as stated in the Charter Oath of the Meiji government. The knowledge sought abroad was closer in nature and spirit to that of the Tokugawa Confucianists than that of the National Scholars. Scientific knowledge was at the bottom of the industrial revolution that had placed Europe and North America so far ahead of Japan, and Japanese leaders understood this. Scientific method had some affinities with Confucian method, which encouraged the rational and systematic investigation of things.

It is true that Confucian metaphysics were destroyed by science. Confucianism differed from science in its confident knowledge that investigation of things would only confirm the Confucian universe and not reveal any new principles that would undermine it. The Confucian method was not experimental; instead, it assumed the reality of what it set out to investigate. The importation of scientific knowledge destroyed completely the Neo-Confucian metaphysical and physical universe composed of the Supreme Ultimate, Principle, Ether, Yin and Yang, and the Five Elements. Japanese scholars in the latter nineteenth century simply abandoned that universe, without regrets and without complications.

But in the study of society and history, as opposed to metaphysical and physical reality, investigation of things was not completely tied up with an obsolete metaphysic. Positivistic research was expected to demonstrate that Heaven approved of good rulers and disapproved of evil ones. We have seen how such beliefs led to failures of positivistic research in the work of Hayashi Razan, the Mito scholars, and Arai Hakuseki. This unscientific element, belief in the will of Heaven, was vigorously attacked by the earliest modern scholars who combined Confucian and Western methods. In 1891 the prominent historian Kume Kunitake (1839-1931) wrote an article entitled 'Let Us Look at History without the Old Practice of Praising the Good,' in which he said, 'Nowadays everyone is aware of the error of viewing history as a record of rewarding the good and punishing the bad.'[6] However, the practical methods of Tokugawa Confucians for handling historical materials – evaluation and authentication of documents and so on – proved to be detachable from Neo-Confucian metaphysics and political theories and survived independently to be reinforced by Western scientific methods.

As we shall see, modern Japanese historians seemed to combine the best of both worlds. In addition to abandoning Confucian metaphysics, they rejected the heavy freight of German political thought that accompanied Western historical method to Japan and accepted only the method.

None of this applied to National Learning. Its method was also scholarly and systematic, especially in the case of Motoori Norinaga, but in historical studies it was completely devoted to demonstrating the truth of the Age of the Gods. Unlike the Confucian method, the method of National Learning actually deteriorated in the nineteenth century when it was confronted by Western learning, because the central historical truths could not be abandoned in the same way as the Confucian universe. They had to be saved by any means whatsoever. Hence, Hirata Atsutane (1776-1843), who claimed to be a disciple of Motoori Norinaga, adopted two approaches to try to accommodate National Learning to Western learning. The first was to update the metaphysics of the Age of the Gods by borrowing features of Christian thought and claiming that they were found in the Age of the Gods. This met with little acclaim. The second was to betray the high standards of scholarly method set by Norinaga, playing fast and loose with the facts. For example, Hirata claimed to have discovered a Japanese writing script from the Age of the Gods [*jindai moji*] that antedated Chinese writing.[7] If true it would have been a sensational discovery indeed, revolutionizing thought about ancient Japanese history. But apart from a small following, no one was convinced, and modern scholars have shown that the script was a forgery. Since his work represents such a sad decline from high standards, it is difficult to see why Hirata Atsutane is always included as a major figure in studies of Japanese thought and is frequently listed as one of the four great National Scholars, after Kada Azumamaro, Kamo Mabuchi, and Motoori Norinaga. Probably this exaggerated esteem arises from the undoubted political importance of Hirata followers, who were active in the movement toward the Meiji Restoration.[8]

Finally Western learning introduced a new element of universalism that did not clash with Tokugawa Confucian method. We have seen Bitō Masahide's view that Hayashi Razan argued for the theory of Wu Taibo partly because it placed Japan in a more universal setting, that of the Chinese-dominated East Asian world. In the nineteenth century, Japan was lifted again by Western learning into the truly universal setting of the globe, and Confucian historical method was able to take that in its stride. However, universalism was antagonistic to the faith and ethnocentrism of National Learning, which affirmed that Japan was the only country in the world that had been founded by the gods. The result was that in historical scholarship, Western scientific learning and Confucian positivistic research combined after the Meiji Restoration to shoot far ahead in the race by 1890.

Part 2
The Modern Century

6
European Influences on Meiji Historical Writing

Fukuzawa Yukichi: An Outline of a Theory of Civilization

In outward appearance, the Meiji Restoration was regressive, as it destroyed the bakufu and restored the emperor to the status quo of the Nara period (710-94). The emperor formally retrieved all the powers that he had held under the ancient law codes, and the Council of State was reconstituted to govern the country.

However, the form of government was temporary and would be radically revised to suit the needs of a modern nation of the nineteenth century. Within twenty years, a political settlement was reached in the Constitution of 1889. During those twenty years, Japan changed greatly in every respect: political, social, economic, intellectual. The models for these changes lay in the West, more precisely in England, France, Germany, and the United States. Japanese leaders acknowledged that superior organization and learning existed in those countries, and they seemed to have no emotional difficulty in regarding the Japanese past as unproductive, or backward, or benighted. As the Englishman Basil Hall Chamberlain warned Westerners in 1891, 'Whatever you do, don't expatiate, in the presence of Japanese of the new school, on those old, quaint, and beautiful things Japanese which rouse our most genuine admiration ... Speaking generally, the educated Japanese have done with their past. They want to be somebody else and something else than what they have been and still partly are.'[1]

The European Enlightenment and its nineteenth-century heritage were brought to Japan through swift translation of works during the 1870s and 1880s and by the study of Japanese abroad. For the first time, through study and experience, Japanese encountered forms of civilization outside the ancient East Asian world that was dominated by Chinese culture. If Chinese learning in the Tokugawa period had given a wider intellectual perspective to Japanese views of their origins and history, Western learning in the Meiji period jolted Japanese into awareness of their place in the development of human civilization. Japanese intellectuals seem simply to have accepted, with little criticism, the views of Western intellectuals about the superiority of Western societies to all others, because they seemed manifestly true. However, Japanese intellectuals were not discouraged by this discovery of the inferiority of their civilization. The opposite was true: they believed that, through the combined efforts of Japanese people, their level of civilization could be elevated to that of Western societies. This possibility was held out to them by the theories of the Westerners themselves.

The youthful Tokutomi Sohō (1863-1957) was typical of early Meiji intellectuals in his enthusiasm for Western civilization. Tokutomi, a journalist, teacher, and later a popular historian, adopted the theory of Herbert Spencer. He held that civilization progressed in stages and that Western society had progressed beyond the militant stage to the industrial stage, in which wars would cease, industrial production would provide material and intellectual welfare for everyone, and democracy would find its fullest development. Tokutomi equated the Tokugawa period with the militant stage of development and believed that Japan had now gone beyond that stage and was headed toward industrialism, peace, and liberty.[2]

Equally prominent was Fukuzawa Yukichi (1835-1901), an educator and journalist. His writings of the 1870s emphasized the superiority of Western civilization and the undoubted capability of Japan to catch up through the efforts of its people. In *Bunmeiron no Gairyaku* [An Outline of the Theory of Civilization, 1874], Fukuzawa adopted the idea that societies could be grouped into three categories: civilized, represented by Europe and the United States; semideveloped, represented by countries such as China, Japan, and Turkey; and primitive, represented by numerous tribal societies of Africa and Australia.[3] Japan, he thought, could move swiftly from the semi-developed stage to the civilized stage. Fukuzawa was not interested in the development of civilization for its own sake but as a means to protect the sovereignty and integrity of the Japanese nation: the last chapter of *Bunmeiron no Gairyaku* is 'A Discussion of Our National Independence.' Thus, Fukuzawa's thought may be distinguished from the more purely theoretical positions of many of the European Enlightenment scholars whom he cited.

Very little was original with Fukuzawa. His models were *Histoire de la civilization en Europe* (1828), by François Guizot, and *History of Civilization in England* (1871), by Henry Thomas Buckle. Chapters 3 and 8 of Fukuzawa's *Bunmeiron no Gairyaku* were based on Guizot, while Chapter 4 employs Buckle's ideas about social statistics; in addition, the general theory of Buckle suffuses the work.[4]

Buckle's *History of Civilization in England*, of which the first volume appeared in 1857, started from the assumption that history was not the doings of elites, the record of kings and warlords and their edicts and battles, or even the story beloved to Englishmen of the development of the English Constitution, but the progress of civilization as found in various peoples of

Earth. I have noted Fukuzawa's criticism that Arai Hakuseki's highly original history, with its nine stages of imperial history and its five stages of military history, was nothing more than the same play written fourteen times over. In this he followed Buckle, who cited approvingly an eighteenth-century French historian, Mallet. Mallet wrote, 'For why should history be only a recital of battles, sieges, intrigues, and negotiations? And why should it contain merely a heap of petty facts and dates, rather than a great picture of the opinions, customs, and even inclinations of a people?'[5] Guizot expressed similar views. Buckle also held that some societies had developed to far more advanced stages than others, and he had no doubt that England was the most advanced. Similarly, Guizot thought that France lay at the heart of European civilization: France was 'The most complete, the most true, the most civilized.'[6] However, what interested Fukuzawa and others was Buckle's search for principles or laws to explain why the advanced societies had got that way.

Having vigorously disposed of all theological causes for the development of civilizations, Buckle turned to a search for secular laws, confident that modern learning had progressed so far that he would find them. Of the physical determinants of a society, he cited climate, food, soil, and the general aspects of nature. By the last, he meant that nature excites two forms of mental activity, imagination and intellect. When people encounter nature that is violent and intimidating, the imagination is stimulated, giving rise to a society filled with superstitions and beliefs. When a milder form of nature is met, intellect is stimulated, and progress is the result. Buckle held that the ideal form of nature for stimulating intellect was found in the temperate zones, particularly in western Europe and especially in England.[7]

Japanese scholars agreed with Buckle that some societies, including Japan, had generated far too much from the imagination, since Japan was filled with useless superstitions and beliefs. However, they appear to have discounted Buckle's idea that only the temperate zone of Europe, and not the monsoon lands of Asia, could stimulate intellect. Without giving much thought to Buckle's geographic limitations, the men of the Japanese Enlightenment in the 1870s thought that Japanese could easily turn to activities of the intellect and generate progress.

German Influence: Ludwig Riess (1861-1928)

While English and French historians such as Buckle and Guizot pioneered in writing the history of civilization, German historians developed modern scientific historical method as well as the concept of the university professor as historical researcher. Leopold von Ranke (1795-1886), professor at Berlin University, led the field in both conducting research and producing voluminous works on European history and articulating historical method and philosophy.

The goal of the German school was objectivity. One of Ranke's predecessors, Wilhelm von Humboldt (1767-1835), put it clearly in 1821: 'The historian's task is to present what actually happened. The more purely and completely he achieves this, the more perfectly he has solved his problem.'[8] Ranke's own sayings about objectivity have achieved the status of aphorisms. He wanted, he said, to write history 'as it had really been.' He held that 'Every epoch is immediate to God, and its value in no way depends on what it has produced, but in its existence itself, in its very self.'[9]

The way to objectivity was through scientific method, which Ranke held to be as feasible in history as in any other field. The sciences of geography and geology made clear and indisputable the history of the earth itself, and the science of history did the same for the record of its human inhabitants. The natural scientists had to disregard received truth – for example, about the date and process of creation of Earth – and proceed under their improved method in the field and the laboratory. Similarly Ranke did not simply accept established narratives but went to the archives, where he worked through mountains of unexamined documents, correlating and cross-checking them, subjecting them to tests for authenticity and accuracy, and producing a new narrative from scratch. He wrote model histories, such as *History of the Popes*, on subjects previously filled with errors, untruths, unfounded theories, and deliberate falsifications. It was said of Ranke that he was 'contemporary with Lyell and Wallace, Darwin and Renan, who were applying the analytical and critical method with startling results in their particular fields. He turned the lecture room into a laboratory, using documents instead of "bushels of clams."'[10]

Ranke remains best known for his aspiration to objectivity and his scientific method, but his ideas about history did not end there. His main aim was to seek the facts, but he also believed that the facts of history were interrelated and expressed a spiritual reality that cohered in a nation. The spirit of a nation was to be understood intuitively, not scientifically. Furthermore, historical understanding required religious faith, for he believed that God ultimately orchestrates history, for good and for bad. In 1820 Ranke wrote: 'God dwells, lives, is recognized in all history. Every act testifies of him, every moment preaches his name, but most of all, it seems to me, the context of history. Good cheer then. No matter how it goes, let us try to reveal for our part the sacred hieroglyphs. In that too we serve God, in that too we are priests, in that too teachers.'[11]

The Japanese historians who received scientific method, by way of Ranke's disciple, Ludwig Riess, were not especially interested in these spiritual aspects. They had no Christian belief, and they already had their fill of Confucian moral purpose in history. They were looking for a way out of that and were attracted only by the pure scientific method of Ranke, detached from his metaphysics. Their instructor, Riess, may have shared their view

Ludwig Riess (1861-1928) and his wife Ōtsuka
Fuku. Riess taught scientific historical method
at Tokyo Imperial University from 1887 to 1902.
(Courtesy of Kanai Madoka, Professor Emeritus,
Historiographical Institute, Tokyo University)

since he was not Christian either but Jewish. In this respect, the Japanese
historians were like those in the United States who were also in the process
of establishing history as an academic discipline. The Americans too were
drawn by Ranke's idea of history as empirical science and not as philosophy. While many of the Americans shared Ranke's Christian beliefs, they
were not interested in his focus on political power, involving a bias toward
the monarchical state, the German state in particular.[12]

The most important influence on method in Japanese history was provided by Ludwig Riess, who went to Japan in 1887 on a three-year government contract. This was unusual, since most foreigners hired under the
government's program for bringing experts to Japan were under one-year
contracts. Even more unusual, Riess's contract was repeatedly extended until
1902 because of the importance of his work. Riess had been a history student at Berlin University and worked as a copyist for Leopold von Ranke,
though he met the old man only twice. Riess's field was English history, and
he was in England for research in November 1886 when he received a tele-
gram inviting him to Japan. According to *Encyclopaedia Judaica*, although
his 1885 doctoral dissertation, 'History of the English Electoral Law in the
Middle Ages,' 'was widely hailed for its brilliant scholarship, Riess was

unable to obtain a university position because he was a Jew. He therefore accepted an appointment at Tokyo Imperial University in 1887.'[13]

Riess went to Japan under a government program of hiring foreign experts in order to modernize Japanese knowledge, technology, and institutions, so he was received as a peerless authority in his field.[14] Bunka Daigaku, a college of Tokyo Imperial University, had four divisions: philosophy, Japanese literature, Chinese literature, and linguistics; history, German, and English were added in 1887. Students in history already had a broad curriculum in subjects outside history; Riess proposed great intensification of historical studies in a memo of 20 November 1888 submitted at the request of the university president. Riess held that Japanese history was not different in nature from any other and should be studied by the same scientific methods. In addition to pure historical research, he advocated historical geography and historiography, as well as ancillary studies, including English. The study of ancient Japanese documents [komonjogaku] was to be maintained as a field, but with improvements in method according to Western practice.[15]

Riess's personal influence was more important than memos on systems and methods. Tokyo Imperial University was small in 1888, and the professors and history students in all fields of history knew each other. A photograph shows Riess and forty-seven Japanese men, mostly young, assembled on the wooded campus of Tokyo Imperial University; they may have numbered all of the history professors and students.[16] Shigeno Yasutsugu, Hoshino Hisashi, and Kume Kunitake were colleagues. The students who came under his instruction included Mikami Sanji, Japan's most influential prewar historian; the great Tokyo Imperial University scholar of documents, Kuroita Katsumi; Tsuji Zennosuke, who became Japan's most eminent cultural historian; and Murakami Naojirō (1868-1966), a postwar president of Sophia University and a member of the Japan Academy. Others were Uchida Ginzō (1872-1919), who specialized in modern economic history, and the legal historian Miura Hiroyuki (1871-1931), who both taught at Kyoto Imperial University.

Riess was active in the Historical Association, a learned society founded in 1889 with Shigeno Yasutsugu as president. Academic papers were given, and in the same year the society began publishing *Shigakukai Zasshi* [Journal of the Historical Scholarship Association], which was originally devoted to Japanese history but was later expanded to cover world history. It was renamed *Shigaku Zasshi* [Journal of Historical Scholarship] in 1892 and has continued as Japan's leading historical journal to the present. Japanese historians were thus abreast of world developments in scholarly publishing.

Riess also participated in the social life of the university, and he married a Japanese woman, Ōtsuka Fuku, with whom he raised five children. Unfortunately, when his last contract expired and he departed from Japan in 1902, he left the family behind; Kanai Madoka suggests that the social life in Germany of a Jew married to a Japanese would have been too difficult.[17] He returned to Japan once in 1909 to visit, and his son Otto went to Germany to study, but his contact with the family was otherwise limited to correspondence until his death in 1928. However, his scholarly influence was further disseminated through his family, for his son-in-law Abe Hidesuke became a lecturer in Western history at Keiō University, where he taught Riess's method.

Riess's Methodology of History

Riess took the lead in setting up the history curriculum at Tokyo Imperial University. He taught extensively on Western history, lecturing on the English Constitution, the French Revolution, the modern history of Europe by country, and Tacitus' *History of the German People* in English translation. He used the materials of the Franco-Prussian War to illustrate methods of documentary study. Lectures on method, as well as on historical geography, were given.[18] Remarkably all his lectures were in English, which must have been a great struggle for most of the students. Murakami Naojirō, linguistically gifted, reported that they were excellent, while Kōda Shigetomo (1873-1954) said that Riess stammered and could not pronounce 'this.'[19]

Most of my information is based on the memories of colleagues and students. However, notes of his lectures on method were taken by Murakami Naojirō, who showed them to Riess for correction. Copies for distribution were then made on a hectograph by Tsuji Zennosuke, and the result was a short book, *Methodology of History*. Only a few passages are unintelligible because of this process of transcription by Japanese of the English lectures of a native German speaker; the stuffy, prolix style presumably was Riess's. No copies survived in Japan, but in 1937 Tokyo Imperial University Library purchased in Germany a copy from the personal library of a friend of Riess named Liebermann.[20]

The opening paragraph unambiguously states the purpose of the book:

1 THE SCIENTIFIC CHARACTER OF HISTORY

That historical studies of the type as they are now carried on in France, England, and other countries, but most extensively in Germany, are of a *scientific* character, will be admitted by anybody who is thoroughly acquainted with them and competent to judge about this point. On this basis we venture to build the generalization, that all historical subjects and problems are capable, and in need, of scientific treatment; that historical treatises everywhere ought to partake, as a matter of course, of similar requirements and thereby justify their being credited as *scientific* productions.[21]

Methodology is divided into Elementary Methodology and Higher Methodology. Elementary Methodology consists of

(1) moulding the question
(2) heuristics
(3) critique
(4) hermeneutics or interpretation.

All of them are rather advanced, and a chapter is devoted to each. Higher Methodology consists of

(1) systematic survey of historical phenomena
(2) topik [sic]
(3) philosophy of history.

Presumably a chapter was devoted to each, but the last one was either omitted or lost by the time that this copy was acquired by Tokyo Imperial University Library.

The book is a thorough survey of the types of historical materials commonly found: relics, including language and state papers, monuments, and every other sort of written source. Numerous criteria for evaluation are discussed; methods of collation and correlation are outlined; and methods of reasoning and hypothesizing are given for the detection of errors and frauds and for the exclusion of possibilities. Not the least useful are hints for note taking: one only per piece of paper, with source and date conspicuously entered. Four types of narrative are suggested, following Theodore Droysen: pragmatic, biographic, monographic, and catastrophic ('a highly exciting style of narrative much used in poetry and fiction'). The discussion throughout is detailed and well illustrated by practical examples:

> If we observe the process of transferring a tale from mouth to mouth, we find the most wonderful alterations ... [One type is] assimilation to well known types and repetition of individual tracts. A notorious tyrant like Nero is charged with almost all tyrannical acts that people ever knew of. Adversaries of Emperor Henry IV charge him with hideous acts in order to stamp him a tyrant. Nearly all absent-minded professors are credited with having thrown their watch into the boiling water and kept an egg in their hand for seeing when five minutes will have past [sic].[22]

There is no need to evaluate this treatise on scientific history in terms of science. Few North American and European historians now aspire to the objectivity that Ranke thought resulted from scientific method, and most are happy to write from a well-acknowledged, deliberately chosen position.[23] The more forgiving will concede that history may have looked more like a science in the late nineteenth century than it does now. The less forgiving will immediately observe the weak points of Riess's discussion and might conclude that it is so flawed that the entire work has no value. The militant might conclude that, if this is what masqueraded as scientific method in history, it is little wonder that much Japanese scholarship in the twentieth century was marred by nationalism, racism, and sexism.

The most obvious case of unscientific method is 'Systematic Survey of Historical Phenomena,' the first chapter in Higher Methodology, which deals with problems of individuals and their times. 'The difficulty in nearly all these cases is, that any other man in the position of Charles I, Cromwell, James II, Wallenstein or Luther, Louis XIV, Louis XVI, Frederick William IV, and Bismarck would certainly have acted differently and thereby produced another result. Since the actions of these men seem to be the turning point of an event, we must be quite sure, that we comprehend their actions.'[24] According to Riess, the experience and maturity of the historian will be critical for comprehending the actions of an individual, but he may have realized that he was venturing into unscientific subjective judgment as a historical method. To give scientific aid to the historian's judgment, he identified types of personality with characteristic behavioural traits. These are the Choleric, Sanguinic, Phlegmatic, and Anaematic (chosen to 'avoid the misleading term Melancholic'). The associated behavioural categories, respectively, are Spontaneity (strong or feeble), Receptibility (quick or slow), Impressibility (deep or superficial), and Reagibility (persevering or intermittent). I have found no dictionary that lists reagibility and think that it was an error of transcription.

Contemporary psychology and psychiatry continue to use types, of course, but they are thought to be more scientifically derived than Riess's types; like his, however, they may not be considered scientific 100 years hence.[25] Riess's types would also be unacceptable now, with no second thought, because of the examples that illustrate them. The strong, quick, deep, and persevering Choleric type is illustrated by 'Heroes like Luther,' while the strong, quick, deep, and intermittent Choleric individual is to be found in '"Paddy" [presumably Irish]. The Pole. The Italian.' Under Phlegmatic types,[26] we find the following:

Spontaneity	Receptibility	Impressibility	Reagibility	Instance
strong	slow	superficial	persevering	The energetic Cunctator. Englishmen.
feeble	slow	superficial	persevering	Lazy Men. Quiet women.
strong	slow	deep	persevering	The Swabian. The fanatic.

Riess's teaching was not the only factor in moving Japanese historians into a more critical mode, since Japanese were going throughout the world and imbibing scientific knowledge everywhere. In addition, it is possible to overestimate the importance of the scientific methods that he taught, since they were not greatly different in practice from the methods of traditional positivistic research.

Nevertheless, Riess's scientific methods had profound impact on Japanese scholarship. The new methods had the cachet of international authority. They also opened the eyes of Japanese historians to the limits of their traditional positivistic research. It was rational and systematic but was carried out in the Confucian framework that affirmed existing authority and the invariable triumph of officially defined goodness. Scientific research, however, could be applied to any topic whatsoever, without preconceptions about the results. In 1891 Kume Kunitake wrote, 'Nowadays everyone is aware of the error of viewing history as a record of rewarding the good and punishing the bad.'[27]

Certainly the new history had the effect of clearing out what I termed failures of positivistic research in the work of Hayashi Razan and the Mito scholars. Because they thought in Confucian categories, the Tokugawa scholars never questioned the goodness of Emperor Nintoku and the wickedness of Emperor Buretsu and uncritically repeated the tales about the Hōjō regents suffering attacks of conscience when opposing Go Toba in the Jōkyū War of 1221. The new scientific scholars did not attack the Tokugawa scholars on these points. Viewing history with their new scientific lenses, they saw that these topics were not worth pursuing and simply abandoned discussion of them.

Whatever the relative importance of positivistic research and scientific history, the presence of Riess at Tokyo Imperial University was a catalyst in the development of history. Shigeno Yasutsugu, Kume Kunitake, and Hoshino Hisashi moved there in 1888 in dual roles as professors in the university and as compilers of *Dai Nihon Hennen Shi*. The establishment of the Historical Association and *Shigaku Zasshi* stimulated their activity, and they began teaching and publishing critical articles on long-established historical truths and theories. By the time that Riess left Japan, the historical profession was well established, and all its members acknowledged their debt to him. Fifty-four men were present at his farewell party on 9 September 1902, and they included the great names of twentieth-century Japanese historical scholarship, such as Kuroita Katsumi, Mikami Sanji, and Tsuji Zennosuke. Mikami Sanji thanked Riess, in English, on behalf of the Japanese history department, and Shigeno Yasutsugu thanked him, also in English, on behalf of the Historical Association.[28]

7
The Beginning of Academic History

Government History Projects

In keeping with its early nature as a restoration government, the Meiji
government planned to resume the writing of history as it had been practised in the Heian period. History writing then was an official government
undertaking, with projects defined by the government and carried out by
people specifically appointed to the task. There were no professional historians; instead, well-educated people all possessed knowledge of history and
literary composition and were expected to be able to write history. Funding
in the modern sense was not an issue. The system worked well, and six
official histories were produced between 720 and 901, after which the enterprise lapsed. The books are formally known as the Six National Histories;
the best known is the first, *Nihon Shoki* [Chronicles of Japan, 720], which
covered history from the Age of the Gods to 697, and the last in the series is
Nihon Sandai Jitsuroku [Veritable Records of Three Reigns of Japan, 901],
which covered the period from 858 to 887.[1] The Six National Histories obviously can be criticized by modern standards for their concentration on the
emperor and the court and for the absence of explanation of historical causes.
In their time, however, they stood out as serious, high-minded scholarship
aiming at objective historical truth. The devotion of the authors to the imperial state, which was not uncritical, was a fair reflection of the dominant
political and social ideology of the period. To the new rulers of Meiji, the
excellent scholarship and devotion to the state displayed by the ancient
historians seemed natural and exemplary.

The Meiji government therefore set about writing history, taking up where
Nihon Sandai Jitsuroku left off. It appointed official historians who were sala-
ried civil servants and expected them to produce factual histories of imperial government that were based on documents and written in Classical
Chinese [*kanbun*]. The highest standards of positivistic research were expected to be observed, and no one thought that this would result in anything but affirmation of the legitimacy of the imperial government. In 1868

there was not the least suspicion in government that the scholarship envisaged was obsolete in many respects and that in twenty-five years the scholars appointed to the task would have to be disciplined.

In 1869 Emperor Meiji gave a written order to the distinguished court noble Sanjō Sanetomi (1837-91) to start a history beginning from 887, 'to set right the relation between monarch and subject, to make clear the distinction between civilization and barbarity, and to implant the principle of virtue throughout the empire.'[2] The old-fashioned moral purpose of the work is evident. An office was set up to do the work, and this went through many reorganizations before achieving final form as the Shūshikan [Bureau of Historiogaphy] in 1877.[3] The major project planned was *Dai Nihon Hennen Shi* [Great Chronological History of Japan], an annalistic work to be written in Classical Chinese. Later it was recognized that *Dai Nihon Shi* provided excellent coverage from 887, where the Six National Histories left off, up to 1392, so the task was redefined as a history from 1392 to Meiji. Intensive work was begun, but *Dai Nihon Hennen Shi* was never completed; it was suspended in 1893, when the historians had fallen into disgrace on other accounts. Two other works were completed and published: *Fukkōki* [Record of the Restoration] and *Meiji Shiyō* [Outline of Meiji History].[4] They are now entirely neglected.

The director of the *Dai Nihon Hennen Shi* was Shigeno Yasutsugu (1827-1910), a former samurai of Satsuma who had received training in the Hayashi academy. He became well practiced in positivistic research, and like the *Dai Nihon Shi* scholars of the seventeenth century, he embarked on research trips all over Japan. His research made him increasingly sceptical of *Dai Nihon Shi* itself. I have noted in detail only a few instances of uncritical scholarship in *Dai Nihon Shi*, the accounts of the virtuous Emperor Nintoku and the awful Emperor Buretsu, and the case of the Hōjō warriors worrying about opposing the emperor in 1221. Shigeno and his colleagues began to compile a great number of such cases and to publish critical articles, especially after becoming professors at newly established Tokyo Imperial University in 1888.

This critical attitude arising from positivistic research was greatly reinforced by Western historical scholarship. A work of particular interest to Shigeno was Augustus Mounsey's *The Satsuma Rebellion: An Episode of Modern Japanese History* (1879), which treated the last great feudal uprising in Japan in 1877. In his discussion of this history of events that occurred in his native domain, Shigeno noted, 'Unlike Chinese and Japanese histories, which confine themselves to factual statement, Western histories inquire into causes and consider effects, provide detailed accounts of their subjects and vivid pictures of the times with which they are concerned. There can be no doubt that their form and method embody many points of value to us.'[5] Shigeno set out systematically to learn the form and method of Western historical writing. The influence of Ludwig Riess was timely. Shigeno's combination of Japanese positivistic research with Western form and method brought him recognition in his lifetime as the pioneer of modern Japanese academic method.[6]

Private Scholarship:
Taguchi Ukichi and *A Short History of Enlightenment in Japan*
Like Fukuzawa Yukichi, Taguchi Ukichi (1855-1905) was a child of the European Enlightenment, but his scholarship was more thorough, original, and sophisticated. In his short life of fifty years, he realized to the full the new possibilities for life in Meiji Japan. He learned English as a youth from missionaries and traders in Yokohama and was an ardent follower of the nineteenth-century English school of liberal economics, becoming known as the Adam Smith of Japan. Taguchi began his career as a bureaucrat in the Ministry of Finance and then founded an economics journal, *Tokyo Keizai Zasshi* [Tokyo Economic Journal], contributing many of the articles himself. *Nihon Kaika Shōshi* [A Short History of Enlightenment in Japan] was published in six instalments between 1877 and 1882 during his period as an active journalist. In 1891 he founded a historical journal, *Shikai* [Sea of History], intended to be more popular than the academic journal *Shigaku Zasshi* [Journal of Historical Scholarship] established by the professors of Tokyo Imperial University. Next he went on to electoral politics, first at the Tokyo local level and then as a member of the House of Representatives, being first elected in 1894 and reelected in 1898 and 1904. In his political life, he continued to advocate classical liberal economics. At the same time, he carried on a career as a businessman.

Taguchi found time to edit major historical works that still remain useful. The first was *Dainihon Jinmei Jisho* [Dictionary of Japanese Biography], which he produced between 1884 and 1886. In 1893 he started *Gunsho Ruijū* [Classified Collection of Books], a modern printed edition of the huge collection of historical texts compiled in the Tokugawa period by Hanawa Hokinoichi (1746-1821). In 1896 he started *Kokushi Taikei* [Compendium of Japanese History], consisting of critically collated editions of major historical works and documentary sources from ancient times. Both of these projects were finished in 1902.

In his brief study of Taguchi, Sakamoto Tarō was less impressed by Taguchi's other historical writing than by this work of editing texts and documents for use by advanced scholars.[7] In neither *Gunsho Ruijū* nor *Kokushi Taikei* were annotations or explanations provided. Thus, many of them have long been superseded by superior critical editions, but they continue to stand as authentic texts. A supplementary series *Gunsho Kaidai* [Bibliography of Classified Collection of Books, 1962-] is devoted to critical introductions to the texts in *Gunsho Ruijū*. The work of continuing and enlarging the *Kokushi*

Taikei series was carried on at Tokyo Imperial University in the Taisho and early Showa periods and is best known under the name of the editor in that period, Kuroita Katsumi, instead of Taguchi. Kuroita, who entered the Tokyo Imperial University Department of History in 1896, assisted Taguchi on both *Gunsho Ruijū* and *Kokushi Taikei.*

In summary, in addition to being a follower of the new civilization history, Taguchi was also qualified in the new stream of academic history, devoted to documentary and textual study, that was emerging at Tokyo Imperial University.

Taguchi's *Nihon Kaika Shōshi* covered all of Japanese history in the customary manner of traditional Japanese historians, who started at the beginning of history and carried the story up to their own time. However, it was the first Japanese work to treat ancient history in a completely objective manner; it might as well have been the history of England or Germany, so far as any special view of the origins of society was concerned. The first chapter, 'From the Origins of Shinto to the Spread of Buddhism,' far from recounting how the islands were formed by deities, explained instead how myths originate out of the social and economic conditions of a people. In early hunting and fishing society, said Taguchi, people were concerned with survival and were hardly different from other animals, with no time for speculation about their ancestors or about life after death. With the advance of technical skills and the improvement of material life, however, came awareness of human illness, belief in the existence of a spirit, and the idea that the spirit can survive the death of the body. Taguchi illustrated this stage by the myths of Izanami and Izanagi, the only Japanese gods who went to a nether world of the dead. At this stage, the Japanese people, according to Taguchi, were still far from imagining and worshipping the gods of Heaven and Earth. With the development of agriculture and the establishment of settled society, they entered a stage in which the myths were transmitted orally, in such a way that the ancestors were transmogrified into deities. Taguchi held implicitly that these stages of development in primitive society were universal and that the Japanese myths were representations of this truth.

Next Taguchi regarded the Emperor Jinmu myth as a representation of the attainment of agricultural and other material prosperity. A distinction between gods and humans continued to develop and was formalized to such an extent that humans came to depend on the gods for protection from calamity. Government was now understood as a religious undertaking to secure that protection: this was Shinto. Subsequently the intellectual and spiritual shortcomings of Shinto were supplemented by Buddhism, which came from abroad. Buddhism suited the psychological needs of people by connecting paradises and hells with their deeds in present and past lives, thereby making goodness rewarding. Death remained inescapable, but an afterlife was provided in compensation. Thereafter, said Taguchi, the Shinto imagination did not develop further; it completely abandoned the field of religious thought to Buddhism. Prince Shōtoku encouraged Buddhism but had nothing at all to say about Shinto. In the seventh century AD, government shifted toward Buddhist worship.[8]

It is easy to see how Taguchi, with this rational and objective attitude toward Shinto, came to the support of Kume Kunitake when the latter fell into trouble for asserting that Shinto was 'an ancient custom of Heaven worship' and unworthy of classification with highly developed religions. Taguchi went far beyond Date Chihiro, who had used the materials in *Kojiki* and *Nihon Shoki* to elucidate the social and political system of ancient times. Date did not use the materials from the Age of the Gods but accepted without question the account of history starting with Emperor Jinmu. He cited the materials extensively, in an original way, to advance his narrative and support his points about the ancient social system. But he did not perceive any of his materials as myth, and accordingly he had no interest in trying to account for the origins of the myths as such. Instead of quoting them as Date had done, Taguchi interpreted both the myths of the Age of the Gods and the accounts of the early emperors as evidence of the stages of thought and social organization of a primitive people.

A classical liberal economist, Taguchi introduced principles of economics as his fundamental law of history. However, he was not a strict materialist.

> It is human nature to preserve life and avoid death. To accomplish this desire, clothing, food, and dwellings are necessary. However, it is not enough merely to obtain clothing, food, and shelter to avert hunger and cold. We desire to clothe our nakedness with fine fabrics, to eat sweet things, and to keep out wind and rain by living in well-serviced centres.
>
> To accomplish these desires, humans must exert their intellectual powers. And in proportion as material wealth accumulates, the inner qualities of humans increase. If the inner qualities of humans do not increase, material wealth by itself cannot accumulate. So long as wealth does not decrease, human qualities by themselves do not decrease. It is material wealth that causes the development of intellectual capacity; and it is human qualities that preserve and augment material wealth.[9]

In the development of his argument, Taguchi did not adhere to a purely materialist interpretation. For example, his chapters on the manifestation of enlightenment in the Tokugawa period make a thorough survey of the various schools of thought and works of literature, with little reference to the economic trends of the time. This work of intellectual history was the first of a kind that is now commonplace.

There was, however, one matter in which Taguchi was completely traditional, because it was beyond his control: the dating of events. He was forced to count from the reign of Emperor Jinmu in 660 BC, having no other reference point, and this resulted in an unwieldy system. The first date that he mentions is the year 700 after Jinmu, which the modern editor converted into 40 AD. The last date mentioned, 2518, was 1858 AD. It was not until 1897 that Japanese scholarship completed the conversion of dates, with Naka Michiyo's *Jōsei Nenki Kō* [On Ancient Chronology], fifteen years after Taguchi's pioneering work of 1882.

Kuroita Katsumi placed *Nihon Kaika Shōshi* in a class with the great works of Japanese tradition, *Jinnō Shōtōki* by Kitabatake Chikafusa and *Tokushi Yoron* by Arai Hakuseki. However, Kuroita observed that Kitabatake wrote his tract to instruct the young Emperor Go Murakami (r. 1339-68), and Hakuseki drew his work from lectures on history to the Shogun Ienobu. Taguchi's work belonged to a new age because he wrote for the Japanese people [*kokumin*].[10]

In a work called *Rekishi Gairon* [General Theory of History], Taguchi noted that there are three types of historical writing: (1) chronicles of the traditional Japanese type; (2) histories centred on the exploits of heroes and great men; and (3) comprehensive histories of social and economic organization, based on objective study of cause and effect.[11] His own work clearly belongs to the third category.

Dangerous Attacks by Shigeno Yasutsugu and Kume Kunitake

Taguchi Ukichi's book, inherently destructive of Japanese political values based on the sacred origins of the imperial house, passed without comment. Possibly the implications of his argument were not understood. On the other hand, Shigeno Yasutsugu attracted much attention for his attacks on cherished historical verities and traditional heroes, freshly viewed through the lenses of scientific history. Perhaps this was because his discussions were more specific than those of Taguchi Ukichi and thus were more easily grasped by those who missed the implications of myth interpretation by Taguchi, but believed without second thought in the heroes of Japanese history. In addition, Taguchi was a private scholar, while Shigeno worked as a civil servant at Tokyo Imperial University and was therefore expected to support imperial values.

Shigeno earned the title Dr. Obliteration [*Massatsu hakase*]. The bestowal of this sobriquet after the age of sixty reveals the profound impact of Western scientific history on him. Japanese people were accustomed to think of scholarly influences in personal terms, tracing the transmission of ideas from senior teacher to junior disciple, and not in the more abstract, comprehensive terms of the impact of theories and methods that are common in the West. It must have been astounding and improper to many that the senior scholar Shigeno, over sixty years old, was so influenced by the junior Riess, only twenty-six when he came to Japan. Kume Kunitake, who got into even more trouble than Shigeno, was over fifty when he began his assaults on traditional truths.

Shigeno's most spectacular attack was on a fourteenth-century hero, Kojima Takanori, whose exploits as a loyal supporter of the emperor are told in the war tale *Taiheiki* [Chronicle of Grand Pacification]. Like most of the medieval war tales with literary flourishes, *Taiheiki* is filled with embellishments and fabrications that are now obvious at first reading, but in 1890 its historical veracity was still largely unquestioned. Kojima Takanori was a devoted retainer of Emperor Go Daigo (r. 1318-39), celebrated in Japanese history for the Kenmu Restoration, in which the bakufu was overthrown and power was restored to the imperial court. The restoration enterprise was difficult, and Go Daigo ended up in exile after the first attempt. According to *Taiheiki*, Kojima Takanori encouraged Go Daigo in exile by carving a loyalist poem on a cherry tree; it involved a recondite allusion to Chinese history that only Go Daigo understood, and it cheered him up.[12] In a lecture on 15 May 1890, before the Japan Historical Society, Shigeno claimed that there was no historical evidence to show that Kojima Takanori had

Shigeno Yasutsugu (1827-1910) was called Dr. Obliteration for his attacks on traditional historical beliefs. (Courtesy of the Historiographical Institute, Tokyo University)

existed and theorized that he was invented by the author, a priest named Kojima Hōshi, for the purpose of getting the Kojima family name into the narrative.[13]

This was asking for trouble. The Kenmu Restoration of the fourteenth century provided a model and inspiration for the Meiji Restoration of the nineteenth century, so critical discussion on any aspect of Go Daigo's reign was widely unpopular. The Meiji government had adopted a policy of systematic posthumous promotion in court rank, and enshrinement, for the men who supported Go Daigo and the Southern Court in the fourteenth-century struggles. This left no doubt about which side the government was on and on which side it intended the people of Japan to be. Between 1876 and 1909, court ranks and promotions were posthumously awarded to thirty-five heroes of the Southern Court, and between 1869 and 1893, Shinto shrines were established to worship fourteen of them.[14] In 1889 Yoshino Shrine was established to worship Emperor Go Daigo; it was upgraded to a Grand Shrine in 1918. At one of its subsidiary shrines, none other than Kojima Takanori was worshipped.[15] In allied policies, the Meiji government promoted imperial loyalism through the promulgation of the 1889 Constitution, the 1890 Imperial Rescript on Education, and the adoption of imperial ceremonies and celebrations in the national educational system. Thus, in extinguishing the loyalist hero Kojima Takanori in 1890, Shigeno displayed an ineffable sense of bad timing.

The government did nothing, but there was much public criticism.[16] Shigeno became identified with the scholarly murder of Kojima Takanori and was the object of vehement but uninformed criticism. Kume Kunitake reported that Shigeno received letters challenging him to duels but was not intimidated. Kume pointed out that there was also a real danger of attack by armed political Shintoists, one of whom had assassinated Minister of Education Mori Arinori on 11 February 1889.[17] Mikami Sanji also wrote that there was fear of physical injury.[18] The 1890 lecture stayed with Shigeno, and he had to explain and defend it many times over the next twenty years. He was utterly certain about both the truth of his assertion and its public importance. On a research trip to Okayama in 1896 with Mikami Sanji, Shigeno said that, if proof of the existence of Kojima Takanori were found, he would bow his white head to the ground and apologize to the whole nation. Mikami was able to reassure him that no evidence had been found.[19]

In 1890 Kume Kunitake went even further. Agreeing with Shigeno's views on Kojima Takanori, he proceeded to question the historical veracity of *Taiheiki* in its entirety. In a *Shigaku Zasshi* article entitled '*Taiheiki* Is Worthless for the Study of History,'[20] Kume used two main approaches to show the unreliability of *Taiheiki* and other texts. First, parts of the narrative were disproved by documents. Second, parts of the narrative were not supported by documents, and since distortions could be shown – borrowings from other texts, inventions, anomalies, anachronisms – the narrative was suspect. Kume was not out to kill the text without motive. In 1910, as a scientific historian, he modified his ideas about Kojima Takanori when Tanaka Yoshinari (1860-1919) reported some evidence that a Kojima family had existed. However, Kume did not change his views about the general worthlessness of *Taiheiki.*[21] It is not clear whether Shigeno, who died in 1910, learned of Tanaka's argument.[22]

In this way, the Tokyo Imperial University historians were chipping away at various corners of the edifice of Japanese historical truth. There was much to do, and they studied what seemed important and what came to hand. They had no overall plan of attack. Yet it seemed inevitable that they would soon cast a critical look at the fundamental questions of Japanese history, the Age of the Gods and the succession of emperors. We have seen how Tokugawa scholars, through sheer rationality and incremental study, had cast serious doubt on the reality of the gods. Then the nineteenth-century infusion of scientific method into Japanese positivistic research produced deadly publications on diverse subjects by Shigeno, Kume, and, as we shall see, Hoshino Hisashi. It was only a matter of time until they too would question the Age of the Gods and the emperors. Finally, a new direction was taken in the early Meiji period, when a different basis for reexamining ancient history was laid in a way that Japanese scholars could not have accomplished by themselves. The foreigners in Japan used archeology to reconstruct ancient history. The combination of archeology and scientific historical method had the potential utterly to destroy the myths of the Age of the Gods and the early emperors.

Archeology

Tokugawa Mitsukuni pioneered in archeology, as in positivistic research, when he excavated tombs in Nasu, Tochigi Prefecture, in order to explicate a stone inscription of an ancient ruler in the area. According to Kanaseki Hiroshi, 'The fact that Mitsukuni reburied the excavated artifacts after making his records and diagrams deserves special note as a landmark in the advance of scholarship.'[23] Other Tokugawa-period scholars in Japan, and scholars in China, understood the importance of digging up the past, but none reached the conclusion that archeology could reveal the origins and development of human civilization. Nor could they develop the scientific method practised by the foreigners.

The ground was broken by *The Shell Mounds of Omori,* published in 1879 by the American Edward S. Morse (1838-1925).[24] It is clear from his observations of Japanese life in *Japan Day by Day* that Morse was a scientist by nature, interested in everything he saw, gifted with acute powers of observation and an ability to grasp the rationale behind the unfamiliar things that he observed in Japan.[25] A zoologist, he went to Japan because he was interested in its brachiopods. He organized and taught at the zoology department of Tokyo Imperial University in 1877-9. Morse was the first to distinguish ancient shell middens from natural landforms and conducted excavations to reveal the remains of an ancient society now called Jōmon [Cord-mark], after the characteristic cord-mark patterns impressed in its unglazed pottery. This society is now fixed at roughly 10,000-250 BC.

Many of the foreigners were interested in archeology. Starting in the mid-1870s, scholars, diplomats, teachers, and missionaries gathered for papers and discussions in English at regular meetings of the Asiatic Society of Japan, and they published the results in the *Transactions* of the society. Early numbers of the *Transactions* contain papers on archeology. In his 1880 article 'Notes on Stone Implements from Otaru and Hakodate, with a Few General Remarks on the Prehistoric Remains in Japan,' John Milne covered pits, shell mounds, inscriptions, arrowheads, tumuli, and caves, with illustrations. The same volume contained an article by Ernest Satow, 'Ancient Sepulchral Mounds in KAUDZUKE.'[26]

Japanese scholars soon entered the field. The first site of the Yayoi period (250 BC-250 AD), succeeding the Jōmon, was found in 1884 at Mukōgaoka in Tokyo. Interpretation of both the Jōmon and Yayoi periods was retarded, however, by a fixation on the cultural identity of the people whose remains were dug up. Japanese and foreigners alike started with the assumption that Jōmon remains were those of the Ainu, aboriginal people who survived in northern Japan. They were racially and linguistically distinct from the Japanese and retained a primitive culture. Since the Japanese were regarded as a superior race, it was natural to assume that the primitive society that underlay Japanese society 2,000 years ago was not Japanese. Scholars divided on the further point of whether there was a pre-Ainu society called Koropokguru, whose members, according to Ainu myth, had lived in Hokkaido before the Ainu came. The Koropok-guru thesis was laid to rest in 1912 with its main supporter, Tsuboi Shōgoro (1863-1912), founder of the Department of Anthropology at Tokyo Imperial University.[27]

In 1890 it appeared that archeology had the potential to destroy the myths as sources for ancient history. The interpretation of archeological remains would later go through many stages, involving numerous theories of race, movements of peoples, and invasions, many of them ill founded and pointless. But no matter how the remains were interpreted, the central point of archeological research was clear: the earliest society in Japan was human, like everywhere else in the world, and there was no physical evidence for the Age of the Gods. As I have noted, Taguchi Ukichi had already proceeded in 1882, wholly without the benefit of archeology, to a new interpretation of the only other evidence, the myths in *Kojiki* and *Nihon Shoki*. He viewed them as the products of an early stage common to all societies, and since they were myths, the question whether they contained any historical truth appears not to have occurred to him. Now around 1890, with the truth laid bare by archeology, it seemed that only religious believers, politicians looking for an edge, and administrators committed to stability might hold out for the truth of the myths.

8
The Kume Kunitake Incident, 1890-2

Professors as Civil Servants

A powerful constraint lay on the scholars at Tokyo Imperial University: professors were civil servants. The university seemed to be at arm's length from the government, and the Ministry of Education did not normally intervene in matters of appointment, promotion, and curriculum; yet the minister of education retained the power of dismissal. In the twentieth century, it became increasingly difficult to exercise that power as professors and administrators learned how to put up a solid front to protect their autonomy.[1] However, ministerial authority was exercised in 1892, when Kume Kunitake was dismissed, and the effect on historical scholarship was profound.

When Mori Arinori (1847-89), as minister of education, set up the system, he was clear that the purpose of primary and secondary education was to create obedient, loyal, and productive citizens of the Japanese state. However, he seems to have distinguished between education and scholarship. Without much thought on the point, he believed that it was possible to cap off an educational system devoted to training the people, with no special regard for historical truth, by a university dedicated to the unhindered pursuit of scholarship. Personally he was not troubled by what went on in the university, and his biographer says that 'no other single appointment ... better revealed Mori's ideological position than that of Basil Hall Chamberlain, a historical positivist who interpreted the ancient legends straightforwardly as myth, to the chair of Japanese literature.'[2]

Yet Mori, his successors in the Ministry of Education, and his fellow politicians agreed that an invigorating, unifying view of Japanese history and institutions, especially the imperial throne, was more important than academic theory. They were prepared to exercise authority over professors and make them refrain from academic theory that might damage the foundations of an emerging sacerdotal state. The elements of such a state were provided by the Constitution of 1889. Sovereignty was established not in the people but in the emperor, strictly on the basis of his uninterrupted

故 久米 博士 倚像 并 筆蹟

Kume Kunitake (1839-1931), as shown in an
obituary photograph, and with an example of
his calligraphy. Kume was dismissed from
Tokyo Imperial University in 1892 for sceptical
writing about Shinto. (Courtesy of the
Historiographical Institute, Tokyo University)

descent from Emperor Jinmu. The preamble to the Constitution did not
mention the Age of the Gods, in which the Sun Goddess chartered the
imperial line with a vow of eternal protection. A number of proposed drafts
for the Constitution had explicitly stated the chartering of the imperial
house by the Sun Goddess, but the final text did not. Nevertheless, in 1889
everyone in Japan understood that its reality was affirmed.

The point was the same one with which the Mito scholars wrestled: accepting Emperor Jinmu entailed his ancestry going back to the Sun Goddess. We have seen that the Mito scholars compromised their rationalism
and positivism by grudgingly starting their history with a collapsed genealogy of the Age of the Gods, leading up to Emperor Jinmu. It remained to be
seen how the modern sceptical scholars at Tokyo Imperial University would
deal with it. They were in a worse position than the Mito scholars, who had
struggled in private with the issues. The Meiji scholars were civil servants in
a modern state with a Constitution that affirmed the myths.

Moreover, the Constitution provided a legal basis for protecting both the person and the reputation of the reigning emperor with its vague definition in Article 3 of the emperor as 'sacred and inviolable.' It was not clear whether this meant strictly the person of the emperor, who should be venerated as descended from the Sun Goddess and should not be physically attacked, or whether it pertained to his responsibilities under constitutional law. In 1889 some newspapers held a narrow view, in the good legal sense of narrow, that the purpose of the article was simply to clear the emperor of political responsibility for unpopular policies and decisions. They maintained that Article 3 should be seen in conjunction with Article 55, which provided that ministers of state 'assist the emperor' [*hohitsu*] and take responsibility for policies good or bad.[3] The sacred emperor was always in the clear, and the assisting ministers of state were always responsible. Had this narrow view prevailed, discussion of the imperial institution and its foundation in ancient myths might have developed more freely in the twentieth century.

There was a good basis for such a positive narrow view in the discussions preceding the final drafting of the Constitution. For example, constitutional drafts by the House of Elders [*Genrōin*] in 1876 and 1880 had paired the two concepts of the emperor's sacredness and immunity from responsibility: 'The emperor is sacred and inviolable and is not responsible for any acts whatsoever' (1880 draft).[4] The point of stating his sacredness was not simply to affirm it but to make sacredness the basis for immunity of the emperor from political responsibility. In between, an 1878 draft by the House of Elders had separated the two concepts of sacredness and responsibility, thereby making imperial sacredness absolute, but by 1880 the elders had thought better of it.

Similarly an 1880 draft by the conservative Confucian scholar Motoda Eifu (1818-91), tutor of the Meiji emperor, linked the two ideas: 'The emperor is sacred and inviolable, and no disturbances whatsoever are the responsibility of his sacred person.'[5] The most explicit draft was by Tamura Kan'ichirō: 'The emperor is sacred and inviolable, *and therefore* is not responsible. The responsibility for government matters rests upon the cabinet and the ministers of state.'[6] The majority of constitutional drafts proposed this understanding of the sacredness of the emperor.

However, in the Constitution of 1889, the two concepts of sacredness and political responsibility ended up widely separated. No doubt this was decided by Itō Hirobumi (1841-1909), the main author of the Constitution and thrice prime minister under it. Article 3 stated simply that the emperor is sacred and inviolable. Article 5 stated that the emperor passes laws with the cooperation of the Imperial Diet, while Article 55 stated that the ministers of state 'assist the emperor and take responsibility.' Thus, there was a basis for the broad view that the emperor's sacredness, stated clearly and without qualification in Article 3, was absolute and unrelated to any other aspect of the Constitution. This was reinforced by the phrase in the preamble in which the emperor referred to his 'divine ancestors' [*shinsei no sosō*]. If his ancestors were divine under the preamble, then so was the emperor under Article 3.

The most influential interpretation was that of Itō Hirobumi himself. In his *Commentaries on the Constitution*, he came down hard in favour of absolute sanctity:

Article III The Emperor is sacred and inviolable

'The Sacred Throne was established at the time when the heavens and the earth became separated.' (*Kojiki*) The Emperor is Heaven-descended, divine, and sacred; He is pre-eminent above all his subjects. He must be reverenced and is inviolable. He has indeed to pay due respect to the law but the law has no power to hold Him accountable to it. Not only shall there be no irreverence for the Emperor's person, but also shall He neither be made a topic of derogatory comment nor one of discussion.[7]

This extraordinarily hard view was only an interpretation of the Constitution by its main author, Itō Hirobumi, not law or policy. But it was in line with developing trends of nationalistic thought about Japan, the Constitution, and the emperor. Itō's views were enthusiastically supported by many nationalists and Shintoists, who were eager to affirm the absolute sacredness of the emperor and the necessity of unquestioning submission.

As matters developed after 1889, critical remarks about the imperial institution and its entire history became unacceptable because they insulted the imperial dignity. Criticism of the historical emperors could, by association, be considered criticism of the reigning emperor and therefore treasonable. Moreover, Itō Hirobumi cited a *Kojiki* passage from the Age of the Gods to prove the sacredness of the emperor. Thus, by extension, critical discussion of the Age of the Gods might also be considered criticism of the emperor. In these circumstances, the massacring scholars of Tokyo Imperial University were on a collision course with the authorities in charge of the imperial institution and with their supporters in the public.

Kume's Offensive Article:
'Shinto Is an Ancient Custom of Heaven Worship'
In March 1899, Kume Kunitake was hired as a lecturer at Waseda University, then known as Tōkyō Senmon Gakkō [Tokyo Specialty School]. His curriculum vitae to that time is stored at Waseda University. The latter portion reads,

1888 September.	Invited from the History Compilation Bureau to Tokyo Imperial University; appointed professor in the Faculty of Arts; second-grade official. Assigned to the Special Chronological History Project; established Department of History and occupied chair.
1889 February 23.	Promoted to first-grade official.
February 27.	Awarded Fifth Order of Merit. Awarded Order of the Sacred Treasure.
1892 February 29.	Awarded junior fifth rank.
March 4.	Ordered to resign position.
March 30.	Resigned as ordered.[8]

A productive history professor at Tokyo Imperial University, full of honours, was fired. Why?

In 1891 Kume Kunitake published an article that offended nationalists and political Shintoists, who brought much pressure on the Ministry of Education to dismiss him. The article in *Shigaku Zasshi* was titled 'Shinto Is an Ancient Custom of Heaven Worship.'[9] But as Kume himself said ten years later, in 1901, it was not his article alone that caused his dismissal but the development of the modern school of critical history at Tokyo Imperial University. Shigeno Yasutsugu acquired the nickname Dr. Obliteration, but the historical method that earned him the name was shared by the whole group at the Historical Compilation Bureau, which moved on to Tokyo Imperial University in 1888. When Shigeno published his article on Kojima Takanori, it became evident that the new method threatened believers in the Japanese national essence centred on the emperor. The trouble, said Kume, was that academic freedom was an import from the West and not a Japanese product.[10]

As the immediate background of the incident, Kume singled out the work of Hoshino Hisashi. It was equally offensive to an opposition whom Kume regarded as benighted. In October 1890, Hoshino published an article in *Shigaku Zasshi*, 'A Question from an Old Man for Sincere Patriots Concerning Japanese Race and Language,' that he knew would rouse opposition.[11] It was the practice of *Shigaku Zasshi* to publish long articles serially, but Hoshino sensed trouble and requested that this article be published all in one issue so that no misunderstanding would arise. The argument of the article was simple: one of the deities in the Age of the Gods was Korean. The discussion was extremely complex. The deity in question was Masakatsukachi Hayahi Ame no Oshimimi no Mikoto, Oshimimi for short, who was a child of Amaterasu Ōmikami, the Sun Goddess, founder of the Japanese imperial line. Hoshino was explicit on the significance of his contention: it meant that an ancestor of the imperial house had come from Korea. Furthermore, Hoshino stated that Japan and Korea had not been separate countries in ancient times and noted that he shared this view with Kume Kunitake.

Hoshino's discussion began from a variant text on the Age of the Gods in *Nihon Shoki*, in which the deity Susano-O was expelled from the Plain of High Heaven for violent behaviour and went with his son Iso Takeru to the kingdom of Silla in Korea. Not liking it there, he soon returned to Japan in the province of Izumo.[12] This type of story was not uncommon in other Japanese records besides *Kojiki* and *Nihon Shoki*, especially those of the seventh and eighth centuries. That was a time of heavy immigration from Korea to Japan, and by the eighth century the Korean immigrants discovered that the Japanese government was prepared to admit them to full citizenship upon their adoption of Japanese names. Many of them presented documents to the Japanese government for certification, showing how they had come by their Japanese names. One method was to claim that their distant ancestors were originally Japanese, but had gone to Korea, and that at some point members of the family had returned to Japan, just like Susano-O, to reclaim their names. His story may have been a model. Thus, the immigrants added to the rich Japanese store of records, legends, distortions, fabrications, and lies about genealogies.[13]

For a scholar like Hoshino who was familiar with the ancient records, Korean ancestry in historical times was not implausible in any individual case. Probably unaware of where his method was leading him, he extended the principle to the Age of the Gods. In the case of Oshimimi, Hoshino held that records other than *Kojiki* and *Nihon Shoki* demonstrated his Korean origin, including *Bungo Fudoki* [Geographical Record of Bungo Province, early eighth century] and such impeccable sources as *Shoku Nihon Kōki*, *Engi Shiki*, and *Shinsen Shōjiroku* [New Compilation of the Register of Families, 815].

Kume provided the background to Hoshino's article in a 1911 talk entitled 'Japan and Korea Together Constituted the Divine Country of Japan.'[14] The Historical Compilation Bureau employed an old-fashioned scholar of the National Studies school named Suzuki Shinnen, much esteemed by his more modern colleagues for his photographic memory and unrivalled knowledge of genealogy. Kume and Hoshino consulted Suzuki about the authenticity of the variant text of *Nihon Shoki* telling of Susano-O's adventure in Korea, which neither they nor any other scholars had noticed before. They asked whether it meant that Susano-O was Korean, and they were astounded to hear Suzuki confirm with equanimity that such a theory existed. They realized the importance of the topic, and Hoshino went ahead with his own demonstration by scientific method of the Korean origins of Oshimimi and the unity of Japan and Korea in ancient times. This view was purely scholarly, without consideration of the current relations between Japan and Korea, in which Japan demonstrated imperial ambitions.

Unscholarly opposition materialized, as soon as Hoshino's article appeared, from nationalist scholars, patriots, and political Shintoists. According to Kume, in 1890 they were offended by the idea that Korea was part of the divine country of Japan in ancient times. Kume characterized the scholars of National Studies, whom he never precisely identified, as still living in the Tokugawa era: 'They absolutely refused to consider Korea part of the country of the gods. They ostracized it as a foreign country. Moreover, they hated viewing Japanese history from an international perspective and doing comparative studies. This bigoted attitude derived from the closed country of the Tokugawa period. The Meiji period had arrived, but Japanese history alone remained in the Tokugawa period.'[15] Peter Duus has shown that by 1910 a strong body of Japanese thought had developed that believed in the unity of Korea and Japan in ancient times. This unity was commonly understood as the racial unity of the two peoples or as the possession of Korea by Japan in ancient times, and it was used as a reason to rejoin the countries in modern times. In short it was a justification for Japanese imperialism in Korea and thus an extremely attractive idea in 1910, the year of Japan's annexation of Korea.[16] However, no one showed up twenty years earlier in 1890, either to defend or to exploit the political implications of the position of Hoshino and Kume. Kume was not wrong in his view that only those hostile to the notion spoke up, mainly political Shintoists and latter-day National Scholars. While they agreed that Japan had rightly possessed Korea in ancient times, they refused to accept that Korea had been part of the divine nation in the first place. That was a different matter; no one but Japanese could share in the divine nation.

Kume believed that there was still much anger about Hoshino's article when he went ahead with his own offensive article in October 1891. That was the last straw:

> We three professors, Shigeno, Hoshino, and myself, who started the Department of Japanese History were all considered bad. I was the most hateful of the three, and in the following year, when I expressed myself too lightly in the matter of Shinto, I had to resign the prestigious position of professor at the Imperial University. Looking back, I would say that I was a victim of the merger of Japan and Korea.[17]

In this article, Kume wrote that Shinto was nothing more than ancient nature worship and had not developed religious importance in the Western sense. This implied that Shinto institutions and articles associated with the imperial house had little significance. They included the Great Shrine of Ise, where the Sun Goddess is worshipped, and the sacred mirror, jewel, and sword that are the insignia of the imperial house. Kume maintained that Japanese thought had otherwise progressed beyond ancient primitive religion, thanks to the advent of Confucianism, Buddhism, and Yin-Yang thought.

Taguchi Ukichi deepened the impact of the article by reprinting it in his own more popular historical journal *Shikai* [Sea of History] on 25 January 1892. He said that he did so because he believed in the principle of freedom of research and required such freedom for his own historical writing. But 'to tell the truth, I was opposed to the contents of the article.'[18] Taguchi then entered the lists to defend Kume's article in an ensuing battle in print, claiming that the article was not disrespectful toward Shinto or the imperial house and proclaiming the necessity for freedom of research and publication.[19]

Kume was vague about the opponents of the Hoshino article, but there is no difficulty in identifying those who opposed his article on Shinto as primitive Heaven worship. The Kume article provoked an extraordinary amount of discussion in newspapers and journals, with blasts and criticisms, symposia, and a few counterblasts, mainly by Taguchi Ukichi. A survey of the literature lists 340 items on the subject between 20 October 1891 and 9 June 1893.[20] It is difficult to summarize the intellectual position of the opposition since much of it resonates like cries of pain personally suffered from a great wound inflicted on the sacred nation by a traitor within.

A representative statement is provided by Miyaji Itsuo, a ritualist in the Imperial Household Ministry, in 'Arguments on the Theory of Shinto as an Ancient Custom of Heaven Worship,' a contribution to an 1892 book. Miyaji wrote that Kume, holding the position of teacher at the Imperial University and receiving many honours, bore a great responsibility as a teacher of the nation. He ought to be making clear 'the right relations between the emperor and his subjects.' Yet, said Miyaji, Kume proclaimed that the great shrines and holy places of the empire did not worship the imperial ancestors, that the three sacred regalia of the imperial house were mere altar decorations, that the imperial Great Feast of Accession worshipped a mere Heaven of Kume's imagining. In addition to accusing Kume of religious blasphemy, he also challenged Kume on a fundamental point of historical scholarship that lay at the basis of Japanese religion and politics: 'Kume also claims that the imperial ancestor Oshimimi came from Korea to prosper, and that the descent of the heavenly founder of the imperial line occurred about 100 years before Emperor Jinmu.'[21]

The opposition not only filled the press but also implored the Imperial Household Ministry, the Ministry of Home Affairs, and the Ministry of Education to press for Kume's dismissal and suspension of the journals. The most prominent suitors for dismissal were four members of an organization called Dōseikan [Path of Life Institute], founded by Watanabe Ikarimaru

(1837-1915), a follower of Hirata Shinto, the school of Hirata Atsutane. The four were Kuramochi Jikyū, Hongō Sadao, Fujino Tatsuji, and Hangyūda Morio, about whom nothing is known.

The four visited Kume for a discussion at his Tokyo home on 28 February 1892; although they were not welcome guests, they stayed for five hours to make their points. Kume, who noted the potential for violence against Shigeno Yasutsugu by inflamed political Shintoists, regarded the visit as threatening, but he was not afraid. It was one of a series of appearances at his home by *sōshi*, normally translated as 'political bullies' or 'henchmen.' Kume said that his wife begged him to stop talking to these people, but he replied that he was confident in argument and could overturn five or ten of them. However, he thought that at one point the discussion with the members of the Path of Life Institute would come to blows.[22]

Only the visitors' version of the encounter was made public, in a piece that appeared in several newspapers, 'The Complete Record of Questions and Answers on the Article "Shinto Is an Ancient Custom of Heaven Worship."'[23] They were quite specific, accusing Kume of claiming that the Shinto gods were imaginary, that the Great Shrine of Ise did not worship the Sun Goddess, that the deity Oshimimi came from Korea, and that Buddhism had provided the foundation of the country in ancient times. They also said that the disgusting theory of Wu Taibo, introduced by the Tokugawa Confucianists, had finally been cleared away, but now Kume wanted to show that the ancestor of the imperial line came not from China but from Korea.

According to this account, Kume's replies were feeble. This is not surprising since such conclusions could be drawn from his article. Kume claimed that the account was full of errors.[24] Nevertheless, there was no way for him to refute it. The professor lived in a different world from the Shinto believers, and he could not explain to them the level of intellectual apprehension of religion on which his assertions were intelligible. The best that he could do was to deny that he had any intention of insulting the imperial dignity, which no doubt was true.

Apart from Taguchi Ukichi, the only support for Kume came from students at Tokyo Imperial University. Ōmori Kingorō (1867-1937), who later became a specialist in Kamakura-period history, led a group of four to visit Kume at his home and offer help. At first they were turned away, being taken for another group of political bullies. When they did get in to talk, it was too late to help; Kume showed them a letter from the Ministry of Education ordering his resignation. Ōmori then led another group to visit Katō Hiroyuki (1836-1916), the president of Tokyo Imperial University, and got a gruff response. Katō, a strong liberal in his youth, had long since become a tough-minded conservative. As president of the university, he was purely an administrator and not a professor, so he had little sympathy with the argument for academic freedom.[25] He said that he had not read all of the article on Heaven worship because it was too long, and he could not judge it in any case because he was not a historian, but he thought that Kume was wrong on one point about the Great Shrine of Ise. Kume, he said, was dealt with because of public outrage. The students asked if that did not injure the dignity of the university, and Katō replied that it was only an internal matter [*uchimaku*], with no principles involved. In any case, said Katō, Kume could be reinstated after public outrage died down; in fact, though, Katō had no intention of doing so.[26] There was nothing left for the students to do. Nonetheless, their response was the strongest expression of support for Kume and the principles involved in the case. Even at that, Ōmori waited for forty years until Kume's death to tell the story.

On 3 March 1892, Kume published a retraction in the newspapers; on 4 March, he was ordered by the Ministry of Education to resign as professor; and on 5 March, an order was given by the Home Ministry for the suspension of publication of both *Shigaku Zasshi* and *Shikai*. Kume's retraction was brief:

My positivistic research on Shinto, published in *Shigaku Zasshi*, numbers 23 to 28, and in *Shikai* number 8, has received public criticism. In light of this, I am obliged to develop more fully the intent of the article, which was not achieved in its original form. Therefore, I retract the article in its entirety.

Kume Kunitake
3 March 1892.[27]

With Kume's resignation on 30 March, the affair was closed.

Shigeno and Hoshino, the other murderous scholars, were not asked to resign from the university, but the Ministry of Education terminated the *Dai Nihon Hennen Shi* project on 29 March 1893, and both men were temporarily cleared out, along with Tanaka Yoshinari. *Dai Nihon Hennen Shi* was ended partly because of the disgrace of the whole group of professors. However, it was also recognized that an annalistic history written in Chinese, on the model of the Six National Histories of ancient times and *Dai Nihon Shi* of Tokugawa times, was simply out of date. Mikami Sanji, director of the succeeding Historiographical Institute from 1899 to 1919, acknowledged both of these reasons.[28]

After his dismissal from Tokyo Imperial University, Kume Kunitake was invited to the more liberal Waseda University, founded by a friend from his youth, Ōkuma Shigenobu (1838-1923). Ōkuma was a successful politician, liberal in his youth, who became prime minister in 1898 and again in 1914. By then his liberalism had entirely disappeared. Kume was hired as a lecturer in 1899, and in 1918, when he was eighty, he was promoted to professor. He remained a pure scholar, so distinguished as a founder of the study of ancient documents that a later historian awards him an Olympic gold medal in the field, with Shigeno Yasutsugu taking the silver and Hoshino Hisashi the bronze.[29] Kume Kunitake retired in 1922, was succeeded by Kuroita Katsumi as the authority on ancient documents, and was gradually forgotten – in the postwar era, hardly anyone was aware of him.[30]

Kume was not deeply disturbed by the incident. He placed it in the wider context of the lingering influence of Japan's seclusion from world affairs in the Tokugawa period, during which a narrow and intolerant school of National Studies came to dominate. He never abandoned his fundamental commitment to scientific research, and he believed that academic freedom would eventually prevail. He wrote his memoirs in 1929 at the age of ninety, dwelling mainly on his youth and his trip to Europe as recorder of the 1871-3 Iwakura mission. The memoirs consist of two thick volumes, with more than 1,100 pages, of which only the last two are devoted to the Heaven-worship incident. He attributed the uproar to personal resentments, misunderstandings, and deliberate distortions and said nothing at all about the relations among state, society, and scholars. The memoirs conclude, 'As the world gradually opens up and scholarship advances, freedom of research becomes wider. Incidents like the one I have described will become fewer.'[31]

Kume's faith and forbearance are all the more remarkable in view of later government censorship of his writing. In 1907 he contributed *Naracho Shi* [History of the Nara Court] to a comprehensive history series. As early as 1915, the Ministry of Home Affairs observed passages disrespectful to the imperial house [*fukei*]: lewd and lascivious accounts of Empress Shotoku (r. 764-70) and the priest Dokyo (?-772), who was said to be her lover. But the ministry did nothing because the author, while citing these accounts, disavowed their historical accuracy. In 1926, however, the Imperial Household Ministry could stand it no longer and complained, so a representative of the publisher, Waseda University Press, was summoned and ordered to make deletions. Since it was a subscription work, going directly to purchasers, it was not possible to retrieve all the copies from booksellers. The Ministry of Home Affairs and the Ministry of Education therefore cooperated in prohibiting the work from being read in libraries and schools.[32]

Kume's purpose in including the lascivious passages was to show the difference between ancient and modern historical practice. He cited the indecent tales directly from ancient works: *Nihon Ryoiki* [Miraculous Tales of Japan, an early Heian collection of Buddhist legends], *Kojidan* [Chats of Oe Masafusa on History, an early Kamakura collection of legends], and *Mizukagami* [The Water Mirror, an early Kamakura collection of historical tales]. It is apparent at first sight, wrote Kume, that the stories are untrue, but in those days there was no distinction between history and literature, and the result was confusion. Kume said that modern scholarship disposed of these sources as unhistorical, and he concluded that scholarly endeavour to separate history from literature must continue.[33] The Ministry of Home Affairs respected Kume's position in the early editions, but by 1926 the Imperial Household Ministry could not bear the repetition of these slanders about an empress in ancient times, even to make a point about scholarly method.

There is no record of any reaction by Kume to this censorship. It must have been fresh in his mind when he wrote his memoirs in 1929, but he said nothing. This was consistent with his attitude toward the Heaven-worship incident. To the end, he displayed an innocence about the power of the state that was also shown by Tsuda Sōkichi during his trial for lese-majesty in 1941.

One aspect of Kume's later scholarship is relevant to the story of developing nationalism among academic historians in the twentieth century. In 1903 Ōkuma Shigenobu edited an important volume, *Kaikoku Gojūnenshi* [History of Fifty Years since the Opening of the Country], and asked Kume to contribute an article on Shinto. The choice of Kume may have surprised some, in light of the Heaven-worship incident that had established his reputation as hostile to the religion. We lack information on the reason for Ōkuma's choice of author, but in any case Kume did not produce another attack on Shinto. His piece strove for objectivity, and far from being hostile it was more sympathetic than might have been predicted.

In his 1890 article 'Shinto Is an Ancient Custom of Heaven Worship,' Kume had adopted a universal approach to religion based on contemporary scholarly standards and had concluded that Shinto belonged in the category of primitive religions, not developed ones. In the 1903 article 'Shinto to Kundō' [Shinto and the Way of the Ruler], he adopted different criteria for evaluating religions; unfortunately they were not very well thought out.[34] The Shinto under discussion was not the ancient Shinto characterized as Heaven worship in the earlier article but the religion termed Shinto, the Way of the Gods, in *Nihon Shoki* in the reign of Emperor Yomei in 585.[35] This was the first recorded use of the term, and it was used to distinguish Shinto from Buddhism. Using a definition of religion drawn from the ancient Chinese classic, the *Yi Jing* [Book of Changes], Kume held that in its nature Shinto was not unique to Japan:

> The *Yi Jing* is the source for the Chinese word *god* [*kami*]. The commentary on the twentieth hexagram *guan,* 'to observe,' says that in the Way of the Gods of Heaven, the four seasons occur in their regular order, and the sage employs the Way of the Gods to establish a teaching to which the empire submits. Religious ceremonies should be understood in the same sense as the Way of the Gods in this hexagram [that is, they embody a teaching patterned after Heaven and bring order to nature and society]. In China a

teaching based on the Way of the Gods was established 3,000 years ago, and thus the Way of the Gods is not exclusive to Japan. Also, the Song-dynasty monk Xie Song said that the Buddha established his teaching on the inner meaning of the Way of the Gods. Christianity is also one form of the Way of the Gods. The Way of the Gods is worldwide; religion itself is the Way of the Gods.[36]

Thus, Kume abandoned the terms of contemporary scholarship to define religion in terms from the most obscure and least rational of the Chinese classics. He was not good at religion. It has been observed that his 1890 article on Heaven worship also suffered from a lack of the rigour that he applied to historical topics other than religious history.[37] Kume probably used this definition of religion in the *Yi Jing* because his senior colleague Shigeno Yasutsugu had already done so in an 1898 article on Shinto in *Shigaku Zasshi*, with satisfactory results.[38] However, Shigeno confined the discussion of Shinto to the proper application of the term within Japanese history, while Kume was trying to place Shinto in the perspective of world religions. His argument was incomparably weaker than Shigeno's. *Yi Jing* did not provide the conceptual framework for such an endeavour.

In any case, in 1903 Shinto was not dismissed by Kume as in the 1890 article on Heaven worship but taken seriously as a major religion of the world. Probably Kume changed his mind about Shinto, not because he was chastened by his dismissal from Tokyo Imperial University, but because he had become more nationalistic. The youthful Kume had written a brilliant account of conditions in the West in his capacity as recorder of the Iwakura mission of 1871-3. But his obituaries in 1931 noted that the mature Kume had come to dislike the West. Photographs always show him dressed in traditional Japanese clothes, not Western garb. Eccentrically he came to dislike things such as electricity and automobiles, though he retained a taste for rich Western foods. This suggests a growing acceptance of twentieth-century Japanese nationalism that rejected the westernizing trends of the early Meiji period. His higher regard for Shinto in 1903 was consistent with his acceptance of state purposes in firing him in 1892. On that occasion, thirty-seven people attended a farewell party and feared a lugubrious occasion. But Kume was not downcast, the evening went well, and they all ended up singing songs and reciting poems.[39] And in 1926, his 1907 book on the history of the Nara court was censored without protest or remark from Kume. Probably he believed that all these things were done in the proper interests of the Japanese nation. He did not perceive any evil aspects of the Japanese imperial state.

Interpretation of the Kume Incident
The immediate significance of the Kume Kunitake incident needs little

elaboration. The government of Japan, which employed university professors as civil servants, dismissed a professor for publishing an article contrary to political and religious doctrine supporting the state. He also publicly retracted the article. Individual freedom of research and expression was violated, and the autonomy of the university was infringed upon. Kume can be seen variously as a victim of authoritarian government, nationalism, undue religious influence on the state, or nameless dark reaction. The term 'martyr' is sometimes used: 'The incident of Kume Kunitake's "Shinto Is an Ancient Custom of Heaven Worship" may be described in any case as establishing a monument to a martyr of modern historical study in the Meiji period.'[40]

Such views were not publicly expressed until long after the incident – indeed, not until after World War II. Apart from Taguchi Ukichi, who was outside the university, Kume received little support at the time. Tokyo Imperial University, the scene of many stormy episodes in the twentieth century, was not stirred up in 1890-2 by the Kume incident. Byron K. Marshall speculates that this was because Kume and his colleagues Shigeno and Hoshino and the rest held dual positions in the Historical Compilation Bureau and the university. Thus, their colleagues in other departments did not see their cause as a struggle for academic freedom and university autonomy.[41]

Yet neither was Kume supported by his fellow historians. Shigeno Yasutsugu and Hoshino Hisashi wrote nothing about the Kume incident, and younger scholars were not very sympathetic. Tsuji Zennosuke found Kume intemperate and dogmatic, and Miura Hiroyuki, who was a student at the time of the incident, wrote in his 1928 study *Nihon Shigakushi Gaisetsu* [Survey of the History of Japanese Historical Scholarship], 'Among Shigeno, Kume, and Hoshino, Kume was the least prudent in the expression of his scholarly views. The opposite of reserved, he was instead provocative, and this was an example of it.'[42] Kume Kunitake was to blame.

Miura Hiroyuki's brief and dismissive evaluation of the Kume incident is illuminating. A brilliant scholar who established the field of legal history at Kyoto Imperial University, Miura held conventional views about history and the imperial house. He believed that the Yamato race had founded Japan and that the imperial house had ruled it since the beginning. The continuing rule of the imperial house without revolution was the basis of the national essence and the source of pride for Japan among nations. Miura approved of the modern development of social science and the diversification of historical scholarship into political, economic, legal, social, and cultural history. In his view, however, there was no conflict between historical scholarship and the political and religious truths of Japan, which must be upheld without question. The Heaven-worship incident, and the 1911 Southern-Northern Courts incident (which I will discuss), caused disputes between the spheres of scholarship and education. But then things quieted down, and the historians got on with history.[43] In *Nihon Shigakushi Gaisetsu*, Miura saw nothing of principle in Kume's attack on unexceptional truths, attributed it to Kume's character, and passed on to other matters. This was the view of the majority in the prewar era.

Obituaries of Kume in 1931, in *Shigaku Zasshi* and *Rekishi Chiri*, simply referred to 'a serious slip of the pen' [*hikka*] as the cause of the incident and offered no interpretation whatsoever of its meaning.[44] However, the choice of terms implies an interpretation. *Hikka* is an apologetic term, meaning that the author was entirely at fault. It differs from a slip of the tongue, usually unintentional at the conscious level. A serious slip of the pen was intentional in the first place and was made against the retrospective better judgment of the author, who was repentant. No blame was attached to the authorities who took proper procedures to deal with the slip of the pen. This position of the obituary writers was consistent with Kume's view of the incident.

Then, in a 1939 review of the development of historical scholarship in Japan, Tsuji Zennosuke avoided all mention of the Kume incident. Tsuji's was the leading article in a volume celebrating the fiftieth anniversary of the Historical Association, begun in the time of Riess and the massacring scholars. Tsuji surveyed historical writing from ancient times, and for the modern period he emphasized the study and compilation of documents and the establishment of history as an independent discipline at Tokyo Imperial University in the era of Shigeno Yasutsugu. However, if he omitted the Kume incident, he also left out the Southern-Northern Courts problem, censorship, and any other contentious matter.[45] The oppressive nationalism of 1939 may have led Tsuji to discuss only positive aspects of the historical profession that contributed to the national Japanese endeavour. As we shall see, by 1939 Tsuji himself had come more or less happily to share the values of that nationalism. Thus, he expunged untoward incidents such as the Kume affair from the glowing story of historiography, which contributed – like all the arts and sciences – to the great imperial nation.

9
The Development of Academic History

Establishment of the Historiographical Institute

On 1 April 1895, a new institute was set up at Tokyo Imperial University, the Shiryō Hensan Gakari [Historiographical Section], which has continued to the present day under the name Shiryō Hensanjo [Historiographical Institute]. Hoshino Hisashi came back as its first head. The idea for the Historiographical Section was pushed by a new minister of education, Inoue Kaoru (1835-1915), despite the inopportune timing of a request for funds when Japan had just ended a costly war with China. Inoue intended to have a fresh start, with historians who would not cause any trouble. There were five rules for the historians of the new section:

1 Members shall strictly avoid causing public criticism of the work of the section in their published personal historical articles or positivistic research reports.
2 For their personal articles or positivistic research reports, the members will not use any of the time allocated to their public duties, nor even their private time in such a way as to hinder the work of the institute.
3 The materials of the section may not be taken out under any name or by any means whatever.
4 No historical articles, reports of positivistic research, or other publications shall be made elsewhere than in internal reports of the institute [tōbun no uchi], or as hitherto in scholarly journals of the several university faculties and in lectures in the classics research institute.
5 Articles on Chinese and Japanese poetry, literature, and education, et cetera, are exempted from the foregoing provisions.

April 1895.[1]

While these rules were intended to apply for five years, after which it was anticipated that the work of the Historiographical Section would be completed, they had a long-lasting effect. The scholars understood and accepted the purpose of the rules and devoted themselves as public servants to the compilation of documents. Disgruntlement with the new section was expressed only by Hoshino Hisashi, the first head, but not because of its restrictions on scholarship. Formerly associated with the history compilation project when it was attached to the cabinet, he thought that the move to the university was a demotion. He also believed that there was still life in the annalistic history project to be written in *kanbun*, but he won no support from his colleagues.[2]

The purpose of the Historiographical Institute was explicitly acknowledged by Mikami Sanji, its head from 1899 to 1919, who played the greatest part in setting the direction for modern historians. (He is discussed in more detail in Chapter 11.) Mikami devoted most of his career to the great public enterprise of compiling documents designed to enable other forms of modern writing.[3] Mikami himself was a scholar of great ability, but according to Rule 2 he did not turn the work done at the institute to private advantage, and he refrained from extensive publication. He wrote many articles and gave numerous lectures and talks, but his major works *Edo Jidai Shi* [History of the Edo Period] and *Sonnō Ron Hattatsu Shi* [History of the Development of Imperial Loyalism] had to await posthumous publication based on his lecture notes at Tokyo Imperial University. As we shall see, this public-spirited attitude would also affect his views on teaching and scholarship.

The work of the Historiographical Institute, known among Japanese historical scholars as academism, has constituted one of the mainstreams of Japanese historical scholarship. It was based on the combined strengths of Tokugawa positivistic research and modern scientific method. The primary activity has been to retrieve and publish documents for scholarly use, and over the last century thousands of volumes have been produced, laying the basis for all manner of institutional, political, economic, and social studies. Major series produced by the institute include *Dai Nihon Komonjo* [Ancient Japanese Documents], classified according to sources, and *Dai Nihon Shiryō* [Japanese Historical Documents], in which documents from all sources are chronologically collated. The scholars and directors of the Historiographical Institute have been outstanding and productive for a century, and they have rightly been awarded the highest academic and cultural honours. The heads have included Mikami Sanji, Kuroita Katsumi, Tsuji Zennosuke, and Sakamoto Tarō, each in turn distinguished as the outstanding historian of his generation. Shiryō Hensanjo heads active in the period of this study were

Hoshino Hisashi April 1895-January 1899
Mikami Sanji January 1899-July 1919
Kuroita Katsumi July 1919-July 1920

Tsuji Zennosuke   July 1920-March 1938
Ryū Susumu   March 1938-March 1951
Sakamoto Tarō   April 1951-March 1962

After Sakamoto Tarō, the headship was changed from an indefinite term to a three-year term, and from 1971 to the present, a two-year term. Projects have been superbly organized, and the continuous training of new generations of scholars responsive to developments in the field has been a priority. Not least of the accomplishments of the Historiographical Institute has been its welcome reception of foreign scholars of Japanese history for training in reading, interpreting, and classifying Japanese documents.

Thus, in 1895 the scholars of Tokyo Imperial University turned away from controversial topics involving the imperial house to the neutral study of documents on everything else. It is common to view this development as the taming of historical study by the modern state. No one decreed it or even discussed it, but it is evident that after the Kume incident there was a tacit agreement among historians to avoid discussion of Shinto and the imperial house. The term 'taboo' is widely used by postwar Japanese historians.[4] Positivistic research inherited from the Tokugawa period, combined with Western scientific method and inspired by civilization history, had led to fundamental questioning of Japanese historical belief and understanding. But with the firing of Kume Kunitake, the brief era of Dr. Obliteration and his killer colleagues passed. The Age of the Gods and the early emperors got a reprieve from scholarly execution.

Yet there were reasons besides the taboo for this development in Japanese historiography. The compilation of documents was perceived as an essential task in other countries as well. At the same time, there was a movement in the United States toward establishing a centre for the compilation of documents. John Franklin Jameson (1859-1937), who like Mikami Sanji did not publish extensively despite his brilliance, tried to establish an American national centre for historical research. 'The establishment of the Carnegie Institute of Washington in 1902 opened such a possibility.'[5] The Carnegie Institute set up a Department of Historical Research that did much the same thing as the Tokyo Imperial University Historiographical Institute, though without the same strictures on its members. Jameson understood his task in the same way as Mikami Sanji understood his. 'I struggle on,' Jameson told Henry Adams in 1910, 'making bricks without much idea of how the architects will use them, but believing that the best architect that ever was cannot get along without bricks, and therefore trying to make good ones.'[6] The great difference was that Jameson could not get the federal or state governments interested in history and was supported instead by the Carnegie Foundation. He struggled for thirty years to promote a national archives, with bill after bill failing in Congress. At last his dream was realized with the establishment of the National Archives in Washington in 1933, in a magnificent building whose cornerstone was laid by President Herbert Hoover.[7]

The difference between the two countries lay in the fact that Jameson's dream was unrealized for so long. In Japan, on the contrary, the national government was strongly concerned with, and in control of, history from the outset. The government decision to reorganize the Historiographical Institute under strict rules had profound consequences for the professional Japanese historians. They were few in number compared to the Americans, held their positions at the pleasure of the national government, had little professional organization, and were accustomed to traditions of serving the government of the day.

Revising Scholarship on Chronology

The trend at Tokyo Imperial University toward collecting materials and evaluating them by positivistic research was not without critics. Young scholars quickly discerned a certain pointlessness, and a short, sharp note appeared in *Shigaku Zasshi* in 1902. 'There are some,' it said, 'who ridicule the professors who compile historical materials, calling them not scholars of history (*shi* 史) but scholars of death (*shi* 死) ... Compilation after compilation, positivistic research on top of positivistic research: isn't it time this came to an end? That is the word among some young history students.'[8] The note was attributed to two scholars who graduated in 1896, Uchida Ginzō and Hara Katsurō (1871-1924).[9] Both became professors at Kyoto Imperial University and helped to broaden the scope of historical discussion, with Uchida specializing in modern economic history and Hara in medieval history.

The complaint was not unique to Japan. In the twentieth century, and especially after World War I, which destroyed much of nineteenth-century belief and practice, many scholars in Europe and America expressed dissatisfaction with mere fact grubbing. However, the mainstream academic scholars of Japan knew what they were about. Undeterred by minor criticism, they turned to many important and demanding topics. In the early twentieth century, all the modern historical sciences were developed. Tokyo Imperial University published huge numbers of documents and continues to do so. Fundamental reference works were also produced: encyclopedias and dictionaries of history, of names, of historical geography. This laid the basis for other types of scholarship, and narrative histories were written for every period. Specialists on legal history, economic history, and cultural history were well established by the 1920s. Throughout the period to 1945, such work went on unhindered by government interference and was conducted with professional dedication and enthusiasm. The imperial university system was expanded, with Kyoto Imperial University founded in 1897 and Tohoku Imperial University founded in 1907, followed by others in Kyushu, Hokkaido, Osaka, and Nagoya, contributing to the strength and diversity of academic scholarship.

Among the many tasks undertaken by the mainstream academic historians, revising the chronology of the emperors was one of the most important. The Age of the Gods was timeless, and no one proposed to deal with that, but it aided historical understanding to locate the early emperors in known periods. Apparently only a few people were offended by scientific scholarly work to establish the imperial reigns in real historical time, so criticisms did not lead to another major incident, such as Kume's dismissal.[10]

According to *Nihon Shoki*, Emperor Jinmu began his reign in 660 BC. This date did not matter much in the abstract, but problems were posed by the Chinese records that noted the existence of a Queen Himiko in Japan in the third century AD. Since ancient times, Japanese had identified Queen Himiko with Empress Regent Jingū (r. 201-69), but if that was accurate, then the traditional chronology after Emperor Jinmu did not work out correctly.

Also, as archeology progressed, it became important to reexamine, and if necessary revise, the ancient written sources in light of the discoveries made in the excavations. Scholars sought a match between the people and places of the traditional sources and the new information yielded by archeology. This was similar to some of the archeology of the Near East, where scholars dug up the desert in order to prove the events of the Old Testament.[11] The first step in achieving this match was to revise the chronology of the traditional sources, especially *Nihon Shoki,* thereby relocating events in the periods defined by archeology: Jōmon, Yayoi, Kofun. The chronology of *Nihon Shoki* had long been suspect in any case, having been attacked by Tokugawa scholars as diverse as Motoori Norinaga, Tō Teikan, and Yamagata Bantō.

The first major step in revising chronology was taken in 1897 by Naka Michiyo, a lecturer at Tokyo Imperial University, who published 'Jōsei Nenki Kō' [The Chronology of Ancient Japan].[12] This was a revision of an 1888 study, and scholars in the postwar period still regarded it as an excellent piece of scholarship that stood up for half a century.[13] Naka argued that the dates in *Kojiki* and *Nihon Shoki* were based on Chinese sexagenary cycles, which had been arbitrarily imposed on Japanese history in ancient times. They had taken the year 601 as the basis for calculating dates backward, yielding 660 BC as the date when Emperor Jinmu had inaugurated imperial rule.

Naka's theory gained common acceptance among Japanese historians. Naka himself was less interested in Emperor Jinmu than in the theory that Queen Himiko was Empress Regent Jingū, and he concluded that they were not identical. Many other scholars joined in the general discussion of chronology, including Hoshino Hisashi and Suga Masatomo, and members of the upcoming generation of historians, Yoshida Togō (1864-1918),

Hashimoto Masukichi, and the same Hara Katsurō who had criticized the pointless work of the Tokyo Imperial University scholars. As late as 1970, Sakmoto Tarō expressed satisfaction with the accomplishments of Meiji- and Taishō-period scholars in resolving problems of chronology.[14]

The first step in improving the chronology was to assign reasonable lengths of reign of thirty years to each of the early emperors, most of whom had improbably long lives according to *Kojiki* and *Nihon Shoki*. Twelve of the first sixteen were supposed to have lived more than 100 years, with Emperor Sujin living to 168 according to *Kojiki*. It was also discovered that the ancient chronology had been misplaced backward by two cycles of sixty years each, so that even the dates in the period when dates became reasonable, around the reign of the fourteenth emperor, Chūai, had to be adjusted forward by 120 years.

In the end, a widely accepted chronology was worked out through collective scholarship and was adopted by Western as well as Japanese scholars. In his 1937 work *Early Japanese History*, Robert Karl Reischauer followed Japanese scholarship in listing the first fourteen emperors as follows:

1	Jimmu-Tennō	8	Kōgen Tennō
	ca. 40-10 BC		ca. 170-200
2	Suizei-Tennō	9	Kaika-Tennō
	ca. 10 BC-ca. 20 AD		ca. 200-30
3	Annei-Tennō	10	Sujin-Tennō
	ca. 20-50 AD		ca. 250-8
4	Itoku-Tennō	11	Suinin-Tennō
	ca. 50-80		ca. 259-90
5	Kōshō-Tennō	12	Keikō-Tennō
	ca. 80-110		ca. 291-322
6	Kōan-Tennō	13	Seimu-Tennō
	ca. 110-40		ca. 323-35
7	Kōrei-Tennō	14	Chūai-Tennō
	ca. 140-70		ca. 356-62[15]

Why Scholars Limited Themselves to Chronology

It took much hard work and ingenuity, and the collective efforts of many scholars, to arrive at this revised chronology. Yet a century after Naka Michiyo's first publication, it is obvious that much of the effort was beside the point. Why should an accurate chronology be worked out for the existing list of emperors? How did it help to change Emperor Jinmu's date from 660 BC to 40 BC? Did Emperor Jinmu exist? Should not the first order of business have been to confirm, modify, or reject the list of emperors? It was constructed at an unknown date in ancient times; it may have arisen partly from myth and may have been partly based on actual memory, but no one knows whose myth and whose memory. The list of emperors may have been invented at some point in the forty-year-long process of writing *Kojiki* and *Nihon Shoki,* in the same way that the authors of *Nihon Shoki* imposed on it a Chinese chronology, or perhaps a received list was only tidied up and harmonized. Furthermore, archeology was beginning to reveal the shape of ancient society, raising the question of what it meant to identify the leader of a society in the Jōmon or Yayoi period. Were there societies to be found with rulers resembling the emperors described in *Kojiki* and *Nihon Shoki?* What was the connection between such leaders and the historic emperors who are identifiable from around the sixth century AD? But these questions were not taken up in the prewar period.

One might think that the scholastically murderous scholars of Tokyo Imperial University in 1890 were driving toward the fundamental question of whether the early emperors had existed. They questioned whether such worthies as Kojima Takanori had existed, and the sources for the early emperors were as unreliable as those for Kojima Takanori. The scientific historians, Shigeno, Hoshino, and Kume, were not less daring or less confident than the Tokugawa scholars, who took up the Age of the Gods and the origins of the emperors. If anything they were more confident, convinced that their new scientific method was superior to any method of the past. But as noted, the Meiji scholars had a thousand tasks but no plan of organized attack on dubious subjects. Thus, one view of their work is that they did what came to hand, and they just never got to the emperors before the subject was closed to them. The dampening effect of the 1889 Constitution, the angry public reception of their ideas, the dismissal of Kume in 1892, and the reorganization of the Historiographical Section in 1895 to compile documents and abstain from massacring articles and books all deflected them from the discussion. Circumstances did not allow discussion to proceed, and all scholars until 1945 were forced to work within the established framework of the succession of emperors starting with Emperor Jinmu.

On the other hand, in the absence of such constraints, the Meiji scholars might not have proceeded to question the existence of the early emperors, since many of them accepted as historical the ancestors of the emperors in the Age of the Gods. Around 1890, when the question of massacring the Age of the Gods and the early emperors was still open, the historians did not show eagerness to take on the task. Hoshino Hisashi and Kume Kunitake represent two main approaches to the problem, both demonstrating clearly why modern historians worked on chronology rather than on the fundamental question of the existence of the early emperors.

Hoshino Hisashi probably would not have questioned the existence of the early emperors, because he was uncritical of the Age of the Gods. He appears to have treated both the Age of the Gods and the early emperors simply as historical, and accordingly he applied the same scientific method to both. Hoshino did not deal much with the Age of the Gods, and this limited treatment may account for the simplicity of his method. In his distinguished career, he published fifty-seven articles in *Shigaku Zasshi*, and only the first and last were on the Age of the Gods. The rest covered a wide variety of subjects, including biographical and institutional studies and evaluations of traditional sources. In all he demonstrated mastery of modern historical method and showed sound reasoning based on the deep study of documentary sources. With good reason, he was appointed to the Imperial Japan Academy. He simply extended that method without second thought to the Age of the Gods. In 1891 and 1911, he wrote to justify this method; nothing happened between 1891 and 1911 to modify his views, and his wording was the same in both articles.

The 1891 statement followed his controversial article on the Korean ancestry of Oshimimi, and perhaps the uproar caused him to affirm that the Age of the Gods was historical and that he had no intention of belittling it.

The legends in Chapter 1 of *Kojiki* and in the Age of the Gods in *Nihon Shoki* derive from 2,000 years ago, and it goes without saying that they are priceless and deserving of respect. From the viewpoint of common sense, many of the tales are rambling and full of mystery. However, some of those beings [*mono*] can be discussed in the context of human society, and for some, accomplishments related to human society are recorded. In these cases, they should be studied in the context of human society. In doing so, one should revere the great virtue and deeds by which they governed the country and planned for the benefit of the people.[16]

In the brief discussion that followed, Hoshino took up the passages, which were indeed fantastic, in which the deities Izanami and Izanagi created Japan and Susano-O created forest and agricultural resources. Hoshino held that these deities should not just be pointlessly revered but respected for their contribution to human enterprise. Thus, he tiptoed unawares toward a euhemerist position but left completely untouched all questions of interpretation and method. His method consisted of citing the *Kojiki* and *Nihon Shoki* passages describing the events and then reaching the general conclusion above.

The methodological statements of 1891 and 1911 are nearly identical, and the 1911 article on the separate heavenly deities was executed in the same way as the 1889 article on Oshimimi. The 1911 article similarly took the texts of *Kojiki* and *Nihon Shoki* at face value and proceeded to try to clarify the genealogies of the gods, as premodern Japanese scholars had done for centuries.

Hoshino concluded in the same vein as the 1891 article. The ancient legends in *Kojiki* and *Nihon Shoki,* he repeated, contain many strange stories, but they were not deliberately created by later people. He praised recent scholarly work, particularly comparative studies, but said that their conclusions were incredible, because 'the national polity, geography, and sentiments and customs of every country are different. Thus, minor points of similarity in legends may be discerned, but one should not rush to conclusions.' He then repeated almost exactly words of the 1891 article, that the deeds of some of the beings [*mono*] in ancient times were recorded because of their accomplishments for human society. But, he cautioned, 'By no means should the deeds of the Age of the Gods be reduced to those of ordinary people.'[17]

Thus, Hoshino did not view the Age of the Gods differently from the age of the human emperors, and he saw no need to adjust the standard method based on the study of documents. He seems not to have realized that, in treating the narratives of *Kojiki* and *Nihon Shoki* as documents needing no verification, he placed his discussion on the territory marked out by traditional scholarship. It was therefore easy for National Scholars and political Shintoists to attack his sacrilegious views on Oshimimi. And since Hoshino Hisashi affirmed the reality of the more doubtful Age of the Gods, he was not about to attack the early emperors. His criticism of comparative study, which ignored the special features of Japan, shows that his belief in the historical truth of the Age of the Gods was based on nationalism.

The case of Kume Kunitake is more complex. Harangued for five hours about Shinto by four uninvited opponents in 1892, he seems to have conceded the religious ground on which the discussion was conducted. He made no effort to show how scientific historical methods changed the nature of the discussion. His 1911 reflections on Hoshino's article on Oshimimi dwelled on the narrow-minded attitudes of National Scholars and political Shintoists, not on how Hoshino might have carried the discussion to a higher level. Kume always seemed to be on uncertain ground when dealing with religion, and I have argued that his method had actually deteriorated in his 1903 work on Shinto for Ōkuma's *Fifty Years of New Japan*, a method that Kume based on a concept from *Yi Jing*.

Although Kume's method for the study of religion was weak, he remained a leader in historical scholarship. His method for history differed according to whether the subject was the Age of the Gods or the human emperors. For the Age of the Gods, he used allegorical method.[18] His *Nihon Kodaishi* [The Ancient History of Japan, 1907] is an extended exercise in the euhemerism familiar since Arai Hakuseki. For example, the myths described the gods as giving birth to the land; Kume treated this as the establishment of order over nature by early agricultural society. However, it was a modernized euhemerism, informed not by the linguistic speculations of Hakuseki but by the archeological and anthropological research that was beginning to affect historical interpretation. Much of it involved theories of races, movements of people, and conquests that are no longer valid, but Kume was satisfied that he was at the forefront of scientific history. Just as Arai Hakuseki's euhemerism provoked severe criticism from Motoori Norinaga, Kume's allegorical treatment was attacked as unfounded dogma by Takagi Toshio (1867-1922).[19]

Kume's method changed abruptly when it came to the human emperors. He believed that actual history began with Emperor Jinmu. There was nothing more to it.[20] Therefore, euhemerism was not in order, just the scientific method of which Kume was the acknowledged master. This belief was not the result of chastening by the authorities over the Heaven-worship incident, which he took in stride; all his work points to this conviction as a product of his scholarship. Far from feeling constrained by authority to work within the established list of emperors, he noted with satisfaction in a 1902 article the progress of scholarship on chronology. In the closed society of the Tokugawa period, said Kume, there had been no freedom of scholarship [*gakusetsu no jiyū*] to work out such problems. In Tokugawa Japan, freedom of scholarship was nothing more than a dream, but in Meiji Japan it had been attained. This from a man who had been dismissed ten years previously for a publication offending political values. He praised the chronology theory of Naka Michiyo and contributed to the ongoing collective work of establishing a valid chronology starting from Emperor Jinmu.[21]

The significance of Kume's acceptance of the list of emperors cannot be overestimated. He took great pride in scientific method freely exercised and had established his credentials as the leading slayer of myths. But massacre by scientific history had its natural limits, which were fixed at the historical reality of Emperor Jinmu. The limits were established by nationalism, which was shared by all the eminent scholars of the prewar era. Otherwise, it is difficult to account for the acceptance of the list of emperors from Jinmu onward by everyone except Tsuda Sōkichi.

To summarize, Hoshino Hisashi treated the Age of the Gods and the early emperors as historical; few major historians in the twentieth century followed him. Kume Kunitake treated the Age of the Gods as allegorical and the early emperors as historical, and this approach became all but universal in the prewar era. It was developed to its fullest in the 1920s and 1930s by Mikami Sanji and Kuroita Katsumi. If the tales of the Age of the Gods were allegorical, they were allegories for something real. They thought that there must be a historical basis for those myths, and they searched for it through increasingly complex methods and theories. They too agreed completely with Kume that there was no question about the historical existence of

Emperor Jinmu and the other early emperors. We shall return to Mikami and Kuroita in Chapter 11.

Thus, the mainstream scholars accepted the historical existence of Emperor Jinmu and worked on chronology, to general satisfaction. There were few exceptions, and they were not popular with the leading academic scholars. The outstanding exception was Tsuda Sōkichi of Waseda University. His cumulative research, beginning in 1913 with *Jindaishi no Atarashii Kenkyū* [New Studies on the History of the Age of the Gods], cast doubt on the Age of the Gods and the existence of the first fourteen emperors. His work provoked antagonism among other scholars of Japanese history, especially at Tokyo Imperial University, revealing that they did not simply accept the list of emperors from Jinmu onward but strongly believed in it as an article of national faith. They defended the list of emperors and held, along with the imperial state that sent Tsuda to trial, that to question it was to offer indignity to the imperial house. We shall return to Tsuda Sōkichi in Chapter 13.

10
The Southern and Northern Courts Controversy, 1911

The Problem with the Textbook

After the Kume Kunitake incident, the Southern-Northern Courts controversy of February 1911 was the most important influence on the development of scholarly historical writing. In the fourteenth century, there had been a war between two imperial courts, called the Southern and Northern Courts. In 1911 a raucous public controversy erupted over the fact that school textbooks failed to say which court had been legitimate in the fourteenth century. The controversy had great importance for professional historians.

In the 1892 Kume incident, the government of Japan, by firing a professor, decided what historians must not discuss. In the more tumultuous Southern-Northern Courts incident, which erupted in parliament, the government of Japan decided what authors of elementary school textbooks must say when discussing the imperial courts of the fourteenth century. Some textbook authors who had gotten it wrong were fired, and this had significance for professional historians. One of the textbook authors was Kita Sadakichi (1871-1939), who received his doctor of letters degree in history from Tokyo Imperial University in 1909 and was a special lecturer in history. He was suspended from his position in the Ministry of Education for two years until February 1913. Other Tokyo Imperial University historians had been members of government committees related to writing textbooks. Many were publicly criticized, an ordeal to which most professors were quite unaccustomed. All of them pondered the implications for their own scholarly work, especially Mikami Sanji, head of the Historiographical Institute, and Tanaka Yoshinari (1869-1919), who was responsible for the lectures on the fourteenth century at Tokyo Imperial University.

The controversy arose when it was discovered that school history textbooks, prepared and authorized by the Ministry of Education, did not reflect the support of the government of Japan for the Southern Court. The textbooks called it 'The Period of the Southern and Northern Courts,' rather than the currently approved 'Period of the Yoshino Court.' In 1911 the former term was held to be scandalously improper and insulting to the imperial dignity because it suggested that there had been a time when two imperial courts existed with equal legitimacy. In the 1889 Constitution, imperial sovereignty was absolute and indivisible. Strong voices were raised, claiming that it was disloyal to suggest that imperial sovereignty had ever been other than absolute and indivisible and insisting that interpretation of the fourteenth century must be guided by this doctrine.

First, the facts of the case. During the Kamakura period, there were two legitimate lines within the imperial house, the Daikakuji line and the Jimyōin line. To no one's surprise, they quarrelled over the succession, but they accepted an arrangement for alternating succession devised by the Kamakura Bakufu, which treated it pragmatically and kept the peace. However, in 1333 Emperor Go Daigo overthrew the Kamakura Bakufu and proclaimed the Kenmu Restoration. He intended to keep the succession within his own Daikakuji line, but the plan went awry when the restoration failed, and Ashikaga Takauji (1305-58) set up a new bakufu. Ashikaga Takauji had himself appointed shogun by a pretender from the Jimyōin line, thereby recognizing that line as legitimate. The situation deteriorated into a war between the two lines that lasted for fifty-seven years, with the Daikakuji line establishing a new capital in Yoshino and becoming known as the Southern Court. The Jimyōin line took over the palace in Kyoto and became known as the Northern Court. War between the two courts continued until 1392, when an agreement was reached and the succession was reestablished in the Northern or Jimyōin line.

As noted, *Dai Nihon Shi* had strongly championed the Southern Court, and in the Meiji period the government fostered loyalty to the Southern Court of Go Daigo, making heroes and gods out of its supporters. In doing so, no one seemed troubled by the fact that the reigning emperor, Meiji, was descended from the Northern line. Nevertheless, during the forty years before 1911, the Ministry of Education had apparently failed to get the point, and textbooks had been issued using a variety of approaches and terms for the Southern-Northern Courts period. The earliest text, in 1872, covered the period without assigning a name to it and identified the two courts as Southern and Northern.[1] Subsequent texts used a variety of methods to name the period: the reign names of the Southern Court, era names of the Southern Court or both courts, topics (The Kenmu Restoration, Nitta Yoshisada Destroys the Hōjō, The Failure of Go Daigo's Government), topics with reign names and era names above the text, and names of individuals (Hōjō Tokimune, Kusunoki Masashige, Ashikaga Takauji).

The terms that came under attack first appeared in the 1903 text *Shōgaku Nihon Rekishi* [Japanese History for Elementary Schools], but they were not noticed at the time. The relevant chapters were entitled 'The Kenmu

Restoration' and 'The Southern and Northern Courts.' They provided a factual review of the split in the imperial house that led to the succession quarrel and the effort by Go Daigo to destroy the military government and restore the imperial system. There followed the raising of Emperor Kōmyō in Kyoto by Ashikaga Takauji and the flight of Emperor Go Daigo to Yoshino. 'From this time on,' says the 1903 text, 'there were two emperors simultaneously. The Yoshino Court was called the Southern Court, and the Kyoto Court was called the Northern Court. Thus, the war between the court and the warriors turned into a war between the two imperial lines ... and went on for more than fifty years.'[2] The text did not declare which court was legitimate, but its coverage reflected the dominant sympathies of the Meiji period, giving much attention to heroes of the Southern Court such as Kusunoki Masashige, who gave his life for his emperor.

It was the 1910 text *Jinjō Shōgaku Nihon Rekishi* [Japanese History for Regular Elementary Schools] that caused the trouble, even though it was much the same as the 1903 text. It called the period 'Southern and Northern Courts' and summed up its factual account thus: 'From then on, the Yoshino Court was called the Southern Court, and the Kyoto Court was called the Northern Court. Thus, the war took on the form of a war between the two courts and lasted for fifty-seven years.'[3] Again, the textbook failed to state which was the legitimate court.

The controversy began when the *Yomiuri Shinbun* newspaper was alerted to the impropriety of the text and published a critical editorial on 19 January 1911. This editorial set off a wave of protest in parliament and the press, protest that the government could not ignore because the controversy followed hard on the heels of the Great Treason Incident of 1910. In this incident, an alleged plot to assassinate the Meiji emperor was discovered, arrests were made, trials were conducted, and twelve people were executed, including the anarchist Kōtoku Shūsui (1871-1911). Concerned citizens and politicians saw an obvious connection between the Great Treason Incident and the failure of the educational system to instruct Japanese youth in imperial values. It was universally assumed that no decent Japanese youth, properly educated in imperial values, could even imagine trying to assassinate the emperor. The convicted terrorists, it is true, had not been educated and led astray by the history textbook in question. However, the textbook was regarded as a conspicuous example of educational failure that might lead to similar consequences in the future, because it did not indicate which of the two imperial lines of the fourteenth century was legitimate. Of course everyone who raised the question and attacked the government knew the correct answer, which had been given by the government itself: the Southern Court was legitimate.

Opposition to the government's educational policies led to heated public discussion and parliamentary confrontation led by independent Diet

Member Fujisawa Genzō. The cabinet of Katsura Tarō (1847-1913) was nearly toppled by the uproar.[4] Prime Minister Katsura, who had been a division commander in the Sino-Japanese War, governor general of Taiwan, and at the forefront of troubles in the Russo-Japanese War, said that nothing in his career had been as worrisome.[5] This seemed out of proportion to the significance of the matter or the ease with which it could be settled. However, this would not be the last time that the attention of Japanese government and society was monopolized by passages in school textbooks. In 1982 protests were heard not only in Japan but also around the world, alleging that Japanese history textbooks glossed over Japan's record of imperialist aggression during World War II. In 1982, however, the government was in no danger of being defeated in parliament over the matter.

The main complaint in 1911 was that scholarship was one thing and the education of the people was another. Someone had let the scholars loose into the field of education, and they brought with them inappropriate standards. During the affair, Kuroita Katsumi wrote, 'The historian's responsibility in professional research is to assemble historical materials and clarify the truth about the facts using his professional judgment.'[6] Anesaki Masaharu (1873-1949), an eminent scholar of religion, reminded the historians that this was not enough, because they could not avoid making moral judgments: 'Historians who think of history only as documents, and the professors of historical materials, say they dislike imposing moral judgments on the past. History, however, is not merely work in the historian's study or the document-compilation room. History affects the entire thought of society and is closely related to the moral education of the people, and therefore it is unalterably connected with such judgments.'[7] Isawa Shūji put more strongly his opposition to the attitude carried into education by the professional historians: 'Of course when scholars do historical research they must dig out the facts, and there is no objection to this in principle. But they cannot insinuate this into the education of the people and destroy the basis of history. History in the education of the people must be centred primarily on moral education that makes clear *taigi meibun* [the right relations between the emperor and his subjects]. That is not open to discussion.'[8] Others disputed the narrow definition of facts employed by historians. Baron Kitabatake Harufusa (1833-1921) argued that the facts of history extended far beyond the formal description in the textbook, which only amounted to a statement that there had been two opposing courts in the fourteenth century. Baron Kitabatake asserted that the facts of history included the existence of an unwritten Japanese constitution [*kenpō*]: 'If the facts written in the textbook are included because they are facts, why have the authors tried so hard to suppress any number of other facts? Why have they included only the opposition between the Southern and Northern Courts? Why has the Ministry of Education, in the name of the facts, destroyed our unwritten constitution – our constitution since the founding of the country that says that there cannot be two sovereigns in the land?'[9]

The conservative Tokyo Imperial University philosopher Inoue Tetsujirō pointed out to his historian colleagues the worst possible result of their scientific study of the facts. Morichika Unpei (1881-1911), convicted and executed for his part in the Great Treason Incident, had been made into a radical by reading the works of modern Japanese historians about the imperial house, of which the most influential was Kume Kunitake's *Nihon Kodaishi* [Ancient History of Japan]. Historians, said Inoue, ought to preserve their scientific attitude as historians, but when it came to the real world [*zokuji*], this often gave rise to appalling errors.[10] This was off topic since Morichika had been made into a radical by scholarly publications, not by school textbooks. Nevertheless, Inoue broadened the discussion to include the dangers of all works by historians, and his point may have given them pause and prompted greater circumspection in their scholarly publications.

Amid heated discussion, the matter went to the cabinet, which made a decision about history: the Southern Court had been the legitimate one in the fourteenth century, and thenceforth this must be stated in textbooks. This was presented to the nation as a decision by the Meiji emperor. Nevertheless, it did not escape notice that the affair had been conducted under principles that were less than enlightened and that the behaviour of some of the principals had been bizarre, especially that of Diet Member Fujisawa Genzō. Most important for our purposes, the government of Japan had decided the facts of history for political reasons.

On 14 March 1911, Minister of Education Komatsubara Eitarō (1852-1918) ordered revision of the text, and the new version was out by December. Chapter 23 was called 'The Yoshino Court' rather than 'The Period of the Southern and Northern Courts,' thereby indicating that the Southern Court at Yoshino had been the legitimate one. The title was everything. The factual account did not change much, but the imperial presence and its divine ancestry were given greater emphasis: 'Emperor Go Daigo secretly took the imperial regalia to Yoshino and set up his court. This was the first year of Engen (1336), and the 1,996th year since the founding of the empire by Emperor Jinmu. Thereafter the Yoshino Court was called the Southern Court and the Kyoto Court was called the Northern Court.' Previous texts had noted that Ashikaga Takauji had set up the Northern emperor and had prevailed upon that emperor to appoint him shogun in order to avoid being called a rebel. Since the Northern emperor was no longer a legitimate emperor, the new text called Takauji's bluff and proceeded to label him just that – a rebel. It also enlarged on the heroes of the Southern Court and made it clear why they were important to Meiji people: 'During this period, there were many who took upon themselves the travails of the emperor. They were families such as the Kitabatake, Nitta, Kusunoki, Nawa, and

Kikuchi, fathers and sons, brothers and brothers, and their bravery and loyalty are models for later generations. Thus, in the reign of Emperor Meiji, their loyalty was rewarded, as they were given court ranks and are worshipped as deities.'[11]

The Historians Divided on the Two Courts

Scholars were divided on the question of legitimacy in the fourteenth century. With the work of Kume Kunitake, historical research on the period had become modern in its method and sophisticated in its interpretation. Thus, for historians there were no easy answers like those announced by politicians and moralists. In the preface to his 1907 study *Nanboku Chō Jidai Shi* [History of the Southern-Northern Courts Period], Kume wrote that the history of the period was not simple and that its development could not be explained by one or two causes. He criticized the earlier histories, especially Rai Sanyō's moralistic *Nihon Gaishi* [Private History of Japan, 1827], which he described as nothing more than a script for a play [*geki hon*]. The real story would be revealed, he said, by research into political and economic history, research that would entirely supersede the unreliable *Taiheiki* and the more reliable *Baishōron* [Tale of the Plums and Pines, ca. 1349].[12]

As more became known about the period, it became even more difficult to reach conclusions about the legitimacy of the two imperial courts. Kume Kunitake, Hoshino Hisashi, Mikami Sanji, and Kita Sadakichi favoured recognizing the two courts equally. Kuroita Katsumi thought that the Southern Court should be recognized because of the authority that it exercised, while Miura Hiroyuki thought that they were about equal in power and in law but that the Southern Court had a stronger moral claim. Kita Sadakichi held that the main issue of fourteenth-century politics was not the courts at all but the struggle for power between the imperial system and the warrior system.

One of the perennial questions that exercised historians concerned the imperial regalia of mirror, sword, and jewel, which were possessed by the legitimate occupant of the throne according to universal belief. To enter into the question of the origins, location, and authenticity of the regalia was about as fruitful as discussing the genealogies of the gods in *Kojiki* and *Nihon Shoki*: nothing could be resolved. Thus, most scholars took notice of the assertions about the imperial regalia that had been made over the centuries, but this provided no consensus on the legitimacy of the fourteenth-century courts. The leading authority, Tanaka Yoshinari, dismissed the regalia from considerations of legitimacy, writing that 'The authenticity of the regalia is not clear, and therefore theories that determine the legitimate line on the basis of their whereabouts have no merit.'[13] However, everyone agreed with relief that the Northern emperor had come into proper possession of the regalia in 1392, when the two imperial lines were unified.

Most historians were not tempted by current political theory to find answers to the problem of legitimacy. For historians only ancient and medieval political theory would have sufficed, not contemporary ideas. Unfortunately, in the law and the writings of the ancient and medieval periods, there was no constitutional theory that went beyond asserting the legitimacy of the imperial house because of its divine ancestry. This did not help with the problem of two courts. In Japan there was no tradition of abstract political thought and hence no theory that might clarify the possible division of sovereignty. The distribution of powers in the state had been described only once, in the law codes issued at the beginning of the imperial state in the early eighth century. No division of powers between emperors had been contemplated. From the late eleventh century to the reign of Go Daigo in 1333, sovereignty had been shared by the emperor and the retired emperors, who conducted business at a separate court [*insei*] or courts. Between 1298 and 1304, there were no fewer than five retired emperors, and this number would seem to make urgent the need to clarify their respective powers.[14] Yet nothing was ever settled in theory. There are not even any records of discussion of the subject.

In light of this poverty of theory, it is not surprising that only one historian, Kuroita Katsumi, even attempted discussion of a theory of sovereignty. However, his essay was really only a limited and undeveloped analysis of the location of political power.[15] Otherwise, the historians refrained from the question of sovereignty because they fully realized that the theories put forth by politicians and the press in the 1911 controversy were anachronistic for the fourteenth century. They declined to apply contemporary theories to fourteenth-century problems, confining themselves to discussing the facts of history, the most important of which was that two courts had existed. In the eyes of their critics, this refusal to extend discussion beyond the facts made the historians appear narrow in their professional concerns and insensitive to greater issues of national importance such as loyalty to the imperial house.

The scholar whose views mattered the most was Tanaka Yoshinari, a mild-mannered professor who was responsible for the lectures on the Southern-Northern Courts period at Tokyo Imperial University. Tanaka started as a copyist in the old Historical Compilation Bureau and moved with it to Tokyo Imperial University in 1888. He continued on as a member of the Historiographical Institute when it was reorganized in 1895, doubling as an assistant professor according to the system, and he obtained his doctor of letters degree in 1903, finally becoming a professor in 1905. In a eulogy for Professor Tanaka in 1920, Mikami Sanji observed that Tanaka spent forty years in the History Compilation Bureau, as well as twenty-eight years as a teacher, and served on textbook committees in the Ministry of Education, all of which Mikami considered as devoted public service.[16] Contrary to those who considered historical compilation as brainless, mechanical work, Tanaka's scholarship was of the highest calibre; his findings have not been challenged by later scholars but amplified by succeeding research. His writing style was excellent. His works on the period from the fourteenth through the sixteenth centuries are in the narrative style now in disfavour in the West but still appreciated in Japan for elegance, clarity, and explanatory power.[17]

Tanaka's *Nanboku Chō Jidai Shi* [History of the Era of the Southern and Northern Courts, 1922] was a posthumous publication, but it had been assembled mainly by Tanaka himself from his lecture notes at Tokyo Imperial University. He went straight to the point and opened the work with discussion of his choice of title. He noted that, while the Ministry of Education had decreed the use of 'Yoshino Court' for textbooks, the university remained a place of academic freedom, and scholars must follow the facts. In the fourteenth century, there were two courts, Southern and Northern; that was a fact, and so the period was aptly described by the term 'Southern and Northern Courts.' Tanaka noted that the principal reason for adopting the term 'Period of the Yoshino Court' was the political theory of *taigi meibun* [the right relations between the emperor and his subjects], which arose in the Tokugawa period. But he said, 'Historical facts cannot be ignored. I see no necessity to sacrifice the facts completely to *taigi meibun*. We must argue on the basis of facts, and for that reason I use the term 'Southern and Northern Courts.'[18]

Tanaka also rejected the argument that titles for periods were no more than arbitrary inventions by historians and therefore should be chosen to reflect contemporary needs. He agreed that all titles of periods arise in later times and are assigned by historians. But he insisted that they are not arbitrary and arise from the facts of the period. This position was clearly based on his confidence in the competence of professional historians. In his writing, therefore, Tanaka firmly upheld the independence, freedom, and responsibility of scholars.

The Effect of the Controversy at Tokyo Imperial University

Teaching was another matter. Following the 1911 textbook incident, Tanaka changed the title of his university lecture series from 'Southern and Northern Courts' to 'Yoshino Court.' Mikami Sanji explained this in his eulogy:

> The problem of the Southern and Northern Courts in the textbooks of the Ministry of Education ... made a great deal of difficulty for Professor Tanaka. It was decided that the Southern Court was legitimate and that in elementary school textbooks it must not be known as such, but rather as the Yoshino Court, and this created a problem about lectures in the university.

Professor Tanaka and others of us held that university lectures are pure scholarship and need not follow the example of elementary school textbooks, so we thought that it would be acceptable to continue calling the lectures 'History of the Southern and Northern Courts.' However, the dean of the Faculty of Letters, Ueda Kazutoshi,[19] ... and others were somewhat opposed, suggesting that it would be better to title them 'The Yoshino Court.' Professor Tanaka was a man who was firm in his principles, but ... he was always disposed toward harmony and would not offend others unnecessarily. Thinking that it might not make much difference, he titled his lectures 'History of the Yoshino Court' from that time on. He was truly harmonious and big hearted and would never display his anger.[20]

Mikami's eulogy was disingenuous. Tanaka did not just yield because he was big hearted but because all the historians, including Mikami Sanji, caved in together under public and government pressure. For that reason, the Tanaka case raised a critical question: were university professors subject to the same government teaching requirements as elementary school teachers? The university had been conceived as a place of academic freedom, but it was paid for by the Ministry of Education, and professors were public servants. The Kume incident had made it clear that, while the Ministry of Education did not determine the content of writing and teaching, professors had to respect political and social sensitivities or put their principles and their jobs at risk. Now, with the Southern-Northern Courts incident, the Ministry of Education intended to determine some of the content of university teaching.

We know nothing about how the Ministry of Education communicated with Dean Ueda or how he decided to request Tanaka to change the title of his lecture series. Since the affair had become such a serious political issue, doubtless there was pressure from above; it is unlikely that the dean merely pondered the matter and came up with the idea.

The discussion among the professors is more clear. According to the diary of Kita Sadakichi, one of the authors of the textbook, he paid a New Year's visit to Mikami Sanji in January 1911, when wind of the affair was coming up. Mikami said that the problem was being discussed by the professors, and Kita went away feeling downcast.[21] A number of Tokyo Imperial University professors were in fact directly involved in the case. Mikami himself was a member of a committee struck by the Ministry of the Imperial Household, called the Committee of Inquiry into the Draft of an Imperial Chronology [*Teikoku Nenpyō Sōan Chōsa Iinkai*], along with the historians Shigeno Yasutsugu, Hoshino Hisashi, Tsuboi Kumezō (1858-1936), the philosopher Inoue Tetsujirō, and others. Their business was to review all the difficult points of imperial history that involved legitimacy, such as the reign of Empress Regent Jingū and the Southern-Northern Courts period, and come up with a chronology that reflected the legitimate succession of emperors. The committee was divided on the Southern-Northern Courts question, and during the discussions the members became fully aware of the political implications of their work. In the end, the committee decided on a chronology giving equal recognition to the era names of the Southern and Northern Courts.[22]

Then, during the Southern-Northern Courts controversy, Mikami wrote newspaper articles summarizing his views that the two courts were equally legitimate. He was attacked in turn by half a dozen writers of newspaper articles supporting the Southern Court.[23] He was also seen as the ringleader of the Ministry of Education Textbook Examining Committee [*Kyōkasho Chōsa Iinkai*], of which Tanaka Yoshinari was also a member. It was this committee that had let pass the offending work. Because of this, Mikami and Kita Sadakichi, together with two Ministry of Education officials, received a visit on 10 February 1911 from Diet Member Fujisawa Genzō, who was pressing the case in parliament. Fujisawa was accompanied by two Waseda University professors who supported his position, Makino Kenjirō and Matsudaira Yasukuni.

According to separate accounts of Kita and Mikami, Fujisawa Genzō was drunk.[24] Despite verging occasionally on comedy, the discussion went on, with Mikami and Kita trying to show how the historians confined themselves to the facts, of which the principal one was that two courts had existed. Mikami introduced his favourite idea that the division between the two courts was not like the existence of two suns in the sky but like a river that branched into two streams and then rejoined. Which stream was the true river during the time of separation could not be determined. This analogy confused Fujisawa, so Mikami withdrew it. He also brought up another of his ideas, that discussion of legitimate and illegitimate did not apply to the Japanese imperial house but only to countries such as China, where revolutions had taken place and where one imperial house had displaced another. Fujisawa, having missed the point, then asked whether they would allow that two suns could exist in the sky, and Kita, losing patience, replied that, for all he knew, in the future there might be two suns or even three. Undeterred, Fujisawa squarely posed the problem facing the professional historians:

Fujisawa: This is a textbook compiled by the state. Since it is compiled by the state, historical discussion from now on should take it as the standard. That's why we are here to discuss the matter. If it weren't compiled by the state, we would have no reason to be involved. What do you gentlemen understand by the term 'compiled by the state'?

Mikami/Kita: No reply.[25]

After the announcement by the minister of education on correct terminology had closed the textbook controversy, Mikami Sanji resigned from the Textbook Examining Committee and was followed shortly by Tanaka Yoshinari. It appears that they were unsettled by the entire affair and subsequently trimmed their sails at the university to fit the prevailing wind.

Thus, on two levels there was wide concern and much discussion among the Tokyo Imperial University history professors. First, they continued to argue the evidence about the fourteenth century and tried without success to reach a scholarly consensus. Second, they discussed whether Ministry of Education decisions about elementary education were relevant to university teaching. The involvement of half a dozen of them in the textbook affair, exposing them to a cantankerous public and a nervous, cautious government, influenced their views. Decisions by university deans were not the final word; the faculty had considerable power over appointments, promotions, and curriculum, and Dean Ueda's suggestion to change the title of Tanaka's lecture series could have been resisted. There is no record of a decision at a faculty meeting, but clearly the majority decided not to resist. They concluded that, in a case involving imperial legitimacy, it would be best to put aside scholarly scruples and accept Ministry of Education guidelines. This view was communicated to Tanaka Yoshinari, who duly changed the title of the lectures to 'The Yoshino Court.'

The Meaning of the Incident
The Southern-Northern Courts controversy of 1911 is generally seen as reinforcing the taboo on discussion about the imperial house. In 1892 Kume Kunitake had been alone in his brush with authority and got no support from his fellow historians. They thought that he was intemperate. In 1911 all the leading professional historians were involved, even though they were not intemperate, and they learned the depth of public feeling about the imperial house and the extent of state power. The unsettling experience seems to have recalled them to a sense of their position as Japanese citizens and servants of the state. Employed in the imperial university, they had no business contradicting government decisions about education. All of them thenceforth accepted a distinction between education [kyōiku], under which the people of Japan were to be taught useful and inspiring fictions appropriate to a sacerdotal state, and scholarship [gakumon].

The professional historians were to practise scholarship, proceeding unhindered to determine pure scholarly truth. Yet they had yielded to the state the power to decide historical truth in an important matter related to the emperor, not only in school textbooks but also at the university level. It was a bad precedent. None could foresee that, twenty-five years later, scholarship would be completely reduced to the same level as education. The distinction between education and scholarship, newly arrived at in 1911, seemed workable for the time being. At the university, only the title of a lecture series was changed, and neither the titles nor the contents of publications were affected. The contents of the lectures were unchanged, and no doubt Tanaka told the students the reason for the new title and made it clear to them that academic freedom remained intact, as shown by the posthumous book based on the lectures.

The scholars at the Historiographical Institute at Tokyo Imperial University, headed by the nervous Mikami Sanji, were all aware of the problem. They had to take it into account when compiling volume 6, part 10, of *Dai Nihon Shiryō*, which covered the period. No interpretation of history was advanced in that series, but a position about the legitimacy of the fourteenth-century courts could be inferred from the organization and presentation of documents. The historians were bound by the 1895 rules of the institute not to enter into public controversies, and a personal chronology by Tsuji Zennosuke reveals their worries: '1911. Age thirty-five. Between February and April, the Southern-Northern Courts dispute was raucous. In the Historiographical Institute, there were many discussions between colleagues. However, nothing was said in public out of fear.'[26] There was no place to hide when an inquiry came from Tokyo Imperial University President Hamao Shin and Dean of the Faculty of Arts Ueda Kazutoshi about whether the historians should proceed as intended with volume 6, part 10. But the institute sturdily replied that its work was based on the objective nature of the documents [*shiryō honshitsu shugi*] and was beyond criticisms based on legitimacy of the respective courts.[27] They were right. The materials were presented chronologically according to the design of the series, under both the Southern and Northern Courts. Volume 6, part 10, which came out on 31 March 1911, was not controversial.[28]

During the Taishō period (1912-26), other scholarly studies that contradicted the government ruling on usage in school textbooks were published without incident. Tanaka Yoshinari's posthumous *Nanboku Chō Jidai Shi* [History of the Southern-Northern Courts Period] was published in 1922. In the same year, Nakamura Naokatsu (1890-1976), a young scholar at Kyoto Imperial University who was taught by Uchida Ginzō and Miura Hiroyuki, used the title *Nanboku Chō Jidai* [The Period of the Southern-Northern Courts] for a book published in a twelve-volume series called *Nihon Bunka Shi* [Cultural History of Japan].[29] No difficulty arose.

No further incidents occurred regarding the Southern and Northern Courts, and the situation remained unchanged during the early 1920s. Scholars proceeded with their work, and the government left them alone. This was in keeping with the liberal trend in Japanese society in the period of Taishō Democracy. This period in intellectual history ended in 1925 with the passage of the Peace Preservation Law, aimed at the extirpation of communism, that made it a crime to discuss critically the national essence or the capitalist system. This law, enforced by newly established thought-control police and courts, also had a dampening effect on liberal thought in general and inevitably upon historical scholarship.

Then, in the 1930s, the rising forces of nationalism and militarism affected every aspect of Japanese life, including historical scholarship. As noted, Nakamura Naokatsu's 1922 book on the fourteenth century used the title *Nanboku Chō Jidai* [The Period of the Southern and Northern Courts] without provoking criticism. In the preface, Nakamura wrote, 'The historian's head must be cool, but his heart must be on fire. His standpoint must be disinterested and impartial ... History is a science, but at the same time it must be an art.'[30]

Nakamura moved along with the nationalist times, and in 1935 he published another history of the period under the title *Yoshino Chō Shi* [History of the Yoshino Court]. It was decidedly loyalist in interpretation and opened with a florid preface:

> Is there anyone who does not prostrate himself in worship before the majestic portrait of the wise and virtuous Emperor Go Daigo? Is there a Japanese who is not drawn near the warmth of that figure? Is there anyone who comes in touch with the personal writings of Kusunoki Masashige and sees his beautiful and fascinating handwriting who does not worship him? Is there a Japanese who is not filled with deep emotion by that vigorous and full style?
>
> It is the Yoshino period, blooming like a flower, that is the essence of Japanese history in all its 3,000 years. It is the living flesh and blood of the Japanese people. In this period, the brilliant Japanese national essence, unparalleled anywhere in ancient or modern times, first came to its realization. In this period, it first became clear that the people of Japan always and forever hold the imperial house at the bottom of their hearts.[31]

In 1942, when Japan was at war, the *Nihon Bunka Shi* series was reissued under the title New Cultural History of Japan. Nakamura made some changes but intended to keep the title *Nanboku Chō Jidai*. However, according to Hayashiya Tatsusaburō, he changed it to *Yoshino Jidai* [The Yoshino Period] 'in accordance with the demands of the time,' and some deletions of the contents were also made. Nakamura also rewrote the preface, deleting the discussion of history as science and art and writing instead of history as 'training' [*kunren*].[32] After the war, the original title, preface, and text of Nakamura's *Nanboku Chō Jidai* were all restored.

11
Eminent Historians in the 1930s: The Betrayal of Scientific History

The 1930s

Japan became a great power by its victories in wars against China in 1894-5 and Russia in 1904-5. It acquired Taiwan as a colony in 1895 and annexed Korea in 1910, and after World War I it was the dominant power in East Asia. In the 1920s, however, Japan did not seek unhindered control of East Asia; instead, it participated in international organizations and signed treaties intended to preserve order and protect the interests of all parties. Japan recognized the importance of collective world security by joining the League of Nations, and it acknowledged the need for arms control by signing the naval limitations agreements that arose from the Washington Conference of 1921. Most important, in 1922 it agreed to a Nine Power treaty designed to secure the territorial integrity of China, despite domestic criticisms that none of the other powers had a strong commitment to enforcing it, leaving Japan at a disadvantage.

These signs of international good citizenship were accompanied by domestic democratic developments that were not anticipated by the makers of the 1889 Constitution. The emperor remained the acknowledged sovereign, and no liberal ever thought of asserting the sovereignty of the people. However, democracy developed in the British direction of cabinet responsibility in a parliamentary system, which was compatible with a monarchy. Responsible government is generally dated from the Hara Kei cabinet of 1918, and it continued to develop until 1925. Cabinet responsibility to the elected House of Representatives was accompanied by the gradual broadening of the electoral franchise, until universal male suffrage was achieved in 1925 (female suffrage was not achieved until the 1947 Constitution). In the early 1920s, there was also considerable broadening of social and intellectual freedom.

However, in Japan there was powerful criticism of both international and domestic developments. Japan agreed to arms limitations and the Nine Power treaty, and it was claimed by opponents that Japan's government had done nothing more than tie its own hands by the treaty. The most disgruntled were factions of army leadership, who watched with horror the continuing chaos of China in its warlord period, menacing Japan's strategic and economic interests as well as Japanese settlements. Other soldiers and politicians perceived that warlord competition was to Japan's advantage, permitting easier exploitation, and that the unification of China was more dangerous to Japan's interests. A new threat arose in 1926 when the Guomintang led by Chiang Kai-Shek launched its northward expedition. By mid-1927 it looked as if a strong, centralized, nationalistic government might soon be in control of much of China and ready to reassert China's interests against the treaty powers, Britain and Japan foremost. Moreover, it was clear that Japan's long-time rival, Russia, under an aggressive communist regime openly seeking to destroy all non-communist states in the world, was fishing in troubled waters in China.

At home, parliamentary democracy was widely unpopular with both elites and the Japanese people because it was achieved by political parties for their own interest, not in response to popular demand. Party politics, necessary in a liberal democracy, require a great amount of tolerance and faith on the part of the governed, and Japan in the 1920s did not develop such traditions. Leadership seemed to have declined from the standards set by the old Meiji men, then receding into a haze of glory enhanced by dimming memories. They were perceived as men of principle and action, utterly devoted to Japan and the emperor, unswerving in their uprightness, ready to die for their beliefs. In contrast, the parties and their leaders were perceived as unprincipled, self-seeking, opportunistic, and corrupt, ever ready to compromise for no apparent gain except making an agreement, even when Japan's national interest was involved. The system of parliamentary government itself was held as the cause of national decline, and radicals such as Kita Ikki (1883-1937) began to call for fundamental reforms.

Some used force to try to destroy the parliamentary system and restore an imagined imperial authority. Political assassination became rife. Prime Minister Hara Kei was assassinated in 1921, and there was an attempt on the life of Regent Hirohito in 1923. In November 1930, Prime Minister Hamaguchi Osachi (1870-1931) was attacked and wounded, dying in August 1931, for signing the London naval arms limitation agreement. On 9 February 1932, Finance Minister Inoue Junnosuke (1869-1932) was assassinated by Onuma Shō, a member of a radical group called Ketsumeidan [League of Blood]. The Ketsumeidan struck again on 5 March 1932, assassinating Dan Takuma (1858-1932), the director general of the Mitsui holding company. In May 1932, the murder of Prime Minister Inukai Tsuyoshi (1855-1932) at his official residence by army and navy officers brought to an end the dominance of political parties in the parliamentary system. Governance by the parties was replaced by unstable coalitions among parties, bureaucrats, and leaders of the army and navy. No one was safe: on 12 August 1935, an army officer, Nagata Tetsuzan, was killed by a rival army faction. More prominent politicians and armed forces moderates were killed in the infamous army mutiny in Tokyo on 26 February 1936. No one knew where it would all end, and thus anyone involved in public affairs must have had a realistic fear for his or her life, especially those involved in any controversial matter. Little wonder that professors feared controversy.

There were yet more causes of intellectual timidity. At the height of parliamentary democracy in 1925, the government took the first step toward the political and intellectual authoritarianism that characterized the 1930s. Every government in Britain, France, Germany, the United States, and Canada was worried about communism, but the government of Japan took the most extreme measures to control it. The Peace Preservation Law of 1925 made it a crime to discuss the national essence and the capitalist system, which was the entire agenda of the communists. Mass arrests without warrants were made on 15 March 1928, and suspects were held for years without bail or trial. Thought-control police and a thought-control court system were established, and by 1945 more than 60,000 suspects were processed. There were many cases of cruel and unnecessary treatment, although execution for thought crimes was unknown.[1]

In addition to the close attention given to communists, government censorship, practised since the Meiji period, deepened into systematic policy in the 1930s. Every type of public expression was severely controlled. With the army's seizure of Manchuria in 1931, Japan was placed in a wartime situation, and the emergency justified unlimited expansion of censorship of every medium. Thousands of works were censored every year after 1931. The press was subjected to both prepublication and postpublication censorship. Postpublication censorship involving the retrieval of all copies was more expensive, so the press tried to anticipate official reaction by self-censorship, thus in effect cooperating in prepublication censorship. *Fuseji* [blanked-out characters] were originally used by the authorities to delete offending materials, with an X or O replacing each deleted Japanese character. The use of *fuseji* by editors themselves became common in the 1930s, and sometimes this use produced passages consisting mostly of *fuseji* (XXXXXXXXXXX). The authorities became unhappy with this method since it alerted readers to the fact of censorship, and anyway readers learned by deduction the secret codes of *fuseji* (the most common was the use of XX for *kakumei*, 'revolution'). Therefore, simple banishment of the work became more common in the late 1930s. Both central and regional officials maintained extensive files on writers and intellectuals in order to keep watch; in the 1940s, they were happy to share with editors their information on who should not be published. The fundamental categories for newspaper censorship announced by the Home Minister Adachi Kenzō in 1931 were comprehensive enough for all media: 'news connected with the imperial house, arrest cases involving important criminals, situations in which there was a risk of upsetting the financial world, and news involving the military or diplomacy. Sometime later the Minister added a fifth category of matters which might cause general unrest and seriously disturb public peace.'[2] Amazingly in 1941 two works by the conservative Tokyo Imperial University historian Kuroita Katsumi were found to disturb the public peace: his *Kokushi no Kenkyū* [Research in Japanese History], and volume five of his collected essays.

In the 1930s, the extirpation of communism and the censorship of liberal expression were accompanied by a positive effort to promote emperor-centred nationalism as an exclusive ideology. Throughout the twentieth century, the Ministry of Education had taught the children of Japan about the divine origins of Japan, the special qualities of its emperor and its people, and the need for each person to contribute sincerely and voluntarily to the greater glory of Japan. In the 1930s, though, this approach proved insufficient. Authorities were shocked by the extent of communist belief among university students, revealed by the presence of students among those arrested in March 1928. Study commissions were set up with a view to educational reform, and comprehensive measures were taken.

Among them was the establishment in 1932 of the Research Centre on Japanese Spiritual Culture [Kokumin Seishin Bunka Kenkyūjo], a well-funded organization that acquired much prestige. It had nine divisions: history, literature, art, philosophy, education, law and government, economics, natural science, and thought. It published a monthly bulletin, pamphlets and studies, and major scholarly works on subjects such as historical commentaries on *Nihon Shoki,* letters of Emperors Go Daigo and Go Nara (r. 1526-57), works of Yamaga Sokō, and various works on Shinto. The administration division also undertook the nation-wide reeducation of middle-school teachers.[3] The leading historian who joined the Research Centre was Nishida Naojirō (1886-1946) of Kyoto Imperial University, a brilliant cultural historian who was radicalized into a right-winger by the 1935 Takikawa incident at Kyoto Imperial University. In that incident, the university attempted to dismiss Takikawa Yukitoki (1891-1962) from its law department for leftist views, provoking wide protest. Nishida left the university for more congenial surroundings in the Research Centre on Japanese Spiritual Culture.

Despite the work of the Research Centre, the 1935 Minobe incident showed once again the incompleteness of belief and generated a Movement to Clarify the National Essence [*Kokutai Meichō Undō*]. The incident involved Minobe Tatsukichi (1873-1948), professor emeritus of law at Tokyo Imperial University and a member of the House of Peers. His interpretation of the Meiji Constitution, describing the emperor as an organ of the state, had long been the dominant doctrine, and Minobe had lectured at the imperial palace in the early 1930s. However, the organ theory was suddenly attacked in 1935 by the rising forces of nationalism because it subordinated the emperor to the Constitution. Nationalist thought held that the emperor was the core of the national essence, which originated in the Age of the Gods, and that no constitution could circumscribe his powers. Minobe's position was considered disrespectful and blasphemous. The attack on him resembled that on Kume Kunitake in its vociferousness and venom and exceeded that on the Ministry of Education in 1911 in its wide scale, spreading through parliament and the press and interest groups such as the Army Reserve Association. Minobe resigned from the House of Peers, an act that was widely taken as his defeat, and he suffered a leg wound in an attempted assassination. The ensuing Movement to Clarify the National Essence culminated in 1937 when the Ministry of Education produced a definitive statement for all Japanese, *Kokutai no Hongi* [Cardinal Principles of the National Essence of Japan], which made it clear that the emperor was superior to all law. The source of the emperor's authority was his direct descent from the Sun Goddess, and the book opened with a statement of the Age of the Gods as historical fact.[4] Nearly 300,000 copies were distributed.

At Tokyo Imperial University, there was pressure on academic freedom from the government and agitators without and from administrators and faculty members within. From without, professors were subject to arrest and prosecution for their views, as shown by the indictment of Morito Tatsuo (1888-1984) and Ōuchi Hyōe (1888-1980) in 1920. They were sentenced to fines and jail terms of two months and one month respectively, but the government appealed, and their cases dragged on through 1940, effectively silencing them for the whole period until the end of the Pacific War.[5] Besides the police and the courts, the powers of the Ministry of Education had been feared ever since the Kume Kunitake case. In the same way as government censorship induced self-censorship by the press, attempts by the ministry to intervene in the universities had the strange result of making university administrators more stringent in controlling wayward faculty and thereby preventing ministry intervention. As summarized by Byron K. Marshall,

> By the end of the 1920s university officers and the majority of the faculties at the imperial universities were all too frequently willing to sacrifice freedoms of speech and press to avoid a threat to their control of their elite institutions. To prevent external authorities from intervening on campus, leftist study groups were disbanded, militant students were suspended, and radical professors were persuaded to resign. Thus, university autonomy came to be identified with such compromises with external enemies.[6]

In the 1930s, major events occurred at both Kyoto and Tokyo Imperial Universities. At Kyoto Imperial University, an attempt to discipline Professor Takikawa (also pronounced Takigawa) Yukitoki of the law department for leftist views, starting in April 1933, led to protracted trouble. Amid angry controversy and clashes between leftist and rightist groups, the incident eventually resulted in the resignation of the president of the university and twenty of thirty-one department members. No clear winner was declared. The Kyoto incident, significant because Takikawa was no communist, only a liberal, roused little support at Tokyo Imperial University even though everyone knew about it. Tokyo had its own incidents in the economics department. In February 1938, three professors were indicted; and in 1939, in connection with the indictment of Professor Kawai Eijirō for subversion, the economics department was purged of seven of its twelve professors by the new university president, Hiraga Yuzuru (1873-1943).[7]

While the Faculties of Law and Economics at Tokyo and Kyoto went through much uproar, there were few attacks on the historians of the imperial universities. Typically the historians did not go to the aid of their colleagues in other faculties. They had been cautious since the 1911 Southern-Northern Courts controversy and displayed ever more circumspection as the times became more difficult, intent on giving no cause for criticism. But no scholars in the humanities and social sciences were immune from nationalist criticism. Danger lurked for the historians because the government had ideas for projects, such as the celebration in 1940 of the 2,600th anniversary of the founding of the empire by Emperor Jinmu. For this celebration, it expected cooperation from the historians. They all thought that 660 BC was not the correct date for the founding of the empire, but stating that view would surely have brought trouble upon themselves. As we shall see, the historians chose to avoid trouble.

Pressure from without also came from propagandists such as Minoda Muneki (1894-1946), the founder of the nationalist journal *Genri Nippon* [Principles of the Japanese Nation], which kept a special watch over intellectuals and scholars to denounce any deviance from emperor-centred nationalism.[8] Probably Minoda's fierce and unpredictable denunciations made the historians nervous because of their positions on the Age of the Gods and Emperor Jinmu, even though Minoda found few targets among them. As discussed below, in 1935 *Genri Nippon* attacked Tsuji Zennosuke for praising Ashikaga Takauji, and Kuroita Katsumi for praising Hōjō Yasutoki. Kuroita had already retired, but apparently the attack on him helped to make Tsuji and the others tread very carefully.

The historians kept their distance in October 1939 when the historian Tsuda Sōkichi was invited from Waseda University to give a series of lectures at a new chair of Oriental thought in the Faculty of Law. Minoda

Muneki unloaded heavy broadside attacks; the cover of *Genri Nippon* on 24 December 1939 read:

> On the eve of the 2,600th anniversary of the empire,
> Blasphemy unprecedented in the scholarly world!
> Doctor of letters, professor at Waseda University,
> Lectures at Tokyo Imperial University Faculty of Law.
>
> TREASONOUS THOUGHT OF TSUDA SŌKICHI
>
> Our arts and science critique of massacre of the Age of the Gods.[9]

This attack on Tsuda eventually led to his legal prosecution in 1941 for works dating from 1913 that violated the publication law by insulting the imperial dignity. Most of the Tokyo Imperial University historians did not go to Tsuda's support because they did not accept his radical theories; they never invited him to lecture in the history department. Instead, it was the liberal law professor Nanbara Shigeru (1889-1974) who had invited him to lecture in the Faculty of Law. Among the major historians, only Tsuji Zennosuke went to the aid of Tsuda by adding his name, along with those of eighty-eight others, to a petition to the court supporting the scholarship and character of Tsuda.[10]

In addition to the wild critics outside the university, there were professors within every faculty of Tokyo Imperial University who promoted the imperial ideology with vigour. This made life difficult for sceptical or merely uninterested colleagues. In the Department of History, the historian Hiraizumi Kiyoshi rose to power in the 1930s by professing perfectly correct nationalist beliefs and insisting on their universal observance. Because his colleagues and all the other historians formally professed the imperial ideology, they had no grounds on which to resist him. Thus, they found themselves pushed more or less unhappily toward extreme positions.

Throughout the 1930s, then, there was a widespread fear of censorship of incorrect statements about Japan and the emperors, fear of denunciation, and beyond that fear for position, liberty, and life. As put in 1938 by Tanaka Kōtaru (1890-1974), the chairman of the Department of Law at Tokyo Imperial University, 'This is not a climate for scholarship. If you so much as show the top of your head, it gets shot at. What honor is there to stay on at such a university?'[11] Let us observe some of the historians in the 1930s to illustrate their responses to troubled times.

Mikami Sanji (1865-1939): Conscientious Civil Servant

In 1895 the Ministry of Education reorganized the Historiographical

Institute to make it conform more closely to the requirements of the government. The one who best understood the purpose of the new institute, and laboured the hardest to achieve it, was Mikami Sanji, its head from 1899 to 1919. He set a personal example, devoting his excellent mind and skills as a historian not to the writing of his own books but to the institute's work of collecting, compiling, and publishing historical materials for other scholars to use in writing the history of Japan. This dedication, and the intelligence and diplomacy with which he carried out the task, were so widely recognized that he achieved a fame as great as if he had written his own books. 'He left enormous footprints on the history of scholarship in Japan,' wrote Takayanagi Mitsutoshi (1892-1969) upon Mikami's death in 1939, 'and I believe his fame will long be known in times to come.'[12] Mikami's dedication to the public good was based on a deep sense of service to imperial Japan.

Mikami was a member of the first generation of scientific scholars trained by Riess, Shigeno, Kume, and Hoshino. A native of Himeji in Hyōgo Prefecture, he graduated in literature in 1889 and entered the graduate school in

Mikami Sanji (1865-1939), the most eminent historian of his time, held that sceptical scholarship must be kept apart from education. (Courtesy of the Historiographical Institute, Tokyo University)

history, where he excelled. By 1892 he was an assistant professor; in 1895 he received his doctorate of letters [*bungaku hakase*], was promoted to professor, and joined the new Historiographical Institute headed by Hoshino Hisashi. In 1899 he succeeded Hoshino as head. In 1902 he travelled to Hamburg as the Japanese representative to the International Congress of Orientalists, and in 1908 he was appointed to the Imperial Japan Academy. All this academic success came in recognition of his excellence as a modern scholar, rationalistic and positivistic. Many articles from those early years are found in the journals *Shigaku Zasshi* and *Rekishi Chiri,* covering a wide variety of topics in the style of his teachers. In his later years, he was renowned for his teaching, which was patient, thorough, and stimulating. His disciple Nakamura Kōya described him as tirelessly devoted to the revision of his lecture notes in a room piled everywhere with documents and records. He brought stacks of them to the classroom. 'The lectures were grounded in the documents, and he made sure that his listeners understood every word and every phrase, not stopping until they all understood the conclusion of the reasoning.'[13]

On the Age of the Gods, our main topic, Mikami stood between Hoshino, who treated it all as history, and Kume, who treated it all as allegory. For Mikami some of it was history, and the business of scientific historians was to find out which parts those were. His approach was the most common among his generation, and it persisted to the end of the 1980s among some historians trained in the prewar era, notably Sakamoto Tarō. However, it would be hard to find a historian trained in the postwar period who agrees with Mikami's view. Most of them just ignore the myths of the Age of the Gods as potential sources for history, leaving the territory to scholars of literature, myth studies, and religion, for whom historical truth is irrelevant. Mikami's ideas are well summarized in a posthumous publication entitled *Kokushi Gaisetsu* [Outline of Japanese History]:

The Age of the Gods is broad and unbounded and cannot be simply understood as historical fact. Among its historical parts are mixed varied and complicated alien elements, much of which must be understood by the rigorous application of auxiliary historical sciences such as historical geography, myth studies, anthropology, archeology, ethnography, and linguistics ... *Kojiki, Nihon Shoki, Kogo Shūi, Kujiki,* and so on have been handed down as books of history; all of them are later recordings of materials originally transmitted orally, and doubt remains about the extent to which their accounts of the Age of the Gods can be relied on. Granted that the legends were faithfully recorded at the time of writing, it cannot be denied that much misinformation had crept into the original legends with the passage of time ... It is extremely difficult at the present to decide which parts of the legends contain misinformation, but at any rate there is no call for deciding beforehand whether the Age of the Gods is completely true or completely mythical.[14]

Like Kume Kunitake, Mikami changed his thinking when it came to Emperor Jinmu and accepted *Nihon Shoki*'s account as completely historical. In *Kokushi Gaisetsu*, Mikami narrates the facts of Jinmu's eastern expedition, and cites his rhetorical speech on the founding of the empire, without even suggesting that there were Chinese sources for the speech as recorded in *Nihon Shoki*. The work goes into archeology, not to determine the level of civilization in Jinmu's time, an assessment that would have been useful, but to try to identify the primitive people encountered by Jinmu. They were Stone Age people, and Mikami cites four theories about their identity that are no longer accepted.[15] Like the other historians, he distinguished between facts and their dates and had no difficulty accepting revision of Emperor Jinmu's date from 660 BC to 40 BC.

Kokushi Gaisetsu provides insight into Mikami's political thinking, which may have influenced his successor, Kuroita Katsumi. As a historian, Mikami found it necessary to scrutinize *Kojiki* and *Nihon Shoki* rigorously, but as a Japanese citizen, he accepted them as the source of religious and political truth. 'The records of the gods,' he wrote, 'are contained in *Kojiki* and *Nihon Shoki*. The gods are the ancestors of the imperial house, which reigns for ages eternal, and of its subjects. Therefore, *Kojiki* and *Nihon Shoki should be honoured outside of history* and ultimately considered as sacred scripture.'[16]

This position, involving fierce scrutiny of the books as works of history, alongside uncritical acceptance of them as sources of political and religious values, has not been unusual in the twentieth century. Many a Western historian has judged the events of the Bible unhistorical yet continued to accept the Bible as the source of religious truth. The position was stated succinctly at the outset of modern science by Sir Francis Bacon (1561-1626), who refrained from applying scientific methods to the Bible, observing that 'sacred theology must be drawn from the word and works of God, not from the light of nature or the dictates of reason.'[17] In *The Great Instauration*, Bacon's announcement of the new science that would change the world, he wrote:

Wherefore, seeing that these things do not depend upon myself, at the outset of the work I most humbly and fervently pray to God the Father, God the Son, and God the Holy Ghost, that remembering the sorrows of mankind and the pilgrimage of this our life wherein we wear out days few and evil, they will vouchsafe through my hands to endow the human family with new mercies. This likewise I humbly pray, that things human may not interfere with things divine, and that from the opening of the ways of sense and increase of natural light there may arise in our minds no incredulity or darkness with regard to the divine mysteries; but rather that the understanding being purified and purged of fancies and vanity, and yet not the less subject and entirely submissive to the divine oracles, may give to faith that which is faith's.[18]

Mikami was a firm supporter of the imperial house, and up to the Southern-Northern Courts controversy of 1911, he found no difficulty in reconciling scholarship and political values. He had risen to high position and honour for outstanding practice of scientific history. This was combined with patriotic devotion to the work of the Historiographical Institute. He was taken aback by the Southern-Northern Courts controversy of 1911 when he was criticized for insufficient loyalty to the imperial house. As noted in Chapter 10, Mikami was unable to declare one or the other court legitimate in the fourteenth century because the historical evidence was not persuasive. However, he was satisfied that he was as loyal as anyone, and he fully believed in his favourite analogy that the division of the imperial house into Southern and Northern lines was not like two suns in the sky but like two branches of a river that divided and then rejoined. To suggest that one of the two branches lacked legitimacy was to imply similarity to the Chinese throne, where emperors were forever being overthrown and usurped by rebels. To his mind, that suggestion was disloyal. Thus, a somewhat theoretical Mikami misunderstood the political forces of his time. He did not comprehend the legitimacy of the Southern line as the only position compatible with the restorationist nature of the Meiji reign. Mikami must have been mortified when he was identified as the ringleader of the disloyal people responsible for the offensive textbook and cornered by the simple-minded, drunken Diet Member Fujisawa Genzō, who could not understand his river analogy.

As noted, Mikami defended himself at the time by writing his own account in *Taiyō*, which was reprinted in *Shigaku Zasshi*. However, he also learned from the affair. Thereafter until the end of his life, he made a rigorous distinction between education of the people [*kokumin kyōiku*], in which the truth as determined by the government must be taught to the Japanese people, and scholarship [*gakumon*], in which scholars freely conducted research and sought different truths. He saw this as the solution to all problems for scholars, and in 1938 he noted that Dr. Obliteration, Shigeno Yasutsugu, had encountered trouble over Kojima Takanori in 1890 because this distinction had not yet been clearly made.[19] Thus, the people of Japan should be taught that the Southern Court was legitimate in the fourteenth century, while scholars should be free to hold whatever view they reached on the basis of scientific research. He realized that this distinction required circumspection on the part of scholars, but he never attempted to define the occasions or limits of circumspection. Mikami summed up these views in the 1911 article in *Taiyō* and never deviated from them.

The Southern-Northern Courts question in the textbooks unexpectedly became a major problem. As a scholar and an educator, I always try to bear in mind the good of the imperial house and the Japanese people when presenting my arguments. Until there is an opportunity to clarify how many reigns there were, on the basis of the Southern and Northern Courts, of course I shall continue to argue according to my principles without regard to which court was legitimate. For now, however, the government has made a firm and important decision on the legitimacy of the Southern Court, and the textbooks will be revised accordingly. Should this doctrine extend to the state as well, I will respectfully follow it. My research as a historian on the Southern-Northern Courts is of course free, but now is not the best time to express it.[20]

Mikami found that this position served him well. As a teacher at Tokyo Imperial University, he was always careful to distinguish the positions reserved for the ears of scholars alone from those that could be taught to the nation at large. In his admiring account of Mikami as a teacher, cited above, Nakamura Kōya noted that Mikami would sometimes close the windows in order to give his lectures. He did this whenever he spoke on a topic containing a contradiction between education and scholarship.[21] Nakamura Kōya, however, could not remember any examples. Another student, Akiyama Kenzō, was able to remember an example of Mikami's circumspection: 'When it came to delicate problems ... especially relations between the imperial house and the bakufu, he was careful to shut the door tightly.'[22]

From this behaviour, it must have been well known that Mikami's scholarly views differed from those that he professed as a citizen, but he was never challenged for disloyalty. Moreover, he made his position clear not only at the university but also in public forums. As Japan's leading scientific historian, he served on the fifty-seven-member Education Reform Council [*Kyōgaku Sasshin Hyōgikai*] that was set up in response to the Minobe Tatsukichi incident of 1935. Its mandate was to review Japan's educational system and recommend improvements. At the meetings, Mikami argued against teaching scientific history to the nation, reserving scientific method only for scholarly research. In making his argument, he went as far as exposing the doubts about the founding of the empire in 660 BC that were shared by all historians:

The idea that there are no national boundaries in scholarship, and that scholarly research must be absolutely free, comes from the natural sciences. In the spiritual sciences [*seishin kagaku*], a very clear distinction must be made between research and the teaching of students ... The fourth-year university students will carry out ceremonies observing the 2,600th anniversary of the empire. Now, if the 2,600th anniversary is studied by scientific history, its doubtfulness is apparent to anyone. However, when it comes to teaching, I would like to have a firm distinction drawn, under which we refrain from discussing this doubtfulness.[23]

Nobody was startled by the spectacle of Japan's leading historian arguing that historical truth should not be taught to the nation. Such were the times that people were more likely to be offended by the statement that, in the view of scholars, the 2,600th anniversary of the empire was doubtful. Yet Mikami was not attacked. It was not his high position and great honour that protected him. Minobe Tatsukichi held a similar high position and great honour, but he was not spared: the nationalist ideologues of the 1930s were great levellers. Perhaps ideological vigilantes such as Minoda Muneki, burdened by the work of exposing many disloyal scholars, just never got around to Mikami Sanji. Similarly I suggested that the emperor may have been spared from direct attack by the murderous rationalist scholars of 1890 because they never got to the subject before they were interrupted by the Kume incident.

There is a lingering suspicion that members of the Historiographical Institute such as Mikami Sanji, who were subjected to such strict rules for avoiding public criticism, must have had private reservations. This is put provocatively by Miyachi Masato:

> The enterprise was reestablished in April 1895 as the Historiographical Institute. There were taboos against publicly affirming that untruths were untruths and against study and discussion of the overall shape of history. While brandishing the nationalist view of history and education, the members sarcastically cut it apart in private. As far as possible, they avoided conflict with the outside, and while taking pride in their abilities in comprehending and critically studying historical materials, what they did was indefatigably compile materials in an extremely conservative manner.[24]

This view of the nature of their work is valid, though the author himself confirms that it is hard to find documentary evidence that they mocked imperial values in private.[25] The suspicion lingers all the same. However, it does not apply at all to Mikami Sanji; it is clear that he had the greatest respect for the views of history required by the imperial state and society that he did not accept as a scholar.

Mikami's position came out strongly during the writing of *Kokutai no Hongi* [Cardinal Principles of the National Entity of Japan, 1937] by a committee appointed by the Ministry of Education. *Kokutai no Hongi* affirmed the imperial values in which Mikami believed. However, it also based these values directly, without qualification, on the myths as facts of history. The first page left no doubt about this:

Our nation was founded when its Founder, Amaterasu Ohmikami (Heavenly-Shining-Great August Deity), handed the Oracle to her Imperial Grandson Ninigi no Mikoto and descended to Mizuho no Kuni (Land of Fresh Rice-ears) at Toyoashihara (Rich Reed-plain). And in relating the facts of the founding of our Land by the Founder of our Empire, the *Kojiki* and the *Nihon-shoki* tell first of all of the beginning of heaven and earth and of the making and consolidating, and the *Kojiki* says ... [26]

Hisamatsu Sen'ichi, a professor of Japanese literature at Tokyo Imperial University, wrote most of the drafts and seems to have had no doubts about the Age of the Gods and Emperor Jinmu. Kuroita Katsumi, Mikami's colleague at Tokyo Imperial University, fell ill six months after his appointment to the committee, and he attended none of the general meetings. That left Mikami Sanji as the only major historian. He played the greatest part in affirming the presentation of the myths as history for the benefit of the Japanese people. He attended all three of the plenary sessions of the committee, in ex officio capacity as a member of the related Education Reform Council. There were many disagreements between the members of the committee, but the greatest was between Mikami and Kihira Tadayoshi (1874-1949), another ex officio member from the Education Reform Council and a member of the Research Centre on Japanese Spiritual Culture. Apparently their battles on the *Kokutai no Hongi* committee were a re-enactment of their exchanges on the Education Reform Council, of which there is no record.[27] Kihira, a Hegelian, wanted to distinguish between fact and myth for philosophical reasons, while Mikami thought that his approach was woolly minded and failed to appreciate the social reasons for the distinction between scholarship and education that Mikami had learned so well. Mikami won.

His position was never challenged by his colleagues. It took a student to point out what he was doing. Inoue Kiyoshi (b. 1913), now professor emeritus of history at Kyoto University, entered Tokyo Imperial University as a history student in 1933. Mikami Sanji was then professor emeritus. He gave a talk to the new students, about twenty-five of them, at a meeting of the Eleventh Club, which met on the eleventh day of each month. He told them that the university is a place of scholarship and that the truth must be pursued. However, many of them would graduate and go on to become schoolteachers and would occasionally find themselves unprepared for teaching their history classes. At such times, they might recall what they studied at university and teach it to their students. That, said Mikami, would not do. He gave two examples. First, the anniversary of the empire was fixed at 660 BC. Tokugawa and Meiji scholars had found that the date was off by 600 years, but Mikami told the students that they must never teach that. Second, the Southern-Northern Courts controversy. He explained that he himself thought the courts equally legitimate, but he went over the 1911 controversy and said that it was settled not by scholars but by the Meiji emperor. Therefore, for the purpose of national education, the Southern emperor alone was legitimate, and the period must be termed 'The Yoshino Court.'

Probably Mikami offered this advice in a helpful grandfatherly way to the students. But young Inoue Kiyoshi was offended and outraged, concluding that the eminent professor wanted to teach lies [*uso*] to the Japanese people. Inoue's faith in the university was destroyed, and he was unable to continue his studies. For two years, he scarcely appeared at the university, leaving his lodgings daily with the pretence of going to class but mainly hanging around Ueno. If he went to the university, he visited other departments, especially the Faculty of Law, where Minobe Tatsukichi taught, or read newspapers and magazines in the library. He bought lecture notes and managed to pass the examinations. Inoue did not come alive until he encountered the Marxist historian Hani Gorō (1901-83) and was introduced to the sceptical historical works of Tsuda Sōkichi.[28]

Mikami was never aware of Inoue's criticism and passed on from glory to glory. In 1932 he was appointed to the House of Peers; there is no record that he supported his former Tokyo Imperial University colleague Minobe Tatsukichi when the latter was attacked in the House for describing the emperor as an organ of the state. Mikami gave lectures at the imperial palace, and he was head of the *Meiji Tennō Ki* [Record of Emperor Meiji, thirteen volumes] project, begun in 1914 and completed in 1933. Finally, in December 1938, he became head of the Commission of Inquiry into Historical Sites Related to Emperor Jinmu, a grand project of the Ministry of Education that was part of the anticipated 2,600th anniversary celebrations in 1940. Like most other Japanese historians, Mikami did not believe that 660 BC was the correct date of the founding of the empire by Emperor Jinmu.

Mikami Sanji died on 7 June 1939 at the age of seventy-five. To the end, he maintained his distinction between education and scholarship, and he never showed any apprehension that the distinction was being steadily erased in favour of the standards for education. His separation of education and scholarship is reminiscent of Hayashi Razan's distinction between public and private.

Kuroita Katsumi (1874-1946): From Rationalism to Nationalism

Rationalism

Kuroita Katsumi succeeded Kume Kunitake as the greatest authority on ancient history. Born in Nagasaki Prefecture, he went to Tokyo Imperial University and graduated from the history department in 1896, having learned

Kuroita Katsumi (1874-1946) gradually
abandoned a distinction between rationalism
and nationalism, in favour of nationalism.
(Courtesy of the Historiographical Institute,
Tokyo University)

scientific history in the era of Riess. He then worked for Taguchi Ukichi, compiling the first edition of *Kokushi Taikei* [Compendium of Japanese History]. As noted, in later years Kuroita undertook a revised and enlarged version, with the help of colleagues at the Historiographical Institute, and the series is now identified with Kuroita's name, not Taguchi's. It is easy now to underestimate the importance of this work, but Tsuji Zennosuke noted that, until *Kokushi Taikei* came out, not even the text of *Nihon Shoki* was at hand, and scholars had to go and use library copies.[29]

In 1901 Kuroita joined the Historiographical Institute and in 1902 was appointed lecturer in Japanese history in the university. He received his doctor of letters degree in 1905 for a dissertation on the forms of ancient documents, and in the same year he was promoted to assistant professor. His tour of the United States and Europe came in 1908-9, mainly to visit historical sites and museums, but it also included an international history congress in Berlin in 1908 and an international Esperanto meeting in Dresden. Kuroita had helped to found an Esperanto society in Japan in 1906, and in 1914 he was joint author of the first Esperanto-Japanese dictionary. This Esperanto work may be taken as a sign of internationalism, but his critics contend that he promoted Esperanto precisely because he was a nationalist. They claim that he hoped the Japanese language would thrive if all nations equally adopted an artificial international language rather than permitting English to displace all other languages.[30] The overseas tour may have sown the seeds of conservative nationalism, as he noted the problems of Japanese immigrants in the United States and sensed a general dislike of Japan. Now that Japan had become a great power, Americans were no longer eager to take Japanese visitors by the hand and show them around factories. Kuroita opined in 1911 that Japan could no longer import Western civilization. It must develop its own culture and power, and this development would require much study and large-scale planning.[31]

Kuroita's *Kokushi no Kenkyū* [Research in Japanese History] came out in 1908 and was revised in 1913 and 1931, becoming the standard work for professionals in Japanese history. He was appointed a full professor at Tokyo Imperial University in 1919, and in the same year he succeeded Mikami Sanji as head of the Historiographical Institute. After only one year, he resigned from that position and continued as a professor of history until his retirement in 1935. His reason for resigning is not known, but Sakamoto Tarō noted that Kuroita always had an independent streak.[32] He may have found the restrictions of the institute more burdensome than Mikami had. The students respected him but found him distant and uninvolved, always occupied with research. Ōkubo Toshiaki described his lectures as disorganized; he had always just rushed back from research in the Kansai and was about to run over to a meeting in the Imperial Household Ministry.[33] His lifelong passion was collecting, editing, and conserving documents, especially those of ancient and medieval institutions such as the temples of Nara and Kyoto.

Only two years of his diary survive, covering 1927 and 1928, and they reveal a busy life of travel, appointments, committee meetings, and lectures about history, though without indicating the substance of it all.[34] A loyal subject of great scholarly distinction, Kuroita was rewarded with the same public honours that fell upon Mikami and upon his successor, Tsuji Zennosuke.

Kuroita's *Kokushi no Kenkyū* (1931) succeeded Kume's *Nihon Kodaishi* as the standard work and represents the highest stage of scientific history in prewar Japan. It is divided into two parts: *Sōsetsu*, or 'General Theory,' and two volumes of *Kakusetsu*, or 'Detailed Discussion.' The General Theory volume, devoted to periodization and methods, is a work for professional scholars and is not likely to interest readers looking for the substance of history or political values. It covers the fields of ancient documents, historical geography, calendars East and West, genealogy, and archeology. A review of the historical development of Japanese scholarship places modern work in context, including scholarship on the Age of the Gods. Kuroita covers the scholarship of the Edo period, including that of Arai Hakuseki, Motoori

Norinaga, Hirata Atsutane, and the rest. Native scholarship had come to a dead end, until the arrival of foreigners in nineteenth-century Japan set it in new directions; Kuroita mentions W.G. Aston, Karl Florenz, John Batchelor, Edwin Baelz. Then came the Japanese of 1890 – Shigeno, Hoshino, Kume, Suga – whose work was not perfectly scholarly but who opened new fields. The Kume incident made a pause, but Japanese scholars had learned the methods and proceeded to anthropology, philology, archeology, myth studies, linguistics, et cetera. The fruit of it all was Kume's *Nihon Kodaishi*, which Kuroita likened to Arai Hakuseki's work in treating the Age of the Gods as the history of humans, of which Kuroita approved, even though he could not agree with all of Kume's views on the meaning of specific myths. Like nearly everyone else in the prewar period, Kuroita had little to say about the Kume Kunitake incident. He certainly did not see it as the outrageous suppression of scholarship by an authoritarian state. He also reviewed the ideas of Tsuda Sōkichi, who emphasized the later provenance of the myths. Kuroita found too arbitrary Tsuda's view of the construction of the myths by intellectuals of the seventh and eighth centuries. He held that Tsuda had overlooked the long process of development of the myths and had incorrectly dismissed them as containing no history.

Kuroita summarized his position on the ancient myths as follows:

Both *Kojiki* and *Nihon Shoki* were recorded and compiled 1,300 years after the founding of the empire. While they preserve the myths and legends of most ancient times, for the most part they are disordered, and their problems are not confined to the inclusion of Chinese and Korean materials. The contents of the myths and legends cannot be taken at face value as historical phenomena, nor can the contents of *Kojiki* and *Nihon Shoki* in general be understood as historical phenomena. Interpretation must be augmented by myth studies, religious studies, linguistics, archeology, anthropology, ethnography, sociology, and so on, and the myths must be considered in the light of research on their every aspect.[35]

No more enlightened a position was achieved in prewar Japan. He opened volume 1 of the Detailed Discussion by going straight to the point: 'The first problem is whether or not the period hitherto known as the Age of the Gods should be treated as history.'[36] There follows a review of positions taken throughout history, of works such as *Ruijū Kokushi* in the Heian period, a work that treated it as history, and *Dai Nihon Shi*, which did not. Modern scholars were justified in not taking it as history. Elsewhere, in 1934, he repeated his view that the myths of the Age of the Gods, having been recorded 1,000 years after they became current, could not be accepted as historical fact and needed interpretation by the modern auxiliary sciences of history.[37]

However, at the prewar stage of scholarship, it was not intellectually sat-isfying to stop there, and so Kuroita next took up the myths one by one. He did this in an attempt to find some residue of facts, despite the view that they would not constitute history anyway. This position was more emo-tional than rational. The historians of Kuroita's time had been brought up on the myths, and they could not dismiss them even after concluding that they held no historical truth. In addition, prewar historians accepted the reality of the national essence, which was mainly based on the myths of ancient Japan, so they plausibly undertook detailed analysis of the myths to demonstrate the way of thinking of the ancients. Accordingly Kuroita plunged in for extensive discussion of the historical meaning of the main stories, starting with the founding deities Izanagi and Izanami. This ap-proach is now dismissed by historians as fruitless, though it persists in other disciplines, such as literature, religious studies, and anthropology.

Kuroita reiterated his rationalist position in other works. In a 1930 study of ancient Shinto, he placed the religion in historical context by reviewing the influence of China on ancient Japan, the findings of archeology, the effect of Buddhism, the role of naturalized foreigners [*kikajin*], and so on. He did not assume the truth of the myths but considered their provenance, meaning, social significance, and contents. He concluded reasonably that ancient Shinto was not a theoretical construction by intellectuals but a faith of the people, with attendant social roles and obligations.[38]

On Emperor Jinmu, Kuroita had no doubts. Accepting, as Kume did, the historical existence of Jinmu, Kuroita approved the ongoing scholarly work of rationalizing the chronology.

Nationalism

These rationalist scholarly positions contended for place in Kuroita's mind against a nationalist political view of Japan as a country with a distinct national essence, based on unbroken descent of the emperors from the Sun Goddess. The struggle led to a separation between history as viewed by the professional scholar and as viewed by the nationalist political writer. The professional scholar did not accept the myths as historical fact, while for the nationalist political writer the myths held such profound meaning that their historicity must be affirmed. Mikami Sanji had stated this position, in which the historian fiercely scrutinized *Kojiki* and *Nihon Shoki* as works of history but also accorded them a separate status as sacred political docu-ments of the Japanese nation. However, Mikami wrote nothing about their political value, while Kuroita wrote extensively about this value. His politi-cal writings were done in the same period as his main scholarly writings, the 1920s and 1930s, revealing a man of two minds.

Several works show Kuroita's second track of nationalistic thinking. A short 1925 work, *Saisei Itchi no Kokutai* [The National Essence Based on Unity of Government and Religion], asked whether modern critical scholarship had caused unnecessary and harmful doubts about the truths of the imperial house. Criticism of *Kojiki* and *Nihon Shoki,* determination of chronology, and rational interpretation of the myths should have no effect on the political truths of Japan centred on the reality of the imperial house.[39]

The separation of history as history from history as source of political truth is advanced but not completed in Kuroita's major 1925 work, *Kokutai Shinron* [A New Essay on the National Essence]. In this work, he subscribed to the common fallacy of contemporary discussion of the *kokutai.* According to this way of thinking, the basic characteristics of the Japanese nation were held to have originated in ancient times. They were retained as the basis of modern Japan, as if nothing had happened in 1,500 years of history to change the Japanese. These basic values included direct imperial rule [*shinsei*], affirmed by Kuroita in this and in other works. Direct imperial rule did not mean that the emperor actually governed but that there were no legitimate intermediate bodies such as the Fujiwara regency, government by retired emperors, and government by the bakufu that filled up the bulk of Japanese history from the tenth century to the nineteenth century. According to devotees of the idea, direct imperial rule had thankfully been resumed with the Meiji Restoration. Essays on kokutai generally made sense only by omitting or downgrading the importance of 1,000 years of history in which the emperors had been insignificant. Such essays were influential because readers wanted to believe in imperial values affirmed by the Meiji Restoration. Hence, they were prepared to overlook the historical superficiality of the essays.

A statement on the uniqueness of Japan suggests acceptance of the divine founding of the imperial house: 'Our country alone is the imperial nation [*kōkoku*]. Since its founding, the positions of ruler and subjects have been settled. The sovereign governs our country in a line unbroken for ages eternal, coeval with Heaven and Earth. In this is manifested our national essence, which has no parallel in other countries.'[40] In *Kokutai Shinron,* Kuroita does not state unequivocally that the myths are true. However, he extracts from them ideal truths about Japanese society that are equally valid in ancient and modern times. The social reality of the myths persists – the land, the emperor, and the people of Japan, three in one, and one in three. The myths express the love of the emperor for the people – a love that is real and the basis for the absolutism of the emperor, which Kuroita expresses repeatedly as a positive value. Absolutism is not despotism. In the myths, the gods gather to discuss and decide matters, and this preference for discussion reflects the reality that the Japanese emperor has never been a despot, as has the emperor of China. Society is distinguished by equality, even though this equality was repeatedly threatened in history by the emergence of class and honour systems. Speech is free, and everyone's view is considered, whether in the Constitution of Prince Shōtoku or in the Meiji Constitution.

Thus, in 1925 Kuroita presented an idealistic interpretation of Japanese political, social, and intellectual history that did not square with his purely scholarly positions.

In *Kokutai Shinron*, Kuroita reiterates his acceptance of modern scholarly dating but disconnects it from the political significance of the imperial house. Doubts about the dates of Emperor Jinmu have no relation to the reality of the eternal imperial reign. Moreover, it is disrespectful to the *kokutai* to use the Christian chronology, even though it is in use in government documents and textbooks. Chinese systems are also inappropriate, since they were devised for a country of chronic political revolutions. Japan's proper system of dating is the method of counting from the ascension of Emperor Jinmu.[41]

Actually Kuroita did not use that cumbersome system, as his mentor, Taguchi Ukichi, had for lack of alternatives. Some scholars in the 1930s did use the Emperor Jinmu dating system, resulting in incomprehensible dates. For example, Nakamura Naokatsu in his nationalist phase used it in a 1937 biography of Kitabatake Chikafusa (1293-1354 AD). He gave Kitabatake's dates as 1953-2014, and those of his son Akiiye as 1978-1998, ancient Japan time.[42] Hiraizumi Kiyoshi of Tokyo Imperial University also used it in some works.

By 1935 Kuroita had moved to a position where he seldom expressed the reservations of the historian about the myths and proceeded straight to their political truth. A short work, *Kokushi no Taikan* [Overview of Japanese History], opened with a statement, reminiscent of Taguchi Ukichi, in which the economic life of the ancient people came to be based on agriculture and religion arose to secure abundant harvests. But the imperial house swiftly came into view. 'Worshipping the gods,' he wrote, 'was not only to ensure the security of their livelihood; it was simultaneously an act of government. Thus, there was unity of religion and government.' The Sun Goddess therefore came to the fore as the ancestor of the imperial house. 'In our country,' continued Kuroita, 'there is no other centre or power that ranks with the imperial house. It is absolute, and everyone, everywhere, offers service to it. This constitutes the special nature of our national essence, which is unparalleled in other countries.' An account of the founding of Japan by the deities follows, qualified only by the sentence 'These legends express the racial ideas and the political thought of our forebears.' There is no suggestion that the ideas of the forebears are obsolete. The important truth is that 'Everything within our country arose within the imperial house, and everything is embraced by it. This principle that the imperial house is at the centre is expressed in the vow of the Sun Goddess to protect it to eternity. In this vow of the Sun Goddess lies the unparalleled majesty of our national essence; moreover, the three imperial regalia which she bequeathed to her descendants have been handed down as symbols of the imperial throne.'⁴³

Similarly a 1934 paper, 'Emperor Jinmu's Eastern Expedition and Hyūga Province' [*Jinmu Tennō Gotōsen to Hyūga no Kuni*], displays a straightforward acceptance of the historicity of the Sun Goddess and her commission of the imperial line, leading to the conquering work of Emperor Jinmu. No reservations are expressed by terms such as 'the myth says ...'⁴⁴

After ancient times, Kuroita saw the imperial light shining most brightly in the fourteenth century when Emperor Go Daigo achieved the Kenmu Restoration. In Kuroita's selective analysis, the Kenmu Restoration of 1333 was always linked backward to the Taika reform of 645 and forward to the Meiji Restoration of 1868, skipping everything else that happened in between. This method was also practised by other historians of the time when discussing political values, including Hiraizumi Kiyoshi and Sakamoto Tarō of Tokyo Imperial University. In a 1935 essay entitled 'Humble Thoughts on the Achievement of Emperor Go Daigo in the Kenmu Restoration' [Go Daigo Tennō Gochūkō no Seigyō o Omoitatematsuru], Kuroita held that the restoration failed because of the general absence of 'thought fully informed by our sacred kokutai [*waga seishin naru kokutai*].' That is, people in the fourteenth century did not understand the essential nature of Japan as an imperial country in the way that modern people do. Thus, they did not realize the significance of Go Daigo's efforts and failed to support the Kenmu Restoration. However, precisely because the restoration failed, the ideal of the imperial restoration was established, to be nurtured through 600 years of subsequent history and realized in the Meiji Restoration. If Go Daigo and his followers had succeeded, their lessons of bravery and sacrifice would have been of no effect in establishing the sacred kokutai. Their achievements would have been perceived as no more than worldly gains, no better than those of Ashikaga Takauji.⁴⁵

Kuroita was a member of the committee to write *Kokutai no Hongi*. Besides Ministry of Education officials, the professors on the committee included the following:

Tokyo Imperial University:
Fujikake Shizuya (1881-1958), art
Hisamatsu Sen'ichi (1894-1976), Japanese literature
Kuroita Katsumi (1874-1946), Japanese history
Ui Hakuji (1882-1963), Indian philosophy and Buddhism
Watsuji Tetsurō (1889-1960), philosophy

Kyoto Imperial University:
Sakuta Shōichi (1878-1973), economics

Tohoku Imperial University:
Yamada Yoshio (1873-1958), Japanese literature

The Peers School:
Iijima Tadao (1874-1954), professor emeritus, Oriental history

Kokugakuin University:
Kōno Seizō (1882-1963), president.

The only other historian on the committee was a Ministry of Education official, Ōtsuka Takematsu (1878-1946), a specialist on the Meiji Restoration. He could be expected to accept the myths of the Age of the Gods and the founding of the empire. Apart from Mikami's occasional *ex officio* presence, Kuroita was the only university historian on the committee, and thus his views on the historicity or otherwise of the myths ought to have carried much weight.

As we have seen in the section on Mikami Sanji, *Kokutai no Hongi* affirmed without qualification the historical truth of the Age of the Gods in order to justify and define the imperial house. If Kuroita joined in writing this report, it means that by 1937 he had completely abandoned scholarship on the point in favour of political thought. However, we do not know how much he participated in the work. He was appointed as a member of the committee in June 1936 but did not attend the general meeting on 7 July. On 11 November, he suffered a serious stroke while on scholarly business in Takasaki, Gunma Prefecture. He was sixty-two. He could not be removed to Tokyo until 20 December, when he was taken back to hospital and then home to recuperate. Kuroita recovered movement in his arm and leg, but speech impairment persisted.[46] Thus, it was generally understood at Tokyo Imperial University that Kuroita's role in *Kokutai no Hongi* was nominal.[47] It can be speculated that his position was represented on the committee by his adopted son Kuroita Masao, who worked at the Ministry of Education and who later served as one of four secretaries on the 1940 Commission of Inquiry into Historical Sites Related to Emperor Jinmu. However, Kuroita Masao left no records, and the Kuroita family can provide no information on the subject.[48]

Apparently Kuroita Katsumi recovered significantly from the stroke, and he retained his membership on numerous historical boards and committees, not resigning from them until 1940-3. He never repudiated his formal part in *Kokutai no Hongi*. That work did not permit minority opinions, whereby a committee member might affirm the political philosophy of the book but express reservations about the myths on which it was based. By participating Kuroita publicly signified his acceptance of the historical truth of the myths.

Kuroita was subject, like every intellectual of the time, to the powerful forces of the 1930s that demanded conformity to imperial values. In 1935 he was criticized in *Genri Nippon*, along with Tsuji Zennosuke, Nakamura Naokatsu, and Kōda Shigetomo, for allegedly thoughtless praise of Hōjō Yasutoki in his *Kokushi no Kenkyū*.[49] Moreover, his works were censored in 1941, when *Kokushi no Kenkyū* (1931) was deemed a disturbance of the public peace [*annei*].[50] We have seen that it presented the most rational and balanced treatment of the national myths in prewar Japan. In 1941 this was unacceptable to the government. The more radical Tsuda Sōkichi, whose position Kuroita could not support, was not only censored but also prosecuted in 1941. The censor also found that volume 5 of Kuroita's collected works, *Kyoshin Bunshū* (1941), endangered public peace. The reasons are obscure, since volume 5 was a technical work for professional scholars, unlikely to disturb the public peace because it was unlikely to be read. It contained the following chapters: 'General Essay on the Study of Ancient Documents,' 'On the Names and Titles of Officials in the Taihō Code of 701,' 'Culture in the Kyoto-Osaka Area as Seen in the Distribution of Ancient Documents,' and 'On the Ancient Documents Related to Military Offices.' Kuroita, a nationalist and whole-hearted supporter of the imperial ideology, seems an unlikely target for censorship. But as the Minobe incident showed in 1935, when an honoured professor who had lectured before the emperor was driven from the House of Peers and wounded in an attempted assassination, neither the imperial state nor nationalist fanatics were respecters of persons in these matters.

There is no record of Kuroita's response to this rebuke by the government. However, it certainly was not the cause of his nationalist position. By 1941 one of Japan's greatest historians of the 1920s and 1930s had already come voluntarily to affirm the myths as historically true because of their political importance.

This seems to have been his final position. One of his last scholarly tasks was supervising a chapter on the Age of the Gods for a 1940 book prepared by Kagoshima Prefecture. Like many prefectures, Kagoshima wanted to prove its claims for recognition of historical sites associated with Emperor Jinmu, which were under consideration by the high-powered Commission of Inquiry into Historical Sites Related to Emperor Jinmu. The prefecture obtained the services of Kuroita, Naganuma Kenkai (1883-1980) of Kyushu Imperial University, and other historians. The opening chapter on the Age of the Gods termed the materials myths [*shinwa*] and noted confusions in their accounts. It then went on to treat them as history in order to establish a convincing link between the Sun Goddess and Emperor Jinmu in Kagoshima.[51]

Kuroita's complete subscription to the political values of imperial Japan, and eventually to the historical truth of the myths, did not interfere with his scientific study of neutral topics. For example, he was a leader in archeology of the historic period. In his 1934-41 study of the Fujiwara palace site, he pioneered in tracing 'the structures from underground foundations even in the absence of surface features.'[52]

Kuroita Katsumi died on 21 December 1946, at the age of seventy-three. He did not have to face the repudiation of his nationalist values in the postwar era. The only biography of Kuroita, a brief essay by Matsushima Ei'ichi, says that he did not have the narrow, mean nationalism of his successor in the Tokyo Imperial University history department, Hiraizumi Kiyoshi. The essay praises Kuroita's openness, energy, scientific method, and scholarly achievements.[53]

Tsuji Zennosuke (1877-1955): Anguished Convert to Nationalism
Everyone liked and admired Tsuji Zennosuke. He was a protégé of Mikami Sanji, since both were natives of Himeji in Hyōgo Prefecture, and he surpassed both Mikami and Kuroita in quantity and quality of scholarly production. Like them he laboured faithfully at the Historiographical Institute, in his case for thirty-six years. He was renowned as head of the institute for invigorating the *Dai Nihon Shiryō* and *Dai Nihon Komonjo* projects. The days were over when scholars refrained from writing their own works, according to the 1895 rules for the Historiographical Institute. Tsuji found time of his own to write about twenty-three books; two multivolume studies, *Nihon Bukkyō Shi* [History of Japanese Buddhism] and *Nihon Bunka Shi* [History of Japanese Culture]; sixteen critical editions of texts; about 190 scholarly articles; and about sixty-five miscellaneous pieces. His scholarly awards spanned the prewar and postwar periods, apparently making him a scholar above nationalistic considerations. He was given the Imperial Japan Academy Prize for *Nihon Bukkyō Shi* in 1921, the Order of Culture in 1952, and the Asahi Culture Prize in 1954. He became a member of the Imperial Japan Academy in 1932, and in the 1920s and 1930s he was invited to the imperial palace for lectures and ceremonies. A devoted admirer of the imperial house, in 1933 Tsuji participated in the ceremonial bathing of the crown prince, now Emperor Akihito.

Tsuji entered Tokyo Imperial University in 1896 and graduated in 1899 from the history department, winning the emperor's prize of a silver watch, presented by the emperor himself. In 1904 his graduate thesis signalled the theme and method of his life work: 'The History of Japanese Buddhism as Seen from the Aspect of Politics: The Early Tokugawa Period.' As Tsuji noted in his 1953 reminiscences, when he started there were very few histories of Buddhism, and they were all done by members of the sects and bore no relation to the history of society.[54] Tsuji's work was the first to consider the history of the religion as a social phenomenon and to apply the methods of modern scientific history. He was especially skilled in the

Tsuji Zennosuke (1877-1955) dressed for the 1933 ceremonial bathing of the Crown Prince, now Emperor Akihito. Japan's leading cultural historian, Tsuji affirmed the national myths in 1940. (Courtesy of Tsuji Tatsuya, Professor Emeritus, Yokohama City University)

study of documents, which were found in abundance in the old temples of Nara and Kyoto and gave a solid basis to his institutional history. At the same time, his interpretation of the development of thought was sound and imaginative. His *Nihon Bukkyō Shi* remains in print forty years after its completion.

Tsuji entered the Historiographical Institute in 1902 and remained there until 1938, serving as its director from 1920 to 1938. In 1911 he visited Europe and the United States. From 1926 he was a full professor at Tokyo Imperial University, occupying a chair in Japanese history and forming a famous team with Kuroita Katsumi. Tsuji learned his teaching style from his mentor, Mikami Sanji, always bringing documents to the classroom, while Kuroita just lectured. Both Tsuji and Kuroita had the custom of inviting the students to their homes for discussions and guidance in selecting thesis topics, and it became known that Tsuji was generous with alcohol, so that inexperienced students were forewarned.

Tsuji's main concerns were with periods undoubtedly historical, so he wrote little on the Age of the Gods and Emperor Jinmu. However, his *Nihon Bunka Shi* began at the beginning, so he had to make up his mind about them. Volume 1 of *Nihon Bunka Shi*, published in 1950, reveals an enlightened position.[55] Chapter 1, 'The Special Features of Japanese Culture,' reflects a highly original approach, starting with discussion of essential arts of civilization such as printing and proceeding to painting, music, architecture, and astronomy. Next came one of his major themes, the adoption and adaptation by Japanese society of elements of foreign cultures such as Confucianism and Buddhism. These, he held, were Japanized but were also preserved in their original form in Japan, and 'Thus the view exists that the essence of Eastern culture is contained in Japan alone. In reality Japan can be called the museum of Eastern culture.'[56]

Chapter 2, 'The Core of Japanese Culture,' covers the racial origins of the Japanese, discussing the Ainu, the Yamato people, and the Izumo people, using theories of regional development, architecture, and language. The myths of *Kojiki* and *Nihon Shoki* are explained as the beliefs of the Yamato people, who took the Sun Goddess as their founder, and the Izumo people, who held Ōkuninushi as their founder. Tsuji divides them into the Takamagahara myths and the Izumo myths. There is no suggestion that they have any relevance to the modern Japanese state. The Emperor Jinmu myth represents an effort by the Yamato people to recover the central region of the Kinki, including Ise. Chapter 3, 'The Chronology of the Ancient Period,' notes how the chronology based on Emperor Jinmu was constructed by *Nihon Shoki* and reviews the criticisms of chronology through the Tokugawa and Meiji periods, observing that a few problems remain. Such were his views in 1950.

This enlightened position was not the same as his prewar position. As we shall see, in 1940 Tsuji affirmed the historicity of the Age of the Gods and Emperor Jinmu's date of accession as 660 BC. But to what degree did he, like Kuroita Katsumi, voluntarily come to accept the founding myths as historical truth? To what degree was he obliged by nationalist pressures to conform to conventional values? Like Mikami and Kuroita, he believed in the imperial house and the Japanese nation, and like them he received many public honours for his devoted service. This was the necessary cause of his subscription to the beliefs of the 1930s. On the other hand, among the historians of Tokyo Imperial University, Tsuji suffered the most from public criticism and government censorship. Was this sufficient cause for moving to accept the historicity of the myths? Let us review Tsuji's scholarly positions in light of the pressures placed on him.

It was Tsuji's originality and fair-mindedness that first got him into trouble. In 1917 he published an article entitled 'Ashikaga Takauji no Shinkyō ni tsuite' [The Religious Faith of Ashikaga Takauji] that viewed Takauji objectively and not through the lenses of imperial morality, in which he invariably appeared as the worst villain in history. Tsuji discovered a vow that Takauji had made at Kiyomizu Temple in Kyoto in 1336, in which he desired to leave the secular world and give affairs over to his younger brother Ashikaga Tadayoshi (1305-52). Tsuji also reviewed other evidence of Takauji's religious faith: poems indicating religious belief, his relationship with the Zen priest Musō Kokushi (1275-1351), his plan to build pagodas and temples in every province, his establishment of Tenryūji in Kyoto, and his copying of sutras. Tsuji's conclusion was quite modest: 'In my view, Takauji's character, and his fight against the Southern Court, must be viewed in the light of research on his religious faith and various other aspects. In recent times, the judgement on Takauji has been bad, but I would like to see more research on whether he deserves such a degree of rejection and criticism.'[57] This view was reasonable, but it may have been impolitic of Tsuji to rank him among the five or six greatest men of Japanese history, along with Nakatomi no Kamatari, Taira Kiyomori, Minamoto Yoritomo, Oda Nobunaga, Toyotomi Hideyoshi, and Tokugawa Ieyasu, none of whom, he said, equalled Takauji in religious faith.[58]

Tsuji's views on Ashikaga Takauji brought heavy criticism in 1934-5, when nationalist fervour and terrorist activity were coming to their height. The political importance of correct views on Ashikaga Takauji was demonstrated in February 1934 by the Nakajima incident, in which Nakajima Kumakichi (1873-1960) was forced to resign as minister of trade and commerce for publishing an article sympathetic to Ashikaga Takauji. It came about that Nakajima had based his article on Tsuji's 1917 article, and thus the critics turned their attention to Tsuji. In an entry for June 1935 in his personal chronology, Tsuji noted that he had been attacked the previous year by the *Ōsaka Mainichi* newspaper and by Minoda Muneki in a series of articles in the journal *Nippon* [Japan].[59]

The strongest attack came from Saitō Takashi in Minoda's journal *Genri Nippon*. Saitō cut a wide swath, criticizing Nakamura Naokatsu of Kyoto Imperial University, Kuroita Katsumi, and Kōda Shigetomi of Tokyo Commerce University in addition to Tsuji. Kuroita and Kōda had praised Hōjō Yasutoki as well as Ashikaga Takauji. Hōjō Yasutoki had a reputation for fair and honest government and for institutional innovation in the Kamakura Bakufu. However, he had risen to power through the Jōkyū War of 1221, when he led bakufu forces against Retired Emperor Go Toba, defeated the imperial army, and imposed punishments on the losers, including Go Toba and two other retired emperors, who were all exiled. We have seen how the interpretation of this incident troubled medieval writers and confused the authors of *Honchō Tsugan* and *Dai Nihon Shi*. Saitō Takashi took a strong view, stating that it was illogical of the professors to separate the personal qualities of Takauji and Yasutoki from their disloyal political actions. Once again the difficult problem of school textbooks was raised, for Tsuji and Kōda had also written their views in middle-school textbooks. Saitō concluded by saying that the authors should be more mindful of the national spirit, citing three poems by Emperor Meiji that illuminated that spirit. He darkly criticized the home minister and the education minister for leaving the textbook problem unattended and the disloyal professors in their university positions.[60] There is no record of a response by Tsuji or the others.

While these criticisms swirled around Tsuji, other events showed the perilous nature of the times. As noted, the Minobe incident of 1935 brought about Minobe Tatsukichi's resignation from the House of Peers and the only physical attack on a professional scholar that occurred in those threatening times. Minobe was not killed, but he suffered a crippling leg wound. The nationalist trend of thought that resulted from the Minobe incident was clear in the Movement to Clarify the Kokutai, which produced *Kokutai no Hongi* in 1937. Uproar continued with the 26 February 1936 army mutiny, in which 1,500 soldiers led by young officers seized the centre of Tokyo. Their aim was to bring down the constitutional government and establish direct rule by the emperor, conducted by army generals. Tsuji was not involved, but an uncharacteristic note in his papers, which otherwise contain no political items, observes the emperor's intervention to condemn the uprising.[61]

Tsuji began to take cover. There are no documents, but it must have been his decision as head of the Historiographical Institute to suspend the publication of volume 6 of *Dai Nihon Shiryō*. The problem was simply that the series presented documents of the Northern Court as well as the Southern Court, and there was no telling who might be offended and take action. In 1911 the historians had decided to keep going despite possible danger, and the series came out at regular intervals (see table below). After 1937, however, publication was suspended for fifteen years.

Dai Nihon Shiryō, Southern-Northern Courts Period

Volume 6,	part 10	1911
	part 11	1912
	part 12	1913
	part 13	1914
	– – – – –	– – –
	part 25	1931
	part 26	1933
	part 27	1935
	part 28	1937
	part 29	1952

The next indication of Tsuji's fear of criticism was censorship of the works of Shigeno Yasutsugu. The Tokyo Imperial University professors decided to publish the complete works of Shigeno, whom they rightly considered a great founder of modern historiography. Tsuji Zennosuke was the editor, while Ōkubo Toshiaki (b. 1900) and Takeuchi Rizō (1910-80), representing the Historical Association, did the work. To avoid giving offence, they censored passages from two of Shigeno's articles.

First, an article titled 'Kojima Takanori Dan Hoi' [Supplement to a Talk on Kojima Takanori], which appeared in volume 15, number 4, of *Rekishi Chiri* [History and Geography] in 1910. Two references to Emperor Go Daigo as 'prisoner' were deleted. He was in fact held prisoner by his opponents. One reference to Go Daigo as a 'rebel' was deleted. This was a strange case, similar to the 1911 controversy over the Southern and Northern Courts. In the fourteenth century, the doctrine that there could not be two legitimate courts was not common, but in 1911 it was retroactively applied as eternal truth. Similarly, in fourteenth-century usage, any act of opposition against established authority could be described as rebellion, whether committed by an emperor or a commoner, but this was not acceptable in the 1930s.

In the fourteenth century, it was not oxymoronic to speak of an emperor's rebellion. *Taiheiki* referred three times to Emperor Go Daigo's uprising against the Kamakura Bakufu, twice calling it *Kimi no gomuhon* [His Majesty's rebellion] and *Gomuhon no koto* [His Majesty's act of rebellion].[62] Even Retired Emperor Hanazono (r. 1308-18) used the term, referring to Emperor Go Daigo's act as *seishu no muhon* [the rebellion of the wise and virtuous emperor].[63] The usage persisted into the late middle ages, as *Hōjō Kudaiki* [Record of Nine Reigns of the Hōjō Regents] described Emperor Go Daigo's action as *Goinbō* [His Majesty's plot].[64] However, the professors editing Shigeno's works decided that it would be fatal to describe the military actions of an emperor as rebellion.

Second, deletions were made from the following passages in Shigeno's article '*Dai Nihon Shi* no Tokuhitsu ni tsuki Shiken o Nobu' [My View of the Special Features of *Dai Nihon Shi*], published in volume 22, number 3, of *Tokyo Gakushi Kaiin Zasshi* in 1900. The text was restored in the 1989 edition, with the passages that had been deleted in 1938 marked with crosses (†). The deleted passages are italicized in the following. It will be observed that Shigeno by no means supported rebellion and disloyalty, but the editors thought that his mere use of the words *dispute, war, rebel, disloyal*, and so forth would be dangerous.

Page 78
The fourth special feature of *Dai Nihon Shi* is *the war* between the Southern and Northern Courts.

Page 78
Thereafter the two courts *disputed each other's claim* without end.

Page 80
In Chinese history, there is much raucous dispute over terms such as 'legitimate line,' 'illegitimate line,' and 'hegemon,' but it is not thought *necessary*
in Japan. The reason is that the [character not restored – occupant?] of our
imperial throne always belonged to the imperial house, and the succession
to the throne was by command of the retired emperor. It goes without
saying that this should hardly be compared to the *rebels* of China. Even in
the case of Emperor Tenmu, he was the emperor's younger brother and
crown prince, and at the time of succession he was refused enthronement,
and so a short war resulted; to consider this *usurpation* is wrong.

Page 82
The war between the Southern and Northern Courts was originally a struggle between imperial lines, but it ended up as a conflict between the Nitta
and Ashikaga houses and dragged on through sixty long years of ups and
downs. The disturbances spread through the whole country. On examination, it is clear that *they ignored questions of obedience and disobedience and
right relations* [*meibun*] and just fought for territory and the honour of
their family names, which determined the respective sides, until it was
settled. Among the aristocrats was Kitabatake Chikafusa, and among the
warriors was Kusunoki Masashige; they had learning and consciousness of
duty and right relations, but the rest were mostly ignorant, doing no more
than using public causes for private benefit. The wars of 1182-5 were also
no more than battles between two families, the Heike and the Genji, but
later historians distinguished between supporters of the imperial court
and the bakufu, and some of them wrote accounts of rebels, thereby praising the good and condemning the wicked. But in a situation where what
was changed in the morning was restored by evening, and it was never
clear who had resisted and who had remained obedient, how can *such
distinctions clearly* be made? The attempt to do so is a vice of mimicking
Chinese historians.
   To summarize my views: Empress Regent Jingū should be restored to the
imperial reigns; the three wars, between Emperor Kobun and Emperor
Tenmu, in the period 1182-5, and between the Southern and Northern
Courts, are all to be regarded as wars between imperial lines. Furthermore,
our imperial house is now descended from the Northern line and *cannot be
considered* a succession in the Southern line. Reckoning on this basis, the
number of reigns from Emperor Jinmu to the present comes to 124 (122
according to *Dai Nihon Shi*).

Page 84

There is a story in *San'yō Gyōjō* [The Life of Rai San'yō]. Rai San'yō was ill when Inokai Keisho came to call. Keisho was a supporter of the Northern Court and earnestly argued his position. Because Keisho was his senior, San'yō did not oppose him. But after Keisho went home, San'yō let forth in a loud voice until late at night, saying that, if the Northern Court were legitimate, then would people such as Nitta Yoshisada and Kusunoki Masashige have to be considered rebels? Even if one side is held legitimate, it is not possible indiscriminately to call *this one and that one a rebel*. All the worse if both sides are legitimate. The ancient writings used 'enemy' or 'outlaw' for foes and antagonists. These terms should be used for Chinese translations too, and the term 'rebel' should not be misused.

Those who support loyalty to the emperor despise the Hōjō and the Ashikaga, as well as their supporters. As the saying goes, hate the priest, and hate even his neck-stole. The Hōjō and Ashikaga conducted the government, and it lasted for several hundred years. Although they committed many tyrannous acts, their accomplishments were not inconsiderable. It is not fair to discuss only their evils and leave out their accomplishments. That goes even more for their supporters, who acted under orders from the retired emperors, which inadvertently brought problems with the imperial succession, *but they acted in accord with right relations and did not harm the succession at all.* This being the case, why then do writers tend to make choices on the basis of *likes and dislikes*? However excellent their principles, what historians must fear most is bias on the basis of *likes and dislikes.*[65]

In addition to the deletion of passages that might cause offence, Mikami Sanji wrote in an introductory note, 'There are some points in Dr. Shigeno's historical argument with which I do not completely agree.' Ōkubo Toshiaki confesses that he did not know whether this indicated genuine scholarly disagreement or was intended to put distance between Shigeno's views and those of the compilers of his historical collection, for the protection of the compilers.[66]

Ōkubo Toshiaki provides the only explanation of this strange incident, in which the professors of Tokyo Imperial University anticipated criticism of their revered predecessor and censored him themselves.

What I want to mention is Shigeno's handling of the emperor when discussing *taigi meibun* in *Dai Nihon Shi's* criticism of the Southern-Northern Courts. It was the period of the 1935 political problem of the emperor-as-organ theory of Minobe Tatsukichi, and the eve of the Tsuda Sōkichi incident, so there was fear about reprinting Shigeno's articles and talks as they stood. If something should happen, it would cause terrible trouble for the Historical Society, Professor Mikami, and Professor Tsuji. So I sought

Professor Tsuji's private views and put in empty spaces for the words at the dangerous places. Entire deletion was unacceptable in a scholarly work, and besides the reader could look up the empty spaces in the original works and understand them. That was a common device at the time in left-wing publications and works injurious to public morals. Nowadays this is unimaginable, but that is just how it was in 1938.[67]

Censorship and criticism continued to fall upon the beleaguered Tsuji despite his obvious position as a wholehearted supporter of imperial Japan. In March 1941, he was asked by the Ministry of Education voluntarily to withdraw *Jinbutsu Ronsō*, a collection of biographies published in 1925. Since the alternative was banning of the work, Tsuji complied. His son, Tsuji Tatsuya, writes that Tsuji understood from telephone discussions that the problem was his discussion of Taira Kiyomori (1118-81), which was critical of the emperor of the time. However, the Ministry of Education later explained that the problem was the chronology of the empire, which Tsuji discussed in an essay on Prince Shōtoku (574-622). During Shōtoku's regency, the ancient dates were determined, according to the long scholarly discussion since Naka Michiyo. In 1941 the Ministry of Education did not want further discussion of the arbitrary nature of the dating of the empire, of which the 2,600th anniversary had been celebrated in 1940.[68] If so, then it was too little, too late, for the Ministry of Education. It had no hope of wiping out all the scholarly discussion of the date of the empire over the preceding fifty years, and there was no point in picking on Tsuji Zennosuke. However, by 1941 the wartime government was censoring everything, whether or not it made sense to do so.

Next, in 1943, Tsuji was requested by the Ministry of Education voluntarily to withdraw *Nihon Bukkyō Shi no Kenkyū* [Studies in the History of Buddhism] because it contained the notorious article on 'The Religious Faith of Ashikaga Takauji.'[69] Finally Tsuji's personal chronology notes that in November 1943 he was once again attacked in *Teikoku Shinpō* [Imperial News] by members of the Minoda Muneki group for the article on Ashikaga Takauji.[70]

Thus, Tsuji Zennosuke was the object of consistent and vehement criticism and censorship in the 1930s and 1940s. This was the sufficient cause of his accommodating attitude toward authorities, public opinion, and public affirmation in 1940 of the historicity of the founding myths. In those times, it was not only frustrating but also dangerous to be the object of public criticism. Tsuji had noted during the 1911 Southern-Northern Courts controversy that the scholars at the Historiographical Institute were afraid; this fear was multiplied many times during the 1930s and 1940s. It is the view of his son that scholars in the 1930s had less freedom of expression than in the days of Arai Hakuseki.[71]

Despite his fears, Tsuji Zennosuke was perceived as an oasis of sanity by those students of the time who felt oppressed by the fierce and insistent nationalism of Professor Hiraizumi Kiyoshi, who dominated the history department after 1935.[72] They used to gather for refuge and study in a room in the Historiographical Institute, 100 yards away from the history department.[73]

We have seen that the continuous criticism of Tsuji was a sufficient cause of his positive support of the imperial state and its enterprises, based on the historicity of the founding myths. There are three examples of this support.

First, we find the following in his personal chronology: '11 August 1939. Appointed part-time member of committee to edit foreign-language version of *Kokutai no Hongi*.'[74] As discussed, *Kokutai no Hongi* was a shameless piece of government propaganda despite being compiled by Japan's leading scholars. No professional historian could honestly have endorsed the view of history contained therein without betraying professionalism for nationalism. Was Tsuji somehow coerced into joining the committee? There is no further information; in fact, there is no evidence that a foreign-language version of *Kokutai no Hongi* was ever done.

Second, Tsuji joined the other leading historians in writing *Nihon Bunka Taikan* [Survey of Japanese Culture], a Ministry of Education project started in 1938 to celebrate the 2,600th anniversary of the empire in 1940. Because of the war, only one volume was published, in 1942. Tsuji's part in the enterprise is not clear, but his papers contain a great deal of material about the project, on which the analysis of Miyachi Masato is based. Miyachi concludes that the work did not approach the scholarly standards achieved by contemporary works such as Endō Motoo's *Nihon Bunka Shi Sōron* [Outline of the Cultural History of Japan, 1939]. That work 'was based on the results of archeology and discussed ancient culture as that of a classless society, explained early religion as animism and totemism, and trained a steady view on the arts and the role of women. In comparison, *Nihon Bunka Taikan* in its overall structure is, in my view, plainly nothing but a government publication on culture and cultural history by the fascist state organized under the emperor system.'[75]

Third, Tsuji was a member of the Ministry of Education Commission of Inquiry into Historical Sites Related to Emperor Jinmu, discussed in the next chapter. All of Japan's most eminent historians were invited to join this commission. In considering the invitation, they had three choices.

(1) They could have declined on the ground of professional difference of views. That is, by 1940 all the professional historians believed that Emperor Jinmu's reign was inaugurated not in 660 BC but around 40 BC. None of the professional historians stood up to say this, and they all joined the commission.

(2) They could join the commission and hold their tongues despite awareness of the significance of their participation. After all, Emperor Jinmu's name means 'Divine Warrior,' and nationalists were not slow to connect his conquering exploits to the current war in China. Minister of Education Kawarada Kakichi (1886-1955) made sure that the historians could not mistake this significance by sending a letter to the members on 8 November 1939.

> At present our country is striving to establish the eternal peace of East Asia and accomplish the great work of unification in order to contribute to the welfare of the peoples of the world. The people of Japan are united under the august imperial authority to reap magnificent results from the war, and now after three years of war, the emperor's beloved people join hands in an effort to realize peace, and so we now see progress toward the establishment of the new order in East Asia. This autumn we are preparing to welcome next year's 2,600th anniversary of our flourishing empire, and by clarifying the historical sites related to Emperor Jinmu, we declare our admiration for his great achievement. For our country, this will deepen the overwhelming significance of our celebrations.
>
> It is my earnest desire that the members of the commission fully bear in mind the great significance for every Japanese of this work of commemoration and strive together toward the goal.
>
> These are my greetings to you during war.[76]

Most of the members took this choice of joining the commission and saying nothing about its meaning, which they all understood.

(3) The historians could join with enthusiasm. Hiraizumi Kiyoshi did, and apparently so did Tsuji Zennosuke.

Tsuji's enthusiasm is suggested by the fact that he not only joined the commission but also published an article in 1940, 'The Significance of the 2,600th Anniversary of the Empire.' The views about cultural history are consistent with his writings elsewhere and thus are unmistakeably his own. The article opens:

> The long-awaited 2,600th year has come at last. The people of the nation all celebrate it together and pray for the prosperity of the country and the eternal glory of the imperial throne. Let us explain a little of its significance and why we celebrate this 2,600th year.
>
> We observe the 2,600th anniversary of our eternally unchanging national essence. It is the celebration of the founding of our system, which is unparalleled in the world. The Heavenly Grandchild descended to begin the imperial line, and after three generations at Hyūga, Emperor Jinmu set

out upon the eastern expedition and pacified Yamato in the end. He ascended the throne at Kashihara, and there he firmly laid the foundation to realize the vow of the Sun Goddess that the imperial line would be coeval with Heaven and Earth.[77]

Thus, Tsuji affirmed without qualification the imperial founding myth of the Age of the Gods and Emperor Jinmu.

In the body of the article, he developed a favourite theme that foreigners had come to Japan and contributed much to its culture. They were the naturalized immigrants [*kikajin*] who came from China and Korea in ancient times, adopting Japanese names and culture and eventually becoming Japanese. The culture that they brought became Japanese [*Nihon-teki*], but at the same time Japan performed for Asia the valuable function of retaining some culture in its original form. Tsuji's main example is an imperial poetry collection of the Tang dynasty, *Bunkan Shirin* (*Wenguan cilin*), which was lost in China itself but preserved in Japan since the early ninth century. As we have seen, Tsuji repeated this view of Japan as a museum culture in his postwar work *Nihon Bunka Shi* (1950), purging it of military significance.

In 1940 this view of the ecumenical nature of Japanese civilization led to a startling conclusion, in which Tsuji arrived at the same military significance that was stated by Minister of Education Kawarada Kakichi:

> During 2,600 years, many foreign peoples have been fused with the Japanese, and all manner of foreign civilizations have been assimilated, and much ancient culture has been accumulated thanks to our national essence. At the present time, the imperial Japanese army is advancing on the field in the north, centre, and south of China, and the war has become protracted. We are now at the great dividing line of our history. That we welcome the 2,600th anniversary at this point bears a great significance. It is most apposite that 2,600 years in our past Emperor Jinmu carried out the great intention of the Sun Goddess by coming from distant Kyushu to pacify Yamato. In the same way, the people of China will now be fused into our brilliant national essence and bathe in the blessings of our emperor. I believe that this will establish the eternal peace of East Asia and contribute to world culture.[78]

Since this 1940 essay is inconsistent with the peaceable image of Tsuji that is generally held, one searches for evidence that he was compelled to write it. There is none. The evidence is to the contrary. The Tsuji Zennosuke papers contain a draft of the article, consisting of a fair copy in someone else's hand, with amendments in Tsuji's hand. The substance is the same as the 1940 article, except that the opening sentence of the 1940 article was updated from 'We look forward to and prepare for the anniversary of the empire' to 'The long-awaited anniversary has come.'[79] Since the date of this draft is 11 February 1938, it is likely that Tsuji wrote the article sometime in 1937, and thus he had much time to think about it. Since he could have refrained from writing on the subject, probably he meant it.

The last example of Tsuji's support for imperial projects came on 6 December 1941. He became a member of the Commission of Inquiry into Historical Sites Related to the Founding of the Nation [Chōkoku Seiseki Chōsa Iinkai].[80] This referred to the creation of the islands and the founding of the nation by the gods in *Kojiki* and *Nihon Shoki*. In the case of Emperor Jinmu, to study the historical sites meant acceptance of the traditional founding date of 660 BC. To study the historical sites related to the founding of the nation would signify unqualified acceptance of the myths of the Age of the Gods as historical fact. There is no further information about this commission beyond the fact that Sakamoto Tarō was also appointed.[81] Everybody has forgotten about it. It must have been sponsored by the Ministry of Education, but it seems that no work was done because of the exigencies of war or because the exercise was inherently preposterous. Since this commission has been entirely forgotten, it must be discounted in the evaluation of Tsuji Zennosuke.

In light of his membership on the committee to translate *Kokutai no Hongi,* his work on *Nihon Bunka Taikan,* his participation in the Commission of Inquiry into Historical Sites Related to Emperor Jinmu, and his 1940 article on the significance of the 2,600th anniversary of the empire, it is difficult to avoid the conclusion that Tsuji had come to believe without reservation in the nationalist values of prewar Japan. Therefore, he accepted the historical truth of the myths of the Age of the Gods and Emperor Jinmu.

Finally we must consider the possibility that Tsuji's unqualified acceptance of the national myths in 1940 was based on a separation of historical fact from political truth in the manner of Mikami Sanji and Kuroita Katsumi. In their cases, however, the separation of historical fact from the political truth of the myths was developed over thirty years and became the foundation of their way of thinking. Mikami maintained the separation in a clear-minded fashion to the end of his life. Kuroita, however, gradually lost track of the separation, and by the mid-1930s he affirmed without any distinctions both the political truth and the historical reality of the myths.

In Tsuji's case, the acceptance of the historical truth of the myths by 1938 was anomalous. A devoted servant of the imperial house and a Japanese nationalist, he had nevertheless refrained from political writing throughout his scholarly career. Because his field of study was later cultural history, he had not addressed the question of the founding myths and their relation to political values, in the manner of Mikami and Kuroita. Instead, throughout his career he addressed questions of cultural history in an elegant and rational style. In 1937 he was finally moved to draft a political article on the significance of the 2,600th anniversary of the founding of the empire. Perhaps the times were too far advanced into uncritical nationalism, and he was too battered by criticism, to offer distinctions between historical fact and political truth. This is the most charitable interpretation.

Tsuji was pounded by criticism and fearful of it. Even so, in 1940 his use of the founding myths of Japan to justify the war against China was not worthy of a great professional historian.

Hiraizumi Kiyoshi (1895-1984): Passionate Nationalist

Hiraizumi Kiyoshi was the foremost exponent of *Kōkoku goji shikan*, the view of Japanese history centred on preservation of the imperial nation.[82] He was brilliant, but he placed the religious and political values of his country before objectivity and the rationalist scholarly method. He used his position as a professor of history at Tokyo Imperial University to spread national values and invigorate the nation, not to seek the truth about history. Hiraizumi thought that he already knew the truth. Such attitudes may be appropriate in a private university dedicated to the study and promotion of a religion, of which there are many examples, but it is questionable whether they belonged in a secular university such as Tokyo Imperial University. However, precisely because of his strong beliefs and methods, Hiraizumi raised up a generation of devoted disciples working for the greatness of Japan. As the first disciples now depart from the scene, they in turn have brought on a new generation, who think of Hiraizumi as a great leader.

Hiraizumi Kiyoshi was born in Heisenji-chō, Katsuyama City, Fukui Prefecture, as the son of the head priest at Hakusan Shrine. This shrine was founded in 717 during the reign of Empress Genshō (r. 715-24) by the Buddhist priest Taichō (ca. 681-767). Its principal deity is Izanami no Mikoto, one of the main founding deities of Japan according to the myths of the Age of the Gods. Thus, Hiraizumi was disposed by birth and education to unquestioning acceptance of the myths. As a scholar, he did not write about the history of the Age of the Gods, but it formed the basis of his thought about the Japanese nation. Hakusan Shrine also contains the grave of Kusunoki Masashige (?-1336), the most famous hero of the fourteenth-century Southern Court and the very model of the values of *Bushidō*, the Way of the Warrior.[83] Kusunoki Masashige is renowned for his loyalty to Emperor Go Daigo, his lofty willingness to die for the nation, and his death by suicide [*hara-kiri*] after defeat in a brave but hopeless battle at the Minato River in 1336. This devotion may have influenced Hiraizumi to make the Kenmu Restoration of Emperor Go Daigo his scholarly specialty. In the 1930s and 1940s, he also urged the example of the selfless fourteenth-century restoration heroes on his students, the army, and the nation at large.

At Hiraizumi's funeral in 1984, his follower Nagoshi Tokimasa said in a eulogy that Hiraizumi was deeply shocked by the Great Treason Incident of

Hiraizumi Kiyoshi (1895-1984), a vigorous nationalist, as Assistant Professor at Tokyo Imperial University in the early 1930s. (Courtesy of Mrs Hiraizumi Akira)

1910, in which a plot to assassinate the Meiji emperor was discovered. Thereupon Hiraizumi 'raised a great ambition to protect the national essence of the imperial nation.'[84] His teachers at Tokyo Imperial University, from which Hiraizumi graduated in 1918, might have been aware that this bright young man had unusually strong patriotic feelings. Mikami Sanji, Kuroita Katsumi, and Tsuji Zennosuke evaluated his graduation thesis, 'Shinto Shrines and Society in the Middle Ages,' finding it original and sufficiently scholarly. However, six pages of their twenty-page report are crossed out; they seem to contain reservations or criticisms, which the three professors then decided not to leave on the record.[85] They accepted him into the profession and later promoted him to assistant professor in 1926 and full professor in 1935. If they came to regret his ubiquitous and combative presence in the 1930s, which is not certain, then it was their own fault.

Hiraizumi's best scholarly work was the book that resulted in 1926 from his thesis, *Chūsei ni okeru Shaji to Shakai to no Kankei* [Medieval Shrines and Temples and Their Relation to Society]. It was highly original, taking up the

Shinto shrines and Buddhist temples in several aspects: organization, economy, learning, and education. In the preface, he noted that most scholarly works on the middle ages dealt with the warriors; his was the first to take society itself as the starting point and to detail the involvement of shrines and temples in every aspect of the life of the people. It was also distinguished by references to the Middle Ages in Europe, especially to document the idea and institutions of asylum. Thus, Chapter 3, on the social organization of the shrines and temples, is peppered with the names of contemporary foreign scholars – Zech, Helfrecht, Wallon, Leist, Viollet, Westermarck – and the titles of their works, all given in original roman type, not *katakana*. This westernization must have dismayed some Japanese readers, but it signalled one of Hiraizumi's great scholarly assets, his extraordinary fluency in Western languages. The conclusion was sound: after the middle ages, the shrines and temples declined in importance, becoming inward looking and defensive, while the great unifying military force of Oda Nobunaga (1534-82) held sway, and Confucianism replaced the old religions as the source of learning and education.

The only peculiarity of the work was the rejection of the Western calendar for dates; Japanese-era names were used throughout. On page 1, Hiraizumi gave the starting and ending dates of his study according to the chronology of the Japanese empire starting at Emperor Jinmu. His study started in Hōgen 1 (1156 AD) during the reign of Emperor Go Shirakawa, which converted to the year 1816 since Emperor Jinmu, and ended on Tenshō 1 (1573 AD) in the reign of Emperor Ōgimachi, which converted to 2233.[86] In 1926 AD, this dating system was already eccentric though still intelligible. It signalled a strong nationalist stance.

Hiraizumi wrote a number of scholarly articles, but by 1925 he was already showing impatience with the methods of scientific history at Tokyo Imperial University. He summed up his discontent at the conclusion of a May 1925 article, 'Fact and Truth in History,' which was reminiscent of the anonymous 1902 article that called the Tokyo Imperial University professors of 'history' (shi 史) professors of 'death' (*shi* 死):

> The scholarly style since Meiji has been mainly to work at searching out the facts. This is called scientific research. The research method is analytical. Analysis is autopsy. Autopsies are for the dead. The opposite, searching for truth, is unifying. Unifying is life. But it is not science; rather, it is art, and taken to its end, it is faith. In truth history has many aspects. It goes without saying that a cool scientific attitude and meticulous research are necessary. But if history is analyzed by that alone, it dies. What makes history live, and continue, is the mysterious spiritual power of living people who believe in it. By this spiritual power, fact becomes truth. Such truth is what

the historian must search for. Thus, the historian will become the priest for the past, present, and future and will assist in the development of Heaven and Earth.[87]

Faith in history, he pointed out, is shared by everyone. Throughout his career, he used homely examples, and to illustrate this point he reminded readers that they could not prove the fundamental truths about their own existence. There is only the word of one's parents that they are indeed one's parents. The family register [*koseki*] that documents every Japanese person could be mistaken or forged.

As a teacher at Tokyo Imperial University, Hiraizumi used the same example to discomfit students who expressed scepticism about the Age of the Gods. Asking leading questions, he would show them that they accepted the facts about their own existence on faith in the words of their parents and family registers. Then, he would say, at the bottom of knowledge and action lies faith. The same applies to the founding of the country. When we come to accept the books that tell the history of the Age of the Gods, we become Japanese.[88] We do not know how many students he convinced, but there were indeed some.

In his dissatisfaction with scientific history, Hiraizumi turned for answers to Europe, ironically the source of Japan's scientific history at the time of Ludwig Riess. A November 1925 article entitled 'My View of History' [*Waga Rekishikan*] placed the discussion of historical method entirely in European terms. The names of Voltaire, Montesquieu, Hegel, Marx and Engels, Thomas Carlyle, August Comte, Karl Lamprecht, and so on all appear, but not the name of a single Japanese historian or work of history. No Japanese historian of his time was as well versed in European history. The ground that he covered in the article was already well trodden – history is different in purpose and methods from the social sciences, seeking not general laws and universal explanations but knowledge of concrete facts conveyed in discrete narratives. He concluded, 'I do not stand outside of history but live within it. I do not possess history but actually make it. Formerly human character was sought in the object of history. Now it is sought in the subject of history. In this movement toward introspection is found the special characteristic of the contemporary view of history.'[89]

In 1925 Hiraizumi did not yet know how to fill up history with subjective material. He found out during his visit to Europe from March 1930 to July 1931 that the Japanese imperial nation was the answer to every question. Everyone at Tokyo Imperial University noticed that he went to Europe as a dissatisfied young assistant professor and came back as a pure and ebullient Japanese nationalist [*kokusui shugisha*], eager to spread his views. He visited Germany, Austria, Italy, France, and England and returned by way of the

United States. He went to the usual historic sites and monuments and called on scholars. The most influential scholar was the Italian philosopher Benedetto Croce (1866-1952).

Croce's ideas, ranging over aesthetics, religion, and history, are now hard to classify, leading recently to terms such as 'mundane idealism' and 'radical immanence,' which themselves require explanation.[90] However, an earlier formulation by H. Wildon Carr in 1917 used vague and idealistic language that suggests why Croce's views were attractive to the searching Hiraizumi. Carr wrote of Croce's historical ideas, 'History is the form in which full reality is presented to consciousness. History is not the story of life but the story immanent in the fact that life is an unfolding and expression. History presents to us life or mind in its reality, and, therefore, history and philosophy are in their essence identical.'[91] Writing like this has now almost disappeared, but such discussions encouraged Hiraizumi, who sought spiritual meaning in history. He went to Croce's house in Naples on 29 October 1930, just showing up without an introduction. Croce welcomed him for the next two days, during which they discussed the unity of history and philosophy and their common rejection of Marxist materialism.[92]

In Germany Hiraizumi took lectures from Hellmann at Leipzig University and Friedrich Meinecke (1862-1954) at Berlin. Both were in the tradition of Ranke, and Meinecke was then Germany's most eminent historian and the editor of *Historische Zeitschrifte*. While in Germany, Hiraizumi was not impressed by the Nazi party, which he discounted as a regional party in the fragmented German parliament.[93]

During his European visit, Hiraizumi kept a handwritten journal of his ideas and research separate from his private diary; the latter has not been published. The first page of his journal records his conclusion that race is the most important matter, but race does not dominate the journal. There are some observations on the remarkable staying power of the Jews, who survived for centuries without a country, and a hint that Karl Marx's Jewish origin may have been a factor in his evil theories.[94] On the whole, however, Hiraizumi did not need any confirmation from Europe about the importance of race. To the end of his life in 1984, he remained both ignorant and defiant of biology and evolution and believed that the Japanese constitute a separate race, which was for him the basis of their community.

What puzzled him greatly was the French Revolution based on liberty, equality, and fraternity. He could not understand fraternity without a racial basis and devoted more than a third of his journal to investigation and thought on the matter, finally concluding that the three concepts had different origins: liberty in 1789, equality in 1792, and fraternity in 1793.[95] In any case, Hiraizumi correctly understood that the French Revolution was the turning point in modern history, on which everyone must take a stand. It is not surprising that Hiraizumi, with his communitarian instincts and reverence for the Japanese imperial house, ended up vehemently opposed to the French Revolution.

In Germany Hiraizumi found ideas more congenial and closer to his profession as a historian. He learned more about the nationalist historians Fichte, Ranke, and Treitschke, and on 5 September 1930 he visited a Dr. Reimann, who had compiled a history textbook for youngsters. He was especially impressed by the ending, addressed to all the youth of Germany: 'Believe in the revival of the German race! ... The fate of Germany rests on your shoulders. The responsibility is yours!'[96] Returning to Japan, Hiraizumi took as his own responsibility the inspiration and invigoration of Japan's youth to undertake a great national mission. He realized that he was perfectly situated for the task as a professor at Japan's leading university, and he thought that the task was urgent.

Because of the deteriorating world situation, Hiraizumi cut short his planned two-year trip and went home, by way of the United States, to urge Japan to prepare for trouble. In 1982, in the last speech of his life, Hiraizumi recalled:

> The world was just at the point of heading for great disturbances. And while it was falling into those disturbances, Japan alone did not know it. In Japan in the Taishō-Shōwa period, society was drifting in genial obliviousness, in the midst of worldism, pacificism, democracy, internationalism, and epicureanism, while the rest of the world was glaring fiercely at each other. If it did not get organized as a nation to meet the oncoming disturbances, Japan would be defeated without a fight.[97]

Back at Tokyo Imperial University in the 1930s, Hiraizumi became the nationalist force within that was the counterpart to the nationalist forces without. As we have seen, the other professors were cowed by the combination. Hiraizumi filled the space created by the passing of the old guard. Mikami Sanji had retired; Kuroita Katsumi retired in 1935; Tsuji Zennosuke was fully involved in matters of the Historiographical Institute and becoming distracted besides; and Sakamoto Tarō, who later gave the impression of having been critical of Hiraizumi, was his junior.

Urging the necessity of a university response to the Movement to Clarify the National Essence that arose after the Minobe Tatsukichi incident in 1935, Hiraizumi pressed for the creation of a chair [*kōza*] in Shinto. He proposed this at a faculty meeting on 6 May 1936. It eventually proceeded, with Miyaji Naokazu (1886-1949), a rationalist scholar, as the first occupant. The proposed curriculum, to which Miyaji probably did not adhere, was a survey of Japanese thought, the development of *kokutai* consciousness, *Jinnō Shōtōki*, Mitogaku, and the Tokugawa-period philosophers Yamaga Sokō and Yamazaki Ansai.

Another proposal by Hiraizumi for a chair in Studies of the National Essence [*kokutaigaku*] foundered on opposition and ended up as a chair in History of Japanese Thought [*shisōshi*], with Hiraizumi as the first occupant. The Tokyo Imperial University history professors, who proceeded on the basis of documents, did not think that History of Japanese Thought was a valid subject, but they lost out in the discussions. The proposed curriculum for the new chair in Japanese thought, to which Hiraizumi did not adhere, was clarification of ancient thought, the development of Confucianism, and the development of Bushidō, the Way of the Warrior.[98]

Thus, Hiraizumi had his way, and as the senior professor in the Department of Japanese History after 1935, he conducted what some remember as an ideological reign of terror. Treating national history as a sacred subject, he instituted a custom of removing shoes and wearing slippers in the building. He would not address students as *kun* in the common manner because the character for *kun* was the same as *kimi*, which was reserved for the emperor. In matters of thought, he insisted on uniformity. The works of Tsuda Sōkichi of Waseda University, who was sceptical about the Age of the Gods and the early emperors, were not kept in the department, and students were forbidden to read them.[99] Hiraizumi further controlled the students' thoughts with the threat of failure or refusal to recommend them for positions, though usually he did not carry out the threat.[100]

Students who did not share his views learned to avoid him, gathering for companionship and study in a room at the Historiographical Institute. One who avoided him was Inoue Mitsusada (1917-83), a leading postwar historian of ancient times, who graduated in 1942 with a thesis on Nara Buddhism under Sakamoto Tarō. The thesis was written from the viewpoint of intellectual history, and Inoue intended to continue in intellectual history as a graduate student, extending his studies to the middle ages and modern times. However, Hiraizumi was the teacher on the middle ages, and Inoue could not bear the thought. He went instead to Watsuji Tetsurō, whose field was not even history but ethics.[101]

Ienaga Saburō, who entered the Department of Japanese History in 1934, has strong memories of the time. The history students were taken on field trips, the first-year students to Mito, the home of imperial loyalism, and the second-year students to Nara and Kyoto, rich in monuments and records of ancient history. According to Ienaga, Hiraizumi was cranky and domineering on the December 1935 trip to Nara and Kyoto. They stopped to visit Ise Shrine, which worships the Sun Goddess. When they entered the shrine, Ienaga found to his astonishment that Hiraizumi prostrated himself fully on the ground. Standing right beside Hiraizumi, Ienaga had no choice but to do the same.[102] When they returned to Tokyo, Ienaga had the job of writing up the account of the trip, which duly appeared in *Shigaku Zasshi*. He wanted to make some remarks about placing Japanese history in a wider context and not viewing it as a singular product of Japan without outside influences. To provide protective covering for these remarks, Ienaga dressed up his account of the Kansai trip in phrases acceptable to contemporary enthusiasts of *Kōkoku shikan*. They included the editor of *Shigaku Zasshi* in charge of his report, Hiraizumi's disciple Hirata Toshiharu (b. 1911). Not deceived, Hirata deleted Ienaga's heartfelt remarks on wider history and left in the protective covering in the account of the Kansai trip, making Ienaga look like a supporter of *Kōkoku shikan*.[103]

> *On Ise Shrine*: The simple bark of this pure wood construction, and the splendid ornamental crossed rafters of the Plain of High Heaven, have been handed down unchanged from the Age of the Gods in the distant past.

> *On Kashihara Jingū, worshipping Emperor Jinmu*: This peaceful place, with Mount Unebi in the background, is where the Empire of Japan had its origin.

> *On Yoshino, where Emperor Go Daigo dwelled*: It was from here that Emperor Tenmu set out to accomplish his goal and here that Emperor Go Daigo failed, but for all eternity loyal men of fiery spirit cannot fail to be inspired to action. It is the place where the mountain religion of Shugendō began in the distant past, where the priest Saigyō concealed himself in the wind-blown blossoms, where Minamoto Yoshitsune wept at being exiled. All of them have great significance in the political and spiritual history of Japan.[104]

Hiraizumi thought that his job as a teacher was not to impart facts, theories, and methods about Japanese history, and certainly not to encourage independent theories, but to inspire the students to great deeds for Japan. On 16 April 1935, he started his lecture on the middle ages in Japan, to between fifty and sixty students, thus:

> What you young men aspire to will determine the course of your lives. Moreover, it will determine not only the course of your lives but also the future of our nation. What determines the destiny of a country? Is it abundant harvests, the production of goods, the degree of military preparedness, the rate of population growth? Obviously they all have an important bearing on the future of a country. But the most important foundation is the attitude of the youth of a country. If the youth of a country lack patriotism, and are not burning with desire to repay their debt to the land by offering their lives in time of national emergency, then that country is on the road to inevitable decline, no matter what its size, productivity, military preparedness, or population growth.[105]

This was startling enough. But most widely remembered by the students was that the lectures on the Japanese middle ages then proceeded to a long discourse on the French Revolution and the evils thereof. For those who remained in the course, the lectures eventually arrived at the inspiring stories of the Kenmu Restoration, Hiraizumi's specialty.

By 1934 Hiraizumi's scholarship had become completely subordinated to political values. That year was the 600th anniversary of the Kenmu Restoration of Go Daigo, and the next year was the 600th anniversary of the death of its heroic supporter, Kusunoki Masashige. Both were duly celebrated on campus, with Hiraizumi as organizer and host of visiting army generals. He also wrote a short book, *Kenmu Chūkō no Hongi* [The True Meaning of the Kenmu Restoration], outlining his ideas. Like the later Kuroita Katsumi, he defined a few outstanding incidents such as the Kenmu Restoration and the Meiji Restoration as the essence of Japanese history, ignoring the meaning of all the rest. He held that Emperor Go Daigo's aim in the Kenmu Restoration was to restore the essence of imperial Japan, not to accomplish any personal desires. Like Kuroita, Hiraizumi stated that the restoration failed, not because of lack of virtue in Go Daigo, but because the Japanese people failed to understand its true nature and sought after private benefit and gratification. The great ideal of the restoration was to make Japan truly Japan [*Nippon no Nippon taran to suru dairisō*].[106] This seems tautological, but such language was common at the time. It meant that the nation must become completely and exclusively devoted to all the ideals carried by the imperial house, which exhausted the meaning of Japan according to Hiraizumi and all contemporary nationalists. Nothing could be called truly Japanese that was outside imperial values; that included liberalism, individualism, democracy, communism, and other offensive Western values. He summed up:

> Thus, the Kenmu Restoration arose, and thus it was done. Certainly it did not arise from capitalizing on the decline of the Kamakura Bakufu or from the private desires of the imperial house. Nor was it done by people who follow the times or submit to public opinion. They did it under the great ideal of making Japan truly Japan, following the Way of Japan in which the emperor is the emperor and the subjects are subjects, with no fear of strong enemies, not yielding before a hundred obstacles. Such was the aim of the Kenmu Restoration, the restoration of the true imperial country of Japan.[107]

Like the other Tokyo Imperial University professors, Hiraizumi was happy to be invited to the imperial palace to receive honours. He lectured before the emperor and Prince Chichibu and even went to Japan's puppet state of Manchukuo in 1934 to lecture before its ruler. However, he went far beyond the other professors by participating in politics and military affairs.

He consulted at high levels, meeting four or five times with Tōjō Hideki, general of the army and prime minister, 1941-3, and ten times with Konoe Fumimaro, who was thrice prime minister.[108] It is not clear in what capacity he met them, but he regarded himself as a trusted and close confidant. To be sure that he would never mistakenly disclose confidential matters, he abstained from alcohol, which loosens many a tongue. He knew all their secrets, he said.[109] Hiraizumi took those secrets with him when he died.

He was also in touch with the army and navy, hosting generals on campus for ceremonies and speeches and being invited in turn to lecture to officers at their schools, invitations that surprised him:

> At the army college in particular, no one other than a general was supposed to give lectures. I was barely thirty-five, and as you see I am weak and meagre, giving the appearance of a man who could not run a mile carrying a gun without falling down and dying. Even in my dreams, I never thought that I would receive the welcome accorded to a general of the army. What I said was most presumptuous, but I thought that the army was excellent. To save the nation from great disasters, it took extraordinary measures, and so it welcomed me who had no experience as a soldier.[110]

Hiraizumi also encouraged youth at a private school that he set up in Tokyo in 1933, called Seiseijuku [Green Green School], still remembered for its vigour and inspiration. The school was popular and expanded rapidly, with three more branches in Tokyo and branches in Kyoto and Sendai. Each branch only admitted students from the imperial university in the city concerned. The Tokyo academies had only students from Tokyo Imperial University, the Kyoto academy had students from Kyoto Imperial University, and the Sendai academy had students from Tohoku Imperial University. However, the Tokyo branch had one student from Waseda University, a private institution, because he was from Fukui, Hiraizumi's hometown.[111]

Hiraizumi's ideas of the middle 1930s were summed up in an influential book entitled *Bushidō no Fukkatsu* [The Revival of Bushidō, 1934] and then reduced to simple terms in a six-page pamphlet with the same title. The pamphlet started by citing a French journalist, Marc Chadourne, whose work Hiraizumi had noted in Europe: 'L'Asie n'existe plus!' Asia existed no longer because it was dominated spiritually, economically, and politically by the West. Objectively, said Hiraizumi, for Asia to revive, Japan must first revive in order to lead, nourish, and protect Asia. Japan had adopted too much Western materialistic culture; it must recover its own spiritual culture and 'must return to a truly Japan-like Japan' [*Makoto ni Nippon rashiki Nippon ni kaeri*]. The essence of a Japan-like Japan was Bushidō, the Way of the Warrior. The Meiji reforms had destroyed feudalism and the warrior class, but fortunately conscription had followed, so that every able Japanese man could now be a warrior.

> To sum up, in order to set the world on its correct path once again, Asia must first become Asian. In order for Asia to become Asian, Japan must first become Japanese. In order for Japan to become Japanese, it must stop following the meaningless models of foreign civilization and revive the true spirit of Japan [*tadashiki Nippon seishin*]. To do this positively, we must pay no heed to considerations of life or death, gain or loss, and with united hearts we must awaken the spirit of Bushidō that has slumbered so long in our breasts.[112]

Hiraizumi's message that Japan must take military action in Asia was clear, but in public he always stopped short of explicit recommendations, confining himself to general exhortations about military spirit. They were well received. However, he may have recommended more precise measures on policies and military campaigns in his many discussions with colonels, generals, and prime ministers, discussions that are not documented.

Somehow Hiraizumi was involved in the 26 February 1936 army mutiny by young officers, which seemed to be the sort of revivalist military action that he was urging the youth of Japan to take. On 27 February, Prince Chichibu (1902-53), the younger brother of the emperor and known to be sympathetic to the rebels, took a train from Hirosaki in Aomori Prefecture down to Tokyo to take part in the action. The train stopped at Minakami station in Gunma Prefecture, where Hiraizumi got on to consult with the prince, whom he had formerly instructed in history. What transpired is not known, and Prince Chichibu, upon arriving in Tokyo, remained noncommittal throughout the mutiny.[113] It was, of course, severely put down by the government, while Hiraizumi escaped with undiminished reputation as an authentic spokesman for Japan's nationalist positions.

Finally, at the end of the war, he was also involved with young officers who were dismayed by the impending unconditional surrender to the Allied powers. Because the Potsdam Declaration of 26 July 1945 gave no guarantee about the safety of the emperor or the imperial institution, many believed that the national essence would be destroyed. There was talk of a coup d'etat and a guerrilla war against the Occupation forces. General Anami Korechika (1886-1945) led the group opposing surrender, and on 12 August a group of young officers who had been influenced by Hiraizumi came to him for advice. They included Takeshita Masahiko, Iida Shōkō, Tsuchizaki Jirō, and Hatanaka Kenji. However, Hiraizumi, who had inside information that the decision to surrender was made by the emperor himself, said nothing, and they had to go away and make up their own minds what to do, which ended up being nothing.[114]

On our main topic, the myths of the Age of the Gods and Emperor Jinmu, Hiraizumi had little to say. He just believed them, and by becoming such a powerful spokesman for the emperor-centred view of history that was based on the myths, he gave them immeasurable reinforcement. So great was his reputation as a believer that it was long thought that he had drafted *Kokutai no Hongi* (1937), though it had actually been written by Hisamatsu Sen'ichi, a professor of literature at Tokyo Imperial University. It may have been part of his strategy not to discuss the truth of the myths, not going into whether they were allegorical or whether some truth lay beneath them. Such an approach would acknowledge that problems existed, and he would have none of that. Hiraizumi had no doubts about Emperor Jinmu, though he accepted, like all the professors, the scholarly revision of the founding date of the empire to 40 BC. This date caused him no trouble on the 2,600th anniversary of the empire in 1940, and he served happily on the Commission of Inquiry into Historical Sites Related to Emperor Jinmu.

Hiraizumi Kiyoshi knew where he stood. Japan surrendered on 15 August 1945. On 17 August, he attended a faculty meeting, saying nothing. Then he tendered his resignation to the dean of the Faculty of Arts.[115] He went back to Hakusan Shrine in Fukui Prefecture and became the head priest of the shrine for nearly forty years until 1981, when he turned the position over to his son Hiraizumi Akira (d. 1995). He knew that he was a potential war-crimes suspect, but he was never indicted.

To the end of his life, Hiraizumi never changed his ideas in the least. He worked tirelessly to restore the Japanese spirit and to reestablish the traditional history of Japan based on the founding myths, saying that the history of Japan had been distorted by the American Occupation reforms. He lectured endlessly, founded two journals, and wrote a conservative history of Japan for young people in order to counteract the evil effects of the postwar educational system, *The Story of Japan*, vol. 1: *History from the Founding of the Nation to the Height of Fujiwara Prosperity* (Ise: Seisei Kikaku, 1997).

Takeshita Masahiko, one of the conspirators of August 1945, was surprised to hear from Hiraizumi twenty-five years after the war, when Hiraizumi sent a note of condolence on the death of Takeshita's mother. Takeshita, by then a retired general in Japan's Self-Defence Force, had come to respect Japan's postwar democracy, which he saw as inseparably connected with respect for human rights and commitment to peace. Takeshita reflected on his relationship with Hiraizumi and concluded that Hiraizumi was persisting in an untimely conservatism.[116]

Hiraizumi Kiyoshi died in 1984 at the age of ninety. The 100th anniversary of his birth in 1895 was celebrated at Hakusan Shrine by his followers on 24 September 1995.

12
The Commission of Inquiry into Historical Sites Related to Emperor Jinmu, 1940

By 1940 no professional historian thought that Emperor Jinmu had begun his reign in 660 BC. This was plain to see in publications that stretched over fifty years. There was no effect on the thinking of the government or the people at large, who were all taught about 660 BC in the course of their elementary education. Accordingly government and society set about celebrating the 2,600th anniversary of the empire in 1940. A grand ceremony was held at the imperial palace, attended by dignitaries of Japan and representatives of foreign governments. Everyone thought up a project of greater or lesser grandeur, and the government helped with money. There were exhibits everywhere and a popular song contest, with the prize given by the prime minister. The government also commissioned a serious work by the leading German composer, Richard Strauss, which was performed at the imperial palace and broadcast on the radio.[1]

Amateur historians produced volumes about Emperor Jinmu in appallingly large numbers,[2] but more important, professional scholars also joined in the general celebrations. Some were scholars in other fields who were not perhaps fully aware of the views of historians about the accuracy of the date. Even more remarkable, historians at the imperial universities themselves came up with projects.

The scientists in the Imperial Japan Academy decided on *Meiji Izen Nihon Kagaku Shi* [History of Science in Japan before Meiji], covering topics such as mathematics, physics, astronomy, medicine, agriculture, and engineering. This work drew the attention of all to the fact that Japanese scientific accomplishments had been numerous and important before the advent of Western science. The project was approved in 1940 and went on throughout the war, being suspended during the bombing in March 1945. It was resumed after the war and completed in 1948. The first volume was published in 1954 by Iwanami Shoten, and the complete work of fourteen volumes was in print in 1958.[3]

紀元二千六百年
26th Centennial of Japan
(2s. & 10s.) *Feb. 11, 1940*
(4s. & 20s.) *Nov. 10, 1940*

dark orange

deep green

dark blue

dark rose

Stamps from 1940 commemorating the 2,600th anniversary of the Japanese Empire. The owner of this album managed to collect only the upper right member of the set. (Courtesy of Mr Jarvis Stoddart, Toronto)

The humanists in the Imperial Japan Academy produced an edition of *Shinkan Eiga* [Letters of the Emperors]. Five scholars of literature, language, and history formed an editorial board; the historian was the indefatigable Tsuji Zennosuke, who later became the head of the project. They retrieved materials from the Shōsoin in Nara, the Imperial Household Ministry, temples, shrines, and private archives. During the bombing in March 1945, they moved the project out of Tokyo to a safer place in Iida City, Nagano Prefecture. In 1946 the 2,600th Anniversary Committee of the Japan Academy was dissolved, but the work was deemed still worthy, and a new committee was formed to complete the project in 1950. Besides Tsuji, other historians who worked on it were Iwahashi Koyata (1885-1978) and Aida

Nirō (1897-1945) of Tokyo Imperial University, and Akamatsu Toshihide (1907-79), Nishida Naojirō, and Nakamura Naokatsu of Kyoto Imperial University.[4]

Not to be left behind in a display of public enthusiasm, historians also generated projects. The Department of History at Kyoto Imperial University published a collection of essays called *Kigen Nisen Roppyakunen Kinen Shigaku Ronbun Shū* [Collection of Historical Essays Commemorating the 2,600th Anniversary of the Empire]. Commendably the papers had nothing to do with Emperor Jinmu. Only the first article, by Nishida Naojirō, concerning 'spiritual history' in *Nihon Shoki*, displayed appropriate reverence. However, other works were more in spirit with the occasion; Nishida Naojirō, who was by then deeply involved in a spiritual interpretation of Japanese history, published separately *Yamato Nisen Roppyakunen Shi* [History of 2,600 Years of Yamato].

The leading historians were also invited to join the most important scholarly work on Emperor Jinmu, which was conducted by the Ministry of Education. It established a Commission of Inquiry into Historical Sites Related to Emperor Jinmu [Jinmu Tennō Seiseki Chōsa Iinkai], consisting of about sixty people.[5] The minister of education was officially the head of the commission, signifying its importance, but the work was done by members of the Religion Bureau [Shūkyōkyoku] and university professors. On the actual research team were ten members of the Ministry of Education and eighteen scholars, mainly from the imperial universities, supported by secretaries and clerks. The formal head was Sakatani Yoshirō (1863-1941), an elderly member of the House of Peers. The real head was Mikami Sanji until his death on 7 June 1939, when he was succeeded by Chikuwa Fujimaro, about whom little is known. Not surprisingly Tokyo Imperial University was represented by the greatest number of scholars, including the historians Tsuji Zennosuke, Hiraizumi Kiyoshi, and Sakamoto Tarō. Other Tokyo Imperial University scholars included Miyaji Naokazu, a rationalist professor of Shinto religion; Wakimizu Tetsugorō (1867-1942), a professor of geology; and Tsujimura Tarō (1890-1983), an assistant professor of geography. Representing the other imperial universities were the historian Naganuma Kenkai from Kyushu Imperial University; the historians Nakamura Naokatsu from Kyoto Imperial University and Nishida Naojirō, formerly of Kyoto Imperial University and latterly of the Research Institute on Japanese Spiritual Culture; and Yamada Yoshio of Tohoku Imperial University and later of Jingū Kōgakkan University in Ise, a nationalistic scholar of Japanese language and literature who had also been on the committee to compile *Kokutai no Hongi*. The historian Nishimura Shinji (1879-1943) of Waseda University was the leading representative of the private universities.

The report recognized the problem noted by the ministry – that there were numerous Emperor Jinmu sites identified by tradition in ten prefectures, most of them dubious. Many were claimed for a single act of Jinmu, many were in ruins or greatly altered, most were poorly documented, and confusion and uncertainty abounded. Since everyone in Japan believed that Emperor Jinmu had existed, the ministry's plan to identify the sites once and for all, using the skills and knowledge of modern historians, was indeed an excellent idea. It was carried out thoroughly and intelligently. The ministry got started in 1935, and in 1936 it sent inquiries to ten prefectural governors (Kagoshima, Miyazaki, Ōita, Fukuoka, Hiroshima, Okayama, Nara, Wakayama, Mie, and Ōsaka Urban Prefecture) for information about the location, history, and state of the preservation of sites. The governors responded by identifying 150 sites, which the ministry narrowed down first to eighty-seven and then to twenty-three. The prefectures lobbied for recognition of their sites and sent in great amounts of material, usually in the form of booklets prepared by officials and local scholars. They all supported their cases with citations from ancient documents and with abundant maps and photographs. In December 1937, the order was given to set up the committee of scholars.

The committee started in earnest, working under detailed guidelines from the Ministry of Education. To prevent giving advantage to any of the lobbyists, the guidelines were marked 'Strictly Confidential' when they were sent to the members of the committee, but they were published in the final report. The main criterion was the identification of the sites in ancient documents, starting with *Kojiki* and *Nihon Shoki*. The Ministry of Education had already visited more than ninety places, and the committee of scholars sent out individuals and teams of up to four scholars between May 1939 and May 1940. These visits of eminent scholars were widely reported in the local press.[6] Then they met to discuss the final selection, meeting eleven times up to August 1940 in two- to three-day sessions. The Tsuji Zennosuke papers contain printed reports of these meetings, indicating substantive scholarly discussion.[7]

The committee recognized twenty-one sites related to Emperor Jinmu; it discussed the difficulties of twelve other places that it did not recognize. The twenty-one sites were located in seven prefectures:

Nara	8
Wakayama	5
Ōsaka	4
Ōita	1
Fukuoka	1
Hiroshima	1
Okayama	1

The report includes local maps and photographs, many showing the standard marker that was erected as a result of the committee's work. Granite markers were made, with inscriptions determined by the Ministry of Education in consultation with the local authorities. The front of each marker reads 'Emperor Jinmu Historical Site [place name] Commemorative Stone.' The back gives the details of Jinmu's association with the place. To take the least difficult example, the site at Sanu in Shinmiya City, Wakayama Prefecture, where nothing really existed, was selected on the basis of ten historical records, including *Nihon Shoki, Man'yōshū, Azuma Kagami, Heike Monogatari*, and six minor works. The principal evidence was a passage for 663 BC in the Emperor Jinmu chapter of *Nihon Shoki*: '6th month, 23rd day. The army arrived at the village of Nagusa, where they put to death the Tohe of Nagusa. Finally they crossed the moor of Sano [sic], and arrived at the village of Kami in Kumano.'[8] The standard marker was installed in September 1940 and read: 'In 663 BC, Emperor Jinmu led the imperial army through Sanu on the way to Kumano no kami. The site is in this area.'[9]

Thus, in 1940 the leading historians of Japan participated in a government project to commemorate a historical date in which they did not believe. As we have seen, all the historians believed without second thought that Emperor Jinmu had existed, but none of them accepted 660 BC as the date of his founding of the empire at Kashihara. In 1933 Mikami Sanji had offended the young Inoue Kiyoshi with his recommendation of 660 BC as the date to be taught in the educational system, while rejecting it as a scholar. Now, in 1940, all the leading historians accepted 660 BC as the date to

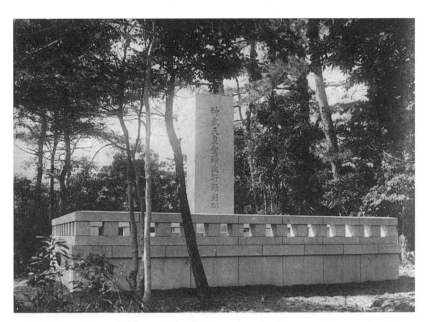

Granite monument marking a historical site related to Emperor Jinmu in Sanu, Wakayama Prefecture, as determined by a commission of scholars.

which they gave formal scholarly recognition. The distinction between education and scholarship had been erased in favour of the date used by the Ministry of Education.

Our study of the historians has shown two things. First, most of them accepted their position as Japanese citizens and public employees and believed that their work contributed to the glory of the Japanese empire. The greatest of them – Mikami, Kuroita, Tsuji, and Sakamoto – were showered with honours. Second, they were cowed by the scholarly tempests going back to Kume Kunitake and the 1911 Southern-Northern Courts controversy, and by the strong forces of nationalism within and without Tokyo Imperial University, that demanded conformity to formal expressions of loyalty. Rightly or wrongly, they saw no alternative to conformity, unlike their colleagues in law and economics, who engaged enthusiastically in battles against the authorities. As the 1930s moved on, the works of the historians were censored by the government and accommodating publishers, and they were so nervous about this that they even censored themselves. As we have seen, in 1938 the Tokyo Imperial University historians published the works of Shigeno Yasutsugu and took out words about the fourteenth-century imperial house that they thought might be offensive to radical nationalists or the government. The ultimate act of conformity by the historians was participation in the commission to identify the sites related to Emperor Jinmu. All of them were made aware of the military significance of joining the commission by the 8 November 1939 letter of the minister of education, Kawarada Kakichi, cited in the section on Tsuji Zennosuke. The minister recalled the significance of Emperor Jinmu's magnificent exploits in uniting Japan by military force at the sites to be confirmed by the commission, and linked these exploits to the war in China.

Only Sakamoto Tarō said anything about conformity after the war, but not until he published his memoirs in 1980. In 1940 he had been a forty-year-old assistant professor at Tokyo Imperial University. He said that he thought it best to avoid controversial topics. Commenting on *Kokutai no Hongi,* he said that he had no idea who was responsible for asserting the historical truth of the Age of the Gods, which astounded him, and that he 'thought the best thing to do with the Age of the Gods was leave it alone.'[10] As for the Commission of Inquiry into Historical Sites Related to Emperor Jinmu, he saw no alternative to participating as requested and observed somewhat ruefully that at least it provided funds for research into those matters, at a time when money was tight.[11] Thus, Sakamoto went as part of different teams on four research trips between October 1939 and April 1940, twice to Mie Prefecture and once each to Fukuoka Prefecture and Miyazaki Prefecture, to find out the truth about Emperor Jinmu.[12] He seems not to have considered the possibility of declining to participate. None of them did.

13
Tsuda Sōkichi (1873-1961): An Innocent on the Loose

Scholarship

Tsuda Sōkichi was not invited to join the Commission of Inquiry into Historical Sites Related to Emperor Jinmu. Quite the opposite. On 21 January 1940, three weeks before the official 2,600th anniversary of the empire, he was summoned to a Tokyo prosecutor's office and questioned for five and a half hours about books that he had written on ancient history. In February the sale of four of his books was prohibited, and on 8 March he was charged with violating the publications law by insulting the imperial dignity. Subsequently he was tried and convicted of lese-majesty. The crime consisted in his casting doubt on the very existence of Emperor Jinmu and the next thirteen of his successors, up to Emperor Chūai (r. 192-200).

Tsuda's background, interests, method, and university position were all different from those of the professors of the imperial universities, who navigated their way through the storms of the 1930s and entered the safe haven of appointment to the Commission of Inquiry into Historical Sites Related to Emperor Jinmu. Tsuda did not graduate from Tokyo Imperial University but from the politics department of Tokyo Senmon Gakkō (later Waseda University) in 1891. Kume Kunitake also went there after his dismissal from Tokyo Imperial University to become the 'Olympic gold medal champion' of ancient documents, but he came too late to influence Tsuda. Thus, Tsuda missed out on the study of documents as the key to history, in the Tokyo Imperial University style. This lack may be accounted a good thing by those who consider the Tokyo style narrow, unimaginative, and boring, but in prewar days, when the Tokyo professors dominated the field, they considered it a defect. Sakamoto Tarō reported the dismissive comment of Tsuji Zennosuke: 'Tsuda is good at reading books, but they are just published works, eh?'[1] Sakamoto himself was more kindly disposed, thinking it necessary to take account of Tsuda's views, but he never came to full agreement with Tsuda and to some extent considered his views destructive of proper attitudes toward history and the Japanese nation.

Tsuda Sōkichi (1873-1961) was convicted of lese-majesty in 1942 for writing sceptically about the existence of the early emperors. (Courtesy of Iwanami Shoten, Tokyo)

Tsuda's irregular path next took him around the country as a high-school teacher, a job that he came to loathe. From ages twenty-three to twenty-seven, he taught, changing schools every year. He wrote in his diary, 'How can I give serious lectures to such little children? Will I have to spend my days on work like this forever? I hate it, I hate it. I hate everything about it.'[2]

Eventually he escaped, and in 1908 he became a researcher at the Tokyo office of the Manchurian Railway Company, in the Manchuria and Korea Geographical and Historical Research Department. There he came under the influence of Shiratori Kurakichi (1865-1942), whose methods and approach to history significantly shaped his work.

Shiratori picked up where Taguchi Ukichi left off, interpreting the myths simply as myths, the product of stages in the development of ancient peoples. Thereby he detoured around the problem of looking for historical truth in the myths that obsessed the mainstream historians. His scholarly credentials were in good order. In 1887 he entered Tokyo Imperial University, then known as Bunka Daigaku, and was one of the first students of Ludwig Riess, from whom he learned Western history and scientific method. He kept his Riess lecture notes, which were later read by Tsuda. After graduating he became a professor at Gakushūin [The Peers School], specializing in Chinese history. The obligatory tour of Europe took place in 1901-3, and he returned in 1904 to positions in both Gakushūin and Bunka Daigaku. In 1908 he moved on to become the head of the Manchurian Railway Research Institute. He was honoured with membership in the Imperial Japan

Academy, senior third-court rank, and the Order of Merit, second grade, and his views were sound enough to make him a tutor to Crown Prince, later Emperor, Hirohito from 1914 to 1921.[3]

Insofar as Emperor Hirohito held enlightened and liberal ideas – a controversial topic – Shiratori may have contributed to them. He wrote a Japanese history text for the edification of the crown prince, a copy of which was retained by a fellow student, Nagazumi Torihiko. It is an idealistic work, organized by the reigns of emperors and emphasizing their special virtues. However, it is also fair and even-handed, noting the deficiencies of infamous villains who opposed the emperors such as Hōjō Yasutoki and Ashikaga Takauji, but also praising their good qualities.[4] As we have seen, praise of these villains became politically unacceptable in the 1930s.

Shiratori's field was Chinese history, but he left an unfinished manuscript entitled 'Jindai Shi no Shin Kenkyū' [New Studies on the Age of the Gods], based on lectures that he gave at Tōyō Bunko in October-November 1928. He took for granted the need to rationalize and secularize the myths in the twentieth century, and he remarked of the National Scholars of the Tokugawa and Meiji periods, 'The Tokugawa-period scholars such as Motoori Norinaga and Hirata Atsutane ... as well as Meiji-period nationalist scholars interpreted the Floating Bridge of Heaven literally, holding that it really spanned Heaven and Earth in the Age of the Gods. In the Shōwa period, not even a school child believes that.' He made a similar contemptuous remark about Motoori Norinaga's interpretation of the Land of the Dead.[5]

Shiratori did not dwell on who wrote *Kojiki* and *Nihon Shoki*, or why, but took the texts as given and used linguistics, anthropology, and comparative mythology to get at their meaning as myth, not as history. Like Taguchi Ukichi, he theorized that religious ideas arose among the ancients and went through stages of development, eventually reaching expression in the idea of creator gods. In Shiratori's view, these gods should not be rationalized into humans, because the ancients really thought that they were gods. Izanami and Izanagi were trees; Amaterasu was the sun; Tsukiyomi was the moon; Susano-O was the wind.[6] The point was to distinguish between the way of thinking of the ancients and the moderns. Tsuda also made this point, saying that the ancients lived in the childhood of humankind. As he put it, their thought differed from modern thought as that of children differs from that of adults. In the world of the ancients, things happened that moderns do not accept; islands and beasts and trees acted like human beings, but they were not human beings, they were islands and beasts and trees.[7]

Shiratori's views were inherently dismissive of the Age of the Gods. But like Mikami Sanji and Kuroita Katsumi, Shiratori was untroubled in revering the imperial house on the basis of the founding myths, separating political truth from historical fact. He provided a straightforward and

orthodox discussion of the symbolism of the imperial regalia, which originated in the Age of the Gods. Possessing the regalia, the imperial house has
love, mercy, and bravery, and so do the people of Japan; these qualities are
special to them. In every country, there are government and religion, civil
arts and military arts, and they tend to become separated. In Japan, however, they remained combined, 'and this is the special quality of our national essence.'[8] Shiratori taught these things to the crown prince.

Tsuda explained how Shiratori was able to conduct scholarship that was
potentially destructive of the imperial ideology and yet remain devoted to
it, and the explanation applied to Tsuda himself:

> Professor Shiratori held that scholarship is the foundation and the origin of
> the deepest knowledge about human life, and the highest activity of the
> human mind. Scholarship in itself possesses significance, value, authority,
> and utility, and he believed that its universal nature is to promote the cul-
> tural progress of the human race. The flourishing of scholarship of any
> kind whatever improves the spiritual life of the nation and enriches culture
> and thereby raises the position of our country in the world and increases
> national prosperity.[9]

This liberal view of scholarship, not entirely uncommon in Japan, could
never have been articulated by Hiraizumi Kiyoshi, who would accept only
scholarship that enhanced the political values of the imperial nation. Tsuda
would later offer this liberal view in his own defence against the charge of
lese-majesty.

Tsuda went to Waseda University in 1918 and remained a professor there
until 1940, when he was forced to retire because of the legal charges against
him. In the years up to 1940, he worked quietly, publishing at a fast pace
the books that would doom him. But he escaped punishment in the 1930s,
when all around were being rooted out for insufficient devotion to the imperial house and the nation. Ienaga Saburō suggests that Tsuda was left
alone because he was in an ivory tower on the margin.[10] In addition, Waseda
University was a private institution, so he was not expected to earn his keep
by praising the state, in the manner of professors in the imperial universities. Yet his ideas were well known by the 1930s, received enthusiastically
by young scholars such as Inoue Kiyoshi and Ienaga Saburō and excoriated
by nationalist scholars such as Hiraizumi Kiyoshi. Opponents of unacceptable works were all too eager to draw them to the attention of the government, so it is unlikely that the censors were unaware of them. Perhaps the
critics and censors just never got around to him.

It is not difficult to summarize Tsuda's ideas. The Tokyo Imperial University scholars approached history by rigorously examining pieces of evidence
one by one and trying to build up a detailed record of events, without

questioning the imperial framework of history. Tsuda cast his eye over the whole process of ancient history and asked when and how the imperial framework came into being. The answer was not far to seek: the main sources for ancient history were Japan's first histories, *Kojiki* and *Nihon Shoki*. Because both were written by bureaucrats and intellectuals, at the command of the emperor, and given the organization and contents of the two works, it was not hard to reason that they were written to legitimize the imperial state. Their historical reliability was compromised.

Let us summarize the historical circumstances of the writing of *Kojiki* and *Nihon Shoki* from the standpoint of the mid-1990s. The origins of the emperors are difficult to pinpoint, but the historical record of the imperial state in the late seventh and early eighth centuries is reasonably clear. From the mid-seventh century, the Yamato court began a drive toward establishing central power, for both external and domestic reasons. Externally Japan had aligned with the losers, Koguryo and Paekche, in centuries-long wars in Korea. Japan lost decisively to Silla in a naval battle in 663, and as a consequence it faced possible invasion by a Korea united under the Silla dynasty, backed by Tang China. According to *Nihon Shoki*, hurried construction of fortifications began. Internally the loose federation of great clans under the Yamato court that governed Japan was not up to the task of defence against such a formidable continental alliance. Struggle in the state was at hand in any case, as the federation of clans was breaking down, with the Soga clan ambitious to replace the Yamato clan as the ruling house. The defenders of the Yamato clan adopted the idea of a more centralized state. A series of battles terminated the Soga clan in 645, and reforms in the latter seventh century led to the establishment of a Chinese-style imperial state. Its forms and procedures were crystallized in the Taihō law code of 701 and embodied in the great capital city of Nara from 710. The whole process marked the last stage of millennia of history in Japan, during which civilization advanced from the Stone Age to the stage of high classical civilization found in China. However, people in the eighth century were not aware of this background of progress through early stages of civilization. To cap off the development of the imperial state, *Kojiki* and *Nihon Shoki* were written by command of the emperors to tell its story. They started with the Age of the Gods.

'It is hardly necessary to say that the history of the Age of the Gods does not contain historical facts,' wrote Tsuda in his first work on the subject, *Jindai Shi no Atarashii Kenkyū* [New Studies on the Age of the Gods, 1913]. Then, in his provocative way, he claimed that the ancients who wrote the histories did not think that the age contained facts either, and precisely for that reason they distinguished between the Age of the Gods and the age of humans.[11] Their reasons, however, were different from those of modern scholars. From the ancient terms in ritual prayers [*norito*] and texts such as

Shoku Nihongi [Chronicles of Japan Continued, 797), it is evident, said Tsuda, that the emperor was considered divine, though the emperor himself was not an object of worship. Hence, the Age of the Gods was an anachronistic creation by the authors of *Kojiki* and *Nihon Shoki* to account for this divinity. The Age of the Gods was located just before the first emperor, Jinmu.[12]

Tsuda wrote at great length on *Kojiki* and *Nihon Shoki* as sources for history and their problems, but he summarized them conveniently in a 1934 work entitled *Jōdai Shi no Kenkyūhō ni tsukite* [Research Methods in Ancient History]:

1 The bulk of the evidence is in the form of legends, which are inherently untrustworthy.

2 Assuming that there is a historical basis to the legends, much time elapsed between the events and the formation of the legends and then between the formation of the legends and the writing of *Kojiki* and *Nihon Shoki*. Many changes in their contents must have occurred.

3 From discrepancies between *Kojiki* and *Nihon Shoki*, and from the variant versions in *Nihon Shoki* ('one book says,' 'another account says'), it is evident that different versions of events existed.

4 Because of the use of Chinese characters, Chinese thought influenced *Kojiki* and *Nihon Shoki*.

5 Since Chinese was known only at the imperial court, they wrote from the perspective of the court, producing a unified view.

6 All dates in *Nihon Shoki* are given according to the Chinese calendar, falsely superimposing a Chinese chronology on Japanese history.[13]

Working from this position, Tsuda dismissed as history the entirety of the Age of the Gods. Furthermore, for the same reasons, he questioned the existence of the early emperors. He was the only major historian in prewar Japan to do so. The drift of the body of his works casts doubt on the existence of the first fourteen emperors from Jinmu to Chūai (r. 192-200), but in places he went as far as the nineteenth emperor, Ingyō (r. 412-53).[14]

Tsuda's position was widely offensive in 1940. He destroyed the myths of the Age of the Gods and the early emperors that all the major historians had come to affirm as historical fact. The legitimacy of the imperial house rested mainly on those myths, so by the standards of 1940 he was properly charged with lese-majesty.

Tsuda also undermined the fundamental sources for Japanese national identity. We have seen how the government sponsored *Kokutai no Hongi* (1937), employing the nation's leading scholars to define once and for all the true nature of the national essence. Those scholars turned without second thought to the myths in *Kojiki* and *Nihon Shoki* as fundamental sources. Much of the work done at the Centre for Research on National Spiritual

Culture was the same. Moreover, the 1930s and 1940s were littered with thousands of books and articles, amateur and professional, defining Japanese national identity. They all shared a belief that its reified essence could be found in ancient times, acknowledging nothing in the subsequent 1,500 years to change the Japanese. They invariably found that the myths showed that the Japanese people were essentially peaceful, clean and pure, properly respectful of authority, worshipful of the gods, disposed toward harmony, and so on.

According to Tsuda, however, what everyone was defining as the essence of the Japanese people was nothing more than the ideas of bureaucrats and intellectuals at the imperial court in the early eighth century. Those ideas were political, created to explain the origins of the imperial house, and did not reflect the everyday beliefs of the Japanese people. 'They are not the crystallization of the feelings and spirit of the Japanese people. Among the gods, there is not one who resembles a hero of the Japanese people.'[15] Tsuda held that the true myths of the ancient Japanese people were childlike in nature, stories about people born from peaches and such. However, this was an assumption. The weak point of his method was that he could not prove this by the myths themselves, to which he had no access: they had all been transmogrified by the intellectuals.

Tsuda was widely read in Western myth studies.[16] But he held that the Japanese myths could not properly be analyzed by Western methods for the study of fundamental myths of peoples because they had been filtered through the compilation process in *Kojiki* and *Nihon Shoki*. They represented the advanced ideas of bureaucrats and intellectuals, not the beliefs that arose spontaneously among the Japanese people. Tsuda was wrong about this, in that Western myth studies do take account of such filtering processes. Possibly he was protective of the Japanese myths, like Hoshino Hisashi, who wanted to guard them from overzealous comparative study.

More important, Tsuda could not maintain this position. Like everyone else, he wanted to know what the myths really meant, and so he ignored his own strictures. Not a euhemerist like Arai Hakuseki, he sought to understand the thought of the people who made the myths, employing a combination of higher criticism, cultural anthropology, racial studies, and folklore studies.[17]

We have seen that Kuroita Katsumi did the same thing in his *Kokushi no Kenkyū*, theoretically dismissing the myths as a source for history and then undertaking extensive analysis to find out if they contained a germ of historical truth. Kuroita and Tsuda differed in the meaning that they attached to the myths, but at bottom they were both Japanese nationalists. They were unable to abandon emotional attachment to the myths on which they had grown up and that formed the basis for the fundamental values of their nation. More generally this was the fundamental cause of the betrayal of scientific history for nationalist history, which we have observed in all the major historians.

Tsuda went along without difficulty until October 1939, when he was invited for the first time to give guest lectures at Tokyo Imperial University. A chair in Oriental Political Thought had been established in the Faculty of Law as the product of recent trends that accompanied the war in China. Government propaganda, popular sentiment, and scholarly opinion all held that the purpose of the war was to unite Asia under Japanese leadership, in opposition to the West. This view involved stressing the common heritage of China and Japan by recognizing Japan's historical roots in an Oriental culture [*Tōyō bunka*]. The new chair in Oriental Political Thought was devoted to that purpose.[18]

Strangely, control of the guest lectures came under Nanbara Shigeru (1889-1974), a specialist in political thought who was well known as a liberal. A scholar of Kant and Fichte, he was opposed to both Japanese nationalist thought based on the national essence and Nazism. In his memoirs, Nanbara said that he was in a quandary over whom to invite. There was no one at the Tokyo Imperial University Faculty of Law in the field, and he considered the Tokyo Imperial University nationalist historian Hiraizumi Kiyoshi, and the philosopher Watsuji Tetsurō, out of the question. Watsuji, whose field was logic, had also moved with the nationalistic times and had come to consider that Japanese logic, based on communitarian values, was superior to Western logic, based on individualistic values. Outside there were Tsuda Sōkichi of Waseda University, who had published much on Chinese thought, and Muraoka Tsunetsugu (1884-1946) of Tohoku Imperial University, a rationalist scholar of National Studies and Shinto. Nanbara chose Tsuda.[19]

The trouble was that Tsuda had already denied the existence of an Oriental culture that embraced Japan as well as China and other Asian countries. Before taking up the study of Japanese history, Tsuda had studied ancient China at the Manchurian Railway Research Institute, and he kept up a life-long interest in the subject, writing extensively on Chinese thought and culture. He had gradually come to conclude that Japan differed greatly from China, despite massive cultural borrowing from China in ancient and medieval times. The concept of an Oriental culture embracing Japan, he wrote in 1938, was nothing more than propaganda, devised by those who wanted to reject the Western culture that had entered Japan in the nineteenth and twentieth centuries. By the same logic, they should reject Asian culture, which had entered Japan from outside in times past and been assimilated, and not enlarge it into a great concept of Oriental culture that included Japan.[20] He did not say so, but if there was no common Oriental culture, of which Japan should take charge in order to defend it against the West, then there was no point to the current war in China. Its purpose was purportedly

to defeat degenerate Chinese forces that failed to recognize Japan's historically necessary leadership of Oriental culture.

In any case, Tsuda gave a series of lectures on the Qin dynasty (221-06
BC) of ancient China, and they were heard politely by sixty to seventy listeners. At the conclusion of the final lecture, he bowed and asked for questions, whereupon hands shot up. Young Maruyama Masao (1914-96, later
Japan's most eminent political scientist), who was present, thought that the
questions were planted. Tsuda was immediately taken to task for denying
the existence of Oriental culture, for which Japanese soldiers overseas were
bravely sacrificing their lives. One questioner asked:

> You completely deny the connection between Confucianism and Japanese
> culture and the existence of an Oriental culture that is common to Japan
> and China. China is awakening from the delusions of the European and
> American doctrine of liberty that has poisoned Asia for many years and
> from 'democratic thought' and communism. At a time when China and
> Japan are cooperating to fight for the establishment of a new order in East
> Asia that will restore the traditions of Oriental culture, and our brothers are
> shedding their blood daily, does your argument not fundamentally deny
> the cultural significance of this holy war?[21]

Maruyama Masao intervened, going to the front of the room to remind the
listeners that Tsuda was an invited guest and to point out that their questions were not scholarly or relevant to the lectures on the Qin dynasty.
They all adjourned to another room, where the questions went on for hours.[22]
It was similar to the extended questioning of Kume Kunitake at his home
by the four Shintoist visitors. Tsuda, like Kume, was not shaken at all and
seemed to enjoy answering the questions; he showed the same attitude at
his trial.

The matter did not end there. Minoda Muneki took up the case of Tsuda's
Tokyo Imperial University lectures in *Genri Nippon*, exposing the treasonous
thought of Tsuda Sōkichi. Mitsui Kōshi led off with a critique of Tsuda's
works in which he compared Tsuda to Shigeno Yasutsugu, Dr. Obliteration.

> This crime of denying the existence of the first emperor and the first four-
> teen ancestors of the present emperor: what shall we make of it? It is nearly
> impossible to find words to express ourselves. In the Meiji period, there was
> 'Dr. Obliteration' Shigeno, but he did no more than deny the existence of
> the loyal subject Kojima Takanori. But Mr. Tsuda's arguments fundamen-
> tally deny the entire historical reality of the Age of the Gods, the fountain-
> head of Japan's national essence. To massacre the first emperor, and the
> first fourteen ancestors of the present emperor, and thereby to massacre

also the imperial shrines and tombs, is an act of treasonous thought completely without precedent in the history of Japan![23]

Then Minoda Muneki weighed in with a seventy-page exposé. It was not difficult to make the case: the article consisted mainly of citations from Tsuda's works that were self-evidently destructive of the imperial mythology, interspersed with apoplectic asides. One method of refuting Tsuda was to cite poems by the Meiji emperor, as if they settled questions of ancient texts and national identity. Minoda's final charges were that Tsuda massacred the Japanese national essence and Oriental culture; Minoda blamed Waseda University, Iwanami Shigeo, who published Tsuda's books, and the Tokyo Imperial University Faculty of Law.[24]

It is widely agreed that Minoda's article was what caused the government of Japan to take legal action against Tsuda. Perhaps if he had not accepted the invitation to lecture at Tokyo Imperial University, Tsuda might have continued to escape censure as he had throughout the 1930s, but of course he could not decline to lecture at the nation's best university. Minoda Muneki's position was perversely correct. The expression of such disloyal views by a guest lecturer was unacceptable at Tokyo Imperial University, where the history professors were public servants who had all learned, one way or another, to deal with the times. The history professors themselves knew, from their several positions, that Tsuda was wrong. They had already demonstrated this by joining, without demur, the Commission of Inquiry into Historical Sites Related to Emperor Jinmu.

Trial
On 10 February 1940, the day before the 2,600th anniversary of the empire, Tsuda's book *Kojiki oyobi Nihon Shoki no Kenkyū* [Studies in *Kojiki* and *Nihon Shoki*, 1919] was banned. On 8 March, charges were laid against him for four books: *Kojiki oyobi Nihon Shoki no Kenkyū, Jindai Shi no Kenkyū, Nihon Jōdai Shi Kenkyū* [Studies in Ancient Japanese History], and *Jōdai Nihon no Shakai oyobi Shisō* [Society and Thought in Ancient Japan]. A preliminary hearing found against him, and he went to trial on 1 November 1941, charged with violating Article 26 of the publication law: 'For books or drawings that profane the dignity of the imperial house, or advocate change in the form of government [*seitai*] or disturbance of the national essence [*kokutai*], the author, publisher, and printer shall be punished by imprisonment from six months to two years.'[25]

Also charged was the publisher, Iwanami Shigeo (1881-1946), the founder of Japan's publishing giant Iwanami Shoten. Iwanami was a man of vision, inspired by the Meiji Charter Oath of 1868, which promised to seek knowledge throughout the world to strengthen the foundations of imperial rule.

Believing that the Japanese nation needed to learn about every subject whatsoever, he published indiscriminately. The right wing and the left wing both appeared in the lists of Iwanami Shoten in the 1930s, and he was in constant trouble with the authorities. However, Iwanami himself was not charged until the Tsuda case. His testimony on behalf of Tsuda showed his wide view of scholarship and of Japan's place in the world. 'Professor Tsuda's character and scholarship are rare in Japan. I firmly believe that his excellent scholarship ranks with the best in the world. While I cannot make a scholarly evaluation of the contents of his work, I believe that publication of his work is in the interest of the scholarly world, of Japan, and of the state and society.'[26]

Tsuda was not without assistance. He was supported by fifty to sixty scholars at Tokyo, Kyoto, Tohoku, and Waseda Universities, some of whom disagreed with his views but supported his right to state them. At Tokyo Imperial University, Nanbara Shigeru mobilized Maruyama Masao to take up a petition, which gathered eighty-nine names, including that of Tsuji Zennosuke. Watsuji Tetsurō, no radical, appeared as a witness to affirm that Tsuda's views did not harm the imperial house.[27] The philosopher Nishida Kitarō of Kyoto Imperial University, himself a perfect nationalist and imperialist by that time, met with Minister of Law Kazami Akira (1886-1961) to discuss the legal prosecution of a scholar. Kazami listened and understood, but he said that the matter was out of his hands because an indictment had already been made.[28] The Marxist historian Hani Gorō showed up to suggest a counterattack: if the court affirmed the historical truth of *Kojiki* and *Nihon Shoki*, then Tsuda should point out that it contained records of the evil Emperor Buretsu, who tortured his subjects.[29]

Tsuda presented a lengthy written defence, covering scholarly method in general and his approach to Japanese history in particular. He affirmed the importance of free inquiry scrupulously conducted according to international professional standards and held that, even if correct conclusions were reached, they were invalid if not arrived at by correct methods. He said that diversity was important, providing a greater service to Japan in the world than uniformity binding the whole nation under a single inclusive ideology. But he affirmed that free inquiry by correct method was ultimately patriotic and therefore necessary in Japan: 'Scholarly research is not an individual matter. It is patriotic work [*kokumin toshite kō no shigoto*]. Its results are significant as contributions to the prosperity of the nation, both direct and indirect. In this sense, scholarly publications are necessary public expressions.'[30]

On the Age of the Gods, Tsuda showed that there had been much disagreement from ancient times to the present. Starting from the ninth-century works *Kogo Shūi* [Gleanings from Ancient Words, by the Imbe family, 807] and *Shinsen Shōjiroku* [New Compilation of the Register of Families, 815], it was clear that the accounts in *Nihon Shoki* had not been accepted as accurate. He then covered scholarship from the Heian period through the Edo period, claiming much support for his doubts about the Age of the Gods.[31] He summarized the main positions of scholars through the ages on the Age of the Gods as follows:

1 No matter how strange the stories, they should be accepted as historical fact. Motoori Norinaga.
2 The strange stories are not true:
   (a) Although they are not historical fact, they have meaning – for example, didactic. Fujitani Mitsue (1768-1823).
   (b) They were concocted, have no meaning, and should be disregarded.
3 Some historical fact lies at the bottom of the strange stories:
   (a) Traces of the ancestors of the imperial house. Arai Hakuseki.
   (b) Traces of the peoples and the origins of the imperial house. Meiji-period scholars.
4 The stories are not historically true but reveal the politics, religion, morals, thought, and customs of the ancients. Scholars of myth, anthropology.[32]

There were fewer supporters to enlist for doubts about Emperor Jinmu, but he raised Yamagata Bantō, Miyake Yonekichi (1860-1929), and Taguchi Ukichi.[33]

Tsuda's position on the existence of the ancient emperors aroused the greatest controversy. The judge listened to all the roundabout discussion about scholarship and the contents of ancient history from the prosecutor, the defendant, and the witnesses, and eventually he came to the following point:

Judge: It seems that, in these passages from Emperor Jinmu to Emperor Chūai, there are things that might cause the reader to doubt the historical existence of the emperors. When the defendant wrote these, did he doubt the existence of the emperors from Jinmu to Chūai?
Tsuda: I do not doubt it.
Judge: Do you believe in their existence as given?
Tsuda: I do.
Judge: Then if the defendant does not doubt their historical existence, would he please explain whether there are passages in *Kojiki oyobi Nihon Shoki no Kenkyū* that were written to give the impression that he affirms it?
Tsuda: I can't find them for you right off, but speaking overall there is no passage in these works of mine that gives the slightest doubt about the historical existence of the emperors.[34]

Tsuda's reply to the judge was bumbling and evasive, giving the impression of falseness, but in my view this statement was mainly consistent with his position. He held that the accounts in *Kojiki* and *Nihon Shoki* were constructed by the bureaucrats and intellectuals of the eighth century, and accordingly their record of history was not reliable. That did not necessarily mean that the early emperors did not exist, only that their existence could not be demonstrated by the evidence. Probably Tsuda, a child of his age, believed in their existence with all his heart, just like the other historians whom I have discussed, Kume Kunitake, Mikami Sanji, Kuroita Katsumi, Tsuji Zennosuke, and Hiraizumi Kiyoshi. However, Tsuda could not find for the judge the passages in his work that affirmed the existence of the early emperors because, as the result of his consistent method, there were none.

Ienaga Saburō thinks that Tsuda betrayed his own position and affirmed the existence of the early emperors in court because he feared conviction and punishment. As evidence Ienaga presents Tsuda's postwar work *Nihon Koten no Kenkyū*, which denies their existence, and Tsuda's unwillingness to talk about the trial after the war. Ienaga attributes this reticence to discomfort over the evasive tactic in court.[35] On the other hand, Tsuda's last disciple, Kimura Tokio of Waseda University, finds him consistent throughout. Kimura says that Tsuda never disbelieved the existence of the early emperors, and this was consistent with his postwar conservatism, in which he affirmed conventional beliefs in the imperial house and Japanese tradition.[36]

To clarify the matter, for his 1972 study Ienaga took a private survey of twelve major historians at Tokyo, Kyoto, and Osaka Universities, asking them to read *Kojiki oyobi Nihon Shoki no Kenkyū*. They replied as follows:

A   Tsuda denied the existence of the early emperors: 6.
B   Tsuda affirmed the existence of the early emperors: 0.
C   Tsuda's discussion was not about existence or non-existence: 3.
D   No reply: 2.[37]

On 21 May 1942, the court found Tsuda guilty on one of nine charges. Three of the four books were found inoffensive, but in four of its sections *Kojiki oyobi Nihon Shoki no Kenkyū* violated the publication law by insulting the imperial dignity. Tsuda and Iwanami Shigeo were sentenced to prison terms of three and two months respectively, with a stay of punishment of two years. The prosecution appealed but failed to meet a two-year deadline, so both men were set free, a remarkable turn of events in wartime Japan.

With the conviction, though not the imprisonment, of Tsuda and Iwanami, the Japanese imperial state completed its grand project of imposing uniformity of thought and supression of dissidence. Yet Tsuda seemed not to understand his case as part of an overall implementation of thought control. In 1952 he discussed it with Ōkubo Toshiaki, saying, 'That event has been misinterpreted. It was not government suppression, as is commonly said. In the court, it became a question of the nature of scholarship and research, which I explained as politely as possible. I felt like I was a teacher explaining to students. They say that I was fighting against the court, but that is wrong.'[38] Like Kume Kunitake, Tsuda blamed personalities for the trouble, explaining that he was prosecuted because right-wingers, whom he did not identify, forced the government into that direction.

We have seen that two of the most celebrated targets of government censorship and thought control, Kume Kunitake and Tsuda Sōkichi, failed to see themselves as victims. This makes it difficult for Japanese critics of the censorship and thought-control policies of the imperial state to make their case in the field of history.

For critics of censorship and thought control, there was worse to come. At his trial, Tsuda could not locate in his own writings the passages that affirmed the existence of the early emperors. But in the postwar era, he began to write positively about the imperial institution, as if he had found the non-existent passages. He found the dogmatism of the postwar communists worse than that of the prewar nationalists, because the communists were out to abolish the imperial institution. In a famous article in April 1946, 'The Circumstances of the Founding of the Nation and the Idea of the Eternal Succession of Emperors,' he affirmed the historical faith of the Japanese people in the imperial house and their special relationship with the emperors. He concluded by saying that the Japanese people love [*ai suru*] the emperor.[39]

Tsuda's case generated an immense amount of literature. Many concluded that Tsuda spontaneously had undergone, in the postwar era, the ideological 'conversion' [*tenkō*] that the state had forced onto communists in the thought-control system of the prewar period. The term was softened by Ienaga Saburō to 'transformation' [*henbō*] since imprisonment and coercion were not involved. The last disciple, Kimura Tokio, holds that neither term applies to Tsuda because he was consistent throughout his career. Kimura claims that a change in thought is attributed to Tsuda by those who expected him to support fundamental reforms as the result of his victimization by the imperial state. They were disappointed in his stance of upholding the imperial house in sentimental terms inappropriate to the postwar era.[40]

I agree with Kimura Tokio on the consistency of Tsuda Sōkichi, though not necessarily for the same reasons. Tsuda was a political innocent, a true product of the ivory tower at Waseda University, as stated by Ienaga Saburō. Absorbed in truly brilliant thought about the past, he did not understand the character and purposes of modern states. Tsuda never apprehended the nature of the systematically authoritarian, militarist, imperialist Japanese state that prosecuted him in 1941. He held a conventional view of Japan's problem, not seeing much wrong with the imperial state. He blamed the Japanese army for the war, just as he blamed unnamed individuals for his own prosecution. In correspondence on 10 September 1945, he said that it was a shame that the Japanese people did not overthrow the army and had to await help from the Americans. The army ought to apologize to the emperor and the people.[41] And so Tsuda forgave the state after the war and tried to help out when abolition of the emperor system was urged after World War II.

Iwanami Shigeo, who received the Order of Culture, died on 25 February 1946 at the age of sixty-six. His publishing house, Iwanami Shoten, has continued to flourish as one of Japan's major publishers. After the war, Tsuda Sōkichi received the Order of Culture and became a member of the Japan Academy. Widely popular at Waseda University, he died with many honours on 4 December 1961 at the age of eighty-eight.

Epilogue:
Historical Scholarship, Education, and Politics in Postwar Japan

Sakamoto Tarō: A Conservative in the Postwar Era

After the war, some of the historians educated in the prewar period continued to accept the founding myths, in the manner of Mikami Sanji and the young Kuroita Katsumi, who wrote *Kokushi no Kenkyū*. The historical scholarship of their successor, Sakamoto Tarō, was distinguished by rationalism. Yet to the end of his life in 1987, he believed that some historical reality lay beneath the myths. The difficulty was to say exactly what it was.

Sakamoto Tarō entered Tokyo Imperial University in 1923 and was taught by Mikami Sanji, Kuroita Katsumi, and Tsuji Zennosuke. In the postwar era, he emerged as the leading scholar of the history of ancient Japan, heading the Historiographical Institute of Tokyo University, publishing voluminously, serving on all manner of committees of historical preservation and investigation, and becoming a member of the Japan Academy.

As we have seen, Sakamoto served on the 1940 Commission of Inquiry into Historical Sites Related to Emperor Jinmu. He waited forty years after the event to express his reservations; even at that, he was the only one to do so. In the postwar era, he remained conservative and was at pains to resist those who dismissed the myths entirely. Sakamoto found them as dogmatic as the prewar scholars who affirmed their literal truth. In *Rikkokushi* [The Six National Histories, 1970], he discussed extensively the myths of the Age of the Gods, claiming that they contained some historical truth. On Emperor Jinmu, Sakamoto wrote a 1974 article for the Japanese version of *Encylopaedia Britannica* in which he acknowledged that the empire was not founded by Jinmu at a stroke. Discussing the founding work of the first nine emperors up to Sujin, he wrote:

> Certainly the unifying of the country by the Yamato court was not accomplished during the single reign of Emperor Sujin (r. 97-30 BC) but was carried out by the strength of the succession of emperors who made their

capitals in Yamato. It follows that we must recognize the existence of the emperors before Sujin. Nor should the stories of the eastern expeditions by the early emperors be dismissed without qualification as nonsense; they should be understood to contain a number of historical facts. A large number of scholars have held that first Emperor Jinmu, and then the first nine reigns up to Emperor Sujin, did not exist, but that is nothing more than scholarly theory, with no evidence whatsoever.[1]

Sakamoto was more logical than Tsuda Sōkichi, whose method destroyed the basis for his own belief in Emperor Jinmu. Sakamoto held that the myths contained some truth and that the burden of proof rested on those who claimed that they were entirely spurious. Probably most scholars of the present day would agree with Sakamoto that the myths were not mainly concocted by the eighth-century intelligentsia, as Tsuda claimed, but somehow originated with the people. However, Sakamoto's documentary method could not yield any specific historical truths that were widely accepted. He accepted archeology for the general shape of ancient history, but for the substance of what actually happened, who lived when, who did what to whom, his materials consisted only of the myths themselves. Thus, he affirmed the existence of the first nine emperors, as noted above. Instead of accepting the account of *Kojiki* and *Nihon Shoki* that Emperor Jinmu did it all, he spread the work of the emperors more reasonably over nine reigns. Sakamoto's work displayed the limitations of the Tokyo University documentary method in dealing with ancient history.

A New History Textbook: 'The Progress of the Nation'
Sakamoto Tarō notwithstanding, the list of emperors did not survive the death of the imperial state. The eminent historians who served on the 1940 Commission of Inquiry into Historical Sites Related to Emperor Jinmu had painted themselves into a corner. However, eighty-nine men – most of them were lesser names – signed a petition in support of Tsuda Sōkichi during his trial. In the postwar era of freedom of inquiry and expression, these men promptly came forward, taking the works of Tsuda as the basis for their position. To borrow a phrase from economics, there was pent-up demand for historical truth. They now began the discussion of ancient Japan with geology, geography, and archeology. There were many centuries of history to cover before the question of political authority in the historical Japanese state, its relation to founding myths, and the sources of the myths could even be taken up. It is now unusual to find a scholarly work that starts the history of Japan with the myths; the few that do, such as the works of Tanaka Takashi (b. 1923) of Ise Kōgakkan University, consciously try to sustain the prewar positions. Otherwise, Tsuda Sōkichi's questioning of the

existence of the early emperors, and the fierce official and scholarly reaction that he provoked, now seem quaint.

Change in the educational system finally erased the distinction between education and scholarship. In the prewar period, ideological demands had drawn scholarship down to the level established for education by the imperial state, and scholars came to affirm what was taught in the schools. In the postwar period, the process was reversed, and the schools were brought up to the standards of academic scholarship. This upgrading proceeded in several stages. First, on 20 September 1945, while the Supreme Command for the Allied Powers (SCAP) was still getting organized, the Ministry of Education gave a directive about the deletion of inappropriate materials from textbooks.

> It is required that all teaching materials that are inappropriate in the light of the intentions of the Imperial Rescript proclaiming the end of the war be struck out in whole or in part or be handled with the utmost care, in accordance with what follows:
> (1) The following are materials which ought to be used with care, amended or eliminated: (a) Materials that emphasise national defence and armaments; (b) materials fostering the fighting spirit; (c) materials that may be harmful to international goodwill; (d) materials that have become obsolete through being entirely removed from present postwar conditions and the everyday life of students; and (e) other materials that are not appropriate in the light of the Imperial Rescript [ordering surrender].[2]

Like Hiraizumi Kiyoshi, who resigned soon after Japan's surrender and expected to be indicted as a war criminal, officials of the Ministry of Education were perfectly aware of the offensive nature of the doctrines taught in Japan's schools. They ordered the deletion of inappropriate parts of the school textbooks in order to prevent more drastic measures by SCAP. The deletion of passages was carried out in schools throughout the nation, sometimes leaving nothing to read on the page.

The second stage was to replace the existing texts with new ones. Again the Ministry of Education took the lead, commissioning Toyoda Takeshi in November 1945 to write a new history text. Among those whom he consulted were Tsuda Sōkichi, Sakamoto Tarō, and Watsuji Tetsurō. Strange companions they would have been, but they never got started. SCAP put a stop to the work, not trusting the Ministry of Education. SCAP had found on 16 November 1945 that uncensored textbooks were still being printed and crated for shipping despite the ministry's instructions for deletions.[3]

This discovery led to the third stage. On 17 May 1946, SCAP gave direct orders to a group of four junior historians to compile a new textbook under

Two boys examine a textbook censored by the Ministry of Education after defeat in 1945, before new texts could be written. (From R.J. Wunderlich, 'The Japanese Textbook Problem and Solution, 1945-46,' PhD diss., Stanford University, 1952)

SCAP guidelines. They were Ienaga Saburō; Ōkubo Toshiaki; Morisue Yoshiaki (1904-77), a scholar of medieval Japanese arts; and Okada Akio (b. 1908), a scholar of Tokugawa foreign relations and Christianity in Japan. A SCAP official, J.C. Trainor, gave them guidelines for the text:

1. It will not be propagandistic.
2. It will not advocate militarism, ultranationalism and Shinto doctrine.
3. The deeds of the emperors are not the whole of history. One supposes that matters connected with economics, inventions, learning and the arts, and other things which arose among the people must have flourished. However, if certain emperors in fact left important works behind them, there is nothing to prevent them from being included. Emperors should not be written about simply because they were emperors.[4]

These guidelines suited the authors very well, and they set to work, producing *Kuni no Ayumi* [The Progress of the Country] in short order. It was published in October 1946.

Ienaga Saburō did most of the work. He had survived the war as a teacher, having been rejected for army service because of his frail constitution. He had to keep his head down during the war years, and as a schoolteacher he was obliged to teach the national myths as historical truth, a task that he found offensive. One of his articles on the thirteenth-century Buddhist priest Dōgen was censored in 1944, not for what Ienaga said but for what Dōgen himself had said.[5] This was no accident. Ienaga studied Dōgen because he was looking for a critical tradition in Japan in order to fight against the smothering nationalism that he encountered as a student at Tokyo Imperial University and during the war years. One of his most important works in this quest was 'The Development of the Logic of Negation in the History of Japanese Thought,' published in 1940.[6] After the war, Ienaga became a champion of liberal democracy, which in his youth had been as radical a political philosophy as socialism and communism. The wartime experience made him a strong believer, and he has retained a lifelong conviction of the need for continuing action to defend liberal democracy. Hence, in 1946 he was eager to reform the nation's historical education and jumped at the chance to write the new textbook.

Kuni no Ayumi finally brought the historical education of the Japanese people in line with the findings of scholars in the universities. The text did not begin, like every prewar text, with the statement that the distant ancestor of the emperor was the Sun Goddess. Instead, it started with geography and archeology and placed the beginnings of Japanese society in a universal human context.

> In the sea to the east of the Asiatic continent there are islands which stretch from north to south in a long thin line. These are the islands of Japan where we live. The heat and cold are not extreme; rain falls in good measure; the trees and grasses grow thick, and the scenery in each of the four seasons has a different appearance.
>
> It was in very ancient times that our ancestors settled down in this country. We do not know just when it was, but without a doubt it was at least several thousand years ago.

The discussion then proceeded to the evidence of early civilization, found in the shell mounds of the Jōmon period. 'From shell mounds, besides shells, the bones of fish and tools ordinarily used by the people of those days are dug out. From these finds we can tell how the people of ancient times lived.'[7] This was certainly not a tale of gods and emperors.

Kuni no Ayumi had its critics, the most prominent of whom was Inoue Kiyoshi. A disgruntled student in the 1930s like Ienaga Saburō, he moved much further to the left in his quest for historical truth. In the postwar era, he became one of Japan's most renowned Marxist historians. Inoue published widely on the Meiji Restoration, the emperor system, the war responsibility of the Shōwa emperor, militarism and imperialism, and social groups neglected by the mainstream academic historians, such as Japan's outcasts.

In May 1947, a year after *Kuni no Ayumi* appeared, Inoue Kiyoshi published a critique called *Kuni no Ayumi Hihan: Tadashii Nihon Rekishi* [Critique of *Kuni no Ayumi*: Truthful Japanese History]. Therein he claimed five purposes: to clarify the vague parts, correct the errors, supply what was missing, suggest how to teach in the classroom, and, most important, 'to add the many things that are completely missing in *Kuni no Ayumi* – most of which relate to the history of the people.'[8] Inoue also criticized, with considerable justification, the process of writing *Kuni no Ayumi*. It was prepared in three months, he pointed out, by a selected group of scholars who worked in isolation from other educators and scholars. To be in line with the Occupation position on freedom and democracy, said Inoue, *Kuni no Ayumi* must be freely exposed to criticism. He offered abundant criticism of its contents.

Inoue claimed that the work was not people centred but emperor centred, just like the old books. *Kuni no Ayumi* used respectful language [*keigo*] for the emperors. In his critique, Inoue used plain language because, he said, his was a scholarly work and the emperor under the new Constitution is 'nothing more than one of the Japanese people.'[9] He severely criticized the opening passages of the book, cited above, which described positively the geography, topography, and climate of Japan as suitable for the development of a civilization. To Inoue this praise of Japan's geographical and topological features was nothing more than sentimental patriotism. He had no patience with the implied position of the authors that they were trying to explain, in simple terms suitable to young students, the origins of Japanese society as advanced by modern theories of geography and anthropology.

For the origins of the Japanese state, Inoue had a clear, concise, and heavily Marxist theory, not necessarily supported by the documentary evidence of Japanese history. He did not even mention the questions about the historicity of the myths that had so exercised prewar historians. Civilization, said Inoue, originated in the following stages: The development of productive capacity → the possibility of exploitation → the separation of social classes → the development of ruling classes and subordinate classes → the origins of tribute → taxation. He contended that the origin of the state is the result of the emergence of the system of private property and that *Kuni no Ayumi* concealed this point.[10]

Inoue was not alone in his criticisms. He chaired a symposium, attended by the proletarian writer and sometimes member of the Communist Party Nakano Shigeharu (1902-79), Hani Gorō, and two lesser-known figures, Tōma Seita and Koike Kikō. Two of the textbook authors, Ōkubo Toshiaki and Okada Akio, were invited to participate. Many criticisms were made from the left-wing position: the myths remained, militarism and the centrality of the emperor had not been expunged, important facts had been concealed or deleted, and the analysis was unscientific.[11] In his memoirs at the age of ninety-six, Ōkubo Toshiaki wrote that he had felt like the defendant at a criminal trial.[12]

These criticisms by the left wing had little effect. The textbooks became standard issue. Despite conservative revisions, the school texts still retain the rational and secular approach to ancient history adopted in *Kuni no Ayumi*. For anyone born since 1940 and educated in Japanese public schools, the Age of the Gods has no historical meaning, unless it is privately acquired for religious or political reasons. However, there may be some confusion about the early emperors starting from Jinmu.

Confusion about the emperors may arise because scholars writing for popular audiences show a carelessness that perpetuates the myth of emperors starting from Jinmu. Examples come easily to hand, as in a 1990 book entitled *Rekidai Tennō 125 Dai* [The Succession of Emperors: 125 Reigns], the first volume in an introductory historical series published by Shin Jinbutsu Ōrai Sha. The very title of the book assumes the reality of Emperor Jinmu, since the number of 125 emperors is arrived at by counting from Jinmu. A chronology at the back of the book starts with 660 BC, when 'Emperor Jinmu ascends the throne at Kashihara (*Nihon Shoki*).' The next six dates list events of Japanese history from archeology and Chinese sources, and no emperor's name appears until Emperor Keitai, 507 AD. Thus, the chronology clearly gives no credence to the traditional list of emperors from Jinmu to Keitai, but the reader is left with the impression that Jinmu's ascension is firm historical fact.

This impression is reinforced by the first three articles: Sakamoto Tarō's 'Nihon Rekishi to Tennō' [Japanese History and the Emperors], Torigoe Kenzaburō's 'Amaterasu Ōmikami: Tennōke no Soshin' [The Sun Goddess: Ancestral Deity of the Imperial House], and Kawasoe Taketani's 'Jinmu Tennō Kami to Hito o Musubu Genten' [Emperor Jinmu: The Point Where Gods and Humans Are Joined Together]. Scholarly qualifications and reservations, expressed throughout these articles, may not overcome the impact of the organization and the titles. Lay Japanese readers, to whom the book is directed, might remember the main points – that the Sun Goddess and Emperor Jinmu stand at the beginning of Japanese history – better than the scholarly qualifications about details.[13]

Postwar Historians and National Founding Day

In general, postwar historians have not been vigilant about the myths. A few, such as Ienaga Saburō and Inoue Kiyoshi, have maintained a watch, but they retired twenty years ago. The universities are now staffed by their successors, trained in the postwar era, who do not appreciate the perils of misstatement or failure to speak out.

An outstanding exception was the opposition of historians to National Founding Day, established in 1966 to celebrate 11 February as the founding of the nation. The idea for National Founding Day was first mooted by the government of Yoshida Shigeru in 1952 and continuously promoted by succeeding Liberal Democratic Party governments until its proclamation in 1966. It was immediately opposed by a historical organization called Nihon Rekishigaku Kyōkai [Japanese Association for Historical Scholarship], which stated, 'The time of the founding of our country has not yet been clarified by historical research. We are currently opposed to the establishment of this commemoration day.'[14] This was true; postwar historical scholarship has not yet identified a time of the founding of Japan. Nor will professional scholarship ever identify such a date; most historians now ignore it as a fruitless question. Only perfect nationalists, or amateurs holding a simplistic view of the nature of a nation, would try to pinpoint its founding in ancient times.

The original legislative proposal did not specify a date for National Founding Day, so a commission of inquiry was set up to look into the question. Its ten members, who did not include a historian, selected 11 February.[15] The protesting historians correctly perceived that this choice was not accidental. According to *Nihon Shoki*, 11 February was the date on which Emperor Jinmu declared his inauguration of imperial rule in 660 BC. The Meiji government had also selected 11 February 1889 as the date for proclaiming the Constitution of Imperial Japan, and 11 February was celebrated in the prewar period as the annual founding-day holiday called Kigen Setsu [Empire Day]. The postwar governments favouring the proposal disingenuously claimed that they had no specific historical event in mind, that they simply preferred 11 February.

During the 1950s, the event was sporadically celebrated by right-wing organizations and in some schools according to the political sentiments of the school principals. Protest was registered by historians' organizations, including left-wing groups such as Rekishigaku Kenkyūkai [Research Association for Historical Scholarship] and some mainstream groups such as Shigakkai [Association for Historical Scholarship]. Discussion and protest also appeared in newspapers, journals, and radio broadcasts; *Yomiuri Shinbun*, a major Tokyo daily newspaper, opposed National Founding Day. Leading historians of ancient Japan, such as Wakamori Tarō (1915-77) and Kadowaki Teiji (1925-), came forward to speak against the proposal. Wakamori is described by one of his interpreters, not as a leftist, but as a pragmatist and an advocate of enlightenment.[16] Wakamori held that it was less a problem of historical accuracy than of the recent militarism and imperialism associated with the former Empire Day. Inoue Mitsusada of Tokyo University, similarly no left-winger, reminded everyone of the wide scholarly doubts about the existence of the first fourteen emperors and the impossibility of fixing the date of founding the empire.[17] Wakamori and Inoue Mitsusada also spoke against the proposal at a 1955 public hearing held by the cabinet, where they were opposed by the Shintoists Ono Sokyo (1904-) and Mori Kiyoto.[18]

Politically the movement to oppose National Founding Day won the support of the socialist and communist parties in parliament. They managed to repel it for a while, but their support may have been the kiss of death. Those parties had a bad odour for the majority of voters for their unrealistic views about Japan's position in the Cold War era. They opposed the existence of Japan's Self-Defence Force, claiming that it was unconstitutional, and the alliance with the United States, claiming that they preferred unarmed neutralism. Many might have reasoned that anything to which the left-wing parties were opposed could not be all bad. In any case, it was reported that the question of National Founding Day, taken seriously by historians, was perceived by the public as a superficial question of when to have a welcome national holiday.[19] February 11 was finally chosen after parliamentary hearings and proclaimed in 1966.

The involvement of professional historians such as Wakamori Tarō, Kadowaki Teiji, and Inoue Mitsusada in public debates has been unusual in the postwar era. Apart from National Founding Day, they have not spoken up on public issues that could benefit from their professional competence. There are many such issues involving the imperial house.

The 1947 Constitution and the Founding Myths

The emperor-centred view of history has few supporters, but it is not yet dead and will continue as long as the imperial house continues. The situation is strange, since the members of the imperial family are all highly educated in secular history, understand thoroughly the democratic constitution of Japan, and take the lead in upholding it. Emperor Akihito's address to the nation at his accession in 1989 was a model of probity and international goodwill: 'Together with all of you, the Japanese people, I will protect the Constitution of Japan and vow to carry out my duties according to its provisions. I will never cease to aspire to the development of our national fortune and to the peace of the world and the further advancement of human welfare.' The Constitution of 1947, which he vowed to defend, pointedly placed sovereignty in the people. It made the emperor only a symbol of the state and of the unity of the Japanese people.

Yet the imperial house does not deny the founding myths of the Age of the Gods and Emperor Jinmu, which were the basis for the absolute sovereignty of the emperors in the Meiji Constitution, and it participates in ceremonies that affirm the truth of the myths. The funeral of the late Emperor Hirohito in 1989, and the accession ceremonies for Emperor Akihito, followed traditions based on belief in the founding of the imperial house by the Sun Goddess and the beginning of imperial rule by Emperor Jinmu in 660 BC.[20] Extreme interpretations of the accession ceremonies held that, at one point in the proceedings, the new emperor spent a night alone with the Sun Goddess and had sexual intercourse with her. Needless to say, the emperor is a modern upright gentleman, and so the ceremony does not provide a proxy for the Sun Goddess. Those who professed this interpretation evidently had no difficulty squaring its meaning with the concept that the Sun Goddess was the ancestress of the new emperor, and thus it was somehow incestuous.

The ceremonies provoked criticism based on the constitutional requirement of separation of state and religion. The government responded by claiming to separate the ceremonies into public secular ceremonies by the state and private religious ceremonies by the imperial family and to pay for only the public secular ceremonies. The distinction was formal and unconvincing, but everyone acquiesced, and the government carried on. This is not extraordinary; similar ceremonies elsewhere infringe upon the constitutional separation of church and state, such as the swearing-in and funeral ceremonies for presidents of the United States, which are Christian, but protest hardly arises. The controversy obscured the more important fact that the Japanese ceremonies, both public and private, followed in exact detail the prewar traditions based on the founding myths that affirmed imperial sovereignty.

The imperial house also affirms the myths in other ways. Envoys from the imperial house attend in official capacity at important Shinto ceremonies at various shrines. Examples are the annual Harvest Thanksgiving Festival [Kanname-sai] at Ise Shrine of the Sun Goddess and the ceremony at Kamigamo Shrine in Kyoto on 19 October 1994 to mark the twenty-year removal of the deities to a new sanctuary. The principal deities at Kamigamo Shrine are from the Age of the Gods. And members of the imperial family still regularly go to the Ise Shrine to announce their weddings and births to the Sun Goddess, and they go to Kashihara Shrine and Emperor Jinmu's official tomb nearby to announce them to Emperor Jinmu.

These activities of the imperial house could conceivably be justified under Article 7 of the Constitution of Japan, covering the performance of unspecified ceremonies:

> The emperor, with the advice and approval of the cabinet, shall perform the following acts of state on behalf of the people:
>   Promulgation of amendments of the Constitution, laws,
>   cabinet orders, and treaties.
>   [Eight other acts of state.]
>   Performance of ceremonial functions.

However, it is not so argued, because the subject is not raised for discussion, for or against, by anyone. No one in the press questions the members of the imperial family or the Imperial Household Agency about what they understand by these procedures. Historians do not stand up to say that the Sun Goddess is the principal deity of a discredited mythology associated with imperialism and that, if Emperor Jinmu existed at all, he was at best a putative tribal leader in prehistoric times before the organization of the Japanese state. Similarly, constitutional scholars and lawyers unanimously accept the emperor as 'a symbol of the state and of the unity of the Japanese people, deriving his position from the will of the people with whom resides sovereign power,' according to Article 1 of the 1947 Constitution of Japan. But they do not protest the association of the emperor with prewar traditions and ceremonies, confirming the absolute sovereignty of the emperor under the 1889 Constitution of Great Imperial Japan.

Instead, millions of people follow on television the journeys of members of the imperial family to Ise and Kashihara. They are greeted by large numbers of solemn officials, barely concealing under the solemnity their pleasure at having their day in the sun. Cheering, flag-waving imperial house groupies, mainly young women who idolize Crown Princess Masako, appear in numbers. The imperial family members arrive smoothly in Kyoto by bullet train, pass before the assembled solemn officials, graciously accept flowers from children, comfort the elderly and disabled, and then proceed to worship at the shrines, another hour distant from Kyoto. Panels of television commentators energetically discuss the outfits worn by the female members of the imperial assembly. Empress Michiko and Crown Princess Masako still wear hats, like the Queen of England, and interesting colourful suits, though the male members of the party wear boring standard-issue suits or tails, with carefully chosen neckties that we cannot see on television. No one asks why the imperial house is reporting to the Sun Goddess and Emperor Jinmu.

It is difficult to say whether this popular adulation of the imperial house proceeds in acceptance, disregard, or ignorance of the significance of the myths that the imperial institution perpetuates. There is no sign of resolution of this contradiction between the behaviour of the imperial house on the one hand and constitutional requirement and general secular knowledge of history on the other hand. Unwillingness to confront any behaviour of the imperial house is almost universal. Criticism of the imperial house for observing Shinto rites would be widely unpopular and might even provoke physical attack from well-organized right-wing groups. In 1989-90 death threats were made against Motoshima Hitoshi, the mayor of Nagasaki, and he was shot and wounded for suggesting that the mortally ill Emperor Hirohito might bear responsibility for the war.[21] I have noted the same threat of physical attack in the cases of Shigeno Yasutsugu and Kume Kunitake, actual attack on Minobe Tatsukichi, and the effects of fear of attack on the historians of the 1930s.

Conservatives capitalize on this situation. There remains in Japan a body of believers and scholars who keep alive the traditions of the prewar era. Some wish to relocate sovereignty in the emperor on the basis of the founding myths. The former Tokyo Imperial University historian Hiraizumi Kiyoshi was prominent and vigorous in this group until his death in 1984, and his followers consciously carry on his beliefs. Tanaka Takashi, professor emeritus and former president of Kōgakkan University in Ise, was Hiraizumi's last disciple at Tokyo Imperial University, graduating in the spring of 1945, just before that world crashed. Fifty years later, he follows the Hiraizumi tradition in his writings and has trained a new generation of followers. The instruction of the students at Ise Kōgakkan University is punctuated by attendance at ceremonies at Ise Shrine, with full explication of their meaning.

These believers disregard the negative implications of reviving the imperial state. Unlike their hero Hiraizumi, who knew perfectly well where he stood, they appear to underestimate the fact that the imperial state was authoritarian at home and aggressive abroad. They understand Shinto as simple, pure, and beautiful and do not appreciate the degree to which its doctrines were incorporated into domestic authoritarianism and brutal imperialism. Knowing that they are few in the general Japanese population, they carry on with the dedication of true believers. There is political capital in this, attracting the support of some conservative members of parliament.

At the present, this support does not matter. Many other countries also have minority movements with quirky and obsolescent political views. There are still monarchists in France and imperialists in Britain. In the future, such support might matter in Japan. The imperial house has had a powerful emotional hold on the Japanese people since the nineteenth century. Now the emperor is merely a head of state, like the queen of England. However, their respective histories are so different as to restrain easy interpretation of their positions as heads of state.

The powers of the English monarch have been gradually, sometimes violently, circumscribed over nearly 1,000 years, accompanied by a change in constitutional doctrine. Cutting off the head of King Charles I in 1649 was very salutary. 'The revolution of 1688 itself was so easily successful because James II remembered all too clearly that he had a joint in his neck. The lesson of January 1649 for the kings of Europe did not need repeating for another 144 years [until the French Revolution].'[22] The queen herself now proclaims the virtues of parliamentary democracy on the basis of modern historical development. She would not dream of suggesting the divine right of kings or queens, even at the time of coronation, when ceremonies signify the special blessing of God upon the monarch. Instead, she shares the view beloved of English people that the most important story of English history is the gradual broadening of parliamentary democracy through the ages. It is now fashionable in some quarters to scorn this view, but it gains renewed strength with the historical collapse of authoritarian forms of government.

The Japanese emperor, however, carries the traditions of 1,500 years of authoritarian history, which were not diminished over time. Instead, they were gradually brought to their height of effectiveness half a century ago. The execution of the English king in 1649 was salutary, and its effect incremental, but the opposite was true in Japan. The assassination of Emperors Ankō in 456 and Sushun in 592 seem to have carried no political significance. Through the ages, they were systematically ignored by historians, starting with *Nihon Shoki,* which simply recorded the events as matters of clan politics. The exile of Retired Emperor Go Toba in 1221 by the conquering Hōjō, which excited sharp political discussion in medieval works, was eventually talked into insignificance by the historians over the centuries. Despite this lack of interest in the personal fate of emperors, imperial loyalism as an ideology began a long, slow ascendancy in the middle ages. Starting with the imperial restoration of Go Daigo in the fourteenth century, loyalism gathered theoretical support in the Tokugawa period and became a widespread ideology in the nineteenth century in order to save Japan from the foreigners by the Meiji Restoration. We have also seen how, after the Meiji Restoration, imperial enthusiasts turned history into a pageant of heroes such as Kojima Takanori who aided the emperors, and villains such as Ashikaga Takauji who opposed them. Government and society pilloried any deviants from this position. In the Constitution of 1889, the emperor was described as 'sacred and inviolable,' and in the twentieth century it came to be understood that he was a living god. Incredibly in 1937, *Kokutai no Hongi,* written by Japan's leading professors, affirmed the emperor's divinity.

This is English history turned on its head, inhibiting interpretation of both English and Japanese monarchs alike as nothing more than symbols of state for the last fifty years of history. Thus, the English coronation ceremonies, signifying God's blessing upon the monarch, do not evoke the divine right of kings of the ancient past, while the Japanese ceremonies, linking the new emperor to the Sun Goddess, recall the powerful ideology of half a century ago.

The day of the imperial loyalists is gone, and Emperor Hirohito seemed to deny his divinity in his 1946 New Year's message to the nation when he said: 'The ties between us and our people have always stood upon mutual trust and affection. They do not depend upon mere legends and myths. They are not predicated on the false conception that the emperor is divine and that the Japanese people are superior to other races and fated to rule the world.'[23] Emperor Akihito now proclaims his fidelity to the democratic constitution. But he never denies the truth of the founding myths and apparently accepted their meaning of absolute sovereignty of the emperor at the time of his coronation ceremonies.

Thus, the situation of the emperor now may be analogous not to the contemporary England of Queen Elizabeth II but to the Tokugawa period. Then the imperial house slumbered in obscurity, with its ancient meanings ignored but undiminished. Nobody in the Tokugawa period could have imagined that the emperor would become the centre of an ideology of nationalism, militarism, and imperialism, affecting the entire world. Few now can imagine that the imperial house could again become the symbol of a resurgent Japanese nationalism, militarism, and imperialism.

But it was the external threat to Japanese national independence in the nineteenth century, from the great powers of the West, that caused the development of extreme nationalism, centred on the imperial institution. Nationalists resurrected and exploited the imperial institution, prevailing from 1868 to 1945. Eventually the nationalists included in their number almost everybody.

The next time, a threat to national independence might come from Asian powers, China, Russia, or Korea, either divided as at present into North Korea and South Korea or united. All have long been identified as potential enemies by Japanese military planners. In a crisis, nationalists seeking a unifying symbol of Japan would have recourse again to the imperial house, precisely because it has not purged itself of its ancient traditions based on the founding myths.

Yet Japan is a modern political democracy. The scenario sketched above, of the revival of emperor-centred nationalism based on the old founding myths, is unlikely to gain support either in parliament or among the people. The question of constitutional revision was opened in 1994, after three decades of silence, and the Constitution may well be revised early in the twenty-first century, specifically Article 9, the famous antiwar clause. However, early discussion of constitutional reform also displays a firm and nearly universal commitment to the sovereignty of the people, strongly stated in the 1947 Constitution. In the forthcoming debates, a few politicians can be expected to support revived imperial sovereignty. Some of them will win their seats by virtue of sincerity and vigour, qualities sometimes prized in Japan more than the validity of the proposal. But most politicians know that they can propose no alternative to popular sovereignty and retain their seats in parliament.

In addition, I have described a strong countertradition, the development of rationalism and secularism about the founding myths of the Age of the Gods and Emperor Jinmu, which authorized imperial sovereignty. The critical tradition was begun nearly 400 years ago by Confucians and taken up with vigour 100 years ago by the scientific historians and developed as their common understanding up to 1930. Academic rationalism and secularism flourished completely outside the educational system, in which the myths were taught as absolute truths. Then academic rationalism and secularism were affected by the ideology and actions of the imperial state and the force of public opinion in the 1930s and 1940s. The eminent historians came to agree with the state and public opinion on everything.

But rationalism and secularism about the founding myths inevitably re-surfaced in 1945. Now further developed and instituted into the national system of education for half a century, rationalism and secularism about the founding myths will provide a sturdy defence against any attempt to resurrect imperial sovereignty. At the least, proponents of imperial sover-eignty would have to come up with some fresh and attractive ideas to sup-port their position. Nothing beyond nostalgia for a comforting authoritar-ian world appears to be available in contemporary conservative political argument.

Notes

Introduction

1 W.G. Aston, trans., *Nihongi: Chronicles of Japan from Earliest Times to A.D. 697* (1896; reprint, Rutland, VT, and Tokyo: Charles E. Tuttle 1972), 1-2.
2 John S. Brownlee, 'Ideological Control in Ancient Japan,' *Historical Reflections* 14.1 (1987).
3 Aston, *Nihongi* 1:77.
4 Arthur Weinberg and Lila Weinberg, *Clarence Darrow: A Sentimental Rebel* (New York: G. Putnam's Sons 1980), 317-18.
5 Ibid., 329.

Chapter 1: Hayashi Razan and Hayashi Gahō

1 Yasukawa Minoru, *Honchō Tsugan no Kenkyū* [Studies on Honchō Tsugan] (Gensōsha 1980), 27.
2 Ishida Ichirō, 'Hayashi Razan no Shisō' [The Thought of Hayashi Razan], in Ishida and Kanaya Osamu, eds., *Fujiwara Seika, Hayashi Razan*, in *Nihon Shisō Taikei* [Compendium of Japanese Thought], vol. 28 (Iwanami Shoten 1975), 471-2.
3 See Herman Ooms, *Tokugawa Ideology: Early Constructs, 1570-1680* (Princeton: Princeton University Press 1985), 72-80, for a discussion of the bakufu and the Hayashi academy. Ooms holds that the Hayashi fostered the view that the academy was the official bakufu school and that it had little basis in reality. Robert L. Backus put it more gingerly: 'we may describe the position of the Ch'eng-Chu [orthodox Neo-Confucianism] with respect to the national government during the seventeenth and eighteenth centuries as one of customary privilege, which on the positive side benefited Ch'eng-Chu greatly when the bakufu was interested in expanding education and at other times guaranteed it at least a modicum of support, and which on the negative side preserved it from official suspicion on the few occasions when the bakufu took action to control the expression of Confucian thought.' 'The Kansei Prohibition of Heterodoxy and Its Effects on Education,' *Harvard Journal of Asiatic Studies* 39.1 (1979):72.
4 The name of the scholar Zhu Xi (1130-1200), after whom the school is named, is given as Chu Hsi in the older Wade-Giles romanization.
5 Masao Maruyama, *Studies in the Intellectual History of Tokugawa Japan*, trans. Mikiso Hane (Princeton: Princeton University Press; Tokyo: University of Tokyo Press 1974), 32-3.
6 Inoue Tetsujirō, *Nihon Shushigakuha no Tetsugaku* [The Philosophy of the Japanese Zhu Xi School], rev. ed. (Fuzanbō 1915), 65.
7 Ishida Ichirō, 'Zenki Bakuhan Taisei no Ideorogii to Shushi Gakuha no Shisō' [The Ideology of the Early Bakuhan System and the Thought of the Zhu Xi School], in Ishida and Kanaya, *Fujiwara Seika, Hayashi Razan*, 415.
8 See Sakamoto Tarō, *The Six National Histories of Japan*, trans. John S. Brownlee (Vancouver: University of British Columbia Press; Tokyo: University of Tokyo Press 1991).
9 In Japan Arai Hakuseki accounted for unwelcome examples such as the rise to supreme power of Toyotomi Hideyoshi, a peasant, with a theory of the irresistible Force of the Times

[*toki no un*], which had no permanent significance; see John S. Brownlee, *Political Thought in Japanese Historical Writing: From* Kojiki *(712) to* Tokushi Yoron *(1712)* (Waterloo, ON: Wilfrid Laurier University Press 1991), 125-8.

10 The development of evidential research in China is discussed in Benjamin A. Elman, *From Philosophy to Philology: Intellectual and Social Aspects of Change in Late Imperial China* (Cambridge: Harvard University Press 1984).

11 Yasukawa Minoru, *Honchō Tsugan no Kenkyū*, 27-38.

12 For a description of the work and its importance, see E.G. Pulleyblank, 'Chinese Historical Criticism: Liu Chih-Chi and Ssu-ma Kuang,' in W.G. Beasley and E.G. Pulleyblank, *Historians of China and Japan* (Oxford: Oxford University Press 1961), 151-9.

13 On Zhu Xi's historical ideas, see Fumoto Yasutaka, 'Shushi no Rekishikan' [Zhu Xi's Views of History], in Morohashi Yasuoka, *Shushigaku Nyūmon* [Introduction to Zhu Xi Studies], *Shushi Taikei* [Zhu Xi Compendium], vol. 1 (Meitokusha 1974), 357-65.

14 Hayashi Gahō also wrote *Nihon Ōdai Ichiran* [Survey of the Sovereigns of Japan, 1663]. Composed in Japanese, it was a far more popular work than *Honchō Tsugan*. Covering from Emperor Jinmu to Emperor Ōgimachi (r. 1557-86), and supplemented by other writers to the mid-nineteenth century, it was used as a major source, both acknowledged and unacknowledged, by Arai Hakuseki; as a source for eighteenth-century Dutch and English works on Japan; and as a history text in early Meiji schools. Ozawa Ei'ichi, *Kinsei Shigaku Shisōshi Kenkyū* [Studies in Modern Historical Thought] (Yoshikawa Kōbunkan 1974), 185-97.

15 Throughout this work, traditional reign dates of emperors are given without reference to their historical accuracy.

16 Sakamoto Tarō, 'Waga Kuni ni okeru Shūshi Jigyō' [The Work of Compiling Histories in Japan, 1973], *Nihon Rekishi no Tokusei* [The Special Characteristics of Japanese History] (Kōdansha Gakugei Bunko 1986), 111-14.

17 *Honchō Tsugan* (Kokusho Kankōkai 1918-19).

18 Ibid., 1:36.

19 Miyazaki Michio, *Kumazawa Banzan no Kenkyū* [Studies on Kumazawa Banzan] (Shibunkaku 1990), 174-5.

20 Hori Isao, *Hayashi Razan* (Yoshikawa Kōbunkan 1964), 352-4. This is the standard biography of Razan.

21 See Brownlee, *Political Thought*, Ch. 7.

22 *Honchō Tsugan*, 9:2493.

23 Ozawa Ei'ichi, *Kinsei Shigaku Shisōshi Kenkyū*, 175.

24 Ibid., 173.

25 Hori, *Hayashi Razan*, 357.

26 'Jinmu Tennō Ron,' *Hayashi Razan Bunshū* [Collected Works of Hayashi Razan] (Osaka: Kōbunsha 1930), 280-1. The essay, written in Classical Chinese, is rendered into Japanese in Hori, *Hayashi Razan*, 363-6, and in *Nihon no Shushigaku* [The Zhu Xi School in Japan], *Shushigaku Taikei*, 13:163-7.

27 Bitō Masahide, *Genroku Jidai* [The Genroku Era], *Nihon no Rekishi* [The History of Japan], vol. 19 (Shogakkan 1975), 192-4; and 'Kōkoku Shikan no Seiritsu' [The Establishment of the Imperial View of History], in Sagara Tōru, Bitō Masahide, and Akiyama Ken, eds., *Jikan* [Time], *Nihon Shisō* [Japanese Thought], vol. 4 (Tokyo Daigaku Shuppankai 1984), 323-4.

28 H.P. Varley, *A Chronicle of Gods and Sovereigns: Jinnō Shōtōki of Kitabatake Chikafusa* (New York: Columbia University Press 1980), 104.

29 Hori, *Hayashi Razan*, 361-2. From ancient times, the imperial court had occasionally ordered destroyed books that disturbed its central claim to legitimacy, the singular descent of the imperial line from the Sun Goddess. See Brownlee, 'Ideological Control.'

30 Hori, *Hayashi Razan*, 366-8.

31 *Shintō Denjū Shō* [Selections from Instructions on Shintō], *Shinto Taikei* [Compendium of Shinto], *Ronsetsu Hen* [Discourse Section], vol. 20, Fujiwara Seika, Hayashi Razan (1988), 336-7.

32 Ibid., 406.

33 Ibid., 353.

34 Ibid., 330.

35 Ooms, *Tokugawa Ideology*, 94.

36 David A. Dilworth, '"Jitsugaku" as an Ontological Conception: Continuities and Discontinuities in Early and Mid-Tokugawa Thought,' in W.T. de Bary and Irene Bloom, eds., *Principle and Practicality: Essays in Neo-Confucianism and Practical Learning* (New York: Columbia University Press 1979), 486.
37 Ishida Ichirō, 'Kaidai' [Explanatory Notes], *Shintō Denjū Shō*, 47-51.
38 *Honchō Tsugan* contains an appendix on the gods of Heaven and Earth, added by Hayashi Gahō, who wrote conventionally, 'Our country is indeed the divine country. A general knowledge of it is necessary.' Hanami Sakumi, 'Honchō Tsugan,' in Shigakkai, ed., *Honpō Shigakushi Ronsō* [Essays on Japanese Historical Scholarship] (Fuzanbō 1939), 2:797.

Chapter 2: *Dai Nihon Shi*
1 Kate Wildman Nakai, *Shogunal Politics: Arai Hakuseki and the Premises of Tokugawa Rule* (Cambridge: Harvard University Press 1988).
2 Herschel Webb, 'What Is the *Dai Nihon Shi*?' *Journal of Asian Studies* 19.2 (1960):136.
3 Ibid.
4 Kate Wildman Nakai, 'Tokugawa Confucian Historiography,' in Peter Nosco, ed., *Confucianism and Tokugawa Culture* (Princeton: Princeton University Press 1984), 86.
5 Sakamoto Tatsunosuke, *Rai Sanyō* (Keibunkan 1913), 200-3.
6 Higo Kazuo, *Mitogaku to Meiji Ishin* [The Mito School and the Meiji Restoration] (Tokiwa Jinja Shamusho 1973), 44; Mogi Hisahiro, *Tennō Ryō no Kenkyū* [Studies of the Emperors' Tombs] (Dōseisha 1990), 93.
7 Matsumoto Sannosuke, 'Kinsei ni okeru Rekishi Jojutsu to sono Shisō' [Early Modern Historical Narrative and Thought], in Matsumoto Sannosuke and Ogura Yoshihiko, *Kinsei Shiron Shū* [Collection of Early Modern Historical Argument], *Nihon Shisō Taikei* [Compendium of Japanese Thought], vol. 48 (Iwanami Shoten 1974), 588.
8 The purity of Mitsukuni's idealism is probably why he is the hero of a popular and long-running television series, *Mito Kōmon*, in which he wanders in disguise among the people of his domain, revealing his identity only to right a weekly incident of evil or injustice.
9 Bitō Masahide, 'Mitogaku no Tokushitsu' [The Special Features of the Mito School], in Imai Usaburō, Seya Yoshihiko, and Bitō Masahide, *Mitogaku* [The Mito School], *Nihon Shisō Taikei* [Compendium of Japanese Thought], vol. 53 (Iwanami Shoten 1973), 64-70.
10 Ogura Yoshihiko, 'Kaidai – *Dai Nihon Shi* Ronsō' [Explanatory Notes: The Assessments in *Dai Nihon Shi*], in Matsumoto Sannosuke and Ogura Yoshihiko, *Kinsei Shiron Shū*, 557-61.
11 Tamagake Hiroyuki, 'Zenki Mito Shigaku no Rekishi Shisō no Ichisokumen – Kuriyama Senpō no Rekishikan' [A Profile of Historical Thought in the Historical Scholarship of the Early Mito School – The Historical View of Kuriyama Senpō], *Nihon Shisō Kenkyū* [Studies in Japanese Thought] 13 (1981):9.
12 Takasu Yoshijirō, *Mitogaku no Shinzui o Kataru* [The Essence of the Mito School], (Ida Shoten 1941), 61-2. Takasu was a latter-day believer in the Mito ideology.
13 On these points, see Bito Masahide, *Genroku Jidai* [The Genroku Era], *Nihon no Rekishi* [The History of Japan], vol. 19 (Shogakukan 1975), 207-8.
14 Matsumoto Sannosuke, 'Kinsei ni okeru Rekishi Jojutsu to sono Shisō,' *Kinsei Shiron Shū*, 580.
15 Matsumoto Sannosuke and Ogura Yoshihiko, *Kinsei Shiron Shū*, 190.
16 Ibid., 199. Although this passage appears to be an exact quotation from *Jinnō Shōtōki*, there is no corresponding passage in that work. The editors of *Kinsei Shiron Shū* identify the following as the closest source: 'Yasutoki had an upright mind and conducted his administration openly. He comforted the people and was not personally extravagant; he attended to the needs of the *kuge* and dispelled the anxieties of the estate holders. Like dust vanishing before the wind, peace was brought to the land [*sic*]. It is said that the succession of tranquil years thereafter was solely the result of Yasutoki's efforts.' Varley, *Chronicle*, 228-9.
17 Nakamura Kōya, *Dai Nihon Shi to Mito Kyōgaku* [*Dai Nihon Shi* and the Mito Learning] (Kyōgakukyoku 1941), 21-2.
18 Ibaraki Kenshi Henshū Iinkai, *Ibaraki Kenshi – Kinseihen* [History of Ibaraki Prefecture: The Early Modern Era] (Seikasha 1985), 316-19.
19 Bitō Masahide, *Genroku Jidai*, 198.

20 For details of the original *Nihon Shoki* accounts, see John S. Brownlee, 'The Origins of Nationalist Historical Writing in Ancient Times,' in Brownlee, ed., *History in the Service of the Japanese Nation* (Toronto: University of Toronto-York University Joint Centre on Modern East Asia 1983), 44-7.

21 *Dai Nihon Shi*, vol. 7 (Dainihon Yūbenkai 1929), 275-6.

22 For my attempt at interpretation, see *Political Thought in Japanese Historical Writing*, Ch. 7.

23 Ozawa Ei'ichi, *Kindai Nihon Shigakushi no Kenkyū, Bakumatsu-hen* [Studies in Modern Japanese Historical Scholarship, the Bakumatsu Period] (Yoshikawa Kōbunkan 1966), 130.

24 Noguchi Takehiko, *Edo no Rekishika* [Edo Historians] (Chikuma Shobō 1979), 32.

25 Imai Usaburō et al., *Mitogaku*, 230.

26 'Kōdōkanki Jutsugi,' ibid., 262-3.

27 *Dai Nihon Shi*, 1:2. The translation of the command of the Sun Goddess is taken from W.G. Aston, *Nihongi*, 1:77. This collapsed account of the Age of the Gods, guaranteed to put Western readers to sleep, was doubtless vivid for Japanese readers. The Mito historians were not completely out of the woods since the narrative of Emperor Jinmu's conquering exploits in 'historical' times still involved people bearing names ending in 'mikoto,' the appellation for deities, but their genealogies were not matters of controversy. For its sources on specific points, *Dai Nihon Shi* cited *Kojiki, Kujiki* [Chronicles of Ancient Matters], *Kogo Shūi* [Gleanings from Ancient Words, 807], *Nihon Shoki*, and *Shoku Nihongi* [Chronicles of Japan Continued, 797]. *Kujiki*, which chronicled Japan from the Age of the Gods, was accepted by the tenth century as equally authoritative with *Kojiki* and *Nihon Shoki*. Since the mid-Tokugawa period, it has been considered a forgery in whole or in part. Among the earliest to conclude thus was Tada Yoshitoshi (1698-1750).

Chapter 3: Arai Hakuseki and Yamagata Bantō

1 There are many studies of Hakuseki, including two biographies by the leading contemporary scholar Miyazaki Michio: *Arai Hakuseki* (Shibundō 1957), and *Arai Hakuseki* (Yoshikawa Kōbunkan 1989).

2 G.B. Sansom, *A History of Japan*, vol. 3, 1615-1867 (Stanford: Stanford University Press 1963), 139.

3 Albert Craig, 'Science and Confucianism in Tokugawa Japan,' in Marius B. Jansen, ed., *Changing Japanese Attitudes toward Modernization* (Princeton: Princeton University Press 1965), 135.

4 Miyazaki Michio, 'Rinke Shigaku to Hakuseki Shigaku' [The Historical Scholarship of the Hayashi Family and Hakuseki], *Nihon Rekishi* [Japanese History] 148 (1960):3-5, and Yasukawa Minoru, *Honchō Tsugan no Kenkyū* [Studies on Honchō Tsugan] (Gensōsha 1980), 236-42.

5 Brownlee, *Political Thought*, Ch. 10.

6 See Kate Wildman Nakai, 'The Naturalization of Confucianism in Tokugawa Japan: The Problem of Sinocentrism,' *Harvard Journal of Asiatic Studies* 40.1 (1980):194.

7 Julia Ching, 'Chu Hsi and Ritual,' *Essais sur le rituel* [Essays on Ritual], Bibliotheque de l'École des Hautes Études, Section des Sciences Religeuses, vol. XCV, 59-60.

8 Miyazaki Michio, *Arai Hakuseki Joron* [Introduction to Arai Hakuseki] (Yoshikawa Kōbunkan 1966), 117.

9 *Kishinron* [Essay on Ghosts and Spirits], *Arai Hakuseki Zenshū* [Complete Works of Arai Hakuseki] (Naigai Insatsu Kabushiki Gaisha 1907), 2.

10 Miyazaki Michio, *Arai Hakuseki no Kenkyū* [Studies on Arai Hakuseki], rev. ed. (Yoshikawa Kōbunkan 1984), 639-40.

11 Ibid., 660-4.

12 *Koshitsū, Arai Hakuseki Zenshū*, 3:219.

13 *Tōga* [The Japanese *Erya*], *Arai Hakuseki Zenshū*, 4:75; Arakawa, 154.

14 Hakuseki's first sentence is taken from *Shaku Nihongi* [Annotated Nihongi, latter Kamakura period], which cites a number of private commentaries on *Nihon Shoki*. See *Kokushi Taikei* [Compendium of Japanese History], vol. 8 (Yoshikawa Kōbunkan 1935), 75. These private commentaries were made on the occasions of lectures on *Nihongi* (*Nihon Shoki*), which were held at the court on seven occasions between 721 and 965. Which private commentary was cited by *Shaku Nihongi* is not known. Hakuseki did not acknowledge *Shaku Nihongi* as his source; perhaps he thought that every scholar would know it.

15 *Hitachi no Kuni Fudoki* was one of many geographical records compiled in response to a court order of 713. Most of the text survives.
16 Modern texts of *Nihon Shoki* give 'Kawakami,' not 'Kahara,' as the reading for these characters. Kawakami is given by Kawamura Hidene (1723-92) in *Shoki Shikkai* [Collected Commentaries on *Nihon Shoki*, 1804]; by Iida Takesato (1827-1900) in *Nihon Shoki Tsūshaku* [Complete Commentary on *Nihon Shoki*, 1899]; and by the Nihon Koten Bungaku Taikei edition of *Nihon Shoki* (Iwanami Shoten 1967).
17 *Koshitsū, Arai Hakuseki Zenshū*, 3:225.
18 Miyazaki Michio, *Arai Hakuseki Joron*, 161.
19 Hoshino Ryōsaku, *Kenkyūshi Jinmu Tennō* [History of Research on Emperor Jinmu] (Yoshikawa Kōbunkan 1980), 36.
20 Mizuta Norihisa and Arisaka Takamichi, *Tominaga Nakamoto, Yamagata Bantō*, in *Nihon Shisō Taikei*, vol. 43 (Iwanami Shoten 1973), 146.
21 Minamoto Ryōen, '"Kindai Shisō" no Seisei' [The Formation of 'Modern Thought'], in Yoshida Hikaru, Sakuta Kei'ichi, and Ikimatsu Keizō, eds., *Kindai Nihon Shakai Shisōshi* [History of Modern Japanese Social Thought] (Yūhikaku 1968), 1:24.
22 Mizuta and Arisaka, *Tominaga Nakamoto, Yamagata Bantō*, 615-16.
23 Ibid., 270.
24 Ibid., 273. The medieval books based on *Kojiki* and *Nihon Shoki* were *Yamato Hime no Mikoto Seiki* [Records of the Deity Yamato Hime], written in the Kamakura period at Ise Shrine, and *Gengenshū* [Fundamentals of Shinto, 1338], by Kitabatake Chikafusa.
25 Aston, *Nihongi*, 1:110.
26 Mizuta and Arisaka, *Tominaga Nakamoto, Yamagata Bantō*, 278.
27 Ibid.
28 Ibid., 272.
29 Ibid., 292.
30 Ibid., 294.
31 Tsuda Sōkichi, 'Jōshinsho' [Written Defence], *Tsuda Sōkichi Zenshū* [Complete Works of Tsuda Sōkichi], vol. 24 (Iwanami Shoten 1965), 581-2, 611-12.

Chapter 4: Date Chihiro

1 Ōkubo Toshiaki, *Nihon Rekishi no Rekishi* [The History of Japanese History] (Shinchōsha 1959), 21.
2 The main works dealing with Date Chihiro are Takase Shigeo, *Date Chihiro* (Sōgensha 1942); Ozawa Ei'ichi, *Kindai Nihon Shigakushi no Kenkyū, Bakumatsu-hen* [Studies in the History of Modern Japanese Historical Studies, Bakumatsu Period] (Yoshikawa Kōbunkan 1969), 380-414; Morita Yasuhiko, *Ban Nobutomo no Shisō* [The Thought of Ban Nobutomo], (Perikansha 1979), 148-54; Arakawa Kusuo, 'Date Chihiro no *Taisei Santenkō* ni tsuite' [Date Chihiro's *Taisei Santenkō*], *Kōgakkan Ronsō* [Kōgakkan University Papers] 13.6 (1980); and Ishige Tadashi, '*Taisei Santenkō* ni okeru Jidai Kubun Hō to sono Shisōteki Konkyo' [The Method for Periodization in *Taisei Santenkō* and Its Foundation in Thought], in Ishida Ichirō, ed., *Jidai Kubun no Shisō* [Thought on Periodization] (Perikansha 1986). I list them because Date is so little known, and others may wish to pursue the subject further.
3 Ozawa Ei'ichi, *Kindai Nihon Shigakushi no Kenkyū, Bakumatsu-hen*, 395.
4 Ishige Tadashi, '*Taisei Santenkō* ni okeru Jidai Kubun Hō to sono Shisōteki Konkyo,' 177-81.
5 *Taisei Santenkō*, in Matsumoto Sannosuke and Ogura Yoshihiko, eds., *Kinsei Shiron Shū* [Historical Essays of the Modern Period], *Nihon Shisō Taikei*, vol. 48 (Iwanami Shoten 1974), 388.
6 Ibid., 395.
7 Aston, *Nihongi*, 2:131.
8 *Taisei Santenkō*, 408-9.
9 Ibid., 418-19.
10 Ibid., 407.
11 Ibid., 516.
12 Ibid., 415.

13 Ozawa, *Kindai Nihon Shigakushi no Kenkyū, Bakumatsu-hen*, 409. Ozawa also points out that Date was influenced by ancient ideas of China and Japan that important changes occur every 500 years. See 398-9.

14 Arakawa Kusuo, 'Date Chihiro no *Taisei Santenkō* ni tsuite' [Date Chihiro's *Taisei Santenkō*], *Kōgakkan Ronsō* [Kōgakkan University Papers] 13.6 (1980).

15 *Taisei Santenkō*, 416. Buddhism in ancient times was not a private religion and was integrated into government systems.

16 See John S. Brownlee, trans., 'The Jeweled Comb-Box: Motoori Norinaga's *Tamakushige*,' *Monumenta Nipponica* 43.1 (1988):42-3, 57-8.

17 Takase Shigeo, *Date Chihiro*, 159-61.

18 Ishige Tadashi, '*Taisei Santenkō* ni okeru Jidai Kubun Hō to sono Shisōteki Konkyo,' 190.

19 *Taisei Santenkō*, 452.

20 Ibid., 461.

21 Chijiwa Makoto, '*Taisei Santenkō* ni okeru Shikan' [The View of History in *Taisei Santenkō*], *Shichō* [Tides of History] 2.2 (1932):71, takes up the question, but the analysis is obscure.

22 Fukuzawa Yukichi, *An Outline of a Theory of Civilization*, trans. D.A. Dilworth and G.C. Hurst (Tokyo: Sophia University Press 1973), 142.

Chapter 5: The Resistance of the National Scholars

1 For Kada's petition to the bakufu, see R. Tsunoda, W.T. de Bary, and D. Keene, eds., *Sources of Japanese Tradition* (New York: Columbia University Press 1958), 514.

2 *Kojiki Den* has not been translated and is perhaps untranslatable, the same as Arai Hakuseki's detailed philological studies. For translations of other works of Motoori Norinaga, see Brownlee, 'Jeweled Comb-Box'; Sey Nishimura, 'First Steps into the Mountains: Motoori Norinaga's *Uiyamabumi*,' *Monumenta Nipponica* 42.4 (1987); and Sey Nishimura, 'The Way of the Gods: Motoori Norinaga's *Naobi no Mitama*,' *Monumenta Nipponica* 46.1 (1991).

3 Brownlee, 'Jeweled Comb-Box,' 47.

4 Motoori Norinaga, 'Kan'kyōjin' [A Pillory for the Madman, 1785], Ōkubo Tadashi, ed., *Motoori Norinaga Zenshū* [Complete Works of Motoori Norinaga], vol. 8 (Chikuma Shobō 1972), 282-5.

5 See Bob T. Wakabayashi, *Anti-Foreignism and Western Learning in Early Modern Japan: The New Theses of 1825* (Cambridge: Harvard University Press 1986).

6 *Kume Kunitake Rekishi Chosakushū* [Collected Historical Writings of Kume Kunitake], vol. 3 (Yoshikawa Kōbunkan 1990), 134.

7 The best study is Tahara Tsuguo, *Hirata Atsutane*, rev. ed. (Yoshikawa Kōbunkan 1986). For the writing of the Age of the Gods, see 244-5.

8 See the startling article about Hirata followers cutting off the heads of statues of the Ashikaga shoguns, considered traitors to the imperial land: Anne Walthall, 'Off with Their Heads! The Hirata Disciples and the Ashikaga Shoguns,' *Monumenta Nipponica* 50.2 (1995).

Chapter 6: European Influences on Meiji Historical Writing

1 K.B. Pyle, *The New Generation in Meiji Japan, 1885-1895* (Stanford: Stanford University Press 1969), 20.

2 See John D. Pierson, *Tokutomi Sohō, 1863-1957: A Journalist for Modern Japan* (Princeton: Princeton University Press 1980); Sinh Vinh, *Tokutomi Sohō (1863-1957): The Later Career* (Toronto: University of Toronto-York University Joint Centre on Modern East Asia 1986); and Sinh Vinh, with Matsuzawa Hiroaki and Nicholas Wickenden, eds., *The Future Japan*, by Tokutomi Sohō (Edmonton: University of Alberta Press 1989). Early in the twentieth century, Tokutomi abandoned these ideas of civilization and progress and became the most prominent of nationalist historians, but his later work, conducted outside the academic establishment, is not directly related to our story.

3 Fukuzawa Yukichi, *An Outline of a Theory of Civilization*, trans. D.A. Dilworth and G.C. Hurst (Tokyo: Sophia University Press 1973), 13-14.

4 Ibid., Preface by Tsuda Sōkichi, xix-xxii.

5 H.T. Buckle, *History of Civilization in England*, vol. 2 (London: Longman's Green 1871), 299-300, citing *Mallet's Northern Antiquities*, 1847. The three-volume *History of Civiliza-*

tion in England seems oddly titled, since volume 2 is a history of France and Spain and volume 3 is a history of Scotland, both for comparative purposes.

6 M.C. O'Connor, *The Historical Thought of François Guizot* (Washington, DC: Catholic University of America Press 1955), 42.

7 Buckle, *History*, 1:130-1.

8 Wilhelm von Humboldt, 'On the Historian's Task,' in Leopold von Ranke, *The Theory and Practice of History*, Georg G. Iggers and Konrad von Moltke, eds. (New York: Bobbs-Merrill 1973), 5.

9 Peter Gay, *Style in History* (New York: Basic Books 1974), 68-9.

10 Georg G. Iggers, *The German Conception of History: The National Tradition of Historical Thought from Herder to the Present* (Middletown, CT: Wesleyan University Press 1968), 64.

11 T.H. Van Laue, *Leopold Ranke: The Formative Years* (Princeton: Princeton University Press 1950), 42. The last Japanese scholar to meet Leopold von Ranke was Mitsukuri Genpachi (1862-1919), who studied under both Heinrich von Trietschke (1834-96) and Ranke in Heidelberg and Berlin. Mitsukuri went to Freiburg University in 1884 as a zoology student but changed fields because poor eyesight made it difficult to do microscopic work. For him, changing from zoology to history was switching from one area of science to another. He took Ranke's lectures for three years in 1884-6, until Ranke's death, and returned to Japan in 1892. Matsushima Ei'ichi, 'Mitsukuri Genpachi,' Kano Masanao and Nagahara Keiji, eds., *Nihon no Rekishika* [Japanese Historians] (Nihon Hyōronsha 1976), 63-9.

12 Peter Novick, *That Noble Dream: The 'Objectivity Question' and the American Historical Profession* (New York: Cambridge University Press 1988), 21-31.

13 *Encyclopaedia Judaica*, 1971 ed., vol. 14, 166.

14 On the program for hiring foreign experts, see Hazel J. Jones, *Live Machines: Hired Foreigners in Meiji Japan* (Vancouver: University of British Columbia Press 1980).

15 Ludwig Riess, Memorandum to President Watanabe Hiromoto, *Tokyo Teikoku Daigaku Gojūnen Shi* [Fifty-Year History of Tokyo Imperial University] (Tokyo Imperial University 1932), 1299-1303.

16 Kanai Madoka, 'Rekishigaku: Ludwig Riess o Megutte,' *Oyatoi Gaikokujin, 17, Jinbun Kagaku* [Hired Foreigners, 17, The Human Sciences], 145.

17 Kanai Madoka, 'Riess,' *Nihon no Kindaika o Ninatta Gaikokujin* [Foreign Leaders of Japanese Modernization], in Kokuritsu Kyōiku Kaikan, ed., *Kyōyō Kōza Shiriizu* [Educational Lecture Series] (Kyōsei 1992), 34-40.

18 Ibid., 28.

19 Kanai Madoka, 'Shigaku: Ludwig Riess o Megutte,' *Oyatoi Gaikokujin, Jinbun Kagaku*, 145-6. Natsume Sōseki also testified that Riess's English was good, and that served as the final word on the subject to the students who found him difficult to understand: the problem lay with them. Fujishiro Sojin, 'Natsume Kun no Henrin' [A Glimpse of Natsume], *Sōseki Zenshū Geppō* [Complete Works of Sōseki, Monthly Bulletin] (Sōseki Zenshū Kankōkai), no. 5, July 1928.

20 Kanai, 'Riess,' 30-1.

21 Ludwig Riess, *Methodology of History* (Tokyo: Tokyo University Library), 1-2.

22 Ibid., 54-5.

23 Important studies of contemporary scholarship are Novick, *That Noble Dream*; Bryan D. Palmer, *Descent into Discourse: The Reification of Language and the Writing of Social History* (Philadelphia: Temple University Press 1990); Russell Jacoby, *The Last Intellectuals: American Culture in the Age of Academe* (New York: Basic Books 1987).

24 Riess, *Methodology*, 68.

25 Having entered a vast and fiercely contested territory, let us tiptoe away under cover of a moderately phrased summary by Charles E. Rosenberg in 1973: 'many of the major figures in twentieth-century American psychiatry have been students of the neuroses and personality disorders, not of the most severe and incapacitating conditions ... Much of our century's most influential psychiatric writing has consisted of general statements about the human condition, in the form of hypothetical etiologies of particular personality types and related modes of behaviour. Such works have been as relevant to the educated community generally as to the narrower constituency of medical men and psychiatrists.' 'The Crisis in

Psychiatric Legitimacy: Reflections on Psychiatry, Medicine, and Public Policy,' *Explaining Epidemics, and Other Studies in the History of Medicine* (Cambridge: Cambridge University Press 1992), 252.

26 Riess, *Methodology*, 73 ff. A cunctator is a procrastinator; Swabia was a medieval German duchy.

27 Kume Kunitake, 'Kanzen no Kyūshū o Aratte Rekishi o Miyo' [Let Us Look at History without the Old Custom of Praising the Good], *Kume Kunitake Rekishi Chosakushū* [Collected Historical Writings of Kume Kunitake], vol. 3 (Yoshikawa Kōbunkan 1989), 134.

28 'Riisu Sōbetsukai' [The Farewell Party for Riess], *Shigaku Zasshi* 13.7 (1902):776-9.

Chapter 7: The Beginning of Academic History

1 See Sakamoto Tarō, *The Six National Histories of Japan*. The works are *Nihon Shoki* [Chronicles of Japan], 720; *Shoku Nihongi* [Chronicles of Japan Continued], 797; *Nihon Kōki* [Later Chronicles of Japan], 840; *Shoku Nihon Kōki* [Later Chronicles of Japan Continued], 869; *Nihon Montoku Tennō Jitsuroku* [Veritable Records of Emperor Montoku of Japan], 879; *Nihon Sandai Jitsuroku* [Veritable Records of Three Reigns of Japan], 901. A seventh work, *Shin Kokushi* [New History of Japan], was begun in the tenth century, but the project ran out of steam, and the manuscript was lost.

2 Jiro Numata, 'Shigeno Yasutsugu and the Modern Tokyo Tradition of Historical Writing,' in W.G. Beasley and E.G. Pulleyblank, eds., *Historians of China and Japan* (Oxford: Oxford University Press 1961), 265.

3 The details of organization are given in ibid., 265-8. See also Margaret Mehl, 'Tradition as Justification for Change: History in the Service of the Japanese Government,' in I. Neary, ed., *War, Revolution, and Japan* (Richmond, UK: Curzon Press 1993).

4 *Fukkōki*, 15 vols. (Naigai Shojaku Kabushiki Gaisha 1930-1); *Meiji Shiyō*, 2 vols. (Tokyo Daigaku Shiryō Hensanjo 1933).

5 Numata, 'Shigeno Yasutsugu,' 277.

6 Kume Kunitake, 'Yo ga Mitaru Shigeno Hakushi' [My View of Dr. Shigeno], in Ōkubo Toshiaki, ed., *Shigeno Hakase Shigaku Ronbun Shū* [Collection of Historical Articles by Dr. Shigeno], rev. and enl. ed., vol. 4 (Meisho Fūkyū Kai 1989), 52-4.

7 Sakamoto Tarō, *Shisho O Yomu* [Reading Historical Works] (Chūō Kōronsha 1981), 224-6.

8 Taguchi Ukichi, *Nihon Kaika Shōshi* (Kōdansha 1981), 19-33.

9 Ibid., 181-2.

10 Kuroita Katsumi, 'Ko Taguchi Ukichi to *Nihon Kaika Shōshi*' [The Late Taguchi Ukichi and *Nihon Kaika Shōshi*], *Rekishi Chiri* [History and Geography] 17.5 (1910):520.

11 Kudō Ei'ichi, 'Rekishika to shite no Taguchi Ukichi' [Taguchi Ukichi as a Historian], in Taguchi Ukichi, *Nihon Kaika Shōshi* (Kōdansha 1981), 263.

12 See H.C. McCullough, *The Taiheiki: A Chronicle of Medieval Japan* (New York: Columbia University Press 1959), 107-25.

13 Shigeno Yasutsugu, 'Kojima Takanori Kō' [On Kojima Takanori], *Shigeno Hakase Shigaku Ronbunshū*, vol. 2 (Yūzankaku 1938), 577-90.

14 For the list of names and shrines, see Murata Masashi, *Nanbokuchō Ron* [Essay on the Southern and Northern Courts] (Shibundō 1962), 254-5.

15 Miyachi Masato, *Tennōsei no Seijiteki Kenkyū* [Studies in the Politics of the Emperor System] (Azekura Shobō 1981), 154. This article also appears as 'Kume Kunitake Jiken no Seijiteki Kōsatsu' [The Politics of the Kume Kunitake Incident], in Tokyo Rekishigakka Kenkyūkai, *Tenkōki no Rekishigaku* [Historical Scholarship on the Tenkō Era] (Godō Shuppan 1979).

16 Miyachi, *Tennōsei no Seijiteki Kenkyū*, 154-64, 173-5, covers state Shinto and some of the statements of Shinto organizations and cites passages from some journals disputing Shigeno.

17 Kume, 'Yo ga Mitaru Shigeno Hakase,' 44-5.

18 Mikami Sanji, 'Hajime' [Foreword], *Shigeno Hakase Shigaku Ronbun shū* (1938), 3:2.

19 Ibid. Shigeno repeated the vow in a letter to Mikami on 20 April 1896: Frontispiece, *Shigeno Hakase Shigaku Ronbunshū*, rev. ed. (1989), vol. 2. In a 1990 book, Iriuchijima Kazutaka incorrectly states that Shigeno only raised the question lightly in 1890 and never referred to it again. Iriuchijima's book is a latter-day loyalist effort to document Kojima Takanori,

whose existence is assumed. *Nanchō Kojima Takanori* [Kojima Takanori of the Southern Court] (Takasaki City, Gunma Prefecture: Asao Sha 1990), 914-15. It contains a congratulatory preface by Hashimoto Ryūtarō, prime minister of Japan, 1996- .

20 Kume Kunitake, '*Taiheiki* wa Shigaku ni Eki Nashi' [*Taiheiki* Is Worthless for the Study of History], *Shigakkai Zasshi* 2.17 (1890):230-40; 2.18, 279-92; 2.20, 420-33; 2.21, 487-501; 2.22, 562-78. Reprinted in *Kume Kunitake Rekishi Chosakushū*, 3:144-80.

21 'Tanaka Hakase no Bizen Kojima Ichizoku Hakken ni tsuite' [On the Discovery by Professor Tanaka of a Kojima Family in Bizen], *Kume Kunitake Rekishi Chosakushū*, 2:338-44.

22 Tanaka's article came out in January 1910; two talks of Shigeno on the subject are recorded in *Rekishi Chiri* in February and April 1910, but they do not refer to Tanaka's article. *Shigeno Hakase Shigaku Ronbun Shū*, vol. 2 (1989), 577-90, 592-3.

23 Kanaseki Hiroshi, 'Protohistoric Archeology,' *Kōdansha Encyclopedia of Japan*, vol. 1 (Kōdansha 1983), 76.

24 E.S. Morse, *Shell Mounds of Ōmori*, Memoirs of the Science Department, University of Tokio [sic], Japan, vol. 1, part 1 (1879).

25 E.S. Morse, *Japan Day by Day* (Boston: Houghton 1917), 2 vols.

26 *Transactions of the Asiatic Society of Japan*, vol. 8, 1880. The Asiatic Society of Japan continues to publish its *Transactions*.

27 Nishimura Masae, 'A Study of the Late Early [sic] Jōmon Culture in the Tone River Area,' in Richard D. Pearson, ed., *Windows on the Japanese Past: Studies in Archeology and Prehistory* (Ann Arbor, MI: Center for Japanese Studies, University of Michigan 1986), 421.

Chapter 8: The Kume Kunitake Incident

1 Byron K. Marshall, *Academic Freedom and the Japanese University, 1868-1939* (Berkeley: University of California Press 1991).

2 Ivan Parker Hall, *Mori Arinori* (Cambridge: Harvard University Press 1973), 14.

3 Suzuki Masayuki, ed., *Kindai no Tennō* [The Modern Emperor] (Yoshikawa Kōbunkan 1993), 48-50.

4 Ienaga Saburō, Matsunaga Shōzō, and Emura Ei'ichi, *Meiji Zenki no Kenpō Kōsō* [Early Meiji Constitutional Ideas], rev. and enl. ed. (Fukumura Shuppan Kabushiki Gaisha 1985), 84.

5 Ibid., 117.

6 Ibid., 326, italics added. The editors do not identify Tamura Kan'ichirō.

7 Itō Hirobumi, *Commentaries on the Constitution of the Empire of Japan*, trans. Baron Miyoji Itō (Chūō Daigaku 1906), 6-7.

8 Satō Yoshimaru, 'Kume Kunitake to Waseda Daigaku' [Kume Kunitake and Waseda University], *Kume Kunitake no Kenkyū*, *Kume Kunitake Rekishi Chosakushū*, supp. vol., 390-2. On Kume's early career, see Marlene J. Mayo, 'The Western Education of Kume Kunitake, 1871-76,' *Monumenta Nipponica* 28.1 (1973).

9 *Shigaku Zasshi* 2.23 (1890):636-50; 2.24, 728-42; 2.25, 799-811. Rpt. in *Kume Kunitake Rekishi Chosakushū*, 3:271-96.

10 Kume Kunitake, 'Shigaku Kōshō no Hei' [The Evils of Historical Scholarship and Positivistic Research], *Shigaku Zasshi* 12.8 (1901):1-28. Rpt. in *Kume Kunitake Rekishi Chosakushū*, 3:58-74.

11 'Honpō no Jinrui Gengo ni tsuite Hikō o Nobete Magokoro Aikokusha ni Tadasu' [A Question from an Old Man for Sincere Patriots Regarding Japanese Race and Language], *Shigaku Zasshi* 11 (1890):17-43.

12 W.G. Aston, *Nihongi*, 1:57-9.

13 For further discussion, see John S. Brownlee, 'Ideological Control in Ancient Japan,' *Historical Reflections* 14.1 (1987).

14 'Wakan tomo ni Shinkoku Naru o Ronzu' [Japan and Korea Together Constituted the Divine Country of Japan], *Shigaku Zasshi* 22.1 (1911):42-62; 22.2 (1911):1-20. Rpt. in *Kume Kunitake Rekishi Chosakushū*, 2:38-59.

15 Ibid., *Kume Kunitake Rekishi Chosakushū*, 2:42.

16 Peter Duus, *The Abacus and the Sword: The Japanese Penetration of Korea, 1895-1910* (Berkeley: University of California Press 1995), 413-23.

17 *Kume Kunitake Rekishi Chosakushū*, 2:44.

226 *Notes to pages 99-104*

18 Kano Masanao and Imai Osamu, 'Nihon Kindai Shisōshi no naka no Kume Jiken' [The Kume Incident in the History of Modern Japanese Thought], *Kume Kunitake Kenkyū, Kume Kunitake Rekishi Chosakushū*, supp. vol., 305, note 28.
19 Taguchi Ukichi, 'Shintōsha Shoshi ni Tsugu' [To Certain Shintoist Gentlemen], ibid., 242-4.
20 Kano and Imai, 'Nihon Kindai Shisōshi no naka no Kume Jiken, ibid., 220-31.
21 Ibid., 235.
22 Ōmori Kingorō, 'Ko Kume Kunitake Sensei o Omou' [Remembering the Late Professor Kume Kunitake], *Rekishi Chiri* 57.4 (1931):561-3.
23 'Shintō wa Saiten no Kozoku to ieru Bunshō ni tsuite Mondō no Shimatsu' [The Complete Record of Questions and Answers on the Article 'Shinto Is an Ancient Custom of Heaven Worship'], in *Meiji Shiron Shū* [Meiji Historical Argument], *Meiji Bungaku Zenshū* [Complete Collection of Meiji Literature], vol. 78 (Chikuma Shobō 1966), 102-5.
24 Ōmori, 'Ko Kume Kunitake Sensei o Omou,' 562.
25 Tahata Shinobu, *Katō Hiroyuki* (Yoshikawa Kōbunkan 1959), 86.
26 Ōmori, 'Ko Kume Kunitake Sensei o Omou,' 563-4.
27 Kano and Imai, 'Nihon Kindai Shisōshi no naka no Kume Jiken,' 218.
28 Mikami Sanji, *Meiji Jidai no Rekishi Gakkai. Mikami Sanji Kyuukaidan* [The World of Historical Scholarship in Meiji. Mikami Sanji Talks about the Old Days] (Yoshikawa Kōbunkan 1992), 58-9. Originally published in the scholarly journal *Nihon Rekishi*, 1936-9.
29 Hagino Minahiko, 'Kume Kunitake to Komonjogaku' [Kume Kunitake and the Study of Ancient Documents], *Kume Kunitake no Kenkyū, Kume Kunitake Rekishi Chosakushū* [Japanese History], supp. vol., 366.
30 Satō Yoshimaru, 'Kume Kunitake to Waseda Daigaku,' *Kume Kunitake Rekishi Chosakushū*, supp. vol., 390.
31 Kume Kunitake, *Kume Hakase Kyūjūnen Kaikoroku* [Memoirs of Dr. Kume at Ninety], vol. 2 (Waseda Daigaku Shuppanbu 1934), 557.
32 Naimushō, Ken'etsuka, Hokan-gakari [Ministry of Home Affairs, Censorship Department, Custody Office], *Jūrokunen Tankōbon Shobun Nisshi, Shōwa Jūrokunen – Shōwa Jūhachinen* [Journals of Actions Taken against Books 1941-3], Hisa Gentarō, ed. (Kohoku 1977). Appendix, 'Narachō Shi Naiyō Fukei Jiken' Genkō [Manuscript, 'The Case of Disrespectful Contents of *History of the Nara Court*'], 255-7. This report wrongly gives the first date of publication of *Narachō Shi* as 1912; it was 1907.
33 Kume Kunitake, *Narachō Shi* [History of the Nara Court] (Waseda Daigaku Shuppanbu 1907), 496-500.
34 *Kaikoku Gojūnenshi* (Waseda Daigaku, Kaikoku Gojūnenshi Hakkōsho 1903); rpt. in *Kume Kunitake Rekishi Chosakushū*, 3:337-53. It is translated as 'Japanese Religious Beliefs: The Kami' in M.B. Huish, ed., *Fifty Years of New Japan*, vol. 2 (London: Smith, Elder 1909), 241. The unidentified translation took such great liberties that the English translation cannot be relied on at all.
35 Aston, *Nihongi*, 2:106.
36 'Shintō to Kundō,' *Kume Kunitake Rekishi Chosakushū*, 3:227. The hexagrams were a system of divination used in ancient China and were committed to writing in the Eastern Zhou dynasty (770-256 BC); the commentary cited by Kume was attributed to Confucius. The term '*kami*' in *Yi Jing* is generally rendered not as 'gods' but as 'spirits' by English translators. Japanese gods all have identities, and there is no basis for rendering kami more abstractly as spirits. Thus, Kume's fundamental position may be questioned. For the *Yi Jing* passage and the commentary, see Suzuki Yūjirō, ed., *Ekikyō* [The Book of Changes], *Zenshaku Kanbun Taikei* [Compendium of Translated Works of Chinese Literature], vol. 1 (Shūeisha 1974), 339-50; in English, Wu Jing-Nuan, trans., *Yi Jing* (Washington, DC: Taoist Center 1991), 104-6; 235.
37 Margaret Mehl, 'Scholarship and Ideology in Conflict: The Kume Affair, 1892,' *Monumenta Nipponica* 48.3 (1993):342-3.
38 Shigeno Yasutsugu, 'Shinto,' *Shigaku Zasshi* 8.1,3,4 (Jan., Mar., Apr. 1898). Reprinted in *Shigeno Hakase Shigaku Bunshū* (1938), 1:261-72.
39 Ōmori, 'Ko Kume Kunitake Sensei o Omou,' 564.

40 Haga Noboru, *Hihan Kindai Nihon Shigaku Shisōshi* [Critical Intellectual History of Modern Japanese Historical Scholarship] (Kashiwa Shobō 1974), 80.
41 Marshall, *Academic Freedom*, 51, note 42.
42 Miura Hiroyuki, 'Nihon Shigakushi Kaisetsu,' *Nihonshi no Kenkyū* [Studies in Japanese History], vol. 2 (Iwanami Shoten 1930), 493.
43 Katsuta Katsutoshi, *Miura Hiroyuki no Rekishigaku* [The Historical Scholarship of Miura Hiroyuki] (Kashiwa Shobō 1981), 119, 217-18, 223.
44 Fujiki Kunihiko, 'Zen Honkai Hyōgiin Bungaku Hakase Kume Kunitake Sensei no Seikyo' [The Death of Dr. Kume Kunitake, Former Council Member of the Historical Association], *Shigaku Zasshi* 42.4 (1931); and Hashimura Hiro, 'Kume Kunitake Hakase no Fu' [Obituary of Dr. Kume Kunitake], *Rekishi Chiri* 57.4 (1931).
45 Tsuji Zennosuke, 'Honpō ni okeru Shūshi no Enkaku to Kokushigaku no Seiritsu' [The Development of Historical Writing in Japan and the Establishment of the Field of Japanese History], *Honpō Shigakushi Ronsō* [Essays on the History of Historical Scholarship in Japan], vol. 1 (Fuzanbō 1939).

Chapter 9: The Development of Academic History

1 Matsushima Ei'ichi, 'Kuroita Katsumi,' in Kano Masanao and Nagahara Keiji, eds., *Nihon no Rekishika* [Japanese Historians] (Nihon Hyōronsha 1976), 128-9.
2 Mikami Sanji, *Meiji Jidai no Rekishi Gakkai. Mikami Sanji Kyukaidan* [The World of Historical Scholarship in Meiji. Mikami Sanji Talks about the Old Days] (Yoshikawa Kōbunkan 1992), 130-1.
3 Tsuji Zennosuke, 'Ko Mikami Sanji Sensei Ryakureki' [Brief Curriculum Vitae of the Late Professor Mikami Sanji], in Mikami Sanji, *Edo Jidai Shi* [History of the Edo Period], vol. 2 (Fuzanbō 1943 5), 692.
4 For example, Noboru Hiraga, 'Historiography,' *Kōdansha Encyclopedia of Japan*, vol. 3 (Kōdansha 1983), 157; Miyachi Masato, 'Meiji Zenki ni okeru Rekishi Ninshiki no Kōzō' [The Structure of Historical Understanding in Early Meiji], in Tanaka Akira and Miyachi Masato, *Rekishi Ninshiki* [Historical Understanding], *Nihon Kindai Shisō Taikei* [Compendium of Modern Japanese Thought], vol. 13 (Iwanami Shoten 1991), 559.
5 John Higham, *History: Professional Scholarship in America*, rev. ed. (Baltimore: Johns Hopkins University Press 1989), 22-5.
6 Ibid., 24-5.
7 Victor Gondos, *J. Franklin Jameson and the Birth of the National Archives, 1906-1926* (Pittsburgh: University of Pennsylvania Press 1981).
8 'Hitsuyō Suji' [Off-Topic but Urgent], *Shigaku Zasshi* 13.4 (1902):105-6.
9 Nagahara Keiji, 'Uchida Ginzō,' in Nagahara and Kano, eds., *Nihon no Rekishika*, 98.
10 For a review of the brief struggle over imperial chronology, see Miyachi Masato, *Tennōsei no Seijiteki Kenkyū*, 171-4.
11 Amihai Mazar, *The Archeology of the Land of the Bible, 10,000-586 B.C.E.* (New York: Doubleday 1992), 31-2. Mazar notes that 'Current archeological research in Palestine tends to be professional, secular, and free from theological prejudices'; this also applies to Japan.
12 *Shigaku Zasshi* 8.8 (1897):29-60; 8.9, 50-76; 8.12, 48-73.
13 Evaluation by Mishina Shōei, in Naka Michiyo, *Jōsei Nenki Kō*, rev. and enl. by Mishina Shōei (Yōtokusha 1948), 92-3. For an excellent English summary of Naka's work, see John Young, *The Location of Yamatai: A Case Study in Japanese Historiography, 720-1945* (Baltimore: Johns Hopkins University Press 1958), 93-6.
14 Sakamoto Tarō, *The Six National Histories of Japan*, trans. John S. Brownlee (Vancouver: University of British Columbia Press; Tokyo: University of Tokyo Press 1991), 88.
15 Robert Karl Reischauer, *Early Japanese History* (Princeton: Princeton University Press 1937), part A, 77-8.
16 'Jōko no Jiseki Tsutomete Jinji o motte Kansatsu Atari' [We Must Try to View the Evidence from Antiquity as Pertaining to Humans], *Shigaku Zasshi* 2.23 (1891).
17 'Kojiki Kaikan no Betsutenjin ni tsukite' [The Separate Heavenly Deities in the Opening Chapter of *Kojiki*], *Shigaku Zasshi* 22.1 (1911).

18 Kume Kunitake, *Nihon Kodaishi* [The Ancient History of Japan] (Waseda Daigaku Shuppanbu 1907), 71-2.
19 Saeki Ariyoshi, 'Kume Kunitake to Nihon Kodaishi' [Kume Kunitake and Ancient Japanese History], *Kume Kunitake no Kenkyū, Kume Kunitake Rekishi Chosakushū*, supp. vol.
20 Kume, *Nihon Kodaishi*, 274, 330.
21 'Chūai Tei Izen Kinen Kō' [Dates before Emperor Chūai], *Shigaku Zasshi* 13 (1902):1-25.

Chapter 10: The Southern and Northern Courts Controversy

1 *Shiryaku* [Outline of History], in Kaigo Tokiomi, *Nihon Kyōkasho Taikei, Kindaihen* [Compendium of Japanese School Textbooks, Modern Period], vol. 18, *Rekishi* [History] (Kōdansha 1963), 15.
2 *Shōgaku Nihon Rekishi*, Kaigo, *Nihon Kyōkasho Taikei*, 19:469-70.
3 *Jinjō Shogaku Nihon Rekishi* [Japanese History for Elementary Schools], Kaigo, *Nihon Kyōkasho Taikei*, 19:519.
4 Shuzo Uyenaka, 'The Textbook Controversy of 1911: National Needs and Historical Truth,' in John S. Brownlee, ed., *History in the Service of the Japanese Nation* (Toronto: University of Toronto-York University Joint Centre on Modern East Asia 1983).
5 Tokutomi Sohō, *Kōshaku Katsura Tarō* [Count Katsura Tarō] (Hara Shobō 1967), 520.
6 Kuroita Katsumi, 'Nanboku Ryōchō Seijunron no Shijitsu to sono Dan'an' [Facts about the Southern-Northern Courts Controversy, and Its Conclusion], *Nihon Oyobi Nihonjin* [Japan and the Japanese], 15 Mar. 1911:97.
7 Anesaki Masaharu, 'Nanboku Chō Mondai ni kansuru Gigi narabi ni Dan'an' [Doubts and Conclusions on the Southern-Northern Courts Problem], *Yomiuri Shinbun*, 23 Feb. 1911, cited in Yamazaki Tōkichi, *Nanbokuchō Seijun Ronsan* [Collected Articles on the Legitimacy of the Southern-Northern Courts] (Kyoto: Yokota Kappansho 1911), 571.
8 Isawa Shūji, 'Seijun Mondai to Kokutei Kyōkasho' [The Legitimacy Problem and the National Textbooks], ibid., 53. Herschel Webb noted that 'The expression "taigi meibun" is used almost as though it were a single indivisible thing. In fact the two words were originally quite different concepts.' *The Japanese Imperial Institution in the Tokugawa Period* (New York: Columbia University Press 1968), 192. *Taigi* had to do with duty and *meibun* with ethical behaviour appropriate to status; the two were combined in the Meiji period. I have adopted Uyenaka's rendering of *taigi meibun* as 'the right relations between the emperor and his subjects.' Uyenaka, 'Textbook Controversy,' 94.
9 Baron Kitabatake Harufusa, 'Nanchō Seitō Ron' [The Legitimacy of the Southern Court], ibid., 21. Baron Kitabatake, a loyalist fighter in the Meiji Restoration and a judicial official, was broad-minded. He called on Kita Sadakichi, who was interested as a historian in Kitabatake's hometown of Hōryūji-mura, to talk about their common interests and avoided discussion of the textbook incident. Ueda Masaaki, *Kita Sadakichi* (Kōdansha 1978), 104.
10 Cited in Kanzaki Kiyoshi, *Taigyaku Jiken, I. Kōtoku Shūsui to Meiji Tennō. Kuroi Bōryaku no Uzumaki* [The Great Treason Incident, I. Kōtoku Shūsui and the Meiji Emperor. The Vortex of the Dark Plot] (Ayumi Shuppan 1976), 48.
11 *Jinjō Shōgaku Nihon Rekishi*, Kaigo, *Nihon Kyōkasho Taikei*, 19:586-7.
12 Kume Kunitake, *Nanboku Chō Jidai Shi* [History of the Period of the Southern and Northern Courts] (Waseda Daigaku Shuppanbu 1907), preface. In fact Kume's work did not contain much economic history.
13 Tanaka Yoshinari, *Nanboku Chō Jidai Shi* [History of the Period of the Southern and Northern Courts] (Meiji Shoin 1922), 140.
14 James Murdoch, *History of Japan*, vol. 1 (Tokyo: Asiatic Society of Japan 1910), 534.
15 Kuroita, 'Nanboku Ryōchō Seijunron no Shijitsu to sono Dan'an,' 108-10.
16 Mikami Sanji, 'Tanaka Hakase no Etsureki' [The Career of Dr. Tanaka], in Tanaka, *Nanboku Chō Jidai Shi*, 7-8.
17 More than seventy years after his death, there is a readership for Tanaka's works, two of which are available in inexpensive paperback editions in the Kōdansha Gakugei Bunko series: *Nanboku Chō Jidai Shi*, and *Ashikaga Jidai Shi* [History of the Ashikaga Period].
18 *Nanboku Chō Jidai Shi*, 2.
19 Ueda Kazutoshi (1867-1937), a scholar of Japanese language, dean of the Faculty of Letters, 18 Mar. 1912-31 Mar. 1921. His interest in the case may have been more than deanly, since

he lectured in 1911 on linguistics of the Ashikaga period. Mikami succeeded him as dean, serving from 14 Sept. 1921 to 12 Sept. 1924.

20 Mikami, 'Tanaka Hakase no Etsureki,' 12-13.
21 Yamada Norio, *Rekishika Kita Sadakichi* [Kita Sadakichi, Historian] (Hōbunkan 1976), 88.
22 Kita Sadakichi, *Rokujūnen no Kaiko* [Recollections of Sixty Years], *Kita Sadakichi Chosakushū* [Collected Works of Kita Sadakichi], vol. 14 (Heibonsha 1982), 142.
23 Mikami wrote in *Tokyo Nichi Nichi Shinbun* [Tokyo Daily News], 15 Feb. 1911, and *Jiji Shinpō* [The Times], 17 Feb. These articles and those of his attackers are found in Yamazaki Tōkichi, *Nanboku Chō Seijun Ronsan.*
24 Kita, *Rokujūnen no Kaiko*, 131-2; and Mikami Sanji, 'Nanboku Seijun Mondai no Yurai' [The Origins of the Southern-Northern Courts Problem], *Shigaku Zasshi* 22.2 (1911):493; rpt. from the journal *Taiyō* [The Sun]. Mikami published this to combat alleged inaccuracies in the newspapers and in *Nihon Oyobi Nihonjin*, note 25, below.
25 'Nanboku Chō Seijun Mondō' [Questions and Answers on the Legitimacy of the Southern and Northern Courts], *Nihon Oyobi Nihonjin*, 15 Mar. 1911:213-15. This version of the discussion was published by Fujisawa/Makino/Matsudaira.
26 Tsuji Zennosuke Sensei Tanjō Hyakunen Kinen Kai [Memorial Society for the 100th Anniversary of the Birthday of Professor Tsuji Zennosuke], *Tsuji Zennosuke Hakase Jireki Nenpu Kō* [Manuscript of the Personal Chronology of Dr. Tsuji Zennosuke] (Heibunsha 1977), 31.
27 *Tokyo Daigaku Hyakunen Shi, Bukyoku Shi*, 4:566.
28 *Dai Nihon Shiryō*, vol. 6, part 10 (1911). See also Murata Masashi, *Nanboku Chō Ron*, 227-9.
29 Tanaka, *Nanboku Chō Jidai Shi*; Nakamura Naokatsu, *Nihon Bunka Shi – Nanboku Chō Jidai* [Cultural History of Japan – The Period of the Southern and Northern Courts], *Nakamura Naokatsu Chosakushū* [Collected Works of Nakamura Naokatsu], vol. 2 (Tankōsha 1978).
30 Nakamura, *Nihon Bunka Shi*, 2:325.
31 Nakamura Naokatsu, *Yoshino Chō Shi* [History of the Yoshino Court] (Kyoto: Hoshino Shoten 1935), 1.
32 Hayashiya Tatsusaburō, 'Kaisetsu' [Commentary], *Nakamura Naokatsu Chosakushū*, 2:560-3.

Chapter 11: Eminent Historians in the 1930s

1 See Richard H. Mitchell, *Thought Control in Prewar Japan* (Ithaca: Cornell University Press 1976) and *Janus-Faced Justice: Political Criminals in Imperial Japan* (Honolulu: University of Hawaii Press 1992); Elise K. Tipton, *The Japanese Police State: The Tokkō in Interwar Japan* (Honolulu: University of Hawaii Press 1990).
2 Richard H. Mitchell, *Censorship in Imperial Japan* (Princeton: Princeton University Press 1983), 266. The substance of this paragraph is taken from the chapter 'The Fifteen-Year War.'
3 Miyachi Masato, 'Tennōsei Fashizumu to Ideorōgu-tachi: Kokumin Seishin Bunka Kenkyūjo o Rei ni totte' [Emperor-System Fascism and Its Ideologues: The Case of the Research Centre on Japanese Spiritual Culture], *Kagaku to Shisō* [Science and Thought] 76 (1990).
4 R.K. Hall, ed., *Kokutai no Hongi: Cardinal Principles of the National Essence of Japan*, trans. J. Gauntlett (Cambridge: Harvard University Press 1949), 59.
5 Byron K. Marshall, *Academic Freedom and the Japanese Imperial University, 1868-1939* (Berkeley: University of California Press 1992), 122-3.
6 Ibid., 143.
7 Ibid., 175-80.
8 See F. Curtis Miles, 'Traditionalist Responses to Modernization in Japan: The Case of Minoda Muneki,' PhD diss., State University of New York at Buffalo, 1989. Minoda has been called a psychopath by Nagao Ryūichi, *Nihon Kokka Shisōshi Kenkyō* [Studies in the History of Thought on the Japanese State] (Sōbunsha 1982), 46.
9 *Genri Nippon*, 24 Dec. 1939.
10 The petition is in Maruyama Masao and Fukuda Kan'ichi, *Kikigaki Nanbara Shigeru Kōkiroku* [Oral Memoirs of Nanbara Shigeru] (Tokyo Daigaku Shuppankai 1989), 256-8.
11 Marshall, *Academic Freedom*, 167.
12 Takayanagi Mitsutoshi, 'Ko Mikami Hakase Tsuitōki' [A Memorial of the Late Dr. Mikami], *Kokushigaku* [Japanese History] 38 (1939):60.

13 Nakamura Kōya, 'Mikami Sensei o Omou' [Remembering Professor Mikami], in Mikami Sanji, *Edo Jidai Shi* [History of the Edo Period], vol. 2 (Fuzanbō 1943-5), 712.

14 Mikami Sanji, *Kokushi Gaisetsu* [Outline of Japanese History] (Fuzanbō 1943), 11-12.

15 Ibid., 25-35.

16 Ibid., 12. Italics added.

17 Maurice Ashley, *England in the Seventeenth Century (1603-1714)*, 3rd ed. (Harmondsworth, UK: Penguin Books 1961), 35.

18 Francis Bacon, 'The Great Instauration,' in E.A. Burtt, ed., *The English Philosophers from Bacon to Mill* (New York: Modern Library 1939), 12.

19 Mikami Sanji, 'Hajime' [Foreword], *Shigeno Hakase Shigaku Bunshū* (1938), 3:2.

20 *Taiyō*, 1 Apr. 1911. Also in *Nanbokuchō Seijun Ronsan*, 344.

21 Nakamura Kōya, 'Mikami Sensei o Omou,' 712-13.

22 Akiyama Kenzō, 'Kaisetsu' [Exposition], in Mikami Sanji, *Edo Jidai Shi* [History of the Edo Period], vol. 3 (Kōdansha Gakugei Bunko 1977), 812.

23 Takano Kunio, *Tennō Kokka no Kyōiku Ron – Kyōgaku Sasshin Hyōgikai no Kenkyū* [Education in the Emperor's State – Studies on the Education Reform Council] (Azumino Shobō 1989), 61-2.

24 Miyachi Masato, 'Bakumatsu-Meiji Shoki ni okeru Rekishi Ninshiki no Kōzō' [The Structure of Historical Consciousness in the Late Tokugawa and Early Meiji Periods], in Miyachi and Tanaka Akira, *Rekishi Ninshiki* [Historical Consciousness], *Nihon Kindai Shisō Taikei* [Compendium of Modern Japanese Thought], vol. 13 (Iwanami Shoten 1991), 559.

25 Interview with Miyachi Masato, 20 Aug. 1994.

26 R.K. Hall, ed., *Kokutai no Hongi: Cardinal Principles of the National Entity of Japan*, trans. J. Gauntlett (Cambridge: Harvard University Press 1949), 59.

27 According to Tsuchiya Tadao, '*Kokutai no Hongi* no Hensan Katei' [The Process of Compiling *Kokutai no Hongi*], *Kantō Kyōiku Gakkai Kiyō* [Bulletin of the Kanta Education Society] 5 (1978), the shorthand notes of proceedings at the Education Reform Council were stopped when contentious matters arose, such as the fight between Mikami and Kihira.

28 Interview with Inoue Kiyoshi, 11 July 1993. See also Inoue Kiyoshi, 'Nihon Teikoku Shugi to Kokushigaku' [Japanese Imperial Ideology and Japanese History], in Inoue and Mori Kōichi, *Yugamerareta Kodaishi* [Ancient History Distorted] (Asahi Shinbunsha 1973), 17-19.

29 Tsuji Zennosuke, 'Kuroita Katsumi Kun' [Professor Kuroita Katsumi], *Omoiizuru Mama* [As I Remember], in Tsuji Zennosuke Sensei Hyakunen Kinenkai [Memorial Society for the 100th Anniversary of the Birth of Professor Tsuji Zennosuke], *Tsuji Zennosuke Hakase Jireki Nenpu Kō* [Manuscript of the Personal Chronology of Dr. Tsuji Zennosuke] (Heibunsha 1977), 163-4.

30 Interview with Inoue Kiyoshi, 11 July 1993.

31 Kuroita Katsumi, 'Ōbei Bunmei Ki' [Record of Civilization in Europe and America], *Kyoshin Bunshū* [Collected Writings of Kuroita Katsumi], vol. 7 (Yoshikawa Kōbunkan 1934), 15-24. 'Kyoshin' was Kuroita's pen name, meaning 'straight from the heart.'

32 Sakamoto Tarō, 'Kuroita Katsumi,' *Kokushi Daijiten* [Dictionary of Japanese History], vol. 4 (Yoshikawa Kōbunkan 1984), 954.

33 Ōkubo Toshiaki, *Nihon Kindai Shigaku Kotohajime: Ichi Rekishika no Kaisō* [The Beginnings of Historical Scholarship in Modern Japan: Reminiscences of a Historian] (Iwanami Shinsho, no. 427, 1996), 60.

34 Kuroita Katsumi, 'Shōwa Ni-sannen Nikki' [Diary for 1927-8], Kuroita Katsumi Sensei Tanjō Hyakunen Kinen Kai [Memorial Society for the 100th Anniversary of the Birth of Professor Kuroita Katsumi], *Kuroita Katsumi Sensei Ibun* [Documents of Professor Kuroita Katsumi] (Yoshikawa Kōbunkan 1974).

35 Kuroita Katsumi, *Kokushi no Kenkyū* (Yoshikawa Kōbunkan 1931), Sōsetsu, 167.

36 Ibid., Kakusetsu, 1:1.

37 Kuroita Katsumi, *Kokushi Hensan Chojutsu no Enkaku* [The Development of Compilation and Writing of Works in Japanese History], *Kyoshin Bunshū*, 3:514.

38 Kuroita Katsumi, *Kodai Shinto ni kansuru Ichikōsatsu* [Survey of Ancient Shinto], *Kyoshin Bunshū*, vol. 3.

39 Kuroita Katsumi, *Saisei Itchi no Kokutai*, *Kyoshin Bunshū*, 1:239-69.

40 Kuroita Katsumi, *Kokutai Shinron, Kyoshin Bunshū*, 1:11.

41 Ibid., 29, 114-15, 172-6.

42 Nakamura Naokatsu, *Kitabatake Chikafusa* (Hokkai Shuppansha 1937), 5, 115.

43 Kuroita Katsumi, *Kokushi no Taikan* (Iwanami Shoten 1935), 1.

44 Kuroita Katsumi, *Jinmu Tennō Gotōsen to Hyūga no Kuni, Kyoshin Bunshū*, 2:37-45.

45 Kuroita Katsumi, *Go Daigo Tennō Gochūkō no Seigyō o Omoitatematsuru* [Humble Thoughts on the Achievement of Emperor Go Daigo in the Kenmu Restoration], Kenmu Chūkō Roppyakunen Kinen Kai [Society for the 600th Anniversary of the Kenmu Restoration], *Kenmu Chūkō* [The Kenmu Restoration] (1934), 179-85.

46 Sakamoto Tarō, *Kodaishi no Michi*, Sakamoto Tarō Chosakushū, 12:86.

47 Interview with Ienaga Saburō, 9 July 1994. Ienaga was a history student at the time.

48 Interview with Kuroita Nobuo, nephew of Kuroita Katsumi, and his wife, Nagai Michiko, novelist, 30 June 1994.

49 Saitō Takashi, 'Kokushika no Takauji, Yasutoki Sanbi Ron o motte "Minsei" Shugi Hōgaku Shisō – Tsuji Zennosuke, Nakamura Naokatsu, Kuroita Katsumi, Kōda Naritomo ra no Shoron o Hyōsu' [Works by Japanese Historians Praising Takauji and Yasutoki Show Legal Thought Based on Principle of 'Public Welfare' – A Critique of the Arguments of Tsuji Zennosuke, Nakamura Naokatsu, Kuroita Katsumi, Kōda Naritomo], *Genri Nippon*, June 1935:39-43. See the discussion of Tsuji Zennosuke below.

50 Naimushō, Ken'etsusho, Hokan-gakari, *Tankōbon Shobun Nisshi*, 87.

51 Kigen Nisen Roppyakunen Kagoshima-ken Hōshuku Kai [Kagoshima Prefecture Committee to Celebrate the 2,600th Anniversary], *Jindai narabi ni Jinmu Tennō Seiseki Kenshō Shiryō* [Materials Demonstrating the Age of the Gods and Historical Sites Related to Emperor Jinmu] (1940), 1-10, in Tsuji Zennosuke Kankei Shiryō [Historical Materials Related to Tsuji Zennosuke], Historiographical Institute, Tokyo University, file 130 (hereafter referred to as TZKS). Naganuma Kenkai was a member of the Commission of Inquiry into Historical Sites Related to Emperor Jinmu, but apparently no charges of conflict of interest were made against him.

52 Yamamoto Tadanao, 'Reflections on the Development of Historical Archeology in Japan,' in R.J. Pearson, ed., *Windows on the Japanese Past: Studies in Archeology and Prehistory* (Ann Arbor, MI: University of Michigan, Center for Japanese Studies 1986), 399.

53 Matsushima Ei'ichi, 'Kuroita Katsumi,' in Nagahara and Kano, *Nihon no Rekishika*, 135.

54 Tsuji Zennosuke, 'Kenkyū Seikatsu no Omoide' [Memories of a Research Life], *Shisō* [Thought] 344 (1953):230.

55 *Tsuji Zennosuke Hakse Jireki Nenpu Kō*, 97, gives Dec. 1948 as the publication of *Nihon Bunka Shi*, vol. 1, but the publication date in the book is 15 Jan. 1950.

56 Tsuji Zennosuke, *Nihon Bunka Shi* [History of Japanese Culture], vol. 1 (Shunjū Sha 1950), 30.

57 Tsuji Zennosuke, 'Ashikaga Takauji no Shinkyō ni tsuite' [The Religious Faith of Ashikaga Takauji], *Shigaku Zasshi* 28.9 (1917):864.

58 Ibid., 866.

59 *Tsuji Zennosuke Hakase Nenpu Kō*, 70.

60 Saitō Takashi, 'Kokushika no Takauji, Yasutoki Sanbi Ron to "Minsei" Shugi Hōgaku Shisō Tsuji Zennosuke, Nakamura Naokatsu, Kuroita Katsumi, Kōda Shigetomo ra no Shoron o Hyōsu' [Historians' Articles Praising Takauji and Yasutoki, and 'Democratic' Scholarly Legal Thought – A Critique of Tsuji Zennosuke, Nakamura Naokatsu, Kuroita Katsumi, and Kōda Shigetomo], *Genri Nippon*, June 1935:39-43.

61 TZKS, 22-8.

62 Gotō Tanji and Okami Masao, eds., *Taiheiki* [Chronicle of Grand Pacification], *Nihon Koten Bungaku Taikei* [Compendium of Classical Japanese Literature] (Iwanami Shoten 1970-2), 34:53, 71; 36:293.

63 Ōta Yoshimaro, ed., *Hanazono Tennō Shinki* [The Diary of Emperor Hanazono], vol. 3 (Zoku Gunsho Ruijū Kanseikai 1986), 81.

64 *Hōjō Kudaiki* [Record of Nine Reigns of the Hōjō Regents], *Zoku Gunsho Ruijū* [Classified Collection of Books Continued], vol. 29, part 1 (Zoku Gunsho Ruijū Kanseikai 1925), Zatsubu [Miscellaneous Section], 448. These references to imperial rebellion were identified by Tsuji Zennosuke, *Nihon Bunka Shi* [Cultural History of Japan], vol. 4 (Shunjū Sha 1960), 4.

65 *Shigeno Hakase Shigaku Ronbun Shū* (1989), vol. 1.
66 Ōkubo Toshiaki, 'Henshū Kōki' [Postscript on the Editing], *Shigeno Hakase Ronbun Shū* (1989), supp. vol., 226.
67 Ibid., 225-6.
68 Tsuji Tatsuya, 'Chichi Zennosuke to Rekishigaku to Watakushi' [My Father Zennosuke, Historical Scholarship, and I], in Tsuji Tatsuya, ed., *Edo Jidai Shiron* [Historical Essays on the Edo Period], by Tsuji Zennosuke (Yusōsha 1991), 255.
69 Ibid.
70 *Tsuji Zennosuke Hakase Jireki Nenpu Kō*, 90.
71 Interview with Tsuji Tatsuya, 7 July 1994.
72 Maruyama Masao, in *Nanbara Shigeru Kaikoroku*, 246; interview with Ienaga Saburō, 9 July 1994.
73 Interview with Tsuji Tatsuya, 7 July 1994.
74 *Tsuji Zennosuke Hakase Jireki Nenpu Kō*, 80.
75 Miyachi Masato, '"Nihon Bunka Taikan" Henshū Shimatsu Ki' [Complete Record of the Compilation of 'Outline of Japanese Culture'], Nihon Kagakusha Kaigi Shisō Bunka Kenkyū Iinkai [Council of Japanese Scientists, Committee for Research in Thought and Culture], *'Nihon Bunka Ron' Hihan – 'Bunka' wo Yosōu Kiken Shisō* [Criticisms of 'Essays on Japanese Culture' – Dangerous Thought Masquerading as 'Culture'] (Suiyō Sha 1991), 221.
76 TZKS, 114-11.
77 Tsuji Zennosuke, 'Kigen Nisen Roppyakunen no Igi' [The Significance of the 2,600th Anniversary of the Empire], *Rekishi Kyōiku* [History and Education] 14.11 (1940):7.
78 Ibid., 13.
79 TZKS, 184-2.
80 *Tsuji Zennosuke Hakase Jireki Nenpu Kō*, 87.
81 'Sakamoto Tarō Hakase Nenpu, Chosaku Mokuroku' [Chronology and Catalogue of Works of Dr. Sakamoto Tarō], *Waga Seishun, Sakamoto Tarō Chosakushū*, 12:309.
82 There has been lively discussion among Japanese scholars about minor distinctions among the prewar nationalist historians and writers. *Kōkoku shikan* [the view of history as the imperial nation] is the most general term for the nationalists. Other terms are also proposed to classify them into subcategories: *kokubika shikan* [the view of history that idealizes the nation]; *kokutai goji shikan* [the view of history that protects the national essence]; *kōkoku goji shikan* [the view of history that protects the imperial nation]. For Hiraizumi, the last one, *kōkoku goji shikan*, is favoured by Tanaka Takashi, Hiraizumi's last disciple, so I have adopted it. Tanaka Takashi, 'Hiraizumi Shigaku no Tokushoku' [The Characteristics of Hiraizumi's Historical Scholarship], *Nippon* [Japan] 45.6 (1995):218.
83 Hakusan Jinja Shi Hensan Iinkai [Committee to Compile the History of Hakusan Shrine], *Hakusan Jinja Shi* [History of Hakusan Shrine] (Hakusan Jinja 1992), 10-11, 148-50. There is also a gravestone at Minatogawa Shrine, built in 1872 by the government to worship Kusunoki Masashige.
84 Tanaka Takashi, 'Hiraizumi Sensei no Shinsōsai ni Sanrei Shite' [As an Attendant at the Shinto Funeral of the Late Dr. Hiraizumi Kiyoshi], *Shinto Shi Kenkyū* [Studies in Shinto History] 32.2 (1984):68-9.
85 TZKS, 40-180.
86 Hiraizumi Kiyoshi, *Chūsei ni okeru Shaji to Shakai to no Kankei* [Medieval Shrines and Temples and Their Relation to Society] (Shibundō 1926), 1.
87 Hiraizumi Kiyoshi, 'Rekishi ni okeru Jitsu to Shin' [Fact and Truth in History], *Shigaku Zasshi* 36.5 (1925):371.
88 Ōkuma Kazuo, 'Nihon no Rekishigaku ni okeru "Gaku" – Hiraizumi Kiyoshi ni tsuite' [The 'Scholarship' in Japanese Historical Scholarship – on Hiraizumi Kiyoshi], *Chūsei Shisōshi no Kōsa* [Concepts of the History of Medieval Thought] (Meicho Kankōkai 1984), 237-8.
89 Hiraizumi Kiyoshi, 'Waga Rekishikan' [My View of History], in *Waga Rekishikan* [My View of History] (Shibundō 1926), 23.
90 David D. Roberts, *Benedetto Croce and the Uses of Historicism* (Berkeley: University of California Press 1987).
91 H. Wildon Carr, *The Philosophy of Benedetto Croce: The Problem of Art and History* (New York: Russell and Russell 1917), 194.

92 Hiraizumi Kiyoshi, 'Napori no Tetsujin' [A Philosopher of Naples], *Geirin* [Journal of Cultural Sciences] 4.3 (1953).
93 Hiraizumi Wataru, 'Chichi Hiraizumi Sensei ni tsuite' [My Father Professor Hiraizumi], *Shintō Shi Kenkyū* 33.1 (1985):1389.
94 Hiraizumi Kiyoshi, *Diary* (privately published by Hiraizumi Akira 1991; not for sale), 65-7.
95 Ibid., 109.
96 Ibid., 33.
97 Hiraizumi Kiyoshi, 'Seishin Kihaku Naki Mono wa Horobu' [Those without Fierce Spiritual Force Shall Perish], *Nippon* [Japan] 45.6 (1995, special issue commemorating the 100th anniversary of the birth of Dr. Hiraizumi Kiyoshi):6.
98 *Tokyo Daigaku Hyakunen Shi* [100-Year History of Tokyo University], *Tsūshi* [General History], vol. 2 (Tokyo Daigaku Shuppankai 1985), 781-5.
99 Inoue Kiyoshi, 'Nihon Teikoku Shugi to Kokushigaku,' *Yugamerareta Kodai Shi*, 30.
100 Interview with Tsuji Tatsuya, 7 July 1994.
101 Inoue Mitsusada, 'Watakushi to Kodai Shigaku' [Scholarship on Ancient Japanese History and I], *Inoue Mitsusada Chosakushū* [Collected Works of Inoue Mitsusada], vol. 11 (Iwanami Shoten 1986), 24-5.
102 Interview with Ienaga Saburō, 9 July 1994.
103 Ienaga Saburō, *Gekidō Nanajūnen no Rekishi o Ikite* [Living through Seventy Tumultuous Years of History] (Shinchi Shobō 1987), 66-71.
104 Ienaga Saburō, 'Tokyo Teidai Kokushi Gakka Kansai Chihō Shūgaku Ryokō Ki' [Record of the Study Trip to the Kansai Region by the Japanese History Department of Tokyo Imperial University], *Shigaku Zasshi* 47.2 (1936):282-3.
105 Sasaki Nozomu, 'Nukazuku to Iu Koto' [The Meaning of Deep Prostration], *Shinto Shi Kenkyū* 33.1 (1985):121-2.
106 Hiraizumi Kiyoshi, *Kenmu Chūkō no Hongi* [The True Meaning of the Kenmu Restoration] (Shibundō 1934), 1-2. This essay, published in Sept. 1934, was a reprint of his essay contained in *Kenmu Chūkō*, Feb. 1934, which also contained essays by Miyaji Naokazu and Kuroita Katsumi, cited in note 45 above.
107 Ibid., 177-8.
108 Hiraizumi Kiyoshi, *Nihon no Higeki to Risō* [The Tragedy and Ideals of Japan] (Hara Shobō 1957), 2, 22-3, 45, 85-6, 127-8, 129.
109 Hiraizumi Kiyoshi, 'Seishin Kihaku Naki Mono Wa Horobu,' 10.
110 Ibid., 7.
111 Hiraizumi Kiyoshi, *Kono Michi o Yuku: Kanrinshi Kaikoroku* [Going This Way: Reminiscences of the Gentleman of the Cold Forest] (Sōzōsha 1995, not for sale), 181. The Gentleman of the Cold Forest was Hiraizumi's pen name, suggesting lofty and principled withdrawal. He was delighted with the American rendering of Seiseijuku as Green Green School. A more restrained rendering would be Youth Academy.
112 Hiraizumi Kiyoshi, *Bushidō no Fukkatsu* [The Revival of Bushidō] (Kokumin Shisō, six-page pamphlet, 1933).
113 Hara Keigo, 'Ni-ni-roku Jiken ni tsuite Hitotsu no Uwasa' [A Rumour concerning the 26 February 1936 Incident], *Kokoro* [Heart], May 1966:67.
114 Yamaguchi Muneyuki, 'Hiraizumi Hakase ni okeru Tennō' [The Emperor in Dr. Hiraizumi's Thought], Kyushu Daigaku Kyōikugakubu, *Rekishigaku Chirigaku Nenpō* [Education Department, Kyushu University, Annual Bulletin on History and Geography] 10 (1986):106-7.
115 Hiraizumi, *Kono Michi o Yuku: Kanrinshi Kaikoroku*, 201-2.
116 Takeshita Masahiko, 'Hiraizumi Shigaku to Rikugun' [Hiraizumi's Historical Scholarship and the Army], *Gunji Shigaku* [Military History] 5.1 (1969). More details on Hiraizumi's political activities are given by Imatani Akira, 'Hiraizumi Kiyoshi,' in Imatani Akira, Ōhama Tetsuya, Ogata Isamu, and Kabayama Kōichi, *Nijū Seiki no Rekishika-tachi, Nihon-hen*, I [Twentieth Century Historians: Japan, 1] Tōsui Shobo (1997), which appeared as this work was in press.

Chapter 12: The Commission of Inquiry into Historical Sites
1 Interview with Klaus Pringsheim, director, Canada-Japan Trade Centre, Ottawa, 10 Oct. 1992.

2   Hoshino Ryōsaku, *Kenkyū Shi Jinmu Tennō*, 186-90.
3   Nihon Gakushiin [Japan Academy], *Nihon Gakushiin Hachijūnen Shi* [Eighty Year History of the Japan Academy] (1962), 585-612, 814-19.
4   Ibid., 619-30.
5   The following information is summarized from *Jinmu Tennō Seiseki Chōsa Hōkoku* [Report of the Inquiry into Historical Sites Related to Emperor Jinmu] (Ministry of Education 1942), and the materials in the Tsuji Zennosuke papers, especially TZKS 92, 102, 103, 105, 114, 115, 125, 169.
6   TZKS, 125-16.
7   TZKS, 115.
8   W.G. Aston, *Nihongi*, 1:114.
9   *Jinmu Tennō Seiseki Chōsa Hōkoku*, 140-6.
10   Sakamoto Tarō, *Kodaishi no Michi* (Yomiuri Shinbun Sha 1980), 125.
11   Ibid., 129.
12   *Jinmu Tennō Seiseki Chōsa Hōkoku*, 42-4.

Chapter 13: Tsuda Sōkichi

1   Sakamoto Tarō, *Kodai Shi no Michi* (Yomiuri Shinbun Sha 1980), 114.
2   Ienaga Saburō, *Tsuda Sōkichi no Shisōshiteki Kenkyū* [Tsuda Sōkichi's Studies in the History of Thought] (Iwanami Shoten 1972), 33-4.
3   This paragraph is based on Oyama Masaaki, 'Shiratori Kurakichi,' in Kano and Nagahara, *Nihon no Rekishika*, and Shiratori Yoshirō and Yawata Ichirō, *Shiratori Kurakichi, Torii Tatsuzō* (Kōdansha 1978). Shiratori is discussed in the context of Oriental, not Japanese, history in Stefan Tanaka, *Japan's Orient: Rendering Pasts into History* (Berkeley: University of California Press 1993).
4   Tokoro Isao, 'Shōwa Tennō ga Mananda "Kokushi" Kyōkasho' [The Textbook in Japanese History Studied by the Shōwa Emperor], *Bungei Shunjū* [Art and Literature, Spring and Autumn], Feb. 1990:130-40.
5   Shiratori Kurakichi, *Jindai Shi no Shin Kenkyū* [New Studies on the Age of the Gods], *Shiratori Kurakichi Zenshū* [Complete Works of Shiratori Kurakichi], vol. 1 (Iwanami Shoten 1969), 291, 384.
6   Ibid., 537-9.
7   Tsuda Sōkichi, *Nihon Koten no Kenkyū* [Studies on the Japanese Classics], vol. 1 (Iwanami Shoten 1948), 6-7.
8   Shiratori, *Jindai Shi no Shin Kenkyū*, 441-2.
9   Tsuda Sōkichi, *Shiratori Kurakichi Shōden* [A Brief Biography of Shiratori Kurakichi], *Tsuda Sōkichi Zenshū* [Complete Works of Tsuda Sōkichi], vol. 24 (Iwanami Shoten 1965), 144-5.
10   Ienaga Saburō, *Tsuda Sōkichi no Shisōshiteki Kenkyū*, 325.
11   Tsuda Sōkichi, *Jindai Shi no Atarashii Kenkyū* [New Studies on the Age of the Gods] (1913), *Tsuda Sōkichi Zenshū*, supp. vol. 1 (1966), 15.
12   Tsuda, *Nihon Koten no Kenkyū*, 279-91.
13   Tsuda Sōkichi, *Jōdai Shi no Kenkyūhō ni Tsukite* [Research Methods in Ancient History], Iwanami Kōza Nihon Rekishi [Iwanami Series on Japanese History] (Iwanami Shoten 1934), 16-17. Kuroita Katsumi was the editor of the series, displaying broad-mindedness in presenting the work of Tsuda, with whom he disagreed.
14   Tsuda, *Nihon Koten no Kenkyū*, 295-6.
15   Tsuda, *Jindai Shi no Atarashii Kenkyū*, 144.
16   The works that Tsuda read are given in Kimura Tokio, 'Nihon ni okeru Kindai Shigaku no Seiritsu (Tsuda Sōkichi)' [The Formation of Modern Historical Scholarship in Japan (Tsuda Sōkichi)], in Waseda Daigaku Sōritsu Hyakushūnen Kinen, Waseda Daigaku Shakai Kagaku Kenkyūjo, Kenkyū Sōsho [Centenary Celebration of Waseda University, Waseda University Social Sciences Research Institute, Research Series], *Kindai Nihon to Waseda Daigaku no Shisō Gunzō* [Modern Japan and Waseda Thinkers], vol. 1 (Waseda Daigaku Shuppankai 1981), 241-3. Many of the books are preserved in the Tsuda Sōkichi Memorial Room at Waseda University.
17   Ienaga, *Tsuda Sōkichi no Shisōshiteki Kenkyū*, 258.

18 Ōkubo Toshiaki, 'Yugamerareta Rekishi' [Distorted History], in Sakisaka Itsurō, *Arashi no naka no Hyakunen: Gakumon Dan'atsu no Shōshi* [A Hundred Years in the Storm: A Short History of Suppression of Scholarship] (Keiso Shobō 1952), 63-4.
19 Maruyama Masao and Fukuda Kan'ichi, *Kikigaki Nanbara Shigeru Kaikoroku* [Oral Memoirs of Nanbara Shigeru] (Tokyo Daigaku Shuppankai 1989), 242-6.
20 Tsuda Sōkichi, 'Shina Shisō to Nihon' [Chinese Thought and Japan] (1938), *Tsuda Sōkichi Zenshū*, 20:323. Tsuda's views on Oriental culture are discussed in a different context in Stefan Tanaka, *Japan's Orient*, 278-81.
21 Ienaga, *Tsuda Sōkichi no Shisōshiteki Kenkyū*, 373-4.
22 *Kikigaki Nanbara Shigeru Kaikoroku*, 249-51; Maruyama Masao, 'Aru Hi no Tsuda Hakase to Watakushi' [Dr. Tsuda and I on One Day], in Ueda, *Tsuda Sōkichi*, 106-9.
23 Mitsui Kōshi, '*Genri Nippon* no Gakugeiteki Hihan Sagyō to Tsuda Sōkichi no Senran Gakusetsu' [*Genri Nippon*'s Scholarly Critique and Tsuda Sōkichi's Criminally Disturbing Theories], *Genri Nippon*, 24 Dec. 1940:23.
24 Minoda Muneki, 'Tsuda Sōkichi no Kamiyo Shi, Jōdai Shi Massatsu Ron Hihan' [Criticism of Tsuda Sōkichi's Massacre of the History of the Age of the Gods and Ancient History], ibid., 92-5.
25 Ienaga, *Tsuda Sōkichi no Shisōshiteki Kenkyū*, 380.
26 Abe Yoshinari, *Iwanami Shigeo Den* [Biography of Iwanami Shigeo] (Iwanami Shoten 1957), 226.
27 Ōkubo, 'Yugamerareta Rekishi,' 70.
28 Ienaga, *Tsuda Sōkichi no Shisōshiteki Kenkyū*, 412.
29 Ibid., 413.
30 Tsuda Sōkichi, 'Jōshinsho' [Written Defence], *Tsuda Sōkichi Zenshū*, 24:294.
31 Ibid., 312-28.
32 Ibid., 573-4.
33 Ibid., 611-18.
34 Ienaga, *Tsuda Sōkichi no Shisōshiteki Kenkyū*, 383.
35 Ibid., 404-5
36 Kimura Tokio, 'Yugamerareta Tsuda Sōkichi Zō,' [The Distorted Image of Tsuda Sōkichi], *Shiden Shiwa: Kindai Nihon no Meian* [Historical Legends, Historical Talks: Light and Darkness in Modern Japan] (Maeno Shoten 1978), 248-51.
37 Ienaga, *Tsuda Sōkichi no Shisōshiteki Kenkyū*, 403. The numbers do not tally, but Ienaga gives no explanation.
38 Ōkubo Toshiaki, 'Tsuda Sōkichi,' Asahi Journal, ed., *Nihon no Shisōka*, 3 [Japanese Thinkers, 3] (Asahi Shinbun Sha 1963), 327-8.
39 Tsuda Sōkichi, 'Kenkoku no Jijō to Bansei Ikkei no Shisō' [The Circumstances of the Founding of the Nation and the Idea of the Eternal Succession of Emperors], *Sekai* [The World], Apr. 1946.
40 Kimura, 'Yugamerareta Tsuda Sōkichi Zō,' 251-3.
41 Letter of 10 Sept. 1945 to Kurita Naomi, *Tsuda Sōkichi Zenshū*, supp. vol. 1 (1989), 311. Kurita Naomi (b. 1903) was a professor of philosophy at Waseda University and the recipient of most of Tsuda's published letters. She wrote a brief study of Tsuda's thought in 1978.

Epilogue: Historical Scholarship
1 Sakamoto Tarō, 'Genshi Kodai no Nihon' [The Origins and Ancient History of Japan], *Sakamoto Tarō Chosakushū* [Collected Works of Sakamoto Tarō], vol. 1 (Yoshikawa Kōbunkan 1989), 358.
2 John G. Caiger, 'Ienaga Saburō and the First Postwar Japanese History Textbook,' *Modern Asian Studies*, vol. 3, part 1 (1969):3.
3 R.J. Wunderlich, 'The Japanese Textbook Problem and Solution, 1945-46,' PhD diss., Stanford University, 1952, 237. Wunderlich, a lieutenant commander in the Occupation forces, was placed in charge of textbook revision on 27 Nov. 1945.
4 Caiger, 'Ienaga Saburō,' 7. J.C. Trainor was quite ignorant of Japanese history, and in his pompous memoirs he could not remember the names of the scholars whom he had commanded to write a new textbook.
5 Ienaga Saburō, *Gekido Nanajūnen no Rekishi o Ikite*, 89-91.

6 See Robert N. Bellah, 'Ienaga Saburō and the Search for Meaning in Modern Japan,' in Marius B. Jansen, ed., *Changing Japanese Attitudes toward Modernization* (Princeton: Princeton University Press 1965).

7 Caiger, 'Ienaga Saburō,' 12.

8 Inoue Kiyoshi, *Kuni no Ayumi Hihan: Tadashii Nihon Rekishi* [Critique of *Kuni no Ayumi*: Truthful Japanese History] (Kaihō Sha 1947), 1-2.

9 Ibid., 1-11.

10 Ibid., 16-17.

11 '*Kuni no Ayumi* no Kentō' [An Examination of *Kuni no Ayumi*], *Asahi Hyōron*, Mar. 1947. Included in Hisano Shū and Shimada Jirō, eds., *Tennōsei* [The Emperor System], vol. 1 (San'ichi Shobō 1975), 26-41.

12 Ōkubo Toshiaki, *Nihon Kindai Shigaku Kotohajime: Ichi Rekishika no Kaisō* [The Beginnings of Historical Scholarship in Modern Japan: The Reminiscences of a Historian] (Iwanami Shinsho, no. 427, 1996), 149-59.

13 *Rekidai Tennō 125 Dai* [The Succession of Emperors: 125 Reigns] (Shin Jinbutsu Ōrai Sha 1990).

14 Satō Nobuo and Umeda Kinji, 'Kokumin no Rekishi Ishiki to Rekishigaku' [The Historical Consciousness of the Japanese People and Historical Scholarship], Rekishigaku Kenkyūkai and Nihonshi Kenkyūkai, *Kōza Nihonshi* [Lectures on Japanese History] (Tokyo Daigaku Shuppankai 1971), 226-7.

15 Wakamori Tarō, 'Kigen Setsu Fukkatsu no Haikei' [The Background of the Revival of Empire Day], *Wakamori Tarō Chosakushū* [Collected Works of Wakamori Tarō], vol. 8 (Kōbunsha 1981), 489-90.

16 Naramoto Tatsuya, 'Wakamori Kun to Nihon oyobi Nihonjin Ron' [Wakamori and the Controversy over Japan and the Japanese], *Wakamori Tarō Chosakushū*, 8:573.

17 Wakamori Tarō, 'Kigen Setsu Mondai no Keika' [Development of the Empire Day Problem], *Wakamori Tarō Chosakushū*, 8:521.

18 Inoue Mitsusada, 'Kenpō to Kigensetsu Mondai' [The Constitution and the Problem of National Founding Day], *Inoue Mitsusada Chosakushū* [Collected Works of Inoue Mitsusada], vol. 11 (Iwanami Shoten 1986), 308-9; originally published in *Heiwa to Minshushugi* [Peace and Democracy] (1966).

19 Satō and Umeda, 'Kokumin no Rekishi Ishiki to Rekishigaku,' 228.

20 See Robert S. Ellwood, *The Feast of Kingship: Accession Ceremonies in Ancient Japan* (Tokyo: Sophia University Press 1973); and D.C. Holtom, *The Japanese Enthronement Ceremonies, with an Account of the Imperial Regalia* (1928; reprint, Tokyo: Sophia University Press 1971).

21 Norma C. Fields, *In the Realm of a Dying Emperor* (New York: Pantheon Books 1991), part 3, 'Nagasaki,' 175-266.

22 Christopher Hill, *God's Englishman: Oliver Cromwell and the English Revolution* (London: Weidenfeld and Nicolson 1970), 255.

23 David John Lu, *Sources of Japanese History*, vol. 2 (New York: McGraw-Hill 1974), 191.

References

Note: All Japanese works were published in Tokyo unless otherwise indicated.

Abe Yoshinari. *Iwanami Shigeo Den* [Biography of Iwanami Shigeo]. Iwanami Shoten 1957

Akiyama Kenzō. 'Kaisetsu' [Exposition]. In Mikami Sanji, *Edo Jidai Shi* [History of the Edo Period], vol. 3. Kōdansha Gakugei Bunko 1977

Anesaki Masaharu. 'Nanboku Chō Mondai ni kansuru Gigi narabi ni Dan'an' [Doubts and Conclusions on the Southern-Northern Courts Problem]. In Yamazaki Tōkichi, *Nanboku Chō Seijun Ronsan* [Collected Articles on the Legitimacy of the Southern-Northern Courts]. Kyoto: Yokota Kappansho 1911

Arai Hakuseki. *Kishinron* [Essay on Ghosts and Spirits]. In *Arai Hakuseki Zenshū* [Complete Works of Arai Hakuseki]. Naigai Insatsu Kabushiki Gaisha 1907

–. *Koshitsū* [The Essence of Ancient History]. In *Arai Hakuseki Zenshū* [Complete Works of Arai Hakuseki], vol. 3. Naigai Insatsu Kabushiki Gaisha 1907

–. *Tōga* [The Japanese *Erya*]. In *Arai Hakuseki Zenshū* [Complete Works of Arai Hakuseki], vol. 4. Naigai Insatsu Kabushiki Gaisha 1907

Arakawa Kusuo. 'Date Chihiro no *Taisei Santenkō* ni tsuite' [On Date Chihiro's *Taisei Santenkō*]. *Kōgakkan Ronsō* [Kōgakkan University Papers] 13.6 (1980)

Ashley, Maurice. *England in the Seventeenth Century (1603-1714)*. 3rd ed. Harmondsworth, UK: Penguin Books 1961

Aston, W.G., trans. *Nihongi: Chronicles of Japan from Earliest Times to A.D. 697*. 1896. Reprint, Rutland, VT, and Tokyo: Charles E. Tuttle 1972

Bacon, Francis. 'The Great Instauration.' In E.A. Burtt, ed., *The English Philosophers from Bacon to Mill*. New York: Modern Library 1939

Backus, Robert L. 'The Kansei Prohibition of Heterodoxy and Its Effects on Education.' *Harvard Journal of Asiatic Studies* 39.1 (1979)

Bellah, Robert N. 'Ienaga Saburō and the Search for Meaning in Modern Japan.' In Marius B. Jansen, ed., *Changing Japanese Attitudes toward Modernization*. Princeton: Princeton University Press 1965

Bitō Masahide. *Genroku Jidai* [The Genroku Era]. *Nihon no Rekishi* [The History of Japan], vol. 19. Shogakkan 1975

–. 'Kōkoku Shikan no Seiritsu' [The Establishment of the Imperial View of History]. In Sagara Tōru, Bitō Masahide, and Akiyama Ken, eds., *Jikan* [Time]. *Nihon Shisō* [Japanese Thought], vol. 4. Tokyo Daigaku Shuppankai 1984

–. 'Mitogaku no Tokushitsu' [The Special Features of the Mito School]. In Imai Usaburō, Seya Yoshihiko, and Bitō Masahide, *Mitogaku* [The Mito School]. *Nihon Shisō Taikei* [Compendium of Japanese Thought], vol. 53. Iwanami Shoten 1973

Brownlee, John S. 'Ideological Control in Ancient Japan.' *Historical Reflections* 14.1 (1987)

–, trans. 'The Jeweled Comb-Box: Motoori Norinaga's *Tamakushige*.' *Monumenta Nipponica* 43.1 (1988)

–. 'The Origins of Nationalist Historical Writing in Ancient Times.' In Brownlee, ed., *History in the Service of the Japanese Nation*. Toronto: University of Toronto-York University Joint Centre on Modern East Asia 1983

–. *Political Thought in Japanese Historical Writing: From Kojiki (712) to Tokushi Yoron (1712)*. Waterloo, ON: Wilfrid Laurier University Press 1991

Buckle, H.T. *History of Civilization in England*, 3 vols. London: Longman's Green 1871

Caiger, John C. 'Ienaga Saburō and the First Postwar Japanese History Textbook.' *Modern Asian Studies*, vol. 3, part 1 (1969)

Carr, H. Wildon. *The Philosophy of Benedetto Croce: The Problem of Art and History*. New York: Russell and Russell 1917

Chijiwa Makoto. 'Taisei Santenkō ni okeru Shikan' [The View of History in *Taisei Santenkō*]. *Shichō* [Tides of History] 2.2 (1932)

Ching, Julia. 'Chu Hsi and Ritual.' *Essais sur le rituel* [Essays on Ritual]. Bibliotheque de l'École des Hautes Études, Section des Sciences Religieuses, vol. XCV

Craig, Albert. 'Science and Confucianism in Tokugawa Japan.' In Marius B. Jansen, ed., *Changing Japanese Attitudes toward Modernization*. Princeton: Princeton University Press 1965

Dai Nihon Shi, vols. 1, 7. Dainihon Yūbenkai 1929

Dai Nihon Shiryō [Japanese Historical Documents], vol. 6, part 10. 1911

Date Chihiro. *Taisei Santenkō* [Three Stages in the History of Japan]. In Matsumoto Sannosuke and Ogura Yoshihiko, eds., *Kinsei Shiron Shū* [Historical Essays of the Modern Period]. *Nihon Shisō Taikei* [Compendium of Japanese Thought], vol. 48. Iwanami Shoten 1974

Dilworth, David A. '"Jitsugaku" as an Ontological Conception: Continuities and Discontinuities in Early and Mid-Tokugawa Thought.' In W.T. de Bary and Irene Bloom, eds., *Principle and Practicality: Essays in Neo-Confucianism and Practical Learning*. New York: Columbia University Press 1979

Duus, Peter. *The Abacus and the Sword: The Japanese Penetration of Korea, 1895-1910*. Berkeley: University of California Press 1995

Elman, Benjamin A. *From Philosophy to Philology: Intellectual and Social Aspects of Change in Late Imperial China*. Cambridge: Harvard University Press 1984

Ellwood, Robert S. *The Feast of Kingship: Accession Ceremonies in Ancient Japan*. Tokyo: Sophia University Press 1973

Encyclopedia Judaica, vol. 14. 1971 ed.

Fields, Norma C. *In the Realm of a Dying Emperor*. New York: Pantheon Books 1991

Fujiki Kunihiko. 'Zen Honkai Hyōgiin Bungaku Hakase Kume Kunitake Sensei no Seikyo' [The Death of Dr. Kume Kunitake, Former Council Member of the Historical Association]. *Shigaku Zasshi* [Journal of Historical Scholarship] 42.4 (1931)

Fujisawa Genzō et al. 'Nanboku Chō Seijun Mondō' [Questions and Answers on the Legitimacy of the Southern and Northern Courts]. *Nihon Oyobi Nihonjin* [Japan and the Japanese], 15 Mar. 1911

Fujishiro Sojin. 'Natsume Kun no Henrin' [A Glimpse of Natsume]. *Sōseki Zenshū Geppō* [Complete Works of Sōseki, Monthly Bulletin]. Sōseki Zenshū Kankōkai 5 (1928)

Fukkōki [Records of the Restoration]. 15 vols. Naigai Shojaku Kabushiki Gaisha 1930-1

Fukuzawa Yukichi. *An Outline of a Theory of Civilization*. Trans. David A. Dilworth and G.C. Hurst. Tokyo: Sophia University Press 1973

Fumoto Yasutaka. 'Shushi no Rekishikan' [Zhu Xi's Views of History]. In Morohashi Yasuoka, *Shushigaku Nyūmon* [Introduction to Zhu Xi Studies]. *Shushi Taikei* [Zhu Xi Compendium], vol. 1. Meitokusha 1974

Gay, Peter. *Style in History*. New York: Basic Books 1974

Gondos, Victor J. *Franklin Jameson and the Birth of the National Archives, 1906-1926*. Pittsburgh: University of Pennsylvania Press 1981

Gotō Tanji and Okami Masao, eds. *Taiheiki* [Chronicle of Grand Pacification]. *Nihon Koten Bungaku Taikei* [Compendium of Classical Japanese Literature], vols. 34, 36. Iwanami Shoten 1970-2

Haga Noboru. *Hihan Kindai Nihon Shigaku Shisōshi* [Critical Intellectual History of Modern Japanese Historical Scholarship]. Kashiwa Shobō 1974

Hagino Minahiko. 'Kume Kunitake to Komonjo' [Kume Kunitake and the Study of Ancient Documents]. *Kume Kunitake Rekishi Chosakushū* [Collected Historical Writing of Kume Kunitake], supp. vol. Yoshikawa Kōbunkan 1989

Hakusan Jinja Shi Hensan Iinkai [Committee to Compile the History of Hakusan Shrine]. *Hakusan Jinja Shi* [History of Hakusan Shrine]. Hakusan Jinja 1992

Hall, Ivan P. *Mori Arinori*. Cambridge: Harvard University Press 1973

Hall, R.K., ed. *Kokutai no Hongi: Cardinal Principles of the National Essence of Japan*. Trans. J. Gauntlett. Cambridge: Harvard University Press 1949

Hanami Sakumi. '*Honchō Tsugan*.' In Shigakkai [Historical Association], ed., *Honpō Shigakushi Ronsō* [Essays on Japanese Historical Scholarship]. Fuzanbō 1939

Hara Keigo. 'Ni-ni-roku Jiken ni tsuite Hitotsu no Uwasa' [A Rumour concerning the 26 February 1936 Incident]. *Kokoro* [Heart], May 1966

Hashimura Hiro. 'Kume Kunitake Hakase no Fu' [Obituary of Dr. Kume Kunitake]. *Rekishi Chiri* [History and Geography] 57.4 (1931)

Hayashi Razan. *Honchō Tsugan*. Kokusho Kankōkai 1918-19

–. 'Jinmu Tennō Ron' [Essay on Emperor Jinmu]. *Hayashi Razan Bunshū* [Collected Works of Hayashi Razan]. Ōsaka: Kōbunsha 1930

–. *Shintō Denjū Shō* [Selections from Instructions on Shintō]. *Shintō Taikei* [Compendium of Shinto], *Ronsetsu Hen* [Discourse Section], vol. 20. Fujiwara Seika, Hayashi Razan 1988

Hayashiya Tatsusaburō. 'Kaisetsu' [Exposition]. *Nakamura Naokatsu Chosakushū* [Collected Works of Nakamura Naokatsu], vol. 2. Tankōsha 1978

Higham, John. *History: Professional Scholarship in America*. Rev. ed. Baltimore: Johns Hopkins University Press 1989

Higo Kazuo. *Mitogaku to Meiji Ishin* [The Mito School and the Meiji Restoration]. Tokiwa Jinja Shamusho 1973

Hill, Christopher. *God's Englishman: Oliver Cromwell and the English Revolution*. London: Weidenfeld and Nicolson 1970

Hiraga Noboru. 'Historiography.' *Kōdansha Encyclopedia of Japan*, vol. 3. Kōdansha 1983

Hiraizumi Kiyoshi. *Bushidō no Fukkatsu* [The Revival of Bushidō, six-page pamphlet]. Kokumin Shisō 1933

–. *Chūsei ni okeru Shaji to Shakai to no Kankei* [Medieval Shrines and Temples and Their Relation to Society]. Shibundō 1926

–. *Diary*. Privately published by Hiraizumi Akira 1991 (not for sale)

–. *Kenmu Chūkō no Hongi* [The True Meaning of the Kenmu Restoration]. Shibundō 1934

–. *Kono Michi o Yuku: Kanrinshi Kaikoroku* [Going This Way: Reminiscences of the Gentleman of the Cold Forest]. Sōzōsha 1995 (not for sale)

–. *Nihon no Higeki to Risō* [The Tragedy and Ideals of Japan]. Hara Shobō 1957

–. 'Napori no Tetsujin' [A Philosopher of Naples]. *Geirin* [Journal of Cultural Sciences] 4.3 (1953)

–. 'Rekishi ni okeru Jitsu to Shin' [Fact and Truth in History]. *Shigaku Zasshi* [Journal of Historical Scholarship] 36.5 (1925)

–. 'Seishin Kihaku Naki Mono wa Horobu' [Those without Spiritual Force Shall Perish]. *Nippon* [Japan] 45.6 (1995) (special issue commemorating the 100th anniversary of the birth of Dr. Hiraizumi Kiyoshi)

–. 'Waga Rekishikan' [My View of History]. In *Waga Rekishikan* [My View of History]. Shibundō 1926

Hiraizumi Wataru. 'Chichi Hiraizumi Sensei ni tsuite' [My Father Professor Hiraizumi]. *Shintō Shi Kenkyū* [Research in Shinto History] 33.1 (1985)

'Hitsuyō Suji' [Off-Topic but Urgent]. *Shigaku Zasshi* [Journal of Historical Scholarship] 13.4 (1902)

Hōjō Kudaiki [Record of Nine Reigns of the Hōjō Regents]. *Zoku Gunsho Ruijū* [Classified Collection of Books Continued], Zatsubu [Miscellaneous Section], vol. 29, part 1. Zoku Gunsho Ruijū Kanseikai 1925

Holtom, D.C. *The Japanese Enthronement Ceremonies, with an Account of the Imperial Regalia*. 1928. Reprint, Tokyo: Sophia University Press 1971

Hori Isao. *Hayashi Razan*. Yoshikawa Kōbunkan 1964

Hoshino Ryōsaku. *Kenkyūshi Jinmu Tennō* [History of Research on Emperor Jinmu]. Yoshikawa Kōbunkan 1980

Hoshino Hisashi. 'Honpō no Jinrui Gengo ni tsuite Hikō o Nobete Magokoro Aikokusha ni Tadasu' [A Question from an Old Man for Sincere Patriots Regarding Japanese Race and Language]. *Shigaku Zasshi* [Journal of Historical Scholarship] 11 (1890)

–. 'Jōko no Jiseki Tsutomete Jinji o motte Kansatsu Atari' [We Must Try to View the Evidence from Antiquity as Pertaining to Humans]. *Shigaku Zasshi* [Journal of Historical Scholarship] 2.3 (1891)

–. '*Kojiki* Kaikan no Betsutenjin ni tsuite' [The Separate Heavenly Deities in the Opening Chapter of *Kojiki*]. *Shigaku Zasshi* [Journal of Historical Scholarship] 22.1 (1911)

Ibaraki Kenshi Henshū Iinkai. *Ibaraki Kenshi – Kinseihen* [History of Ibaraki Prefecture – The Early Modern Era]. Seikōsha 1985

Ienaga Saburō. *Gekidō Nanajūnen no Rekishi o Ikite* [Living through Seventy Tumultuous Years of History]. Shinchi Shobō 1987

–. 'Tokyo Teidai Kokushi Gakka Kansai Chihō Shūgaku Ryokō Ki' [Record of the Study Trip to the Kansai Region by the Japanese History Department of Tokyo Imperial University]. *Shigaku Zasshi* [Journal of Historical Scholarship] 47.2 (1936)

–. *Tsuda Sōkichi no Shisōshiteki Kenkyū* [Tsuda Sōkichi's Studies in the History of Thought]. Iwanami Shoten 1972

Ienaga Saburō, Matsunaga Shōzō, and Emura Ei'ichi. *Meiji Zenki no Kenpō Kōso* [Early Meiji Constitutional Ideas]. Rev. and enl. ed. Fukumura Shuppan Kabushiki Gaisha 1985

Iggers, Georg G. *The German Conception of History: The National Tradition of Historical Thought from Herder to the Present.* Middletown, CT: Wesleyan University Press 1968

Iida Takesato. *Nihon Shoki Tsūshaku* [Complete Commentary on *Nihon Shoki*]. N.p. 1899

Inoue Kiyoshi. *Kuni no Ayumi Hihan: Tadashii Nihon Rekishi* [Critique of *Kuni no Ayumi*: Truthful Japanese History]. Kaihōsha 1947

–. 'Nihon Teikoku Shugi to Kokushigaku' [Japanese Imperial Ideology and Japanese Historical Scholarship]. In Inoue Kiyoshi and Mori Kōichi, *Yugamerareta Kodai Shi* [Ancient History Distorted]. Asahi Shinbunsha 1973

Inoue Mitsusada. 'Kenpō to Kigen Setsu Mondai' [The Constitution and the Problem of Empire Day]. In *Inoue Mitsusada Chosakushū* [Collected Works of Inoue Mitsusada], vol. 11. Iwanami Shoten 1986

–. 'Watakushi to Kodai Shigaku' [Scholarship on Ancient Japanese History and I]. In *Inoue Mitsusada Chosakushū* [Collected Works of Inoue Mitsusada], vol. 11. Iwanami Shoten 1986

Inoue Tetsujirō. *Nihon Shushigakuha no Tetsugaku* [The Philosophy of the Japanese Zhu Xi School]. Rev. ed. Fuzanbō 1915

Iriuchijima Kazutaka. *Nanchō Kojima Takanori* [Kojima Takanori of the Southern Court]. Takasaki City, Gunma Prefecture: Asao Sha 1990

Ishida Ichirō and Kanaya Osamu, eds. *Fujiwara Seika, Hayashi Razan.* In *Nihon Shisō Taikei* [Compendium of Japanese Thought], vol. 28. Iwanami Shoten 1975

Ishige Tadashi. '*Taisei Santenkō* ni okeru Jidai Kubun Hō to sono Shisōteki Konkyo' [The Method for Periodization in *Taisei Santenkō* and Its Foundation in Thought]. In Ishida Ichirō, ed., *Jidai Kubun no Shisō* [Thought on Periodization]. Perikansha 1986

Itō Hirobumi. *Commentaries on the Constitution of the Empire of Japan.* Trans. Baron Miyoji Itō. Chūō Daigaku 1906

Iwasa Shūji. 'Seijun Mondai to Kokutei Kyōkasho' [The Legitimacy Problem and the National Textbooks]. In Yamazaki Tōkichi, ed., *Nanboku Chō Seijun Ronsan* [Collected Articles on the Legitimacy of the Southern-Northern Courts]. Kyoto: Yokota Kappansho 1911

Jacoby, Russell. *The Last Intellectuals: American Culture in the Age of Academe.* New York: Basic Books 1987

Jinmu Tennō Seiseki Chōsa Hōkoku [Report of the Inquiry into Historical Sites Related to Emperor Jinmu]. Ministry of Education 1942

Kaigo Tokiomi. *Nihon Kyōkasho Taikei, Kindaihen* [Compendium of Japanese School Textbooks, Modern Period], vols. 18, 19. Kōdansha 1963

Kanai Madoka. *Oyatoi Gaikokujin, Jinbun Kagaku* [Hired Foreigners, the Human Sciences]. Kajima Shuppankai 1976

–. 'Riisu' [Riess]. *Nihon no Kindaika o Ninatta Gaikokujin* [Foreign Leaders of Japanese Modernization]. In Kokuritsu Kyōiku Kaikan, ed., *Kyōyō Kōza Shiriizu* [Educational Lecture Series]. Kyōsei 1992

Kanaseki Hiroshi. 'Protohistoric Archeology.' *Kōdansha Encyclopedia of Japan*, vol. 1. Kōdansha 1983

Kano Masanao and Imai Osamu. 'Kindai Nihon Shisōshi no naka no Kume Jiken' [The Kume Incident in the History of Modern Japanese Thought]. In *Kume Kunitake Rekishi Chosakushū* [Collected Historical Writing of Kume Kunitake], supp. vol. Yoshikawa Kōbunkan 1989

Kanzaki Kiyoshi. *Taigyaku Jiken, I. Kōtoku Shūsui to Meiji Tennō. Kuroi Bōryaku no Uzumaki* [The Great Treason Incident, I. Kōtoku Shūsui and the Meiji Emperor. The Vortex of the Dark Plot]. Ayumi Shuppan 1976

Katsuta Katsutoshi. *Miura Hiroyuki no Rekishigaku* [The Historical Scholarship of Miura Hiroyuki]. Kashiwa Shobō 1981

Kawamura Hidene. *Shoki Shikkai* [Collected Commentaries on *Nihon Shoki*]. N.p. 1804

Kigen Nisen Roppyakunen Kagoshima-ken Hōshukai [Kagoshima Prefecture Committee to Celebrate the 2,600th Anniversary]. *Jindai narabi ni Jinmu Tennō Seiseki Kenshō Shiryō* [Materials Demonstrating the Age of the Gods and Historical Sites Related to Emperor Jinmu]. In *Tsuji Zennosuke Kankei Shiryō* [Historical Materials Related to Tsuji Zennosuke]. Historiographical Institute, Tokyo University, file 130

Kimura Tokio. 'Nihon ni okeru Kindai Shigaku no Seiritsu (Tsuda Sōkichi)' [The Formation of Modern Historical Scholarship in Japan (Tsuda Sōkichi)]. In Waseda Daigaku Sōritsu Hyakushūnen Kinen, Waseda Daigaku Shakai Kagaku Kenkyūjo, Kenkyū Sōsho [Centenary Celebration of Waseda University, Waseda University Social Sciences Research Institute, Research Series]. In *Kindai Nihon to Waseda Daigaku no Shisō Gunzō* [Modern Japan and Waseda University Thinkers], vol. 1. Waseda Daigaku Shuppankai 1981

–. 'Yugamerareta Tsuda Sōkichi Zō' [The Distorted Image of Tsuda Sōkichi]. In *Shiden Shiwa: Kindai Nihon no Meian* [Historical Legends, Historical Talks: Light and Darkness in Modern Japan]. Maeno Shoten 1978

Kita Sadakichi. *Rokujūnen no Kaiko* [Recollections of Sixty Years]. In *Kita Sadakichi Chosakushū* [Collected Works of Kita Sadakichi], vol. 14. Heibonsha 1982

Kitabatake Harufusa. 'Nanchō Seitō Ron' [The Legitimacy of the Southern Court]. In Yamazaki Tōkichi, ed., *Nanboku Chō Seijun Ronsan* [Collected Articles on the Legitimacy of the Southern-Northern Courts]. Kyoto: Yokota Kappansho 1911

Kudō Ei'ichi. 'Rekishika to shite no Taguchi Ukichi' [Taguchi Ukichi as a Historian]. In Taguchi Ukichi, *Nihon Kaika Shōshi* [A Short Enlightenment History of Japan]. Kōdansha 1981

Kume Kunitake. 'Chūai Tei Izen Kinen Kō' [Dates before Emperor Chūai]. *Shigaku Zasshi* [Journal of Historical Scholarship] 13 (1902)

–. 'Japanese Religious Beliefs: The Kami.' In M.B. Huish, ed., *Fifty Years of New Japan*, vol. 2. London: Smith, Elder 1909

–. 'Kanzen no Kyūshū o Aratte Rekishi o Miyo' [Let Us Look at History without the Old Custom of Praising the Good]. In *Kume Kunitake Rekishi Chosakushū* [Collected Historical Writing of Kume Kunitake], vol. 3. Yoshikawa Kōbunkan 1989

–. *Kume Hakase Kyūjūnen Kaikoroku* [Memoirs of Dr. Kume Kunitake at Ninety]. Waseda Daigaku Shuppanbu 1934

–. *Nanboku Chō Jidai Shi* [History of the Southern-Northern Courts Period]. Waseda Daigaku Shuppanbu 1907

–. *Nara Chō Shi* [History of the Nara Court]. Waseda Daigaku Shuppanbu 1907

–. *Nihon Kodai Shi* [The Ancient History of Japan]. Waseda Daigaku Shuppanbu 1907

–. 'Shigaku Kōshō no Hei' [The Evils of Historical Scholarship and Positivistic Research]. *Shigaku Zasshi* [Journal of Historical Scholarship] 12.8 (1901). Also in *Kume Kunitake Rekishi Chosakushū* [Collected Historical Writing of Kume Kunitake], vol. 3. Yoshikawa Kōbunkan 1989

–. 'Shintō to Kundō' [Shintō and the Way of the Ruler]. In Ōkuma Shigenobu, ed., *Kaikoku Gojūnen Shi* [Fifty-Year History since the Opening of the Country]. Waseda Daigaku, Kaikoku Gojūnen Shi Hakkōsho 1903

–. 'Shinto Wa Saiten no Kozoku' [Shinto Is an Ancient Custom of Heaven Worship]. *Shigaku Zasshi* [Journal of Historical Scholarship] 2.23-5 (1891). Also in *Kume Kunitake Rekishi Chosakushū* [Collected Historical Writing of Kume Kunitake], vol. 3. Yoshikawa Kōbunkan 1989

–. '*Taiheiki* wa Shigaku ni Eki Nashi' [*Taiheiki* Is Worthless for the Study of History]. *Shigakkai Zasshi* [Journal of the Historical Association] 2.17-22 (1890). Also in *Kume Kunitake Rekishi Chosakushū* [Collected Historical Writing of Kume Kunitake], vol. 3. Yoshikawa Kōbunkan 1989

–. 'Tanaka Hakase no Bizen Kojima Ichizoku Hakken ni tsuite' [On the Discovery by Dr. Tanaka of a Kojima Family in Bizen]. In *Kume Kunitake Rekishi Chosakushū* [Collected Historical Writing of Kume Kunitake], vol. 2. Yoshikawa Kōbunkan 1989

–. 'Wakan tomo ni Shinkoku Naru o Ronzu' [Japan and Korea Together Constituted the Divine Country of Japan]. *Shigaku Zasshi* [Journal of Historical Scholarship] 22.1-2 (1911). Also in *Kume Kunitake Rekishi Chosakushū* [Collected Historical Writing of Kume Kunitake], vol. 2. Yoshikawa Kōbunkan 1989

–. 'Yo ga Mitaru Shigeno Hakase' [My View of Dr. Shigeno]. In Ōkubo Toshiaki, ed., *Shigeno Hakase Shigaku Ronbun Shū* [Collection of Historical Articles by Dr. Shigeno], vol. 4. Rev. and enl. ed. Meisho Fūkyū Kai 1989

'*Kuni no Ayumi* no Kentō' [An Examination of *Kuni no Ayumi*]. *Asahi Hyōron* [Asahi Critical Essays], Mar. 1947. Included in Hisano Shū and Shimada Jirō, eds., *Tennōsei* [The Emperor System], vol. 1. San'ichi Shobō 1975

Kuramochi Jikyū et al. 'Shinto wa Saiten no Kozoku to ieru Bunshō ni tsuite Mondō no Shimatsu' [The Complete Record of Questions and Answers on the Article 'Shinto Is an Ancient Custom of Heaven Worship']. In *Meiji Shiron Shū* [Meiji Historical Argument]. *Meiji Bungaku Zenshū* [Complete Collection of Meiji Literature], vol. 78. Chikuma Shobō 1966

Kuroita Katsumi. 'Go Daigo Tennō Gochūkō no Seigyō o Omoitatematsuru' [Humble Thoughts on the Achievement of Emperor Go Daigo in the Restoration]. In Kenmu Chūkō Roppyakunen Kinen Kai [Society for the 600th Anniversary of the Kenmu Restoration], *Kenmu Chūkō* [The Kenmu Restoration]. N.p. 1934

–. *Jinmu Tennō Gotōsen to Hyūga no Kuni* [Emperor Jinmu's Eastern Expedition and Hyūga Province]. In *Kyoshin Bunshū* [Collected Writings of Kuroita Katsumi], vol. 2. Yoshikawa Kōbunkan 1934

–. *Kodai Shintō ni kansuru Ichikōsatsu* [Survey of Ancient Shintō]. In *Kyoshin Bunshū* [Collected Writings of Kuroita Katsumi], vol. 3. Yoshikawa Kōbunkan 1934

–. *Kokushi Hensan Chojutsu no Enkaku* [The Development of Compilation and Writing of Works in Japanese History]. In *Kyoshin Bunshū* [Collected Writings of Kuroita Katsumi], vol. 3. Yoshikawa Kōbunkan 1934

–. *Kokushi no Kenkyū* [Research in Japanese History]. 2 vols. Yoshikawa Kōbunkan 1931

–. *Kokushi no Taikan* [Overview of Japanese History]. Iwanami Shoten 1935

–. *Kokutai Shinron* [A New Essay on the National Essence]. In *Kyoshin Bunshū* [Collected Writings of Kuroita Katsumi], vol. 1. Yoshikawa Kōbunkan 1934

–. 'Ko Taguchi Ukichi to *Nihon Kaika Shōshi*' [The Late Taguchi Ukichi and *Nihon Kaika Shōshi*]. *Rekishi Chiri* [History and Geography] 17.5 (1910)

–. 'Nanboku Ryōchō Seijunron no Shijitsu to sono Dan'an' [Facts about the Southern-Northern Courts Controversy and Its Conclusion]. *Nihon Oyobi Nihonjin* [Japan and the Japanese], 15 Mar. 1911

–. 'Ōbei Bunmei Ki' [Record of Civilization in Europe and America]. In *Kyoshin Bunshū* [Collected Writings of Kuroita Katsumi], vol. 7. Yoshikawa Kōbunkan 1934

–. *Saisei Itchi no Kokutai* [The National Essence Based on Unity of Government and Religion]. In *Kyoshin Bunshū* [Collected Writings of Kuroita Katsumi], vol. 1. Yoshikawa Kōbunkan 1934

–. ed., *Shaku Nihongi* [Annotated *Nihongi*]. In *Kokushi Taikei* [Compendium of Japanese History], vol. 8. Yoshikawa Kōbunkan 1935

–. 'Shōwa Ni-sannen Nikki' [Diary for 1927-8]. In Kuroita Katsumi Sensei Seitan Hyakunen Kinenkai [Memorial Society for the 100th Anniversary of the Birth of Professor Kuroita

Katsumi], *Kuroita Katsumi Sensei Ibun* [Documents of Professor Kuroita Katsumi]. Yoshikawa Kōbunkan 1974

Lu, David John. *Sources of Japanese History*, vol. 2. New York: McGraw-Hill 1974

Mahar, Amihai. *The Archeology of the Land of the Bible, 10,000-586 B.C.E.* New York: Doubleday 1992

Marshall, Byron K. *Academic Freedom and the Japanese University, 1868-1939*. Berkeley: University of California Press 1991

Maruyama Masao. 'Aru Hi no Tsuda Hakase to Watakushi' [Dr. Tsuda and I on One Day]. In Ueda Masaaki, ed., *Tsuda Sōkichi*. San'ichi Shobō 1974

–. *Studies in the Intellectual History of Tokugawa Japan*. Trans. Mikiso Hane. Princeton: Princeton University Press; Tokyo: University of Tokyo Press 1974

Maruyama Masao and Fukuda Kan'ichi. *Kikigaki Nanbara Shigeru Kōkiroku* [Oral Memoirs of Nanbara Shigeru]. Tokyo Daigaku Shuppankai 1989

Matsumoto Sannosuke. 'Kinsei ni okeru Rekishi Jojutsu to sono Shisō' [Early Modern Historical Narrative and Thought]. In Matsumoto Sannosuke and Ogura Yoshihiko, eds., *Kinsei Shiron Shū* [Collection of Early Modern Historical Argument], *Nihon Shisō Taikei* [Compendium of Japanese Thought], vol. 48. Iwanami Shoten 1974

Matsushima Ei'ichi. 'Kuroita Katsumi.' In Kano Masanao and Nagahara Keiji, eds., *Nihon no Rekishika* [Japanese Historians]. Nihon Hyōronsha 1976

–. 'Mitsukuri Genpachi.' In Kano Masanao and Nagahara Keiji, eds., *Nihon no Rekishika* [Japanese Historians]. Nihon Hyōronsha 1976

Mayo, Marlene J. 'The Western Education of Kume Kunitake, 1871-76.' *Monumenta Nipponica* 28.1 (1973)

McCullough, H.C., trans. *The Taiheiki: A Chronicle of Medieval Japan*. New York: Columbia University Press 1959

Mehl, Margaret. 'Scholarship and Ideology in Conflict: The Kume Affair, 1892.' *Monumenta Nipponica* 48.3 (1993)

–. 'Tradition as Justification for Change: History in the Service of the Japanese Government.' In I. Neary, ed., *War, Revolution, and Japan*. Richmond, UK: Curzon Press 1993

Meiji Shiyō [Outline of Meiji History]. 2 vols. Tokyo Daigaku Shuppankai 1933

Mikami Sanji. 'Hajime' [Foreword]. Satsuhan Shi Kenkyūkai, *Shigeno Hakase Shigaku Bunshū* [Collected Works of Historical Scholarship of Dr. Shigeno], vol. 1. Yūzankaku 1938

–. *Kokushi Gaisetsu* [Outline of Japanese History]. Fuzanbō 1943 (posthumous publication)

–. *Meiji Jidai no Rekishi Gakkai: Mikami Sanji Kyukaidan* [The World of Historical Scholarship in Meiji: Mikami Sanji Talks about the Old Days]. Yoshikawa Kōbunkan 1992 (originally published in *Nihon Rekishi* [Japanese History] 1936-9)

–. 'Nanboku Chō Seijun Mondai no Yurai' [The Origins of the Southern-Northern Courts Problem]. *Taiyō* [The Sun], 1 Apr. 1911. Rpt. in *Shigaku Zasshi* [Journal of Historical Scholarship] 22.2 (1911)

–. 'Tanaka Hakase no Etsureki' [The Career of Dr. Tanaka]. In Tanaka Yoshinari, *Nanboku Chō Jidai Shi* [History of the Southern-Northern Courts Period]. Meiji Shoin 1922

Miles, F. Curtis. 'Traditionalist Responses to Modernization in Japan: The Case of Minoda Muneki.' PhD diss., State University of New York at Buffalo, 1989

Minamoto Ryōen. '"Kindai Shisō" no Seisei' [The Formation of 'Modern Thought']. In Yoshida Hikaru, Sakuta Kei'ichi, and Ikimatsu Keizō, eds., *Kindai Nihon Shakai Shisōshi* [History of Modern Japanese Social Thought], vol. 1. Yūhikaku 1968

Minoda Muneki. 'Tsuda Sōkichi Shi no Taigyaku Shisō' [Treasonous Thought of Mr Tsuda Sōkichi']. *Genri Nippon* [Principles of the Japanese Nation]. 24 Dec. 1939

Mitchell, Richard H. *Censorship in Imperial Japan*. Princeton: Princeton University Press 1983

–. *Janus-Faced Justice: Political Criminals in Imperial Japan*. Honolulu: University of Hawaii Press 1992

–. *Thought Control in Prewar Japan*. Ithaca: Cornell University Press 1976

Miura Hiroyuki. 'Nihon Shigakushi Kaisetsu' [Exposition of the History of Japanese Historical Scholarship]. In *Nihonshi no Kenkyū* [Studies in Japanese History]. Iwanami Shoten 1930

Miyachi Masato. 'Bakumatsu-Meiji Shoki ni okeru Rekishi Ninshiki no Kōzō' [The Structure of Historical Consciousness in the Late Tokugawa and Early Meiji Periods]. In Tanaka Akira and Miyachi Masato, eds., *Rekishi Ninshiki* [Historical Consciousness]. *Nihon Kindai Shisō Taikei* [Compendium of Modern Japanese Thought], vol. 13. Iwanami Shoten 1991
–. 'Meiji Zenki ni okeru Rekishi Ninshiki no Kōzō' [The Structure of Historical Understanding in Early Meiji]. In Tanaka Akira and Miyachi Masato, eds., *Rekishi Ninshiki* [Historical Understanding]. *Nihon Kindai Shisō Taikei* [Compendium of Modern Japanese Thought], vol. 13. Iwanami Shoten 1991
–. '"Nihon Bunka Taikan" Henshū Shimatsu Ki' [Complete Record of the Compilation of 'Outline of Japanese Culture']. In Nihon Kagakusha Kaigi Shisō Bunka Kenkyū Iinkai [Council of Japanese Scientists, Committee for Research in Thought and Culture], *'Nihon Bunka Ron' Hihan – 'Bunka' o Yosou Kiken Shisō* [Criticisms of 'Essays on Japanese Culture' – Dangerous Thought Masquerading as 'Culture']. Suiyōsha 1991
–. 'Tennōsei Fashizumu to Ideorōgu-tachi: Kokumin Seishin Kenkūjo o Rei ni totte' [Emperor-System Fascism and Its Ideologues: The Case of the Research Centre on Japanese Spiritual Culture]. *Kagaku to Shisō* [Science and Thought] 76 (1990)
–. *Tennōsei no Seijiteki Kenkyū* [Studies in the Politics of the Emperor System]. Azekura Shobō 1981
Miyazaki Michio. *Arai Hakuseki*. Shibundō 1957
–. *Arai Hakuseki*. Yoshikawa Kōbunkan 1989
–. *Arai Hakuseki Joron* [Introduction to Arai Hakuseki]. Yoshikawa Kōbunkan 1966
–. *Arai Hakuseki no Kenkyū* [Studies on Arai Hakuseki]. Rev. ed. Yoshikawa Kōbunkan 1984
–. *Kumazawa Banzan no Kenkyū* [Studies on Kumazawa Banzan]. Shibunkaku 1990
–. 'Rinke Shigaku to Hakuseki Shigaku' [The Historical Scholarship of the Hayashi Family and Hakuseki]. *Nihon Rekishi* [Japanese History] 148 (1960)
Mizuta Norihisa and Arisaka Takamichi, eds. *Tominaga Nakamoto, Yamagata Bantō. Nihon Shisō Taikei* [Compendium of Modern Japanese Thought], vol. 43. Iwanami Shoten 1973
Mogi Hisahiro. *Tennō Ryō no Kenkyū* [Studies of the Emperors' Tombs]. Dōseisha 1990
Morita Yasunohiko. *Ban Nobutomo no Shisō* [The Thought of Ban Nobutomo]. Perikansha 1979
Morse, E.S. *Shell Mounds of Ōmori*. Memoirs of the Science Department, University of Tokio [sic], Japan, vol. 1, part 1. 1879
–. *Japan Day by Day*. 2 vols. Boston: Houghton 1917
Motoori Norinaga. 'Kan'kyōjin' [A Pillory for the Madman]. In Ōkubo Tadashi, ed., *Motoori Norinaga Zenshū* [Complete Works of Motoori Norinaga], vol. 1. Chikuma Shobō 1972
Murata Masashi. *Nanboku Chō Ron* [Essay on the Southern and Northern Courts]. Shibundō 1962
Murdoch, James. *A History of Japan*, vol. 1. Asiatic Society of Japan 1910
Nagahara Keiji. 'Uchida Ginzō.' In Kano Masanao and Nagahara Keiji, eds., *Nihon no Rekishika* [Japanese Historians]. Nihon Hyōronsha 1976
Nagai Ryūichi. *Nihon Kokka Shisōshi Kenkyū* [Studies in the History of Thought on the Japanese State]. Sōbunsha 1982
Naimushō, Ken'etsuka, Hokan-gakari [Ministry of Home Affairs, Censorship Department, Custody Office]. *Jūrokunen Tankōbon Shobun Nisshi, Shōwa Jūrokunen – Shōwa Jūhachinen* [Journal of Actions Taken against Books 1941-3]. Ed. Hisa Gentarō. Kohoku 1977. Appendix. 'Narachō Shi Naiyō Fukei Jiken' Genkō [Manuscript: 'The Case of Disrespectful Contents of *History of the Nara Court*']
Naka Michiyo. 'Jōsei Nenki Kō' [The Chronology of Ancient Japan]. *Shigaku Zasshi* [Journal of Historical Scholarship] 8.8, 9, 12. 1897
–. *Jōsei Nenki Kō* [The Chronology of Ancient Japan]. Rev. and enl. by Mishina Shōei. Yōtokusha 1948
Nakai, Kate Wildman. 'The Naturalization of Confucianism in Tokugawa Japan: The Problem of Sinocentrism.' *Harvard Journal of Asiatic Studies* 40.1 (1980)
–. *Shogunal Politics: Arai Hakuseki and the Premises of Tokugawa Rule*. Cambridge: Harvard University Press 1988

–. 'Tokugawa Confucian Historiography.' In Peter Nosco, ed., *Confucianism and Tokugawa Culture*. Princeton: Princeton University Press 1984

Nakamura Kōya. *Dai Nihon Shi to Mito Kyōgaku* [*Dai Nihon Shi* and the Mito Learning]. Kyōgakukyoku 1941

–. 'Mikami Sensei o Omou' [Remembering Professor Mikami]. In Mikami Sanji, *Edo Jidai Shi* [History of the Edo Period], vol. 2. Fuzanbō 1943-5 (posthumous publication)

Nakamura Naokatsu. *Kitabatake Chikafusa*. Hokkai Shuppansha 1937

–. *Nihon Bunka Shi – Nanboku Chō Jidai* [Cultural History of Japan – The Period of the Southern and Northern Courts]. *Nakamura Naokatsu Chosakushū* [Collected Works of Nakamura Naokatsu], vol. 2. Tankōsha 1978

–. *Yoshino Chō Shi* [History of the Yoshino Court]. Kyoto: Hoshino Shoten 1935

Naramoto Tatsuya. 'Wakamori Kun to Nihon oyobi Nihonjin Ron' [Wakamori and the Controversy over Japan and the Japanese]. *Wakamori Tarō Chosakushū* [Collected Works of Wakamori Tarō], vol. 8. Kōbunsha 1981

Nishimura Masae. 'A Study of the Late Early [sic] Jōmon Culture in the Tone River Area.' In Richard D. Pearson, ed., *Windows on the Japanese Past: Studies in Archeology and Prehistory*. Ann Arbor, MI: Center for Japanese Studies, University of Michigan 1986

Nishimura Sey. 'First Steps into the Mountains: Motoori Norinaga's *Uiyamabumi*.' *Monumenta Nipponica* 42.4 (1987)

–. 'The Way of the Gods: Motoori Norinaga's *Naobi no Mitama*.' *Monumenta Nippponica* 46.1 (1991)

Noguchi Takehiko. *Edo no Rekishika* [Edo Historians]. Chikuma Shobō 1979

Novick, Peter. *That Noble Dream: The 'Objectivity Question' and the American Historical Profession*. New York: Cambridge University Press 1988

Numata Jiro. 'Shigeno Yasutsugu and the Modern Tokyo Tradition of Historical Writing.' In W.G. Beasley and E.G. Pulleyblank, eds., *Historians of China and Japan*. Oxford: Oxford University Press 1961

O'Connor, M.S. *The Historical Thought of François Guizot*. Washington, DC: Catholic University Press of America 1955

Ogura Yoshihiko. 'Kaidai – *Dai Nihon Shi* Ronsō' [Explanatory Notes: The Assessments in *Dai Nihon Shi*]. In Matsumoto Sannosuke and Ogura Yoshihiko, eds., *Kinsei Shiron Shū* [Collection of Early Modern Historical Argument]. *Nihon Shisō Taikei* [Compendium of Modern Japanese Thought], vol. 48. Iwanami Shoten 1974

Ōkubo Toshiaki. 'Henshū Kōki' [Postscript on the Editing]. In *Shigeno Hakase Shigaku Ronbun Shū* [Collection of Scholarly Historical Articles by Dr. Shigeno], supp. vol. Rev. and enl. ed. Meisho Fūkyūkai 1989

–. *Nihon Kindai Shigaku Kotohajime: Ichi Rekishika no Kaisō* [The Beginnings of Historical Scholarship in Modern Japan: Reminiscences of a Historian]. Iwanami Shinsho 1996

–. *Nihon Rekishi no Rekishi* [The History of Japanese History]. Shinchōsha 1959

–. 'Yugamerareta Rekishi' [Distorted History], in Sakisaka Itsurō, *Arashi no naka no Hyakunen: Gakumon Dan'atsu no Shōshi* [A Hundred Years in the Storm: A Short History of Suppression of Scholarship]. Keiso Shobō 1952

–. 'Tsuda Sōkichi.' In *Nihon no Shisōka* [Japanese Thinkers], vol. 3. Asahi Shinbunsha 1963

Ōkuma Kazuo. 'Nihon no Rekishigaku ni okeru "Gaku" – Hiraizumi Kiyoshi ni tsuite' [The 'Scholarship' in Japanese Historical Scholarship – on Hiraizumi Kiyoshi]. In *Chūsei Shisōshi no Kōsō* [Concepts of the History of Medieval Thought]. Meicho Kankōkai 1984

Ōmori Kingorō. 'Ko Kume Kunitake o Omou' [Remembering the Late Professor Kume Kunitake]. *Rekishi Chiri* [History and Geography] 57.4 (1931)

Ooms, Herman. *Tokugawa Ideology: Early Constructs, 1570-1680*. Princeton: Princeton University Press 1985

Ōta Yoshimaru, ed. *Hanazono Tennō Shinki* [The Diary of Emperor Hanazono], vol. 3. Zoku Gunsho Ruijū Kanseikai 1986

Oyama Masaaki. 'Shiratori Kurakichi.' In Kano Masanao and Nagahara Keiji, eds., *Nihon no Rekishika* [Japanese Historians]. Hyōronsha 1976

Ozawa Ei'ichi. *Kindai Nihon Shigakushi no Kenkyū, Bakumatsu-hen* [Studies in Modern Japanese Historical Scholarship, the Bakumatsu Period]. Yoshikawa Kōbunkan 1966

-. *Kinsei Shigaku Shisōshi Kenkyū* [Studies in Modern Historical Thought]. Yoshikawa Kōbunkan 1974

Palmer, Bryan D. *Descent into Discourse: The Reification of Language and the Writing of Social History*. Philadelphia: Temple University Press 1990

Pierson, John D. *Tokutomi Sohō, 1863-1957: A Journalist for Modern Japan*. Princeton: Princeton University Press 1980

Pulleyblank, E.G. 'Chinese Historical Criticism: Liu Chih-Chi and Ssu-ma Kuang.' In W.G. Beasley and E.G. Pulleyblank, eds., *Historians of China and Japan*. Oxford: Oxford University Press 1961

Pyle, K.B. *The New Generation in Meiji Japan, 1885-1895*. Stanford: Stanford University Press 1969

Reischauer, Robert Karl. *Early Japanese History*, part A. Princeton: Princeton University Press 1937

Rekidai Tennō 125 Dai [The Succession of Emperors: 125 Reigns]. Shin Jinbutsu Ōraisha 1990

Riess, Ludwig. 'Memorandum to President Watanabe Hiromoto.' In *Tokyo Teikoku Daigaku Gojūnen Shi* [Fifty-Year History of Tokyo Imperial University]. Tokyo Imperial University 1932

-. *Methodology of History*. Tokyo University Library. N.d.

'Riisu Sōbetsukai' [The Farewell Party for Ludwig Riess]. *Shigaku Zasshi* [Journal of Historical Scholarship] 13.7 (1902)

Roberts, David D. *Benedetto Croce and the Uses of History*. Berkeley: University of California Press 1987

Rosenberg, Charles E. 'The Crisis in Psychiatric Legitimacy: Reflections on Psychiatry, Medicine, and Public Policy.' In *Explaining Epidemics, and Other Studies in the History of Medicine*. Cambridge: Cambridge University Press 1992

Saitō Takashi. 'Kokushika no Takauji, Yasutoki Sanbi Ron o motte. "Minsei" Shugi Hōgaku Shisō – Tsuji Zennosuke, Nakamura Naokatsu, Kuroita Katsumi, Kōda Naritomo ra no Shoron o Hyōsu' [Works by Japanese Historians Praising Takauji and Yasutoki Show Legal Thought Based on the Principle of 'Public Welfare' – A Critique of the Arguments of Tsuji Zennosuke, Nakamura Naokatsu, Kuroita Katsumi, Kōda Naritomo]. *Genri Nippon* [Principles of the Japanese Nation], June 1935

Sakamoto Tarō. 'Genshi Kodai no Nihon' [The Origins and Ancient History of Japan]. *Sakamoto Tarō Chosakushū* [Collected Works of Sakamoto Tarō], vol. 1. Yoshikawa Kōbunkan 1989

-. *Kodai Shi no Michi* [The Way of Ancient History]. Yomiuri Shinbunsha 1980

-. 'Kuroita Katsumi.' In *Kokushi Daijiten* [Dictionary of Japanese History], vol. 4. Yoshikawa Kōbunkan 1984

-. 'Sakamoto Tarō Hakase Nenpu, Chosaku Mokuroku' [Chronology and Catalogue of Works of Dr. Sakamoto Tarō]. In *Waga Seishun* [My Youth]. *Sakamoto Tarō Chosakushū* [Collected Works of Sakamoto Tarō], vol. 12. Yoshikawa Kōbunkan 1989

-. *Shisho O Yomu* [Reading Historical Works]. Chūō Kōronsha 1981

-. *The Six National Histories of Japan*. Trans. John S. Brownlee. Vancouver: University of British Columbia Press; Tokyo: University of Tokyo Press 1991

-. 'Waga Kuni ni okeru Shūshi Jigyō' [The Work of Compiling Histories in Japan, originally published 1973]. In *Nihon Rekishi no Tokusei* [The Special Characteristics of Japanese History]. Kōdansha Gakugei Bunko 1986

Sakamoto Tarō, Ienaga Saburō, Inoue Mitsusada, and Ōno Susumu, eds. *Nihon Shoki* [Chronicles of Japan]. *Nihon Koten Bungaku Taikei* [Compendium of Classical Japanese Literature], vols. 67-8. Iwanami Shoten 1965-7

Sakamoto Tatsunosuke. *Rai Sanyō*. Keibunkan 1913

Sansom, G.B. *A History of Japan*, vol. 3, 1615-1867. Stanford: Stanford University Press 1963

Sasaki Nozomu. 'Nukazuku to iu Koto' [The Meaning of Deep Prostration]. *Shinto Shi Kenkyū* [Research in Shinto History] 33.1 (1985)

Satō Nobuo and Umeda Kinji. 'Kokumin no Rekishi Ishiki to Rekishigaku' [The Historical Consciousness of the Japanese People and Historical Scholarship]. In Rekishigaku

Kenkyūkai and Nihonshi Kenkyūkai [Association for Historical Scholarship and Association for the Study of Japanese History], eds., *Kōza Nihonshi* [Lectures on Japanese History]. Tokyo Daigaku Shuppankai 1971

Satō Yoshimaru. 'Kume Kunitake to Waseda Daigaku' [Kume Kunitake and Waseda University]. In *Kume Kunitake Rekishi Chosakushū* [Collected Historical Writing of Kume Kunitake], supp. vol. Yoshikawa Kōbunkan 1989

Shigeno Yasutsugu. 'Shinto.' *Shigaku Zasshi* [Journal of Historical Scholarship] 8.1, 3, 4. (1898). Also in Satsuhan Shi Kenkyūkai. *Shigeno Hakase Shigaku Bunshū* [Collected Works of Historical Scholarship of Dr. Shigeno], vol. 1. Yūzankaku 1938

Shiratori Kurakichi. *Jindai Shi no Shin Kenkyū* [New Studies on the History of the Age of the Gods]. *Shiratori Kurakichi Zenshū* [Complete Works of Shiratori Kurakichi], vol. 1. Iwanami Shoten 1969

Shiratori Yoshirō and Yawata Ichirō. *Shiratori Kurakichi, Torii Tatsuzō.* Kōdansha 1978

Suzuki Masayuki, ed. *Kindai no Tennō* [The Modern Emperor]. Yoshikawa Kōbunkan 1993

Suzuki Yūjirō, ed. *Ekikyō* [The Book of Changes]. In *Zenshaku Kanbun Taikei* [Compendium of Translated Works of Chinese Literature]. Shūeisha 1974

Taguchi Ukichi. *Nihon Kaika Shōshi* [A Short Enlightenment History of Japan]. Kōdansha 1981

–. 'Shintōsha Shoshi ni Tsugu' [To Certain Shintoist Gentlemen]. In *Kume Kunitake Rekishi Chosakushū* [Collected Historical Writing of Kume Kunitake], supp. vol. Yoshikawa Kōbunkan 1989

Tahara Tsuguo. *Hirata Atsutane.* Rev. ed. Yoshikawa Kōbunkan 1986

Tahata Shinobu. *Katō Hiroyuki.* Yoshikawa Kōbunkan 1959

Takano Kunio. *Tennō Kokka no Kyōiku Ron – Kyōgaku Sasshin Hyōgikai no Kenkyū* [Education in the Emperor's State – Studies on the Education Reform Council]. Azumino Shobō 1989

Takase Shigeo. *Date Chihiro.* Sōgensha 1942

Takasu Yoshijirō. *Mitogaku no Shinzui o Kataru* [The Essence of the Mito School]. Ida Shoten 1941

Takayanagi Mitsutoshi. 'Ko Mikami Hakase Tsuitōki' [A Memorial of the Late Dr. Mikami]. *Kokushigaku* [Study of Japanese History] 38 (1939).

Takeshita Masahiko. 'Hiraizumi Shigaku to Rikugun' [Hiraizumi's Historical Scholarship and the Army]. *Gunji Shigaku* [Military History] 5.1 (1969)

Tamagake Hiroyuki. 'Zenki Mito Shigaku no Rekishi Shisō no Ichisokumen – Kuriyama Senpō no Rekishikan' [A Profile of Historical Thought in the Historical Scholarship of the Early Mito School – The Historical View of Kuriyama Senpō]. *Nihon Shisō Kenkyū* [Studies in Japanese Thought] 13 (1981)

Tanaka, Stefan. *Japan's Orient: Rendering Pasts into History.* Berkeley: University of California Press 1993

Tanaka Takashi. 'Hiraizumi Sensei no Shinsōsai ni Sanrei Shite' [As an Attendant at the Shinto Funeral of the Late Professor Hiraizumi]. *Shinto Shi Kenkyū* [Research in Shinto History] 32.2 (1984)

Tanaka Yoshinari. *Nanboku Chō Jidai Shi* [History of the Southern-Northern Courts Period]. Meiji Shoin 1922

Tokoro Isao. 'Shōwa Tennō ga Mananda "Kokushi" Kyōkasho' [The Textbook in Japanese History Studied by the Shōwa Emperor]. *Bungei Shunjū* [Art and Literature, Spring and Autumn], Feb. 1990

Tokutomi Sohō. *Kōshaku Katsura Tarō* [Count Katsura Tarō]. Hara Shobō 1967

Tokyo Daigaku Hyakunen Shi [One-Hundred-Year History of Tokyo University]. Tokyo Daigaku Shuppankai 1985

Tsuchiya Tadao. 'Kokutai no Hongi no Hensan Katei' [The Process of Compiling *Kokutai no Hongi*]. *Kantō Kyōiku Gakkai Kiyō* [Bulletin of the Kantō Education Society] 5 (1978)

Tsuda Sōkichi. *Jindai Shi no Atarashii Kenkyū* [New Studies on the History of the Age of the Gods]. *Tsuda Sōkichi Zenshū* [Complete Works of Tsuda Sōkichi], supp. vol. 1. Iwanami Shoten 1965

–. *Jōdai Shi no Kenkyūhō ni tsukite* [Research Methods on Ancient History]. Iwanami Kōza Nihon Rekishi [Iwanami Series on Japanese History]. Iwanami Shoten 1934

–. 'Jōshinsho' [Written Defence]. In *Tsuda Sōkichi Zenshū* [Complete Works of Tsuda Sōkichi], vol. 24. Iwanami Shoten 1965

–. 'Kenkoku no Jijō to Bansei Ikkei no Shisō' [The Circumstances of the Founding of the Nation and the Idea of the Eternal Succession of Emperors]. *Sekai* [The World], Apr. 1946

–. Letter to Kurita Naomi, 10 Sept. 1945. In *Tsuda Sōkichi Zenshū* [Complete Works of Tsuda Sōkichi], supp. vol. 1. Iwanami Shoten 1989

–. *Nihon Koten no Kenkyū* [Studies on the Japanese Classics], vol. 1. Iwanami Shoten 1948

–. *Shina Shisō to Nihon* [Chinese Thought and Japan]. *Tsuda Sōkichi Zenshū* [Complete Works of Tsuda Sōkichi], vol. 20. Iwanami Shoten 1965

–. *Shiratori Kurakichi Shōden* [Brief Biography of Shiratori Kurakichi]. *Tsuda Sōkichi Zenshū* [Complete Works of Tsuda Sōkichi], vol. 24. Iwanami Shoten 1965

Tsuji Tatsuya. 'Chichi Zennosuke to Rekishigaku to Watakushi' [My Father Zennosuke, Historical Scholarship, and I]. In Tsuji Tatsuya, ed., *Edo Jidai Shiron* [Historical Essays on the Edo Period], by Tsuji Zennosuke. Yusōsha 1991

Tsuji Zennosuke. 'Ashikaga Takauji no Shinkyō ni tsuite' [The Religious Faith of Ashikaga Takauji]. *Shigaku Zasshi* [Journal of Historical Scholarship] 28.9 (1917)

–. 'Honpō ni okeru Shūshi no Enkaku to Kokushigaku no Seiritsu' [The Development of Historical Writing in Japan and the Establishment of the Field of Japanese History]. In Shigakkai [Historical Association], ed., *Honpō Shigakushi Ronsō* [Essays on the History of Historical Scholarship in Japan]. Fuzanbō 1939

–. 'Kenkyū Seikatsu no Omoide' [Memories of a Research Life]. *Shisō* [Thought], Feb. 1953

–. 'Kigen Nisen Roppyakunen no Igi' [The Significance of the 2,600th Anniversary of the Empire]. *Rekishi Kyōiku* [History and Education], Feb. 1940

–. 'Ko Mikami Sanji Sensei Ryakureki' [Brief Curriculum Vitae of the Late Professor Mikami Sanji]. In Mikami Sanji, *Edo Jidai Shi* [History of the Edo Period], vol. 2. Fuzanbō 1943-5 (posthumous publication)

–. 'Kuroita Katsumi Kun' [Professor Kuroita Katsumi]. Tsuji Zennosuke Sensei Tanjō Hyakunen Kinenkai [Memorial Society for the 100th Anniversary of the Birthday of Professor Tsuji Zennosuke]. *Tsuji Zennosuke Hakase Jireki Nenpu Kō* [Manuscript of the Personal Chronology of Dr. Tsuji Zennosuke]. Heibunsha 1977

–. *Nihon Bunka Shi* [History of Japanese Culture], vols. 1, 4. Shunjū Sha 1950

Tsunoda, R., W.T. de Bary, and D. Keene, eds. *Sources of Japanese Tradition*. New York: Columbia University Press 1958

Ueda Masaaki. *Tsuda Sōkichi*. San'ichi Shobō 1974

Uyenaka Shuzo. 'The Textbook Controversy of 1911: National Needs and Historical Truth.' In John S. Brownlee, ed., *History in the Service of the Japanese Nation*. Toronto: University of Toronto-York University Joint Centre on Modern East Asia 1983

Van Laue, T.H. *Leopold Ranke: The Formative Years*. Princeton: Princeton University Press 1950

Varley, H.P. *A Chronicle of Gods and Sovereigns: Jinnō Shōtōki of Kitabatake Chikafusa*. New York: Columbia University Press 1980

Vinh, Sinh. *Tokutomi Sohō (1863-1957): The Later Career*. Toronto: University of Toronto-York University Joint Centre on Modern East Asia 1986

Vinh, Sinh, with Matsuzawa Hiroaki and Nicholas Wickenden. *The Future Japan*, by Tokutomi Sohō. Edmonton: University of Alberta Press 1989

von Humboldt, Wilhelm. 'On the Historian's Task.' In Leopold von Ranke, *The Theory and Practice of History*. Ed. Georg G. Iggers and Konrad von Moltke. New York: Bobbs-Merrill 1973

Wakabayashi, Bob T. *Anti-Foreignism and Western Learning in Early Modern Japan: The New Theses of 1825*. Cambridge: Harvard University Press 1986

Wakamori Tarō. 'Kigen Setsu Fukkatsu no Haikei' [The Background of the Revival of Empire Day]. *Wakamori Tarō Chosakushū* [Collected Works of Wakamori Tarō], vol. 8. Kōbunsha 1981

–. 'Kigen Setsu Mondai no Keika' [The Development of the Empire Day Problem]. *Wakamori Tarō Chosakushū* [Collected Works of Wakamori Tarō], vol. 8. Kōbunsha 1981

Walthall, Anne. 'Off with Their Heads! The Hirata Disciples and the Ashikaga Shoguns.' *Monumenta Nipponica* 50.2 (1995)

Webb, Herschel. *The Japanese Imperial Institution in the Tokugawa Period*. New York: Columbia University Press 1968

–. 'What Is the *Dai Nihon Shi?' Journal of Asian Studies* 19.2 (1960)

Weinberg, Arthur, and Lila Weinberg. *Clarence Darrow: A Sentimental Rebel*. New York: G. Putnam's Sons 1980

Wu Jing-Nuan, trans. *Yi Jing*. Washington, DC: Taoist Center 1991

Wunderlich, R.J. 'The Japanese Textbook Problem and Solution, 1945-46.' PhD diss., Stanford

Index

12 February 1936 incident, 133, 159

Accession ceremonies, 210

Age of the Gods: affirmed by Hiraizumi Kiyoshi, 168, 171, 179, by later Kuroita Katsumi, 149-55, by Motoori Norinaga, 63 4, by Tsuji Zennosuke, 166-8; circumspect treatment by Mikami Sanji, 139-40, Confucian treatment by Hayashi Razan, 26-8; confused treatment in *Dai Nihon Shi*, 38-40; denial by Yamagata Bantō, 50-2; euhemerist treatment by Arai Hakuseki, 45-8, by Kume Kunitake, 115-16; importance of genealogies of deities in, 3; literal treatment by Hoshino Hisashi, 113-15, 190-1; rational treatment by early Kuroita Katsumi, 147-8, by postwar Tsuji Zennosuke, 157; scepticism of Asaka Tanpaku, 38, of Tokugawa Mitsukuni, 38, of Tsuda Sōkichi, 117, 190-1

Akihito, Emperor: acceptance of ceremonies signifying sovereignty, 209-13; speech on accession in 1989, 209

Amaterasu Ōmikami (Sun Goddess): recognized by contemporary imperial house, 210-11; sends Heavenly Grandchild to Japan, 5; vow to protect imperial house, 5

Anesaki Masaharu, in Southern-Northern Courts controversy, 121

Arai Hakuseki, 6, 54; career, 42-3; euhemerism on Age of the Gods, 45-8; indifference to Wu Taibo theory, 45; orthodox historical studies, 44; periodization of history, 44-5

Archeology, poses threat to orthodox history, 89-91

Asaka Tanpaku, 33; scepticism about Age of the Gods, 38

Ashikaga Takauji: founder of Ashikaga Bakufu, 32, 119, 122, 152; praised by Tsuji Zennosuke, 157-8

Azuma Kagami [Mirror of the East], account of the Jōkyū War, 23

Bacon, Sir Francis, separation of religion and scholarship, 140-1

Baishōron [Discourse of the Plums and Pines], 123; account of Jōkyū War, 22-3

Buckle, Henry Thomas, 72-3

Bunmeiron no Gairyaku [An Outline of the Theory of Civilization], 72

Buretsu, model evil emperor, 20, 21, 36-7

Censorship, 133-4

Chamberlain, Basil Hall, 71, 92

Chichibu, Prince, advised by Hiraizumi Kiyoshi in 1936 Army Mutiny, 178

Chronology, revised, initiated by Naka Michiyo, 86, 111; general acceptance, 112, 140, 149

Chronology, traditional, dismissed by Yamagata Bantō, 51; problems of, 21, 111-12; used by Hiraizumi Kiyoshi, 152, 170, by Nakamura Naokatsu, 151, by Taguchi Ukichi, 86; wide acceptance of by government and society, 180

Chūgan Engetsu, supports theory of Wu Taibo, 25

Chunqiu [Spring and Autumn Annals], 19, 26

Commission of Inquiry into Historical Sites Related to Emperor Jinmu, 145, 154, 195; choices for scholars invited to join, 164-5; members, 182; proceedings, 180-5

Commission of Inquiry into Historical Sites Related to the Founding of the Nation, 167

Confucius, influence on Hayashi Razan, 26

Confucianism: criticized by Motoori Norinaga, 62-3; relationship to science, 66-7

Constitution of Great Japan of 1889, 7; article 3 on sacred emperor, 94-5

Hoshino Hisashi: does not support Kume Kunitake, 105; head of Historiographical Institute, 108; holds founding myths to be historically true, 8, 113-15; offensive article on deity Oshimimi, 96-8
Huang Zongyi, founder of Chinese positivistic research, 19

Ichijō Kanera, denies theory of Wu Taibo, 25
Ienaga Saburō, 207; career, 204-5; made to appear as nationalist, 174-5; on postwar committee to revise textbooks, 203; on Tsuda Sōkichi's views of Age of the Gods, 198; outraged by historians in 1930s, 9
Imperial house, postwar position, 213-5
Inoue Kaoru, starts Historiographical Institute, 107
Inoue Kiyoshi, 207; outraged by historians in 1930s, 9, 144-5, 184; criticizes postwar history textbook *Kuni no Ayumi*, 205-7
Inoue Mitsusada: intolerance of Hiraizumi Kiyoshi, 174; opposes National Founding Day, 208-9
Inoue Tetsujirō: on Hayashi Razan, 17; in Southern-Northern Courts controversy, 122
Ishida Ichirō, explanation of *Shinto Denjū Shō*, 27-8
Itō Hirobumi, on sacred emperors, 94-5
Iwanami Shigeo, 200; prosecuted with Tsuda Sōkichi, 195-6

Jameson, John Franklin, founds National Archives in USA, 109-10
Japan Day by Day, by Edward Morse, 89
Japanese monarch, history, 213
Jinmu, Emperor: anniversary projects in 1940, 180, by Imperial Japan Academy, 180-2, by historians of Kyoto Imperial University, 182; date of founding revised to 40 BC, 111-12; founds imperial rule in 660 BC, 5; meaning of his name, 5; 2,600th anniversary of his founding of empire, 10, 136, 142, 163, 180
Jinnō Shōtōki [Record of the Legitimate Descent of the Divine Sovereigns], 18, 32, 86, 173; denies theory of Wu Taibo, 25; praises Hōjō Yasutoki, 35
Jōkyū War of 1221: causes and outcome, 21; in *Dai Nihon Shi*, 35, 37; in *Honchō Tsugan*, 22-4
Jōkyūki [Record of the Jōkyū War], 23

Kada Azumamaro, 61
Kadowaki Teiji, opposes National Founding Day, 208

Kaikoku Gojūnenshi [History of Fifty Years since the Opening of the Country], 103
Kamigamo Shrine, 210
Kamo Mabuchi, 61-2
Kashihara Shrine, 5, 210
Katō Hiroyuki, refuses to support Kume Kunitake, 100-1
Katsura Tarō, prime minister during Southern-Northern Courts controversy, 121
Kawamura Hidene, 29
Kawarada Kakichi, Minister of Education, letter to members of Commission of Inquiry into Historical Sites Related to Emperor Jinmu, 165
Keichū, 61
Kihira Tadayoshl, 144
Kimura Tokio, disciple of Tsuda Sōkichi, interpretation of Tsuda trial, 199
Kishinron [Essay on Ghosts and Spirits], by Arai Hakuseki, 46
Kita Sadakichi: dismissed from Ministry of Education, 118; involvement in Southern-Northern Courts controversy, 126-7
Kitabatake Harufusa, in Southern-Northern Courts controversy, 121-2
Kōdōkan Jutsugi [The Rationale of the Kōdōkan], 38-9
Kōdōkan Ki [Record of the Kōdōkan], 39
Kojidan [Chats of Ōe Masafusa on History], 102
Kojiki [Record of Ancient Matters]: creation myths in, 3-4, 39; origins of emperors, 4-5; circumstances of writing, 190
Kojiki Den [Commentary on *Kojiki*], by Motoori Norinaga, 29, 52, 62
Kojima Takanori, 14th-century hero: existence denied by Shigeno Yasutsugu, 87-8; possibly confirmed by Tanaka Yoshinari, 89
Kokugaku [National Learning], 61-2
Kokushi Taikei [Compendium of Japanese History], 83-4, 146
Kokutai [National Essence], 5, 65, 150
Kokutai no Hongi [Cardinal Principles of the National Essence of Japan], 135, 143-4, 191-2, 213; committee members, 152-3; plan for foreign language edition, 164
Komatsubara Eitarō, Minister of Education in Southern-Northern Courts controversy, 122
Koshitsū [The Essence of Ancient History], by Arai Hakuseki, 44, 47
Koshitsū Wakumon [Questions and Answers on the Essence of Ancient History], by Arai Hakuseki, 44

Set in Stone by Irma Rodriguez

Copy editor: Dallas Harrison

Proofreader: Edward Wagstaff

Printed and bound in Canada by Friesens

Sidney Silverman Library
and Learning Resource Center
Bergen Community College
400 Paramus Road
Paramus, NJ 07652-1595

www.bergen.cc.nj.us

Return Postage Guaranteed